THE PURSUIT OF POSSIBILITY

"Thrift's wide experience of and genuine passion for the research university has resulted in this first class exposition of them, identifying the challenges they face and how they might be reimagined in light of these, making this book a genuine 'must read' for all those who care about such institutions."
Mark Smith, Vice-Chancellor, University of Southampton

"Research universities matter! Thrift provides an unashamed, insightful and personal defence. In doing so he raises existential questions about their future, and argues for their purpose and survival. Expect to be provoked and want to argue back. An essential read for those who value research and its vital contribution to our future."
Ken Sloan, Harper Adams University

THE PURSUIT OF POSSIBILITY
Redesigning Research Universities

Nigel Thrift

First published in Great Britain in 2022 by

Policy Press, an imprint of
Bristol University Press
University of Bristol
1–9 Old Park Hill
Bristol
BS2 8BB
UK
t: +44 (0)117 374 6645
e: bup-info@bristol.ac.uk

Details of international sales and distribution partners are available at
policy.bristoluniversitypress.co.uk

© Bristol University Press 2022

British Library Cataloguing in Publication Data
A catalogue record for this book is available from the British Library

ISBN 978-1-4473-6484-9 hardcover
ISBN 978-1-4473-6485-6 paperback
ISBN 978-1-4473-6486-3 ePub
ISBN 978-1-4473-6487-0 ePdf

The right of Nigel Thrift to be identified as author of this work has been asserted by him in accordance with the Copyright, Designs and Patents Act 1988.

All rights reserved: no part of this publication may be reproduced, stored in a retrieval system, or transmitted in any form or by any means, electronic, mechanical, photocopying, recording, or otherwise without the prior permission of Bristol University Press.

Every reasonable effort has been made to obtain permission to reproduce copyrighted material. If, however, anyone knows of an oversight, please contact the publisher.

The statements and opinions contained within this publication are solely those of the author and not of the University of Bristol or Bristol University Press. The University of Bristol and Bristol University Press disclaim responsibility for any injury to persons or property resulting from any material published in this publication.

Bristol University Press and Policy Press work to counter discrimination on grounds of gender, race, disability, age and sexuality.

Cover design: Lyn Davies Design
Front cover image: Getty/ANDRZEJ WOJCICKI/SCIENCE PHOTO LIBRARY

For Lynda

Contents

Preface and acknowledgements — viii

1. Is that a 'university'? I'm not sure — 1

PART I The research university
2. So what is a 'university'? Part 1: Architecture and academics — 23
3. So what is a 'university'? Part 2: Students, parents and other constituencies — 72

PART II The contemporary British university system
4. A new Robbins? Recent changes in British universities — 103
5. The hardy perennials — 123
6. The Australianisation of British higher education — 165
7. On vice-chancelloring – a footnote — 194

PART III The research university of the future
8. So what is a research university? — 213
9. Redesigning the research university — 241

Notes — 259
References — 272
Index — 294

Preface and acknowledgements

I have an awful lot to thank universities for. To begin with, I have had considerable freedom in choosing what to do, with the result that I have been able to think about all kinds of issues and ideas in a way that just isn't open to most people. Then, universities have given me some extraordinary experiences. Just two will suffice. One was a research visit to Vietnam in the early 1980s. The Russians were still there in force and the Air France plane from Saigon/Ho Chi Minh City that I departed on was full of the distraught children of Vietnamese mothers and GI fathers being carried to new homes in the US. The children let out an extraordinary and extraordinarily affecting intake of breath followed by a deep sigh of regret as the plane took off – this was both their first experience of flying and the first jab of grief they experienced on leaving their mothers. Another was a hot and sweaty visit to the Square Kilometre Array in deepest outback Australia, which not only transmitted a deep and brooding sense of the life of the planet but also a keener appreciation of humanity's place in the universe. Universities have enabled me to live an interesting and expansive life too. Because of them, I have been able to teach and do research in locations as varied as Cambridge, Leeds, Lampeter, Bristol, Oxford and Warwick, as well as in a number of overseas locations like ANU. In each of them I have been pushed to think and do new things. Universities have given me the particular privilege of teaching some fearsomely bright students who forced me to bump up against my own prejudices and, most importantly of all, clarify what I meant. Universities have enabled me to work with colleagues who were a genuine inspiration. Some of them seemed to be working in a different dimension from me, one where thought moved at light speed and ideas were sprinkled around like confetti. Universities mean that I have been able to encounter people who I have been pleased just to have sat across from or even been in the same room as. (I still remember sitting opposite Raymond Williams at a college dinner in Cambridge while still a lowly research associate and being too terrified to speak to him in case I said something foolish.) And universities have enabled me to build a network of co-author friendships, many of which I am lucky enough to still be able to call on and some of which I wish so very hard that I still could: Ash Amin, Andrew Barry, Jonathan Beaverstock, Nick Bingham, Martin Boddy, Pat Burnett, Tommy Carlstein, Gordon Clark, Paul Cloke, Stuart Corbridge, Mike Crang, Louise Crewe, Peter Daniels, Peter Dicken, David Drakakis-Smith, J.D. Dewsbury, Dean Forbes, Shaun French, Paul Glennie, Steve Graham, Stephan Harrison, Andrew Leyshon, Peter Jackson, Ron Johnston, Paul Keys, Roger Lee, John Lovering, Doreen Massey, Jon May, Danny Miller, Jeremy Oakes, Kris Olds, Don Parkes, Richard Peet, Martin Phillips, Steve Pile, Allan Pred, Mike

Taylor, Peter Webb, Sarah Whatmore, Colin Williams, Peter Williams and Steve Woolgar. Yes, my life in universities was about hard work. But it was about hard work on things I (mainly) wanted to do with people I liked. Not many people can say that, truth to tell.

In a sense, this book is a thank you for that life. It can't be anything else, really. It is a peculiar kind of thank you in that it is quite critical of both the actuality and trajectory of contemporary universities; but the criticism is there because I care very deeply that these precious institutions aren't destroyed, either by the market or by governments or by their leadership, each of which sometimes seem to be doing their level best to do exactly that, sometimes because of that very human urge to meddle just because it's there. The book isn't an exercise in nostalgia, however. No one wants to go back to 1950 when UK universities awarded first degrees to a paltry 17,300 students and higher degrees to only 2,400 students and universities were the preserve of a very White, very male, and very upper-class establishment. But we can't stay where we are either, at least if we still want to belong to something resembling a university rather than a factory production line. To illustrate that point, in 2019/20 there were 2,532,385 students at UK institutions offering higher education in some form, 1,889,475 of which were undergraduates and 642,915 of which were postgraduates. But we keep on calling most of the serried higher education institutions that teach these students, 'university', a word with cultural resonances, to be sure, but increasingly a busted flush as a description of anything distinctive.

From the 1980s, I was involved in university management as well. I come from a generation who mainly just fell into management. When I started out there weren't that many courses or coaches. There was not much in the way of a policy industry. There was really only learning by picking it up from other people and by making mistakes which you could only hope weren't going to come back to haunt you (a few did, of course). But some of the people I learnt from – and the lessons they provided – were genuinely extraordinary. I learnt head of departmenting from Malcolm Anderson, how to do research assessment from John Enderby, how to be more gracious and generous from Peter Haggett, how to be a vice-chancellor from John Kingman, Eric Thomas, Colin Lucas, and especially John Hood. I also learnt that university management is about being able to rely on other people and I have been very lucky in that regard. In particular, I have to mention Jon Baldwin, Mike Beveridge, Kumar Bhattacharyya, Keith Burnett, Ed Byrne, Giles Carden, Ian Chubb, Tim Clark, George Cox, Stuart Croft, Glyn Davis, Rosie Drinkwater, Stephanie Fahey, Margaret Gardner, Janet Hemingway, Catryn Hemlock, Ray Hudson, Tim Jones, Lily Kong, Koen Lamberts, John Leighfield, Paul O'Prey, Nicola Owen, Stuart Palmer, Dan Persaud, David Rhind, Yvonne Salter-Wright, Anthony Seldon, John Sexton, Ken Sloan, Mark Smith, Adam Tickell and Rick Trainor.

I am also acutely aware that for many academics around the world this is not a typical career trajectory. They lack resources. And they sometimes lack even the most basic freedoms of expression. I have heard colleagues in other countries having to talk either in code ('it's how you say it') or with an ellipsis in order to provide an opinion, the very opposite of what a university is meant to be like. I have been lucky to be part of universities where that isn't the case.

It's always possible to sound too preachy – and with that last paragraph I probably did – but perhaps that's what's necessary as the planet begins to hit the buffers. The fact is that universities are way more important than most people realise and never more so than now as the planet spirals out of our control (not that it was ever within it, truth to tell). But many people in the sector seem embarrassed to make an existential defence. Maybe because it sounds pompous, maybe because they have been worn down by working in institutions which seem to them to privilege the vagaries of management and policy over the extraordinary content which is universities' main gift and responsibility, maybe because the minor miracle that these long-term institutions still exist in a world which often seems to be becoming more chaotic and short term day by day has passed them by, or maybe because cynicism has replaced the passion that they once felt. But, each day, universities produce a storm of ideas, experiments and new designs and maybe, just maybe, there will come a day when out of this treasure trove we can produce a world which isn't just on the take, which gives because giving is the right thing to do. Now, that really is preachy! But it's also true.

A word about the title. I originally wanted to call the book *Is That a University? I'm Not Sure*. Though I agreed with the publisher that it needed changing to something less opaque, I hope that the gist of what I was trying to get at comes through in the book: universities are in danger of losing their way. I truly believe that if we go on as we are, we are in danger of destroying some of the only institutions in the UK (and indeed on the planet) which can claim to be disinterested (or extremely interested, seen in another way) – not motivated by the love of lucre, or by a search after power over others, or simply showing off, but rather by a commitment to, if not the truth, then at least to a search for better and better questions. In the middle of the climate change phoney war, but with messages coming in from the scientific front line every day telling us that the situation is likely to get even worse, those values are not just a nice to have. They are a matter of survival.

To conclude this combined preface and acknowledgments, I should say that my analysis, such as it is, is informed by reading over many decades, by my experience of university management in a number of UK research universities and by continuing discussions with numerous people about where universities should go next, none of whom can be held responsible for what follows. It is also informed by participation in the Institute for Public Policy

Research Independent Commission on the Future of Higher Education. Thank you to the Commission members and especially Nick Pearce. It is informed too by my experience of working in other university systems, most notably in Australia, China, Singapore and the US. Finally, it is informed by experience of belonging to the boards of a number of universities, both in the UK and overseas. This record does at least give me a base to work from and some – some – knowledge of what works and what doesn't. It also means that I believe that, given a following wind, research universities could form a kind of international bastion against the creeping forces of the anti-the-best-of-the-Enlightenment we can see all around us. This is a time when universities can search out new exoplanets, put up a concerted fight against cancer, malaria and Covid-19, and produce remarkable conceptual advances in mathematics and philosophy, even though, all around, a blizzard of witchery and greed blows. T'was always thus, you might say. But there does seem to be an awful lot of thus around at the moment. We ought to be more concerned.

1

Is that a 'university'? I'm not sure

This is a book about universities. There are plenty of those around already, so what makes this book any different? Roughly speaking, books about universities can be divided into four types. First off, there are the jeremiads, lamenting the loss of past glories and criticising much of what is presently occurring. Usually sparked off by opposition to the current wave of so-called marketisation in universities, much of what they have to say has an edge to it but they usually make very little of what universities ought to be like in the future.[1] They are strong on what they don't like but weak on what they would like to replace it with. Then, there are the various volumes that take universities to be businesses of one kind or another whose chief business it is to impart skills, enhance employability and boost innovation and productivity. Universities serve the economy and they are economies. Just as one instance, a whole genre – I won't say business – has grown up around making the case for universities as economic saviours of cities and regions. Usually written by authors who have boosting the gross national or regional product in mind, these volumes can sometimes take on a distinctly instrumental edge. Then there are the books which argue that universities are pretty much a waste of time, populated by slackers and ne'er do wells. They are shams that don't teach much at all of what's needed now and don't provide any noticeable intellectual progression (e.g. Caplan, 2018). Send students straight to work to be re-educated in the university of life. Where have you heard that before? And finally, there are books that try to offer up a new vision of what universities might be, rather than clinging to what they once were or embracing what the powers that be think they should be. This book is from this final stable. It's true, it is written from a position of someone who knows a little of what might be possible. However, this pragmatic bent does not mean that I am any the less idealistic. Indeed, fuelled by not a little frustration at the strangely hostile environment that British and other universities have found themselves in, I am probably more so. But you will have to read this book to ascertain why.

Right from the start, I should point out that this is a book about research universities, the maybe 40 universities[2] in the UK that effectively carry out nearly all of the high-end research in the UK and which are the jewels in this country's university crown.[3] In other countries one finds similar kinds of universities. There are maybe another 300 or 350 in the world as a whole which means that the UK is lucky – nay, extraordinarily lucky – to have so many of them. Universities are routinely differentiated from one another but I realise that concentrating on just these universities is hardly likely to be a popular move. It will no doubt be regarded as balkanisation of a sector which needs to stick together. However, at this point in time, a lack of differentiation means that research universities are in danger of becoming part of a gradual extension of the school system, rather than the research part of a spectrum of institutional diversity, so I believe it to be a necessary move.

Indeed, I will go farther. Yes – takes sharp intake of breath – I want to argue that their research is the most important thing about research universities. There have been a large number of books focussed on the role of teaching in universities (e.g. Sperlinger, McLellan and Pettigrew, 2018, Frank, Gowar and Naef, 2019, Scott, 2021), and this book will touch on teaching issues too. But, relatively speaking, research has been neglected by many commentators. The party line is that teaching and research support each other – and indeed that used to be true. But it has become less and less obvious that it is the case. Student number expansion in many research universities has put the connection under more and more strain and it's now becoming a serious issue.[4] The problem is that the degree of importance attached to research in research universities is being continually pressured and sometimes, implicitly at least, downgraded. Most of this pressure comes from a growth in the importance of teaching occasioned by student number growth. Teaching is where, in many (though not all) research universities, the largest amount of income now comes from – some of it to support research. Where they can, universities have often added more students, and many (though not all) research universities have gone down this path too. As research universities have become positional goods, parents search them out for their offspring and, again not surprisingly, have correspondingly high expectations for their university experience, and that of course means their teaching and issues of 'value for money'. But it isn't just the results of taking in more students that's at issue. There are other factors coming into play that weight activity towards teaching too. For example, as research universities appoint more teaching-only staff they become a lobby in their own right. To summarise, research and teaching are getting out of balance.

None of this is surprising but increasingly it places research universities in golden handcuffs. For some research universities with very large research incomes, the growth in the importance of teaching is not necessarily a problem. Oxford and Cambridge take much less income from teaching than other universities and they have not noticeably increased their undergraduate student numbers. For the others, it means that increasingly they run to the beat of the student drum.

Care needs to be taken here. I am decidedly not saying that teaching isn't important or that it shouldn't be done well: students deserve the best. Nor am I saying that teaching is somehow second best. Rather, I am saying that in a research university there needs to be a balance between research and teaching and that this balance is now being broken. Research universities have tried to keep things on an even keel by appointing many more teaching-only staff but, in certain senses, this breaks the compact between research and teaching in which in a research university you would be taught by people who not only knew stuff but were producing it.[5] (It is also the case that in the best research universities, there are also a large number of staff who are research-only, who often do at least a limited amount of teaching, though that is not their priority.)

Straightaway, I have to adopt a defensive pose. I can hear the criticisms already. This just goes to prove what we always thought – that research universities just don't care about teaching students. And, anyway, where is the money to make up the research deficit going to come from if not from international students? And, in any case, haven't students always been the lifeblood of universities? That I have to be defensive in the face of statements like these shows that things have slipped a gear. I believe that we can only bring teaching and research in research universities back into synch by reimagining the relationship.

In effect, I want to re-examine a judgement that Halsey and Trow (1971, p. 464) made back at the dawn of a system of mass higher education:[6]

> In no society, we suggest, can elite institutions such as … British universities provide for … mass higher education and remain elite institutions … their academic standards are too high … their costs are too high [including] salary scales, … staff/student ratios, amenities, and above all, … expensive provisions for research and scholarship.

Halsey and Trow were generally wrong in their judgement then. I'm not so sure that they are now. For research universities, the chickens have come home to roost. At the scale at which it now operates, mass higher education can be a threat to these universities as much as it can be an opportunity.

I should say straightaway that views of this kind make this into a book that will disappoint pretty much everybody. For the ardent supporters of the research university as it was, I cannot offer much in the way of succour. Things have gone too far. We need to reinvent. For the proponents of a sort of market in higher education, I will counsel deep suspicion about the corrosive forces they have unleashed which are in danger of producing a reversion to the mean. We need to find another way. For those who want to make research universities into just job-training machines (and they do exist, believe me), I will simply say 'no'. That is not their goal. For those who want to shed old shibboleths under the guise of being left behind, I will say be careful that your narrative isn't being used as cover for changes which can only make things worse. Whatever the case, what is clear is that the traditional British idea of a research university based on intensive education in residential institutions coupled with total immersion in research is unlikely to hold for much longer in its current form. Truth to tell, the research universities' monopoly on higher education was decisively broken some time back. What distinguishes them now is really high-quality research.

My main concern, then, is to make sure that British research universities never become a concert of failure but, as this book will show, I am certainly concerned that parts of the orchestra are slipping out of tune. Adding Brexit and coronavirus into the mix has only underlined just how flimsy some of the assumptions on which the success of British research universities have been built actually are and how quickly their pre-eminence could fade if the worst predictions come true.

But threats can be turned into opportunities. What we need now, I will argue, is cooperation, not just competition, cooperation that will make these universities – and their counterparts in other jurisdictions – into a real and cohesive actor in a time when their research is needed more than ever: their future needs to be secured so that their research can provide a future for the planet.

Why more than ever? Well, to begin with there are the pressing issues of climatic and biospheric change and all they portend. Universities are one of the only institutions with the ideas, the novel practices, and the green technologies that can dig us out of the hole that we've made for both ourselves and other beings.

We're talking survival here. Just as the Second World War galvanised the growth of research in many universities, now we find ourselves locked into a similar predicament and research is one of the only escape routes. But there are other issues too – all of them, just like climate and biospheric change, self-inflicted and so open to alteration. Massive technological challenges to full employment. Grotesquely unequal societies. Looming food and water shortages. And now a global pandemic to which it is chiefly university scientists that have found the answers. Research universities can and will provide potential solutions to a number of these threats to humankind and the planet – if they're allowed to. In other words, if anything, the products of research universities are becoming more important, not less.

Things have been made more difficult because of a general fall in public trust in experts and expertise which has hit universities particularly hard, even though universities are still generally well thought of in most countries, certainly when compared with other public institutions. One can, of course, argue that much of the current grumbling about universities is therefore part of a more general zeitgeist. But universities cannot get off quite that easily. They have some self-inflicted problems. For example, the machinery of science is creaking, a point I will return to. And there is the issue of what can sometimes seem like a preternaturally timid leadership, a point to which I will also return.

A resumé

After this brief introductory chapter, the book comprises another eight chapters gathered together in three parts which might be thought of as three separate volumes that, when taken together, should provide the reader with (1) a field guide to what research universities are now, (2) a primer outlining what has happened to them in the last few years, and (3) a map of where they might go next.

In two linked chapters that form the first part of this book, I ask a straightforward question. What actually is a research university at this point of time? Instead of working out from some highfalutin principle or the other, or reaching for grandiose statements about the university's spirit and purpose (as in 'the idea of the university'), in these two chapters I try to document what is actually there – the mechanics which go to make up what we call a research university. That turns out to be an accumulation of a multitude of different communities, spaces and equipment all interacting together within a research university's boundaries. This accumulation has some common goals – research and teaching – but like all conglomerates these goals can hide numerous other priorities, some of which are in conflict – or at least in tension – with each other. In particular, I want to underline just how complex university organisations have become and the substantial problem of serving so many different stakeholders, all of whom claim a degree of ownership. Along the way, in each chapter I also provide brief excursions, in Chapter 2 on online teaching and in Chapter 3 on freedom of speech.

Having got to at least some notion of what a research university is, the second part of the book consists of four linked chapters. Chapter 4 provides an opinionated whistle-stop tour through British higher education, stopping at most of the salient points. Paying particular regard to the research university, the chapter gives a brief account of the main events and the key issues animating the history of the expansion of the UK university sector over the last few decades, culminating in the current sort of market, sort of state, takeover. Hopefully this chapter will serve to orient the reader in the contemporary university landscape.

I then move on in Chapter 5 to identify the salient topics that the history of university expansion throws up which have crystallised out over the last decade – the hardy perennials that have arisen and continue to arise, namely the balance of public and private funding, student access, tuition fees, research funding, research integrity, pensions, league tables, and autonomy (or the lack of it). As a prelude to the next chapter, I then conclude this chapter by describing the high degree of dissatisfaction that can now be found in and with many British research universities, and I try to answer the question of why this dissatisfaction has grown to quite the degree it has.

In Chapter 6, I provide a more general explanation of the recent happenings in British higher education by considering what I call 'Australianisation'. This term is meant to indicate that British research universities have nearly all opted for an Australian model of what has often seemed like helter-skelter student growth, at least when they can, prompted by a government that has instituted a university system which is run on 'market' principles which actually promote a form of nationalisation. This raises two issues which I explore in depth. Should the government be able to hold court over the university system in the exaggerated fashion that now pertains? And should the government then be allowed to turn universities into what is basically an extension of the school system, research universities in particular? Governments have been locked into an uneasy but sometimes productive relationship with the British university system for well over a century now. Until recently that relationship has been – with exceptions like the Thatcher years – a passably good or at least not catastrophically bad one. However, I will argue that, so far as research universities are concerned, the relationship now holds considerable risks, especially of creating distractions from research without delivering any particular teaching dividend. Why research universities have come to such a pass is an interesting question and one that I will also explore. At least a part of the reason for this state of affairs is that the dictates of growth have, more often than not, involved government treating all universities as if they were pretty much the same, and, with this tendency to similitude, has come a misunderstanding of what research universities actually are now. (This tendency sits alongside the fact that as universities have grown, often in a somewhat higgledy-piggledy fashion, they have taken on more and more activities. This has proved to be a shoo-in for government. More and more things can be loaded onto them in what can sometimes seem like a never-ending chain of extra responsibilities. At the same time, all these extra add-ons provide government with more and more reason to become involved.)

In Chapter 7, I try to provide a more personal take on universities' multiple manifestations by considering the role of the vice-chancellor from a former vice-chancellor's perspective. There is remarkably little literature that simply describes what a vice-chancellor does. I begin there. I make an attempt, at least, to catalogue the multifarious activities that go to make up a vice-chancellor's day. I then reflect on what needs to be done to lead a research university. This section of the chapter will be considered either brave or foolhardy but I aim to give an account which may be of sociological interest at least.

Part III returns to a consideration of the university system. It consists of another two chapters which ask what now needs to be done. I am aware that many commentators will see the actions I suggest as overly pragmatic and lacking in idealism. But I would argue that, whereas it's easy to produce a city upon a hill, it's much harder to work into the actual situation research universities now find themselves in so as to recover at least some idealistic ends. In the words of the old saw, I wouldn't start from here – but here is where we are. So Chapter 8 looks at how the duties of universities can be recast to take into account the fact of their existence as multiple entities, as described in Chapter 3, and the means to focus them. I follow this section by considering what must surely be the most important function of the research university, research: the clue's in the title. The conduct of research is changing and I try to highlight some of the challenges that this now presents. The final chapter then considers how modern research universities could be redesigned such that they retain some of the best features of the old and construct new features which fit but also extend them in ways which do not just follow but shape the times. I briefly sketch out some of the policy responses that might be put in place that might start to lead universities towards, if not that city on the hill, at least a better settlement. The watchword is cooperation. Through cooperation, the university system, and research universities themselves, could be recast so that they can become even closer to what they surely ought to be – intellectual lighthouses which produce the ideas and the general wherewithal that can help to save us – and the planet – from ourselves.

As Collini (2012, p. 197) puts it, whatever else we do we need to 'throw off a defensive posture', especially at this point in time. Research universities have changed, sometimes massively, through history and they will, no doubt, change again. My interest is a simple one: ensuring that research is not downgraded as these changes happen. Without that vital element of their existence, under current conditions, they are in danger of becoming simply the next step up in a school system. Nothing wrong with that, you might say. I disagree.

I should apologise in advance to colleagues in the devolved administrations. Most of what is written here is based on the English university experience. Scotland, Wales and Northern Ireland have increasingly pursued their own course and this divergence has its own lessons, both positive and negative, some of which I will address.[7] (A good guide to these increasingly different higher education systems can be found in Scott, 2021.)

The book is scattered with observations from my own experience of universities. I don't apologise for this or for engaging in self-criticism, as I do several times in the book. In our historical moment, when argument is too often subsumed into identity, when conjecture is sure to provide proof of infraction, and when doubt is understood as weakness or hypocrisy, such observations are often interpreted as invitations to attack. But I believe that to defend the conditions under which universities can thrive requires something more than just heroic reinstatements of the past or dubious rhetoric about the power of competition to set things to rights. It requires building the kind of robust networks that can only come about from understanding the complexity of what goes on in universities, and thenceforward gradually building architectures of cooperation that can secure universities' futures, not least because their research will be such a vital element of all of our futures. After all, as Oswald (2001, pp. 2–3) puts it:

> For hundreds of years, the quality of a person's research has been the over-riding criterion for promotion and hiring. Those outside universities often find this puzzling or worse. Yet the norm has grown up not because of any conspiracy or mistake. Rather, universities through the ages have learned that the contribution of a scholar is mainly through the ideas that he or she leaves in the minds of the next generation. British citizens and politicians never think to ask: where do the ideas in high school textbooks actually come from? The answer, though, is from universities.

This thought illustrates just how important university research can be. But it also illustrates the degree of responsibility universities hold in their hands, a responsibility which, by the way, is sometimes much greater than they like to acknowledge. (For example, just think of the many negative consequences of quantitative behavioral science as it has been applied in the conduct of US democracy (Lepore, 2020).)

The research university

There is a prevailing myth that all universities are the same, really, and that other universities can morph into research universities over time if only the juices of competition are allowed to flow. That may have been the case at one time but no longer and for so many reasons: growth in the number of universities, sunk costs, sheer concentration of thought power and the resources to support it, centrality to intellectual networks such that the most accomplished academics tend to move to these universities and take pride in being members of them, even the likelihood of being taken seriously in the first place (Bourdieu, 2004). It is often implied that lack of competition from the other UK universities will somehow induce complacency in British research universities (cf. Willetts, 2017). The Matthew effect means that they will become bloated and complacent. I don't think that this is right either. The top research universities are in a worldwide competition and they know that all too well. They are primarily competing with the other top research universities around the world, not with the other universities in the UK. They are continually alert to what their competitors are doing.

In other words, these universities are not the same as the others and they do themselves and other universities a major disservice when they act like they are.[8] Their research reputation is why foreign faculty and postgraduates flock to them, why thousands of overseas students want to take to themselves a little bit of their lustre, and why many thousands of eminent outside speakers lecture at them each year – as a mark of being serious people who will be taken seriously. It is also why these universities' concentration of intellectual firepower has fuelled numerous innovations which are central both to modern economies and to the common good, most especially as the ordure of climate change is dumped on to the planet.

I can imagine all the cries of elitism and snobbery that will follow on from making a distinction between universities more generally and research universities. But the distinction has become increasingly necessary, and not just because so many different kinds of institution now call themselves universities that the word 'university' has become close to meaningless, or because a peculiar form of marketisation-cum-nationalisation (and the simulations of a student 'market' it has built without giving any real thought to the repercussions for research) has progressed to the point where some degree of triage has to be put in place so that some institutions can still lodge a claim to be world-leading research enterprises, or because universities now function in a diverse division of labour, different parts of which can be structurally opposed and therefore say very different things to government and the world at large. Along with Byrne and Clarke (2020), I would argue forcefully that research universities are fundamentally different kinds of institutions from other universities, most particularly because they are the linchpins of a massive system of *unlearning*.

What might such a word mean? Many commentators still see the acquisition of knowledge as one-way. Knowledge is stacked up in a kind of warehouse and then communicated out as necessary in bite-size chunks. But research-led knowledge is not like this grab-and-go model. Like the active universe it investigates in which agency is 'an elemental feature of the natural world' (Riskin, 2016, p. 368),[9] it is always in action, with the result that it is cumulative – but only to an extent. It is a process not an object, in other words: the truth lies in the *pursuit* of knowledge rather than a terminus. As important as accumulation of knowledge is the process of identifying knowledge which is being superseded by new discoveries or is unreliable or no longer applies or is just plain wrong – learning by unlearning. The fact of the matter is that facts aren't stable: they are not 'inert' as Whitehead (1968) famously put it. In a changing world, they are always going to be perishable. What was wheat can become chaff. Facts arise out of the consensus that exists at any time but they can be revised or even overturned; indeed, science may be described, as it was by Richard Feynman, as 'the belief in the ignorance of experts', a stance that is only underlined by the way in which scientists nowadays are willing to ascribe agency and emergence and the unexpected and unpredictable events arising out of partial connectedness to 'nature's mechanism' in a way that they might not have in the past (Riskin, 2016, p. 374). Even what counts as a problem doesn't stay still but is continually rethought and rearticulated as new ideas and methods emerge (Lury, 2021, Barry, 2021). There are numerous examples just from the last few decades of science of this flux leading to dramatic revisions in underlying assumptions and the consequent appearance of new facts – think just of the extraordinary revolution that has taken place in our knowledge of dinosaurs as more and more fossil specimens and species continue to appear: 50 new species have been named every year over the last two decades. Fossils have been found showing extraordinary detail and especially feathers, and CT scans allow the inner workings of dinosaurs to be revealed for the first time. A parallel process has taken place with the early history of mammals and their ancestors, overturning the now dated belief that dinosaur-era mammals were small and rather boring insectivores, scurrying about under the feet of giant reptiles. Or, similarly, work on Neanderthals, transformed from brute status to culturally sophisticated ancestors inhabiting our DNA. Or the way in which what we think of the agricultural revolution has been transformed as the early history of cities has been rewritten and as hunter-gatherers have been transformed from virginal indigenes into peoples who could set up fields and gardens, produce monuments and carefully manage the environment. Or the way in which bacteria, viruses, archaea and fungi are now seen as major actors in human bodies and as prime movers of the planet. Or how biological entities like junk DNA and glial cells which were previously thought to be of limited consequence have been shown to have important effects in humans. Or the way in which we now know that evolution works on much shorter timescales and in much broader registers than we would once have thought possible, with some animals transforming almost in front of our eyes as they adapt to cities. Or the way in which intensive experiment and observation over the last 30 years has revealed many animals not just as cognate and innovative beings but as knowing things that we don't. Or the revolution in how we think of genes which means that not only are we no longer sure what a gene is but also that we have to acknowledge that not just DNA but also RNA can pass on information from generation to generation and that many epigenetic factors like an unhealthy diet, mental stresses and toxin exposure can reshape our genetic make-up. Or the central role of symbiosis not just in evolution but in the interdependence of life on the planet and the pivotal role of bacteria and viruses in this coevolutionary process, a role so great that scientists often now describe animals as holobionts, hosts in league with symbiotic microbiota, and the nonillions of bacteria and viruses as prime movers in evolution, the human body (an estimated 8 per cent of human DNA is reckoned to be of viral origin), food webs, ecosystems and the atmosphere. Or that the famous rules devised by Linus Pauling to describe the preferred crystal structures adopted by ionic compounds are more like loose guidelines.[10] Or in physics, the claims of a relational interpretation of quantum physics in which the world is made up of relations and events rather than permanent substances. Or in computation, the potential of nano-optics to produce much greater speed of processing and response while using much less power. Or the constant calling into question of certain aspects of astrophysics like, most recently, the competing claims of dark matter and modified or emergent gravity. And all this is before we get to disciplines like history or economics where numerous competing explanations co-exist for events which everyone thinks are done and dusted. As has been pointed out many times now, the causes and consequences of many familiar and not-so-familiar historical events are still in dispute and probably always will be. Beyond some bare chronological facts, no one can be deadly sure they know what happened or why. Think only of the way in which our knowledge of what used to be called the 'dark ages' has been transformed or the way in which the shades of empire and slavery have led to a reworking of the economic, social and cultural history of the eighteenth century (and succeeding centuries too) and especially of early America. As for economics, debates still rage over the causes of various financial crises, both recent and historic. In fact, relatively little economic knowledge is uncontested at all.

In other words, the enterprise of universities isn't a particularly efficient or straightforward path towards 'the truth'. Established knowledge is constantly being battered and revised as a result of the interruptions occasioned by just three little words: 'I don't know'. Truthfulness, not truth, in other words. Take the case of science. It is a collective activity of explanation, of 'socialized cognition' (Oreskes, 2019) depending not just on what is known but how, a how which might be empirical or theoretical, words which themselves cover a litany of different approaches. Individual scientists are fallible and they have their own goals and, occasionally, axes to grind, but science as a collective affair keeps moving on, bolstered by the various mechanisms of trust it has developed and the knowledge that oft times seeking out uncertainty can be the only certainty. Researchers make missteps here and there and sometimes they can get things seriously wrong (Oreskes, 2019). They can take a long time to rigorously vet some claims and establish others. A seemingly promising research programme reaches a dead end. Different methods can produce contradictory results.[11] And so on. But, over time, scientists gradually come to a provisional consensus through processes of critical reception and constant revision of their answers to problems which are never pre-given since problems are always processes and they are therefore transformed as they are investigated and twisted into new shapes: problems are very difficult to contain and that fact by itself drives a lot of invention (Oreskes, 2019, Strevens, 2020, Lury, 2021). Equally, academics may work in traditions which can vary mightily in their theoretical approaches and methods, both so far as individual disciplines are concerned and according to particular national traditions, but, even so, they still rely on evidence (which can, of course, be framed in many different ways) and on strength of argument in some form or the other, with the sure and certain knowledge that without them all they have is an opinion which is no better than anyone else's. Most of all, they rely on ideas. (Nowadays, it's true, there are people who, drunk with the glamour currently radiating from artificial intelligence and big data, argue that data and inference can act as a substitute for ideas, or indeed become ideas (though ones that, in the case of artificial intelligence, we won't necessarily be able to understand), but in the end I still believe that method without theory means that knowledge will not advance (Nurse, 2021)).

Unlearning, as the systematic application of doubt and scepticism, has other characteristics too. For one, its form of knowledge is built on making mistakes and tolerating uncertainties. Mistakes are business as usual in science. They are integral to the system. Bends in the road and cul-de-sacs abound. Out of them, we learn. In some disciplines, they can even be a real positive. For example, 'philosophy [is] an area in which you might be remembered for a thousand years if you managed to make an interesting mistake rather than a stupid one. The only sane aspiration in the field [is] to one day make a useful mistake' (Vogler, 2019, p. 28). The general outcome of a stance which recognises the motive power of mistakes is clear in any case: changing your mind about things is not necessarily a bad thing. Uncertainties continue to persist, as well. I always mention the fact that the precise value of the constant of gravitation (G) is still uncertain despite numerous experiments spanning three centuries, as well as pointing to the fact that scientists are still arguing over exactly what a gene or a particle actually is and to the fact that there are over 20 theories vying to explain why the Sun's corona is a million times dimmer than its surface, yet is at least a million degrees Kelvin hotter (Judge, 2021). Uncertainties point us in the direction of what we still don't know.

In other words, as has been shown many times now, we need to be cautious about the reach and precision of our explanations. Sloterdijk, Latour, and others have argued that the motive force behind the modern quest for knowledge is what they call an aesthetic process of 'explicitation' that satisfies the modern need to perceive the imperceptible by making what was formerly regarded as given (like air or water or land) as explicit as possible, for example through the medium of a data explosion (Lury, 2021). However, this process will always remain an uncertain affair, prone to false readings and over-confident extensions.[12] The web of potential causes and effects expands, and then expands again. As Cartwright and Hardie (2012, p. 52) put it, 'causes work in teams'.[13] Overflow is a constant condition as a result.

Then, unlearning is clearly influenced by social and cultural currents. There is ample evidence of this happening from the history of science and social science. What gets studied and how, what gets adopted and what gets passed over, is a complex mix of interactions between people and methods and materials and different kinds of people may pick up different things and draw different conclusions based on their own particular biases. But none of this is to say that everything is socially constructed and that truth is a phantasm, a problematic stance which seems to have made something of a comeback recently on the back of much misrepresented philosophers like Foucault.[14] As Haraway (2018, p. 84) points out, arguing that something is socially constructed does not make it go away: 'made is not made up'. At its best, unlearning is a means of making you believe what you don't necessarily want to believe by interacting with materials that need to be placed in an alignment which allows them to be asked questions, using all kinds of apparatuses, with the result that they are no longer mute. For example, disciplines like physics, chemistry and the geosciences have no doubt been led in particular directions because of the cultural assumptions made by what has been a largely male and White collective of scientists but that's not the same as saying that everything they have done is therefore somehow negated or that the world they studied just conformed to their White male whims and wishes. Those would be absurd conclusions that lead on to a gross form of reductionism where, sin of all sins, the answer is known in advance. Not everything can be politicised and moralised in the way that it sometimes seems a few academics might wish. That would be a reductio ad absurdum. Writers like Bruno Latour and Isabelle Stengers have spent a good part of their lives showing exactly how, by allowing materials to play an active role rather than being reduced to just social and cultural ciphers, it becomes possible to seek out more interesting problems and ask formative questions.

There is one more element to the production of knowledge as a system of unlearning. Students are introduced to something even more disorienting: the world will, to some degree, stay unknowable. That does not mean just that there is no endpoint to the pursuit of knowledge. That's a trivial insight. It means something much more radical (Blastland, 2019). We will likely never know what is going on quite as well as we think we do because of what is often variously called 'intangible variation' or 'noise' or even just 'irregularities' which have no obvious explanation. This 'hidden half' (Blastland, 2019) just is. But it's not simply a leftover. It's a kind of disordering principle, a positive force for disruption which is a property of the world at large. The result is clear at least: 'we dream of laws and general truths: the practicality is often a patchwork of unexpected anomalies' (Blastland, 2019, p. 21) such that 'We thought we knew something, thought we'd seen our knowledge at work, thought we understood how it worked; then we tried to apply it again, perhaps in only a slightly different context, expecting it to work again, and it didn't' (Blastland, 2019, p. 21) This happens in science more than it might be comfortable to admit. Even more intriguingly, we might, given the advances going on in machine learning and artificial intelligence, be able to formulate explanations that we cannot ourselves understand. For example, having used these kinds of advances, the explanation of dark matter that results may turn out to be incomprehensible to us.

To summarise, let me call on Carl Sagan's famous phrase, 'science is a way of thinking more than it is a body of knowledge', a way of thinking that, for all of its undoubted and illustrious forbears, has really only existed for three centuries or so, a means of living the questions, as Rilke might have put it. Of course, it is a body of knowledge too – and a powerful one – but the archive is constantly mutating, constantly receding, always seeking that surprise around the corner. It has what might be best described as negative capability.[15] That is what makes the pursuit of truth – it would be better if there was a different word for something that will always be tentative and never final – into a beautiful thing. Indeed, in certain senses, 'the eternal mystery of the world is its comprehensibility', as Einstein put it, not its incomprehensibility.

Research universities are the chief agents of this style of thinking, a style that upends the cognitive shortcuts of everyday life – which research shows to be a mix of habit, improvisation, bias, and sheer bravado – but never scorns them. As Peter Salovey (2019) puts it (just substitute any major research university for Yale!):

> There is so much we do not know. Let us embrace, together, our humility – our willingness to admit what we have yet to discover. After all, if [students] knew all the answers, [they] would not need Yale. And if humanity knew all the answers, the world would not need Yale.

Research universities have a responsibility, nay a duty, to carry out this purposely disconcerting research – which is producing a string of intellectual advances and innovations for the UK and indeed the world – as well as to practise the kind of teaching which gives students the skills to live in and enquire after an uncertain world. Research universities exist as part of an enormous global network of thinking about thinking that, as I have pointed out, has existed for only a few centuries in its current form,[16] especially since the adoption of 'experimental philosophy' as a means of construing reliability (Shapin, 1994), a network of practical norms and procedures which give others trust that good work is being done. That puts the onus on staff in research universities to produce world-leading research and then pass the results on via high-quality teaching. It means (or should mean) that undergraduates and postgraduates graduate from courses which are right at the cutting edge of what we know. They don't just have content, these courses, they have substance. These undergraduates are introduced to the realisation not only that what looks like a stable body of knowledge is in constant motion and that considerable parts of that knowledge will be challenged and found wanting but also that this is a good thing which allows them to cast right eyes on the world. At the same time, they learn the qualities they will need most in the coming difficult years: adaptability, seriousness, resilience, creativity, concentration, generosity, and, most of all, humility.

Equally, research universities are one of the institutions that will help to get us out of the current global mess. They are that important. And it does no one any credit to diminish them. Without them, we may not die a terrible death but we shall surely suffer far more. I know that many commentators will think that this is an exaggeration or just good old-fashioned pomposity and mock its pretensions. But think about all the innovations that have been made in or because of universities – all manner of technologies, a host of medical and epidemiological advances, and cultural software – the ideas that we need to think with like, most recently, the Anthropocene. Universities are like cathedrals, institutions that, in some cases, have taken centuries to build but that, instead of aspiring to heaven, honour life and the modest contribution they may be able to make to it. They might be thought of as one of life's blessings. (Sometimes, universities are accused of not living in the 'real world'. The really important stuff is being done by other less ethereal institutions and beings. I see it the other way. At least at this point in time, university researchers often have a much better grasp of the real world than the so-called real world.)

But this way of life is under attack, and in three ways. To begin with, there are all those who want to make research into simply a machine to solve immediate problems immediately, a means of 'making a difference'. Of course, that is what often arises out of research and a good thing too. Who wouldn't want answers to common matters of concern like new vaccines, new drugs, new power sources, or new foods? But to think research is only and just about this is to make it less than it is. 'Fast, mobilised science' (Stengers, 2018) is only one part of what science is, even though governments and research councils increasingly seem to bend that way. Research is a complex ecosystem which is able to succeed because researchers have built up a vast array of different kinds of approach, experiment and speculation, many of which may not seem immediately 'useful' but which have every chance of becoming so given time as they stimulate a theory or method formerly thought to be out of court or become affixed to a particular current of thinking that has only existed in embryo, often for many years. What looks redundant or esoteric now may well be relevant in the future, not least because the fast, mobilised industrialised style of science has itself had all manner of unintended consequences which are showing up now in profusion, and by no means always for the best (Stengers, 2018). Trying to separate this system into 'useful' and 'not useful' is to miss its point, therefore. Unlearning necessarily involves redundancy and out of the loop 'poetic' thinking. What looks like waste may turn out to contain all kinds of intellectual nuggets stored up for future use in a world where uncertainty seems to confront us at every turn, as well as those eureka moments of discovery which every now and then reorient a particular field and which only rarely arise out of fast mobilised science. To argue for science as simply a repair shop for immediate issues or as only a repository of technical and industrial innovation is to reduce it to exactly the thing that has brought us to the current pass. It is to choke off real innovation. (In particular, there is a real irony in wanting to make research universities' research more innovative by increasingly dictating what research they should do.)

Equally, there are those who would like to refigure the work of academics by bunching together what are often the quite different tendencies they favour under the banner of 'new' and anything else under 'old'. Universities need to be 'new' or they will be 'left behind'. This is a standard rhetorical strategy, of course, used by management consultants and the IT industry on what sometimes seems like a daily basis to privilege and justify certain kinds of competition which provide them with advantage by forging a so-called knowledge economy. And such binaries can lead us to some pretty odd places. For example, Grant (2021) suggests that academic jobs need to be refashioned. After a period of grace, they will join together in consortia. They will become new 'gig' academics made up of self-employed research teams freed from the pesky constraints of host universities, with celebrity academics managed through agencies, and consortia offering novel teaching solutions and courses. No longer left behind by the new world, they will be set free to leverage their leverage for themselves.

Then, all around the world, governments are trying to rein in the universities producing this research, either because they are perceived as outright enemies – because they nurture thoughts which are off the beaten track (their primary function) – because they are perceived as bastions of the left, firing off a hail of 'propaganda', or simply because they are victims of collateral damage from short-sighted policies that try to cement the world in place as a market or a state. This is a crucial point in their history, therefore. In the US, the Trump government, when it wasn't conducting what often seemed like a war on science (Wagner, Fisher and Pascual, 2018, Plumer and Davenport, 2019), was insisting that universities certify that they protect free speech, or risk losing federal research funds. Meanwhile, in China, even academics in the most eminent research universities have to take care to toe the party line as increasingly 'student information officers' listen in on lectures for hints of deviant thought while the eight Hong Kong universities are being brought under the auspices of the National Security Law and some professors are being fired. In Turkey, many universities have been purged of academics who disagree with the Erdogan regime and have been saddled with government supporters as rectors. In Hungary, a major university has been closed as the government clamps down on dissent in ways which would be counted as ridiculous if they weren't so tragic. In Iran, academics have been imprisoned for scientific activities even including conservation. In India, academics have been sacked for not having the right views. In the Philippines, 19 universities have been labelled as 'recruitment havens' for communists. In Afghanistan, perhaps the worst of all, universities have become the target of nihilistic mass murder. The list goes on. No wonder that from September 2018 to 31 August 2019, Scholars at Risk (2019) recorded 97 killings, instances of physical violence, and disappearances of academics, as well as 87 instances of imprisonment, and 70 prosecutions. That's before we get to all of the visas refused, sometimes on the flimsiest of grounds, including, I'm afraid, by the UK.

Generally speaking, there have only been muffled complaints from research universities, yet alone universities as a whole, about this state of affairs. There's been a lot of what feels like feet shuffling and looking the other way. Yes, the UK has organisations like the estimable Council for At-Risk Academics and schemes like the University of Sanctuary. But when are we going to get institutions grouping together to fight back jointly against these iniquities? This kind of reticence (or, more likely, fear of offending governments from which overseas students originate) has to stop before it starts to look like complicity. If universities themselves do not have confidence in their values and the resolve to fight for them, who else does? Truth to tell, it has taken the Ukraine war and British universities' entirely admirable attempts to twin with Ukrainian universities and help their academics to prove that this mettle still exists.

What about the other universities?

None of this is meant to denigrate other kinds of university, as though they are somehow lacking because they're not a research university. Rather, they tend to be different kinds of institution from research universities, strong but in different directions, as evidenced by the presence of the various mission groups. They have different goals and different missions. They are not trying to do what research universities are doing – which is not the same as saying that these institutions never do any world-class research. Some clearly do and I am certainly not trying to deny that they have this capacity or that it needs protecting. But, putting that important caveat to one side, these universities are concerned mainly – not all – with more vocationally-oriented teaching and with applied research that shows rapid and visible benefit to stakeholders like companies. They are often extremely innovative in their own terms and their importance in educating large numbers of students and boosting local economies is self-evident. They can often have extraordinary effects on their surrounding cities and regions, as can be seen from the examples of universities like Coventry and Teesside, while some of the smaller universities like Harper Adams and the University for the Creative Arts are immensely valuable in their own specialist fields.

Nor am I suggesting that research universities can just close themselves off from other universities. Research universities and other kinds of university are all part of a general ecosystem that delivers higher education, one in which different institutions can still learn from one another and can, in certain circumstances, cooperate closely. There is an argument to be made that they ought to be brought closer together in a division of labour rather like the system found in California where community colleges, Cal State universities and University of California universities co-exist – mainly happily – in a division of labour which, though not perfect (see Marginson, 2018), allows higher education to become a genuine compact by allowing transfer to higher level institutions at the two-year point of a four-year undergraduate degree. That kind of mobility has been stymied in the UK by a number of factors, including the fiction that all degrees are somehow equal, but it would, for example, provide a second chance for many students to access universities like Oxford or Cambridge when they have been able to show their mettle. (It's not far from that to colleges within each of these universities whose main purpose is to allow people to enter their system who have been excluded.[17] Indeed, Oxford already has something a bit like it in the shape of Ruskin College, an affiliate of the university which is aimed at union members. Within the university, it has a kind of orphan status but if it was brought into the fold it might provide a counter to colleges which mainly, after all, train the British elite.)[18]

Nor am I suggesting that we should call a halt to new kinds of universities. Indeed, I have been heartened by the number of smaller universities like NMITE, TEDI-London and the London Interdisciplinary School that are coming into existence which are modelled, in part, on small US liberal arts and science colleges. I see real hope for the pedagogic future in some of these institutions as they try to get back/go forward to an educational experience which is personal and intensely challenging. For a certain kind of student who is often neglected by the current system, they will be a real boon.

Neither am I intending to disparage vocational education. For example, for a long time now, I have argued for much better links between higher and vocational education (e.g. Commission on the Future of Higher Education, 2013, Burnett and Thrift, 2015) and they have indeed been growing. Certainly, it is difficult to dispute the argument that vocational education has had the rough end of the stick. But the tide is turning as T levels arrive, as the apprenticeship levy (however problematic) provides a boost to funding, as the lifelong loan entitlement rolls out after 2025, and as apprenticeships of various kinds burgeon into a genuine parallel track. Consider just the fact that 18 per cent of those applying for an undergraduate degree in 2021, around 50,000 students, said they were also applying for a degree apprenticeship. That compares to just 3,600 apprentices (aged 19 or younger) who started a higher or degree level apprenticeship in 2020/21 (Cope, 2022).

Excellence

A final point. One of the issues that arises in this brief prelude, as in the book as a whole, will recur over and over again in different guises. When it comes to it, excellence is the guiding principle of a research university. Standards must be high and they must be kept high in both research and teaching. But there is a tension between excellence and what might be called a democratic mindset. This issue will surface over and over again in the book. In research, for example, there are those who argue not so much that such a tension doesn't exist but that excellence needs to be redefined to take in more variables like ability to work in a group, communicate well, acknowledge a broader set of actors, and so on, with the result that academic excellence becomes a group rather than an individual attribute. But it isn't possible to get away from the fact that when research universities are looking for the 'best' researchers, though it might be possible to modulate what is meant by best, the fact remains that some researchers are just better than others at doing research, howsoever defined, period. When it comes to students the tension is even greater. Research universities want to take the 'best', the most excellent, students but using this guide to admit students has – so far at least – produced intakes which are socially skewed. Universities may find all kinds of ways of wriggling off this particular hook but the fact is that decisions are being made that privilege particular groups (though to nothing like the degree that used to be the case). There are systematic biases. Yet, on the other side, most school pupils and their parents want to believe that if they get good examination results they should be able to get into a 'good' university. The tension here is that ridding admission to university of certain biases produces other tensions among those who will now be excluded in ways which are going to be interesting to see work out, to put it but mildly. And another tension related to students. When they get to university, students should expect the very best teaching so that they learn to really think. However, as universities have expanded their numbers, it is a moot point as to whether it is possible to achieve this goal in the way that it once was and to what extent damaging trade-offs are being made.

But before examining these and many other issues concerning the current state of British research universities, let's go back to basics. What exactly is a 'university' in these days when so many institutions claim the title? Actually, there is a straightforward way of addressing this question – empirically – and that's what the next two chapters set out to do.

PART I

The research university

2

So what is a 'university'? Part 1: Architecture and academics

Once upon a time, universities were corporations, like the corporation of a town. They were often vocational, charged with the professional training of administrators, lawyers, doctors, the clergy, and the like. But gradually these institutions coalesced around the idea that they had to represent an 'idea'. They were given an all but sacred mission of valuing knowledge for its own sake a la Newman or Jaspers. They were deemed part of a state apparatus in the manner sometimes ascribed to von Humboldt. (In fact, he was much closer to a libertarian for whom universities would cultivate individuality and freedom of opinion on the grounds that 'the preservation of unlimited freedom to think, to study, to pursue studies and conclusions needs no more defence' (cited in Roberts, 2009, p. 7)). They were counted to be transmitters of a high culture. They were understood as moulders of good citizens and builders of character, a favourite of American universities. Carrying on in the American vein, they could be based around an idea of a 'multiversity' a la Kerr. More recently, they have been defined as though they are commercial actors, not exactly red in teeth and claw but certainly feeding on the juices of competition. And there are the contemporary attempts to revive the idea of universities as civic actors, there to rework the nineteenth-century tradition of the civic university.

But none of these definitions works any more, if indeed they ever did. Universities have become many things for many people and they cannot be thought of singly. As universities have both grown and diversified, functions that used to be regarded as add-ons have become central. Universities have become rather like houses on to which a series of extensions have been tacked, with the process of addition seemingly having no end in sight (A cynic might say that British universities are becoming a kind of safety net for problems which other actors cannot solve.) To say that universities are about one thing is patently false. Equally, because the process of extension has been variable, they differ considerably in what, how, and how much they do of what things. They are aggregates. They are multiples. If you are feeling optimistic they are symbionts, with each different part supporting the other. If you are feeling pessimistic, they are just a cacophony of separate parts which no longer come together as anything approximating a whole.

That universities are multiples is hardly a new insight, of course. Both the Robbins Report in the 1960s (Committee on Higher Education, 1963) and the Dearing Report in the 1990s argued something quite similar in that they suggested that universities pursued a number of missions.[1] And, for a long time, pragmatists have argued that that all that binds universities together is a shared set of relations among their different parts – and an annual struggle over the budget. As Duranti (2013, p. 214) has it:

> universities are complex institutions where individuals, groups, and units of various kinds (e.g. academic departments, research centres and institutes, professional schools, support and external relations staff, administrators) compete for resources both inside and outside of their organizational domain while simultaneously trying to coordinate with or at least not intrude on one another.

That doesn't mean that a university is just the sum of its many parts. It may be that, at their simplest, universities are large organisations which provide employment and inhabitation for numerous people. But they contain numerous different and sometimes conflicting communities which, though they are part of the same university, may not always agree on what the organisation is or what it stands for beyond a few cognitive shortcuts which rarely bear close examination. In other words, universities are coalitions of practices which cohere, in part, because they don't cohere and have to continually argue about which community gets the most attention. They consist of an incredibly complex set of work ecologies – made up of buildings, people, things, and particular geographies – which oft times can have quite different goals in mind. Bringing them together in a functioning whole is always a challenge. Some writers declare that a university has a 'soul' (Brink, 2018). Given that their coherence is only relative, I think that is a bit strong. But I do like to think that, for all of their complexity, the best universities do at least have a beating heart, one that arises out of the better impulses of the people they employ in these communities as well as how they are employed.

To begin with, these different communities are grouped around a series of simple operational pragmatics. They are tied together by the teaching timetable which links teaching rooms and teaching times, an activity which can be fearfully complex and which nowadays requires specialised software, by the annual calendar which gives a rhythm to the year of terms or semesters, especially examinations and various graduation ceremonies, by the less and less quiet period of the summer break when undergraduate students have gone home and research time is at a premium, by the meeting of all kinds of committees, by the deadlines for grant and other funding submissions, and by the annual financial round in which each department puts forward a budget, gets it knocked about, and finally comes to a resolution. They are bound together as well by a devotion to research and teaching. Though more and more actors in universities are not directly involved in these activities, still they are cardinals. And they are bound together by the simple fact of interdependency. Just as linchpins were there to stop the wheel sliding off the axle, so each and every part of the university is (or at least should be) there to keep the other parts running.

Then there is the growing importance of measurement. Whether it is the citation mania of parts of science, the hunger of administration for quantitative comparators, the demands of monetary and fiscal discipline, the apparatuses of relationship management, or the need to display community commitment, each mode of university existence is measured out, quite literally. New modes of data generation and management mean that measurement appears around every corner. Pretty well everything an academic or a student does is increasingly able to be recorded and fed back as management information. For example, data gathered on students might include personal data about medical visits, records of learning activities, assignments and grades, browser histories, patterns of student communication, use of identity cards and, as a result, which buildings have been accessed how many times, even students' movements through a campus (Reich, 2020). And that's just to start with. Meanwhile, pretty well everything in academe has become a means of achieving extra visibility through numbers, whether it is a research identifier system like ORCID (launched in 2012) or a research sharing system like Research Gate (founded in 2008) or the ubiquitous digital object identifier (the doi, introduced in 2000). As these examples show, numbers can be very useful. But the rise of numbers in academe has its downsides too, especially when it comes to measuring research output and quality. The problem, pointed out oh so many times now, is that the numbers don't automatically correlate with quality of invention or importance. So numerical measurement has advantages, of course. It does tell you something. But it has disadvantages too. In particular, 'metrics allow actors external to a field of expertise to make decisions that go against the opinions and proposals of the experts, but do so without directly challenging their knowledge' (Biagoli, 2018, p. 269). This is why context is so important which is why the panoply of academic assessment, indexes like citation counts, impact factors and the like, need to be used very carefully indeed (Aknes, Langfeldt and Wouters, 2019).[2] Take the case of peer review:

> To audiences unwilling or unable to appreciate that communities of expertise tend to be small and relatively closed because of the remarkably lengthy training required to gain membership in them, academic departments may look like incestuous tribes ... with a tendency both to think in a certain way and to hold onto specific local interests. Metrics promise to bypass all of that, sorting true knowledge from mere statements of privilege dressed up as local expert knowledge.

Metrics are knowledge by and for outsiders, understandable to all those who consider themselves external stakeholders in academic scholarship, all the way down to the taxpayers. Metrics can even acknowledge some of their limitations because their transparent methodology allows for criticism, and therefore for corrections. Though not epistemologically superior, metrics claim the rhetorical moral upper hand. (Biagoli, 2018, p. 271)

In other words, when it comes to the prominence of measurement in universities which are continually centralising the watchwords are 'handle with care'.

There are many other ways that universities cohere too. However, in order to get to them, instead of starting from the mountain top of grand ideas and motivations, I want to begin on the plains by noting what universities are currently made up of.[3] Each of these constituent parts has their own history, geography and even ideals.

The infrastructure

So how to characterise a conglomerate? Universities are composed of all kinds of entities and spaces, human and inhuman, each with their own histories. I will begin with the inhuman, with physical infrastructure, including distinctive buildings and physical arrangements. Universities tend to have specific spatial orders which mix the instrumental with the ideal and which go to make up what Asa Briggs called a 'map of learning' (cited in Taylor and Pellew, 2020, p. 4). I will then go on to investigate the different communities that inhabit these various spaces, communities which may fall in with this spatial order or harness it to their own purposes.

Universities have a *basic physical infrastructure*. I will pass by the roads, pipes, cables, electricity substations, and the like which are no different from any other agglomeration (though it is worth remembering just how expensive research university utilities bills often are – big science and medicine use large machines which sometimes require epic amounts of power and water) and move straight to university *buildings*. Many of these buildings are utterly familiar, especially because so many sectors of the economy and welfare state have adopted what was the American university ideal of a campus (a term that originated in 1774 in Princeton to describe a large field adjacent to Nassau Hall that has now become a general descriptor of a concentrated university site). But some of them do have distinctive histories that mark them out as belonging to a university, each history laid out in considerable detail now by historians who are increasingly drawn to thinking of the past not only in terms of the textual, material and visual records that survive, but also the architectural and geographical worlds in which people lived. The university fits this turn. Originally, it was a small, mainly male world of confined spaces and forced relationships – an exceptionally intense environment, in other words (Whyte, 2015). It was, and at least to a degree still is, therefore, a place in which a sense of place has been exceptionally important.

To begin with, there are the spaces of knowledge that have evolved over many generations (e.g. Livingstone, 2003). Science is made through many different kinds of site, and these sites – which vary from the grand and sometimes even imposing like the laboratory, the museum, and the botanical garden to more mundane locales like the refectory and the common room – really matter. Science is made out of a set of somewheres. Universities are brim-full of them, many of them arising from a time when universities rarely eschewed a degree of magnificence and were often, for all of science's secular ambitions, linked to the Church.

There is the library, of course. This used to be a building full of collections of books which included, joy of joys for academics, the often rather dusty stacks in which you could find all kinds of treasures – books not taken out for 50 years, various maps and archives, collections on topics you didn't even know existed which allowed for the joys of semi-random discovery. And also that distinctive library hush and that distinctive library smell.

All this has been changed by the internet which means that really obscure sources can often be found immediately, often via a hyperlink, a word first used in 1987. (I well remember the excitement of finding some recondite works on early navigation. Now they're on the web and translated in a flash.) Indeed, a whole way of doing research in the humanities and social sciences through libraries and archives is gradually fading away, as Keith Thomas (2010) has brilliantly documented. Working methods like gathering materials and note-taking (and shuffling) are changing as reference managers and databases proliferate, as laptops and phone cameras make it much easier to translate material from the archive to the study, and as DOIs mean that one can instantly find a paper.

Meanwhile, it often seems as though many university libraries – not all – have become massive undergraduate and postgraduate study spaces as they adjust to the realities of large volumes of postmillennial students and their modes of collaborative working which involve studying side by side rather than being isolated in their rooms. As a result, use of library space is, if anything, increasing, often markedly. Students meet up in libraries and plan their latest group presentation there. They access journals online instead of having to search through heavy volumes of back issues. They may look at a physical book but that is no longer a necessary accoutrement of a library visit. Their search process usually involves some mix of Google and the online library catalogue: most of them wouldn't know the Dewey decimal classification system if it hit them in the face. Though, as a bibliophile, I personally think a lot of this is sad, the fact is that through history libraries have made constant shifts in content and organisation and this is just the latest stage of their evolution.

All this said, libraries are still manna for many researchers. To begin with, you can't buy all the books you want to use (though I have tried) and there are plenty still to be read. Then, transitioning to the internet has brought undoubted boons. For example, many university libraries have built up valuable archives which are now very often accessible online. And, finally, who wouldn't want to just go and sit in a library like the Bodleian, the first copyright library in the world, which even now has a Mervyn Peake-ish nooks and crannyish air about it?

Then there is the laboratory. In the sixteenth century, *laboratorium* primarily denoted the workshops of alchemists, apothecaries and metallurgists, but it subsequently came to refer to all forms of accommodation in which natural phenomena and processes were investigated by means of various instruments. Around the end of the seventeenth century, the laboratory of the alchemist became a casting-off point for a new type of science whose aim was to discover useful facts about nature via concrete routines (Shapin, 1994). Boyle conducted experiments in chemistry and physics in his own laboratory, establishing a practice in which experiments were performed before a learned audience. They were then published in a manner designed to be easily understandable so that others could repeat them. By the last third of the nineteenth century, buildings especially designed and equipped for the purpose of this kind of science became central institutions of a professionalised science which relied on the pursuit of standardised methods for creating innovations (Livingstone, 2003, Schmidgen, 2018). Since that time, laboratory layout has continued to evolve as what counts as the scientist and their accoutrements have changed, as well as who is allowed access to scientific spaces like the laboratory (Galison and Thompson, 1999). Laboratories are often designed to make cultural statements about the conduct of science. For example, science is now often depicted as an industrialised venture that promotes creativity through enhanced mixing in large teams. The design of many laboratories has fallen in line with this cooperative depiction, with consequently elevated demands on space and equipment. But many of the biggest recent impacts on science buildings have arisen from two sources. One is the demands of equipment. But it's not just the range and complexity of the equipment that's now needed – from microscopes that can see individual atoms to all of the gene-editing technology underlying CRISPR-Cas9. It's that laboratories themselves are becoming equipment. Contemporary laboratories can be far more expensive to set up, often requiring completely new kinds of construction – zero vibration labs to underpin nanotechnology research, clean labs for biological research, negative pressure labs to allow safe use of dangerous biologicals, buildings which can house really big pieces of kit like accelerators and lasers, buildings that eliminate noise – each of these can and invariably does produce eye-watering impacts on the bottom line. Then there is the stamp of health and safety. Some academics think that its impact can be stifling. Hmm. My partner was blown up in one undergraduate lab class in the 1970s and suffered some quite serious injuries. Though the event was certainly seen as problematic at the time, that was about it. Again, I well remember seeing photographs of the back of a refrigerator in the laboratory of one chemistry professor in which various, shall we say interesting, chemicals had been stowed and then been forgotten about with the result that they had started to merge into each other in ways which could only be described as potentially quite exciting. So it's a good thing that nowadays laboratories follow strict protocols which mean that these kinds of event happen much more rarely. Fume cupboards are ubiquitous. Safety glasses are ubiquitous. Check lists and registers are ubiquitous. But, even so, there is still some way to go (see Menard and Trant, 2020).

As already pointed out, in line with a new industrialised dynamic based on team spirit and diversity, new science buildings, often designed by statement architects to make a statement, are frequently set up to allow social mixing. Many buildings have labs on one side, offices on the other and in between all kinds of spaces that don't just allow but actively promote mixing. This has become especially true as multidisciplinary and interdisciplinary work has become more and more common, the idea being to mix and match people hailing from various disciplines and to use this diversity to enhance research. All around the world buildings like these have been added to the roster of university built forms. In some US universities, they often have fantastic food on offer as well. In British universities, not so much.

Another difference is that in many disciplines equipment is now queen. From the earliest experiments, equipment always was a vital component of science but it is now a scientific actor in its own right. Many recent scientific advances have been possible only because of new kinds of equipment becoming available. Scientific equipment doesn't last long (and in any case academics want the latest version), is becoming more complex, and is often subject to serious price inflation. Advances in instrumentation take place continually and many of them are large-scale and very expensive – from satellites to super-computers, from space-borne telescopes to particle accelerators able to work with (and smash) individual particles. The bounds of what can be sensed and measured and how finely it can be sensed and measured put a constant pressure on funds, even when some of these facilities are centralised and require booking. It is a perennial headache for universities to find the money to gain access to these larger facilities and to renew equipment which has become outdated and yet renewal is crucial to keep up with science. At the medium scale, the number of new technologies which continue to line up sometimes seems more like a flood – from

3D printing through LIDAR and ultra high-speed photography, from artificial olfaction using new chemical sensors to a battery of new kinds of microscopes that can see into cells – widefield microscopes, confocal microscopes, light sheet microscopy, structured illumination microscopes, stochastic optical reconstruction microscopes, and electron cryo-microscopes among them (Fleming, 2019).[4] In another example from the life sciences, sequencing technologies, which combine new equipment with new kinds of experimental design and data analysis, enjoyed a boom in the 2010s. In 2013, *Nature Methods'* method of the year, single cell sequencing, highlighted the ability to sequence DNA and RNA, allowing biological differences between cells to be inferred. But by 2019 the method of the year was identified as single-cell multimodal omics which has made it possible to broaden out the view of cellular heterogeneity still further, for example by profiling one cell at a time. Or there are holographic extensions to technologies like optogenetics (a technology which has enjoyed a boom since its emergence in 2005) which allows researchers to shine a light into tissue and see neurons at work. Or the use of protein folding algorithms made possible by AI. Then, last but not least, there is the need to constantly replace mundane pieces of technology like desktop and laptop computers which scientists nowadays expect to be able to support numerous programming languages and command interfaces, and give access to vast data sets supported on the cloud. Of course, some of these facilities and equipment will be shared between many scientists, either because they are a facility held in common between a number of universities or because collaborators have been sought out who have access to these machines but, even so, for most research universities, funding new equipment can often feel like running up the down escalator.

Then there is the office. Offices, even now, give rise to disputes between academics. Often jealously guarded, they were signs of status, havens in which to think, places to conduct tutorials, and defensible spaces from which to fend off all comers. Now these sacred spaces are starting to disappear as universities think more and more about the affordability of their spaces, using financial models which explicitly charge individual university departments for the space they use. After all, although it can be argued that offices are crucial for other kinds of work, many academics aren't necessarily doing research when they're within the embrace of their four walls – I have certainly never been able to do any serious thinking and writing in them and that's true of many other academics too (see Tusting et al., 2019). There are just too many distractions to get up a head of steam. I need a grey day and a blank wall and this is often best found at home, an experience shared by many. That said, some academics do put in a strict nine to five day in the office, five days a week.

Many universities, in line with ideas about flexible working (which, ironically are, at least in part, the product of university business school thinking now coming back to haunt universities), have produced buildings in which individual offices are small (with tutorial functions taking place in seminar rooms) or even non-existent. Some have moved to something that looks suspiciously like, or indeed is, hot-desking – just as the barometer of architectural opinion begins to point away from the idea that these kinds of use of space promote greater cooperation and creativity, with numerous critiques of the increased distraction and stress that results from crowding people together in this manner. Ho-hum.

Then there are the various student habitations. It is a mainly post-war peculiarity of the British university system that most students leave home to go to university (Whyte, 2019). Whereas in 1967 'roughly half the universities had less than 40 per cent of students in residence' (Halseyand Trow, 1971, p. 81), with some of the then new universities like Bath having none, in 2017/18, just over 80 per cent of full-time students left home to study. In 2018/19 48 per cent of these students lived in purpose-built halls while 52 per cent lived in private sector purpose-built accommodation with a further 551,000 students being accommodated in houses in multiple occupation (Jones and Blakey, 2020). Halls of residence used to be spartan affairs. In my first year at university, I shared a room in hall with another student. The toilets and baths were all communal. Meals were just like those at school, so at least that was familiar. With the expansion of the sector, with the advent of the student as consumer, and with the influx of international students, such facilities seem like an artefact of history, a backward glance to student rookeries. In particular, a commercial sector has populated British towns and cities with student apartments, not least because universities cannot afford to build from their own resources all the habitation they need to cope with student expansion. Some student residences, especially in London, are specifically aimed at high-end international students who can afford to pay as much as £579 or even £679 a week for an apartment in a private student accommodation block in a central urban area, complete with a range of amenities which might include a games room, a communal study room, an onsite gym, lounges on each floor and, to cap it all, perhaps a rooftop terrace and even an extravagance like a cinema or bowling alley. That said, most universities operate a ladder of more modest rents for their own properties. At one time, these properties used to give all students a chance of access to relatively low-priced accommodation. But many more students now have to live out in the commercial sector in their second and third years as a result of rapid student number expansion. The resulting building boom, combined with the rise of buy-to-let, has produced major effects on some towns and cities. Just go to cities like Exeter and Coventry and you can see this straightaway.

Another distinctive university space is the lecture theatre. When universities first started, there were few printed resources, and these resources were often prohibitively expensive. The medieval meaning of the word 'lecture' was indeed to read or read aloud. Students sat and listened to someone who read from an authoritative text (and came to be regarded as having authoritative expertise). Students produced their own learning resources in the form of notes. Books were often specifically designed to fit on a podium (or a cathedra as it was then called). Lectures have survived for over 800 years and though their death has been proclaimed many times, they stubbornly persist, as does the lecture theatre. The first permanent lecture theatre, one with concentric galleries provided for spectators, was apparently constructed in Padua in 1594, followed by Leiden in 1597 and then the Barber-Surgeon's Hall in London in 1636. Lecture theatres have varied tremendously in how they are laid out. I well remember giving a talk in an early medical lecture theatre in Edinburgh University that had the most extraordinary rake which gave me a crick in the neck and must have had the onlookers fearing for their lives – one false move and they would plummet several tiers to certain injury. But lecture theatres have evolved since and most are now much of a muchness involving the same layout distinguished mainly by better or worse acoustics, better or worse technology and, in some cases, means of allowing group work by, for example, providing swivelling chairs and desks. Lecturers tend to have favourite places to lecture in – mine was always the Peel Lecture Theatre in the University of Bristol which was light and airy and allowed you to walk all around the room, pontificating as you went.

University buildings can also vary in standard and layout. Business schools are one distinctive element of the built ecology. They are often lavish by university standards. Not surprisingly. Their clientele often expects the best and is willing to pay for it. (In many universities, the result is that they earn a lot of money, some of which subsidises the rest of the university. This produces a mixture of envy about some of the salaries paid, snobbery about the quality of their work, and a tendency to see them as symptomatic of marketisation.) Another example of a distinctive built ecology is provided by medical schools. The largest of these – Oxford, Cambridge, UCL – are effectively universities within universities. Some of them have been around a long time but many are far more recent. Some of them are on separate campuses, even on completely separate sites. Others are threaded through cities. Many of them are both a feather in a university's cap and very often a drain on its finances (unless, that is, they are of sufficient size to generate really substantial income like Oxford or Cambridge). Medical schools are expensive to run. They are quite often extremely complex. And they involve cooperation with National Health Service hospital trusts which can sometimes be challenging. Veterinary schools are another distinctive feature of universities. Until recently, there were just five of them. They maintained what seemed like a very successful fortress against newcomers. Now there are six more. Often sited in rural locations, they also form a distinctive ecology made up of all manner of characteristic facilities and equipment (I well remember the operating suite for horses at Bristol).

Next up are science parks. Since the first one was set up in the UK by Trinity College in Cambridge in 1970 they have grown to well over 100 in number. To begin with, they were very distinctive with a particular emphasis on firms involved in scientific innovation or technology transfer. Most have incubator buildings for nascent small businesses, accelerators, and so on. But, though they often look the same, with their jogging tracks and ponds with ducks and buildings meant to represent the business of science, they are often very different and have different economic effects (McCarthy et al., 2018). Some, like Magdalen College Science Park in Oxford, are giants of their kind, able to sell a 40 per cent stake of their operation to Singapore's sovereign wealth fund for £160 million and then keep on expanding both their operations and the college's endowment. Some others, truth to tell, are really quite similar to the commercial business parks found on the outskirts of many towns and cities.

Then, finally, there are all the university facilities. There are the numerous cafes and restaurants (which for academics have often replaced facilities of yore like the senior common room and the university club). There are the sports centres and playing fields and swimming pools, some of which are magnificent. There are the arts centres and the theatres which often act as cultural centres for the surrounding region and host extremely impressive programmes of events and general entertainment. And there are the museums and galleries. Many of these are of national importance and deserve far more attention than they often get. While I was at Oxford, I used to delight in the Ashmolean, the Natural History Museum and the quirky Pitt Rivers. But many other universities have their equivalents like the Barber Institute of Fine Arts at Birmingham University and the Whitworth Art Gallery at the University of Manchester, as well as smaller gems like the Petrie Museum of Egyptian Archaeology at UCL.

This brief romp through university buildings only goes to illustrate all the different threads that now go to make up a university. Whereas at one time a university looked like a university, with just a few buildings shouting out their function, often communicating a sense of grandeur and enclosure all at once, now they often look more like a small town with a melange of different architectural styles, some impressive, some workaday. Often they are highly connected to their city and region and try to act as beacons of place (Whyte, 2015). For some, they represent the flowering of a new civic tradition, a tradition which, it has to be said, has been exaggerated in the service of the present.[5] (After all, in previous times, 'the relationship between civic universities and the cities they serve was often strained. Many leapt at the chance to escape their local communities and embrace the apparent freedoms offered by a national constituency' (Whyte, 2015, p. 330).) For others, they represent a new age of mass tertiary education, factory-style research, and campuses that have begun to resemble theme parks. As so often, a simple explanation rarely encompasses what is happening. That is even more true when we come to all the communities that inhabit these buildings. In the end, after, all it's the people who galvanise a university. Let's start with *academics,* and then move on in Chapter 4 to *students*, ending with all of the *other communities* that go to make up university life.

Academics

Research is about community. Research academics exist in a tight international web of contacts occasioned by their discipline, a means of asking what are often quite different questions about the world in often quite different ways while keeping at least a degree of coherence. Distance has never been a fatal constraint for disciplines, at least since the early days of Galileo and Newton, as many studies in the history of science have shown all too well. You have to cooperate with others – wherever they might be – to know what's going on, what's what and what isn't. Like any community, research is an imperfect, highly social activity. It happens in labs and offices and seminar rooms, on Teams or Zoom calls, in a multitude of conferences (many of them now virtual), in corridors and in airport lounges, or over pizza or a coffee. And as with any other human endeavour, egos and the vagaries of reputation do play a part. Friendships can be broken over perceived or actual critical slights made in the literature or at conferences. But, more often, friendships not only last but strengthen over the years.

The arenas all this social activity takes place in are twofold. First, there is the department. For most academics, not only is this the place in which potential academics still receive most of their long and often arduous disciplinary training but it is also their main experience of the university at large. Universities can have numerous departments. Just look at the list of 'departments' in the University of Oxford.[6] It seems to go on forever (though, in fact, many of the departments are research centres and programmes). Some universities call themselves 'comprehensive', that is they have this kind of rich disciplinary and subject mix. That said, there is a lively debate about whether most research universities need or indeed can afford this kind of mix. I know of universities with such a large number of departments and courses and units that they must be putting themselves in financial harm's way. Yes, students get a wonderful intellectual palette to work from but staff are put under needless pressure, there is often considerable duplication, and most universities don't have Oxford's resources, especially the collegiate boost to teaching.

Whatever the case, departments – which range in size from five to well over 100 academics and associated administrators – tend to be little worlds complete unto themselves, with their own territory and their own ways of doing things. They are effectively cooperatives – not always very cooperative cooperatives but cooperatives all the same. They have to cooperate around teaching. They have to cooperate around forging a departmental direction. And they rely on each other to keep the department's reputation in good order by publishing the very best research. They have regular staff meetings which can sometimes become a little bit fraught in the manner of small communities. Though the pressure of work dictates less frequency than in the past, they still sometimes gather for morning coffee and gossip but this is gossip that binds. Like all gossip, it is partly social (they did what?) but it is also partly informational (what is the new research being spoken about at the last conference I went to). The best departments foster immense pride in themselves, born out of a shared history and shared success. When they are in good order, their members work for each other even though individual personalities may be very different. Part of the equation is finding a good head of department. That's not always easy. It is one of the most difficult jobs in a university and really good heads of department are always in short supply. A head is near to the colleagues that they are trying to persuade to do things – each and every action is close to the action. This can be intensely problematic! (I well remember my first day as a head of department which included trying to mediate a longstanding feud between two colleagues in the departmental administration and two professors who came in to tell me that they weren't paid enough and what was I going to do about it. I wondered what I had got myself into.)

Second, there is the wider discipline (Becher and Trowler, 2001). Though multidisciplinary and interdisciplinary work has grown to the point where it has become a somewhat tiresome cliché to say that we need more, disciplines are still vital. Even in the most multidisciplinary of environments, you still have to bring something to the party. Nowadays, disciplines are often decried as producing narrow intellectual channels and even narrower minds and as open to capture by intellectual cliques. But all academics are socialised into and undergirded by a particular epistemic history which involves an inherited knowledge base and particular skills. That history and its ways of working are mainly instilled as a postgraduate and never fully leave, not least because they are reinforced by conferences and seminars. In most research universities nowadays, the dominant disciplines are from science or medicine. Their rise since the 1950s to become the dominant disciplines by size has produced an enormous infrastructure of personnel, equipment and funding agencies which acts as a kind of machine for producing research. But, whatever else this science is, it is not one bloc. It is striated by different, sometimes radically different, disciplinary ways of proceeding, from the mass engineering projects like CERN which depend upon agglomerations of scientists and engineers acting as one through the behemoth that is the medical and life sciences through what are sometimes still single scholar disciples like mathematics and statistics, and even some parts of computer science. Then there are the social sciences, again a large and diverse field which ranges all the way from social theory to mass surveys and big data, and from a largely formal discipline like economics to disciplines which rely on qualitative methods like ethnography.

Finally, there are the arts and humanities. Arts and humanities subjects, once counted as the humanistic soul of the university, nowadays occupy around 13 per cent of staff employed. To listen to many commentators, they are being crushed in a philistine vice and battered by the decline of a scholarly apparatus based especially on the monograph and the single researcher (Williams et al., 2009). There is something in this charge, without a doubt: some university managers seem to have a clodhopping view of the humanities. But students also seem to be cooling on the humanities. According to UCAS figures, 7,000 fewer students were accepted for English degrees in 2020, a decrease of a third since 2011. History enrolments fell by a fifth to 12,870. There were only 3,830 modern language acceptances, more than a third lower than in 2011, adding to the ongoing disaster of lack of language skills in the UK. But care needs to be taken before hitting the panic button. Most humanities courses are still in good health at higher tariff providers. But, some concern still needs to be expressed (Mandler, 2015, 2021, Reisz, 2015, Roberts, 2021). Why? Because the humanities are increasingly threatened at many of the newer universities (with the result that fewer and fewer students from lower socio-economic backgrounds are likely to end up studying the humanities), the result of disciplinary choices made by cash-strapped institutions which combine with government actions that are reducing grant levels in favour of supposedly more employable subjects (by a relatively small amount, it's true). The utilitarian attitude of many politicians and the government really doesn't help either. They often disrespect arts and humanities courses as somehow superfluous in the 'real' world of business and the economy. In fact, arts, humanities and social sciences graduates are just as likely to be employed as their STEM counterparts and of the ten fastest growing sectors in the UK economy, eight employ more graduates from the arts, humanities and social science than other disciplines (British Academy, 2020). (Ironically, most of the MPs who have degrees have arts and humanities and social sciences degrees – but we'll pass that one by!)

Much about the character of academic research has changed. To begin with, there is the growth of what might be termed interdisciplines. In my early days at university, departments were like fortresses. I knew very little about what was going on in the wider university and wanted to know less: indeed, sometimes the university administration was regarded as the enemy. I hadn't even set foot in most of the other departments. Many of them I wouldn't have been able to find. That has slowly but decisively changed. Academics tend to be much more outward-looking and some of them now gather together in interdisciplinary research institutes which are often designed specifically to promote disciplinary mixing.

Indeed, much more research now takes place in large collaborative networks, often interdisciplinary and international in character, through access to research grants which have become larger on average but thinner on the ground. The rise of such collaborative interdisciplinary research is driven by several factors. For example, a division of labour is often necessary to complete a project. So a climate change project may require an expert on instrumentation, a statistical and/or computational expert, and a network of academics each of whom have generated data on a particular part of the world. Research on new kinds of agriculture may require the skills of an anthropologist, a geographer, an economist, and an agricultural scientist. A nascent field often outgrows its origins and needs to add new specialisms, as in the case of computational social science or some of the very large humanities databases that have been brought into existence that will require the skills of a computer scientist and a web designer as well as many historians. (The same requirements can apply when producing virtual museum collections.) This overall change to a collaborative style resembling something much closer to industrial production has also been brought about by the requirements of funders for big interdisciplinary projects, the vogue for 'open science' (a term which covers a number of ambitions), the fact that academics brought up in a cooperative system are already habituated to think in this way and an ideology acquired from business that promotes teamwork. (None of this means that lone academics producing single-authored pieces of work are about to become extinct, of course, but they will probably take up a smaller proportion of work in science, though in the arts and humanities and some of the social sciences they will still form an important currency, come what may.) The boundaries of disciplines have changed as well, becoming more porous. For example, science has become far more interdisciplinary. Absent all of the funder incentives, this has been happening naturally in the empirical natural sciences anyway, partly because of the need to group around certain core technologies (for example, most recently, in the life sciences, gene-editing technologies like CRISPR-Cas9), partly because many of these core technologies (from magnets to various forms of atomic microscopy) are very expensive, and partly because modern science, having taken a leaf from the prevailing industrial orthodoxy, often deputes production of research in large teams. It is also happening in the social sciences and humanities. Increasingly, research there also takes in teams of researchers. Again, considerable research nowadays is at the border between science and the social sciences and arts and humanities.[7]

There have been other changes to the character of academic research too. Thus, the god-like principal investigators of yore, who ruled their laboratories like potentates, are becoming much less common and of those that are left many resemble nothing so much as CEOs of research networks, groups sometimes numbering 200 or more. They have their lieutenants. They have their workers. Then there has been a change in methods. For example, in the social sciences, statistics and other analytical techniques are in flux as methods have been developed which are no longer imports from the natural sciences but have been developed to fit their own specific requirements. And one other change. Means of representation have changed their character as well. For example, information technology has allowed new means of representation to become commonplace, as what are often spectacular images glowing from screens,[8] and has enabled new kinds of diagramming to become common. How scientific papers are presented is changing too. One example is the redesign of academic papers as computational notebooks that is now starting to take place in some of the scientific domains where computational puzzles predominate (Somers, 2018). Writers like Wolfram argue that it should be possible to produce an inflection point in the pursuit of science itself. Though most commentators would think that this was an inflated claim, still systems like the cathedral of Mathematica, and the bazaar of open enterprise software like IPython (now Jupyter) and the open-source plotting library Matplotlib, are gradually producing a world in which results and methods are revealed at the same time, an important issue given the current crisis of replication in science in fields as diverse as psychology and genetics.

What about academics themselves? To read many accounts, campus novels, memoirs and the like, you might think that academics are a different breed. But ignore all of the media stereotypes (and especially cringe-inducing words like 'boffin', a word whose origin is obscure but seems to have come into use in the Second World War). Academics are no doubt as heterogeneous as the population at large. They take in people with many different types of work styles and outlooks. There are the grand visionary thinkers. You find them in disciplines as various as biology and social theory. They go for broad, partly speculative sweeps. There are the careful instrumentalists and statisticians poring over machine outputs. There are the polymaths who very often range across disciplines. There are the fieldworkers and country experts who often know certain parts of the world better than those who live there (Lopez, 2019). There are the practitioners of methods like archival research and hermeneutics and the poets and playwrights who buoy up the humanities. There are the research bureaucrats who run the big quasi-academic organisations like the Research Councils and the numerous learned societies like the Royal Society and the British Academy. University research is a broad church, in other words.

Do these different kinds of people have anything in common, then, except that they tend to work in the same places?[9] I suppose you could be flippant and argue that they can display behaviours that are often looked on with some suspicion, even as sins, in the wider culture. Pretension may not be welcomed but it certainly isn't excluded in academe. Earnestness is pretty well a given. Dressing down at work is allowed. Indeed, dressing really smartly is often viewed with a certain suspicion; it's a mark of lack of authenticity – or, worse than that, being a member of management. Less flippantly, here are the primary set of characteristics I would identify:

- Academics probably feature more on the introvert end of the introvert–extrovert scale, though there are plenty of extroverts and even academic introverts are rarely timid.
- They are likely to have better powers of long-term concentration – I talked to one mathematician who remembered going 30 hours non-stop thinking about just one problem, neatly illustrating the aphorism that Plato has Socrates utter in book 7 of the *The Republic*: mathematicians are people who dream that they are awake (though I'd be the first to admit that this particular example might be at the extreme end of things).
- They tend to work very hard. Why? Because, to a greater extent than in most other professions, their work is their life – it is a good part of who they are. In the past, things were easier. Being an academic was a privileged position. Many people worked hard but it was still possible to find relaxation time. It was permissible to sit in the departmental common room drinking coffee for extended periods. Those days are long gone and it is now a struggle to fit in all of the mandated activities with research time which is an academic's joy and, for many of them, one of their main reasons for being.
- Academics are often portrayed as passive-aggressive – I'm not sure. Of course, academics can be as petty as anyone else. There are protocols in place in some universities for how this kind of aggression is framed but, as in many other areas of life, electronic means of communication certainly haven't helped the situation. One of Watson's (2009, p. 140) laws of academic life is that 'courtesy is a one-way street (social–academic language is full of hyperbole, and one result is the confusion of rudeness – or even cruelty – with forthrightness; however, if a manager responds in kind, it's a federal case)' and this law certainly applies twofold to email and Twitter. Equally, academics can enthusiastically impute ill intent where none may exist, though I would need convincing that this tendency is any less than in many other workplaces (Watson, 2009). It may be that any bicker factor is heightened by an ingrained sense of challenge to established authority that all academics must have on one dimension or another or by the sense of frustration that wells up in many people in later middle age as their grand life projects come to seem a little less grand or by a simple need to stand out from the crowd. All I can say is that I have found the departments that I have worked in tended to be

both supportive and friendly for the majority of the time and were often wonderful places to work. In Oxford and Cambridge, quarrels are often conducted in the highest of moral tones which can often conceal baser motives. But luckily, these universities have gone beyond the days when it would be possible for someone to carry out vendettas and feuds quite so personal as those of the historian J.H. Plumb (as delineated in Cannadine's (2004) masterful obituary) but determined coalitions of refuseniks can still do damage, as a number of college spats with their heads of house over the years have shown only too well. These spats are often about issues that might seem inconsequential or just plain tiresome away from the inward-looking college community but can take on gigantic proportions in a forcing house of personal relationships that have marinated for far too long and become overly intense.

- As has happened in many other middle-class professions – only 16 per cent of academics originate from working-class backgrounds (compared with 39 per cent of the general population) (Social Mobility Commission, 2021) – academics tend to have shown a greater political allegiance to the left over time. The percentage of Conservative-voting academics fell from 35 per cent in 1964 to 18 per cent in 1989 to as little as 11 per cent in 2015 (Halsey, 1992). The evidence base is inexact but it seems that nearly all this figure is probably accounted for by moderate/centre left views which are probably quite conservative in their own way. But, whatever the case, this is not an issue that can simply be laughed off. To an extent, it parallels the situation in the US where university faculty have become more liberal over time although in often quite variegated ways (for an excellent review, see Jaschik, 2017), with the result that scholars with more conservative and contrarian views now feel increasingly isolated in a so-called 'spiral of silence' (Norris, 2021). Some commentators argue that academics have been responsible for the surge of what John Gray (2018) calls hyper-liberalism around the world in which liberalism becomes illiberalism via teaching which is implicitly biased to one point of view. Intolerance masquerading as tolerance. Though way too much can be made of this critique – for example, what research there is doesn't really bear out the proposition that a university education makes people more liberal or that students are so pathetically impressionable (Economist, 2020) – I don't think it can just be dismissed out of hand. More ideological heterogeneity would be no bad thing. There have been instances – not many but some – of academics simply dismissing counter-arguments to their own arguments as if they emanated from the spawn of the devil, behaviour often amplified by the Twitter echo chamber.[10] (There have even been instances of historians – just a tiny minority I should add – who have argued that because historians rewrite history it's fine to just go ahead and project their particular views onto the historical record when the historians I know always stick to the evidence and give it the space to contradict their views.) It's important that academics can state their views in class and elsewhere but it is equally important for them to acknowledge that other views exist and that not all of them have been dreamed up in the mines of Moria (and it is also important to note that most students are quite able to judge for themselves whether they think these views are of any consequence). You wouldn't think you'd have to say this. But such are the times. Whatever the issue, it is dangerous if universities are perceived as being captured by faction.[11] Just a few academics need to remember that they are damaging universities by making them appear less than they are as they try to extend what can sometimes seem like quasi-millenarian practices into the academic fabric, for example with some eyebrow-raising messages and retorts on social media.[12]

- Academics' social lives seem no more or less tangled than the mean. Ignore all of those blokey *Lucky Jim/The History Man/Changing Places* campus novels with their outdated stereotypes of jetsetting bon viveur bed-hopping male academics feuding their lives away. They are mainly just a fantasy. Better to turn to the works of Anne Tyler or Zadie Smith.[13]
- There are still more men than women but this proportion has changed quite rapidly from 1989 when women made up only 14 per cent of full-time staff carrying out research and teaching (up from 10 per cent in 1964) (Halsey, 1992) to some 48 per cent now.[14] With the exception of a few disciplines like economics, earth sciences, and mathematics where the situation is still problematic, there is now a more symmetrical situation. Indeed, some disciplines have a majority of women in post. Though this change is still working its way through to the professoriat (where 28 per cent of professorships are held by women, up from 23 per cent five years ago) and higher management (where around 30 per cent of universities are led by women) it will still not be happening fast enough so far as most women are concerned. Gender balance is a live issue in other ways too. There is the issue of equal pay, for example. Mean and median pay is higher for male than women academics (especially in universities with business and medical schools) although the gender wage gap at the very top of the hierarchy seems to have shrunk in recent years (for example, according to Bachan and Bryson (2021), among women vice-chancellors it is now negligible). Then there is the issue of parenting, a responsibility which still tends to involve women to a much greater extent, and often falls right in the period when most people are getting their first grants, establishing the international contact networks that will serve them well in the future, constructing the beginnings of a research reputation and beginning to understand how to organise their professional lives (Barnett, Mewburn and Schroter, 2019). Again, they tend to be generally short of time. Women seem to do more

'academic housework', that is various forms of academic citizenship like mentoring (McFarlane and Burg, 2019). Women tend to be structurally disadvantaged in other ways too. Covid-19 showed this particularly well. So, the proportion of accepted papers with a female first author declined during the Covid-19 pandemic to 26.8 per cent of all papers as women took up greater childrearing duties (Matthews, 2020). (The proportion had been increasing over the past four years.) Equally, when a Canadian grant-funding agency asked researchers to submit Covid-19 proposals in just eight days, only 29 per cent of applications came from women. But when the agency offered another grant round two months later – this time extending the deadline to 19 days and reducing the paperwork that was required – applications from women increased to 39 per cent (Witteman, Haverfield and Tannenbaum, 2021). Meanwhile, Deryugina, Shurchkov and Stearns (2021) found that, during the pandemic, mothers experienced a drop in research hours 33 per cent per cent greater than the reduction faced by fathers. The net effect of all of these pressures is not surprising: research productivity suffers. Women publish less than men (on average, 4 publications to every 7 made by men, though interestingly the impact of their publications is the same), apply for fewer patents, cease publishing at a higher rate, and obtain fewer grants (in a ratio of 2.0 to 1.6) (Elsevier, 2020). They are generally likely to receive less credit for their work too (Ross et al., 2022). All this said, concerted action through schemes which promote gender equality like ATHENA-SWAN are generally acknowledged to have met with some considerable success in changing things for the better although there is clearly still some way to go. (However, comparable Advance HE schemes that exist for ethnicity like the Race Equality Charter are more recent and have had less time to prove their worth.)

- Certainly, there are still some pretty shocking imbalances so far as the representation of some but not all ethnic groups are concerned. There were 217,065 academics working at UK universities in 2018/19. Of the 199,245 whose ethnicity was known, 83 per cent were White and 10 per cent were Asian, while Black, mixed race, and other backgrounds made up about 2 per cent each (HESA, 2020). The comparable figures in the population at large (in 2011 it has to be said) were 80 per cent White, 6.8 per cent Asian, 3.3 per cent Black and 2.0 per cent mixed race (though these figures conceal big geographical variations – for example, in London 45 per cent of the population were of White origin, 18.5 per cent were of Asian origin and 13.3 per cent were Black). In all 17 per cent of academic staff were from minority ethnic groups in 2018/19, a figure about equivalent to the percentage in the UK population, but there was particularly poor representation of Black academics in some disciplines. In 2018/19, for example, 19.2 per cent of STEM staff aged 34 and under were Asian but only 1.8 per cent were Black. In physics and chemistry, the proportion of Black researchers was very close to zero (Joice and Tetlow, 2020). More generally, fewer than 1 per cent of professors were recorded as Black in UK universities, a figure which is moving upwards at a glacial pace, and will continue to do so unless something is done, as the STEM figures demonstrate. But the exact goal that should be aimed for is difficult to judge. In particular, there is the difficulty of using a blunt policy tool like a 'quota' which can actually entrench the category of 'race'[15] as well as the parallel difficulty of deciding when equality will actually have been reached and what this would mean. Is it the proportion of the UK Black population – 3.3 per cent? Is it the percentage in a particular population age cohort?[16] Is it the percentage weighted by the ethnicity of the population in any area? (That would mean that universities in London should aim for 13.3 per cent Black academics and universities in the north east for 0.5 per cent.) And no goal would do much to answer the complaint of many Black professors that there simply aren't enough Black academics in their departments to lean on (in many departments that would still be a very small number given these proportions). As for academics in university management, in 2018/19 there were 540 academics in top managerial jobs and 475 of them were White. A total of 15 were recorded as coming from an Asian background, five from a mixed background and a further five from another background. (The ethnicity of the rest was not known.) In 2021, six vice-chancellors were from a minority ethnic background, though none were Black. Two were vice-chancellors of leading research universities. The lack of representation of Black senior academics and managers may not be entirely surprising, given the declining number of Black students and academics making it through each career pinch point, but it is clearly a serious issue. At the moment universities can certainly point to a considerable degree of ethnic diversity but hard work is still required so far as some ethnic groups are concerned. However, even with the speediest of measures, adjusting imbalances will not be the work of a moment but neither should it be thought of as an impossible task – as the figures for academics from a number of Asian backgrounds generally underline.

- Not all academics are both teachers and researchers, the classical model. There has been a rise in teaching-only academics, even in research universities. Overall, Universities UK estimates that, of the 165,000 academic staff employed in the UK, 26 per cent are working purely in teaching (quite a few being on term contracts), 24 per cent working purely on research (again with quite a few being on term contracts) and 49 per cent working on both teaching and research (and 1 per cent on neither!!). Much of what I say in this book applies to active researchers (and many teaching academics do carry out some research) but the presence of an increasing cadre of teaching-only academics in research universities needs to be kept in mind.

Academics are quick to complain about universities and they can sometimes seem to be a constitutionally unhappy bunch, certain that their working conditions have deteriorated (and will deteriorate further). But then ask them about their work and the answer will often be remarkably positive. (Watson (2009) argues that part of the reason for the negativity stems from not wanting to reduce pressure on managers to do something but it may also be seen as letting the side down.) So, if it's all so awful, what is it about academic work itself that makes people still want to sign up to be academics? I think academics' motivations can be boiled down to five main characteristics: curiosity, obsession, hard work, accumulation of the resources to do their work with (grants and equipment, mainly won in competition), and a desire to make the world into a better place.

Certainly *curiosity*. There is a fierce joy in asking hard questions and in conversing with others about those questions. Academics ask why but, more than that, they dream of another story of why. Curiosity requires one essential skill – imagination. As Montaigne put it, we imagine in order to exist and we are curious in order to feed that imaginative desire. But what academics do is practise that skill in a disciplined way. Though, as I have pointed out, the current vogue is for interdisciplinarity, the fact remains that thinking up new questions requires training and disciplines are still the best way to do this. There are still big differences between disciplines, much bigger than most might imagine. They often have quite distinctive structures and ways of working. For example, economics has an exceptionally tight professional structure with highly competitive hiring rounds, a clear and very tightly defined hierarchy of journals, a strong emphasis on citation counts, a penchant for working papers (not least because it takes a long time to get work published in the top journals), and generous reward structures for those who succeed. Disciplines also remind us that academics always stand on the shoulders of their forebears. Though there may be a current tendency to emphasise the power of groups and group diversity in stimulating innovation there is also a tendency to emphasise the power of individual innovation through a garland of prizes and other acknowledgments. But no one has good ideas de novo. They all come from somewhere, even if it doesn't feel like it. Indeed, parts of academia are precisely about where ideas come from. The humanities, for example, are probably humanity's most skilled communicators with the dead. They make ancient ideas and mores come alive again, reworking them for the present day in an endless chain of reinterpretation. They are curators but they are also reinterpreters.

This is a world which increasingly relies on quicksilver judgements and opinions bouncing around in a system of social vibrations which resemble nothing so much as a resonance and amplification machine, a distributor and retransmitter of energies like envy, adulation, outrage, aggression, fear, hatred, and pleasure and the pat systems of meaning that underlie and bolster them. It often seems as though less and less room is given to autonomous reflection – all that is required is a reaction, preferably an escalation tinged with bitterness. Such a world is totally orthogonal to academic values which are based on what Sloterdijk (2011) calls interruption, suspending continuous processes of cementing meaning, attempting to slow things down. Not so much blocking social vibrations, therefore, as attempting to change gear so that we can see the world in new ways. *Quiet reflection* has to be guarded and curated and universities do this best. But concentration on an issue – single-minded, continuous concentration – is a difficult thing to conjure into existence. It does not come easily and it is easily foregone, lost in a whirlwind of distractions. This is why academics are so jealous of their time. (For example, I have always needed to rev up to write and this process takes me about three days to get to the point where the writing starts to flow.) It cannot be stressed enough that loss of consistent periods of time for research is becoming a serious problem in universities. What might once have been regarded as chipping away at the edges has become something rather more serious.

But it isn't just curiosity. What drives many academics is something much closer to *obsession*, exactly the same kind of obsession experienced by artists or musicians (Davis, 2008). You are inspired by your inspiration. It leads to overwork, in part because the work takes over your life. As Picasso famously put it 'I draw like other people bite their nails'. It leads to other activities too, like the search for greater precision and better calibration which are a kind of art form in themselves and can easily lead to obsessional behaviour (Glennie and Thrift, 2009). The pursuit of science is itself often described as a kind of focused obsession but as a motor of science it is very little discussed (Why is an interesting question in its own right.)

The best academics are fuelled by such obsession. They cannot leave off a problem. They chivvy away at it. Academics probably don't talk enough about obsession but for many of them it is the motor. They are possessed by their questions. At an extreme, this obsession can morph into a kind of madness, something that is acknowledged culturally in all of those novels that feature mad scientists. Indeed, for a writer like Davis (2008, p. 24), academics have become the socially acceptable face of a kind of industrialised obsession:

> Science, scientific medicine, and academic specialization – all of which achieve a kind of dominant formation in the nineteenth century in the Western world – are themselves not objective positions of knowledge but in fact aspects of the new problematics of obsession. This new method of knowledge requires all the hallmarks of obsessive

behaviour – fixation on one thing, repetitive interest in that thing, fixed attention to the details, copious notes, observations, repetitive and fixed habits of study, and a strong compulsion to do all this.

Not that there isn't a limit. Most academics would think that the historian of Germany, the late Professor Tony Nicholls, was taking things a tad too far. According to his obituary, 'except for watching the occasional football match on television, study was Nicholls's sole hobby. It was only the second day of his honeymoon in Munich when he announced to [his partner] Christine that he simply had to go to the archives' (Times, 2020). Again, most academics would quail at the monastic routines of the late Derek Parfit who spent almost all of his waking hours at his desk in All Souls.

> Other than his trips to Venice and St. Petersburg, the only reason he left All Souls for any length of time was to travel to America, to teach. He had appointments at Harvard, Rutgers, and N.Y.U.: he wanted students, because he found that it was discouragingly difficult to persuade older philosophers to change their minds. He also needed students because only they would talk philosophy with him for twelve hours at a stretch and then wake up the next day wanting to do it again. Older philosophers (and his students from past years were now in this category) had children and spouses; they sat on academic committees and barbecued in their back yards. Only he stayed the same—as fervently single-minded as they were, too, when they were young. When he found a bright new student to mentor, he devoted hours to reading his work and writing comments. (He did this for many colleagues as well: he read with astonishing speed, and would often return a manuscript with densely argued comments that were longer than the manuscript itself, even if the manuscript was a book.) (MacFarquhar, 2011)

That said, most academics would recognise at least a little bit of Parfit in themselves. *It is why the most precious gift for an academic is time to think.* Most academics have their thinking routines, they have their ways to focus, they have their timetables, they have their disciplines (what were my own? Hardly surprising: always try to write something each day, come what may, always have more than one project on the boil so that if inspiration slackens on one you can go to another, always be thinking about what comes after what you're doing now), and they have all the anxieties that result from the pressure they have often mainly put themselves under.

Obsession has its downsides. Some academics produce forbiddingly large numbers of papers and books. Just up to October of the year 2020, one academic apparently published 161 mainly co-published papers (Grove,

2020). One other colleague I know was thrilled that they were able to go round the alphabet again with a 27th citation (2016aa). These sumptuary impulses can contribute to a more general issue of overproduction – too many average papers resulting from a system which has sometimes seemed to value quantity over quality. (My old doctoral supervisor, Peter Haggett, always used to argue that academics should be given a lifetime quota of papers and if they wanted to publish more they would have to trade with academics who published less.) Certainly, it is worth examining the North American system where publication norms – in the arts and social sciences at least – tend to bend much more to quality over quantity.

All that said, obsession also includes at least an element of *competition*. True, there are a few people like Nichols and Parfit who seem to single-mindedly follow their own star, oblivious to any but their own concerns, and giving the lie to the idea that no man is an island. But most academics are competitive, if only to a degree. (It may even be that they are more competitive than the average – but better at covering it up too.) They might want to get there first (though first is sometimes very hard to define and is usually fleeting), they might want the respect of their colleagues (few don't), or they might – though I think this is very rare – want to best some of their colleagues. But one needs to be careful here. Academic competition is rarely red in tooth and claw and, let's face it, a modicum of intellectual ambition, though it might be performed in very different ways, is vital. But competition is nearly always paralleled by *cooperation*. A discipline or a part of a discipline is often a very small world in which you know or know of each and every one of the people working in your area of knowledge and every one of them can be both friends and rivals in what Harvie (cited in Graeber, 2015, p. 136) calls a 'convivial competition' which very rarely excludes cooperation or sharing. Of course, some academics feel the need to obsessively tend their citation index (some academics have citation counters on their web page which click up like milometers on cars) while others want to see their name in lights in the media (one academic I know said he was aiming for D list celebrity) but such instances are still rare and, generally speaking, academics are not driven by accolades or awards.

I can hear one response already. But I don't think this competitive edge is solely a masculinity thing – though some of the more egregious examples of these kinds of behaviour clearly are as, very often, is the ability to indulge them, as well as at least some models of what a scientist does and is (Stengers, 2018). Generally speaking, studies show that women are more self-effacing and more collaborative. Again, I don't think that the Hobbesian depiction of academics most famously found in Bourdieu's *Homo Academicus* is correct either. However, given that research is a human enterprise, it's important to pay attention to who gets to decide which phenomena to study, which research earns the major government grants, which big experiments get funded, who gets the speaking opportunities at conferences, who is media savvy, who wins the prominent fellowships and awards, and who gets promoted to high-profile academic positions. These factors – and the biases that still exist in some of them – can sometimes shape the path of knowledge.

But, like it or not, academe is inevitably an ego business. It is not for the faint of heart. When it comes to research, you have to be able to take the oft times bracing comments of journal referees about your paper, the sometimes downright nasty (and what you will, of course, regard as absurdly misconceived or horribly inaccurate or personally motivated) reviews of your books, the occasionally unpleasant comments in the question and answer session after you have given your paper at a conference or at a departmental seminar, the hours of brooding about how people have misunderstood your point or the brilliant riposte you would have given if only you'd thought of it at the time. But things are way better now than they were. I can remember one department, many decades ago now, in which people were often in fear and trembling of giving a talk, so barbed were some of the comments made. Now that kind of disparagement – it was all men doing this stuff, you will not be surprised to hear – has subsided as more women have entered academe and as more kindness has entered the culture.

In any case, to the extent that academics are competitive, the competitive spirit is set within a series of values which are crucial to the progress of knowledge. It's a competition of competing viewpoints without doubt but there are rules about what can be counted as right. The most important of those rules is *objectivity*. Daston and Galison (2007) argue that objectivity has a history which is simultaneously a history of the creation of a scientific selfhood. Using the example of scientific atlases, they set out the emergence of objectivity in the mid-nineteenth-century sciences and show how it differs as a concept from the two alternatives circulating at the time, 'truth-to-nature', which aimed to capture the essentials of creation, and 'trained judgement', which highlighted patterns in the name of a particular ethos and not just an epistemology. In other words, what is worth looking at and how to look at it has a social history in which procedures evolved that showed that some people had better examples and arguments. (There are now just a few academics in the humanities and social sciences who get close to arguing that objectivity is for the birds. The simple riposte is that they can't complain, then, when other people take exactly opposite viewpoints to theirs using the same argument.)

And the result of curiosity and obsession and competition and cooperation? Sheer *hard work*. In my experience, academics work hard, often extraordinarily hard. Much of the drive behind this workload is self-generated so far as research is concerned. More than in many jobs, being an academic requires an investment of self. Work and life often have narrow dividing lines. It is not unusual to find academics that work 60 or 70 hour weeks, skimp on vacations, and devote too little time to other activities. It is not that they want to do this exactly. It is that they feel compelled to do it. Partly, it is true, academics may be pushed along by all the paraphernalia of performance targets and the like but partly it is also because of their obsessive interest in what they are doing and the corollary of the anxiety that they would feel if they stopped with a project unresolved. They have a dedication to a project of the same order as is found among other creative workers like artists and musicians. That is why I am a little bit – a little bit – sceptical about arguments that work–life balance is horribly out of kilter in academe. It frequently is but this is not always about some twisted version of masculinity incarnate – a celebration of a tortured soul who exists on a plane far above childcare and the washing-up (well loading the dishwasher, anyway) and is immune to management pressures. Certainly, it is one reason why women have often found academe to be such a challenge – along with the outright sexism. It can prove harder for them to block out their time so that they can pursue their obsessions with quite the same intensity and stubborn perseverance. But, in my experience, as with women artists and musicians, they can be just as obsessive – although they tend to plan their time better than men, partly because they have to.

All this hard work is filtered through academic working methods which transmute raw material of various kinds into papers and books. As Thomas (2010) points out, all kinds of methods have been used through the centuries to gather and organise the material needed to write, from notes and commonplace books (which became increasingly more sophisticated over time) to immensely complicated systems which in time transmuted into paratextual devices for ordering content like the card file, the bibliography and the index, the latter device being first employed in the fourteenth century (Day, 2014, Duncan, 2021). These reading and writing technologies coordinate what can be communicated and how, not just the larger inventions like the bibliography and the index, which were so crucial to the practice of scholarship, but the actual mechanisms of writing itself like the humble indent. Inevitably, many of these writing, composition and attention mechanisms have been computerised. The bibliography and the index and the commonplace book form a direct lineage leading to various kinds of database and they can be summoned up and compiled far more quickly than in the past. The ability to cross-reference these databases has also expanded. In particular, various forms of search tool have made locating material much more efficient. But academic writing technologies can still persist. Take the example of the footnote (Grafton, 1997, Zerby, 2002). Invented in the sixteenth century, hot on the heels of printing, footnotes were originally a means of annotating a text one had written oneself. In history, they were used to identify sources and texts, to note limitations and to indicate interesting alleyways. Sometimes they 'form a secondary story, which moves with but differs sharply from the primary one' (Grafton, 1997, p. 23). In other disciplines, they were used simply to note down issues that, while not vital to the flow of argument, were either interesting facts off to the side or means of indicating arguments that needed expansion or could not be fitted in, or simply acted as a way of putting references into a book without having to break up the text. Nowadays, after a hiatus when publishers became increasingly hostile to the effort of setting them and the attendant cost, footnotes have returned thanks to software packages that automate a good part of the process. Many academics love footnotes because they both bind and disrupt a text. They can allow them to be quirky and to note down odd thoughts and possible directions of research which might not seem important enough to be placed in the main text but might one day prove to be important. Like indexes, they can even be used to inject a moment of humour.

Of course, you might well ask, what's in it for academics? The answer is ownership of their research projects. They can set the rules. Not as much as they could at one time, for sure. But still they have substantial autonomy of thought and substantial autonomy about what they investigate. What they think up is theirs, not the company's or some boss or the other, feeding off their inventions. And that gives them skin in the game of making however small a part of the world anew – the best game in town. And what else? The question itself. It demands an answer. It won't back off.

But to follow this course increasingly demands the *accumulation of resources* that often have to be generated by the researcher or a team of researchers. That means finding time and money. Time to think up and do the research, of course, time which often has to be bought out from teaching using grants or fellowships. Money to employ research assistants, money to buy science equipment or time on equipment, money for consumables, money in medicine to carry out trials, money in social science to set up and carry out surveys and to access big data sets, and so on. Capturing research grants is the academic equivalent of the great game. It is a game that people more often lose than win – the success rate for grants has declined to something like 25 to 30 per cent in the UK (by value, less by number given out) and lower still in the humanities and social sciences. Each grant application – an application to do your job, in effect – usually takes months to prepare so not getting funded can be crushing, especially for new academics who have yet to grow a protective psychological carapace. But some people are remarkably good at the game and build large portfolios of grants which power large research teams, often using project software like Trello, Jira, Asana and GitHub, based on kanban or scrum boards, in order to organise and complete multiple projects, as well as software like OmniPlan for creating timelines and tracking them. Not all academics need these levels of monetary resource, of course – researchers in some parts of the arts and humanities and the social sciences can get by without them – but grant-getting has now become a part of the landscape in all disciplines and with it new modes of organisation are evolving.

Finally, research is about *making the world a better place*. Colleagues always get a bit embarrassed when this is mentioned. It's not like they wake up every morning thinking 'I must save the world' or 'I will explain what's actually going on with human cultures' or 'I will invent a drug or vaccine or medical procedure that will allow millions to live who otherwise would have died'. But this is still a thought that does crop up whether it be more or less often. More, perhaps, in some disciplines that are on an obvious front line, like medicine and zoology, than in others but I think all academics would agree that their work is about making a positive difference which is more than just schematic. Of course, not everyone achieves that goal but the ambition is there. The other side of the coin is that such knowledge is built on a myriad of contributions, some larger, some smaller. It is collective. The ambition and content is distributed, therefore, even though in our individualistic cultures it can look as though everything worthwhile comes from the lightbulb moments of a few geniuses. And, of course, no one can be sure whether what was a research backwater can suddenly turn into a major focus of attention (like the Golgi apparatus in the wake of Covid-19), what will be the idea that genuinely lasts (like evolution), or the idea that 100 years later turns out to be right (like Alfred Wegener's ideas on continental drift or William James' ideas on consciousness) or the contribution that is horribly misrepresented over many decades or even centuries and then suddenly becomes current again (like the work of Jean-Baptiste Lamarck or Herbert Spencer on evolution or A.N. Whitehead in philosophy). In other words, ambition should always be mixed with humility. Even long-lasting contributions accrue so many additions and changes of emphasis that they can often end up looking very different from when they started. Evolution, for example, has now taken in many new approaches including molecular evidence and systems approaches, the importance of symbiosis, and so-called extended evolution.

Of course, academics who win out can become over-confident, sometimes falling in with Watson's (2009, p. 139) law that 'academics grow in confidence the further away they are from their true fields of expertise (what you really know about is provisional and ambiguous, what other people do is clear-cut and usually wrong)'. For example, there is the well-known phenomenon of Nobel Prize over-reach syndrome, wherein Nobel prizewinners start being treated as founts of all wisdom and, in the worst cases, actually begin to believe that they are.[17] They then spend a large amount of time making banal observations about fields of knowledge they know no more about than the majority of the population – often with predictably embarrassing results. Or they become inhabitants of the 'philosopause', the implication being that they have outlived their most productive years and are now pursuing philosophical speculations in their intellectual dotage.

Myths about academics? There are quite a few. One particularly prominent one concerns the distinction often made between 'basic' or 'discovery' and 'applied' research. It is a much less easy distinction to make than many often assume. In so far as it holds, many academics cannot be easily pigeonholed as doing one or the other. For example, in my career I have done quite a lot of theoretical research but with others I have also done quite a bit of what might be considered as applied research, in so far as applied research is largely empirical and is produced for particular industry or policy audiences, for example on long-distance commuting, local currencies, financial exclusion, producer service companies, the City of London, and shopping malls. One does not preclude the other. Even disciplines which might be considered particularly theoretical often have applied components. For example, think of the growth of ethics in philosophy as applied to biomedicine or artificial intelligence. And sometimes theoretical work in philosophy can prove to have an extraordinary practical purchase. Think only of Peter Singer's formative work on animal rights.

Then there is the old saw that academics fight shy of business and industry. It's an outdated myth, though amazingly one that is even now still peddled by some out-of-touch commentators. That might have been true in the past but it isn't true now, especially in science and medicine departments. That doesn't mean that there are no concerns. There are legitimate worries about letting corporate interests bias research, especially after some high-profile cases in medicine where unfavourable results were simply not reported so as to benefit sponsoring firms. Then, there is a genuine issue over whether generally incremental 'fast' industrialised research might somehow crowd out pathbreaking discovery research, the basic research that is essential for scientific progress. Obviously, that cannot be allowed to happen: 'it's like presuming you don't need new knowledge, you can just keep going to the library and pulling books out. Sooner or later the library will be empty' (Chubb cited in Mannix, 2022). A large literature, at least since the work of famous economists like Nelson and Arrow, shows that discovery research has all of the characteristics of a public good and needs to be funded as such. (More recently economists have shown that there is too little investment in discovery research both nationally and globally. They have also shown that discovery research plays a key role in stimulating more general innovation and that without it levels of innovation decline.) Equally, academics have to beware of taking the corporate shilling and finding themselves subject to explicit or more likely implicit pressure to steer results towards a particular outcome. After all, research in universities will sometimes and rightly have to be critical of corporations' activities. That, of course, is one of the reasons why universities have to be autonomous institutions.

But, all that said, close to industry research can be of great value where it pushes along practical solutions to the world's problems, and we desperately need those solutions at this point in time as examples like the collaboration between the University of Oxford and AstraZeneca to produce a Covid-19 vaccine show. What is also clear is that there is little point in continuing to force this issue in institutions. Some academics are particularly keen on doing close to industry or policy work. Some aren't. Enough now do for it no longer to be an issue. My sense is that the balance is currently about right and that forcing things further will produce diminishing returns and will be counter-productive. In any case, close to industry work is often much better done by academics who are members of dedicated industrial centres which, apart from their own work, are skilled in calling on academics in the rest of the university who they know have the know-how they need.

In other words, people who keep on bemoaning academic culture as not 'relevant' enough are either recalling a culture of the past and trying to insert it into the present or a culture they have read about in novels which provides an easy stereotype. Usually, the people who make this criticism then add a disclaimer of some kind about showing respect for academic values/basic research. But, more often than not, they don't really mean it. It's a hollow reed.

I make no apology for underlining the importance of research in this book but, of course, most academics also teach as an integral part of their work. In other words, they have not one but two jobs – most people rarely consider how very odd this might seem. Of course, at its best, teaching is a real pleasure. When you get through to students, it feels good. When you see a student who has struggled to find their star, but suddenly cottons on, it is a joy to behold. The connection between teaching and research also shows up in the fact that many of the best researchers are also the best teachers. Why? Because they have the genuine spark of being right next to what is happening. They bring news from the front because they are the front. Students can detect this. And it is worth noting that overall teaching in UK universities is pretty good, as are the results. For example, the UK has the lowest university student drop-out rate of any OECD country (Hillman, 2021a).

That said, teaching has been going through major changes, not all of them for the better, it has to be said. It is audited to greater and greater degrees, just as in schools, but with far too much attention to procedure and too little attention to the actual content of teaching. School-style control freakery is becoming the norm just as the balance of opinion swings the other way. Consider some of the latest proposals from the Office for Students (OfS). The latest proposals for the Teaching Excellence Framework (TEF) to be applied once again to English universities are an improvement on the old TEF, especially in their devotion to quality enhancement, their realisation that the

TEF has not really worked as a means of applicant choice and their emphasis on greater contextualisation; however, they nowhere really address the actual content of courses, are not grounded in actual observation of teaching, and are shaky on understanding the mass of psychological research which questions whether teacher evaluations correlate well with learning: based on objective assessments, popular doesn't necessarily mean best and teachers who get worse evaluations often end up teaching students far more. As for the somewhat heavy-handed proposals on measuring student outcomes which would set minimum requirements for the teaching outcomes that universities deliver for students, after hundreds of pages it is difficult not to come to the conclusion that judgements will be based rather too firmly on a measure for measure mindset which sometimes seems to forget the old saw that 'not everything that matters can be measured and not everything that can be measured matters' and which often wants to add yet more data when many studies show that restraint works best.

Online learning

According to some commentators, the real action in teaching now is online with the advent of an information technology 'revolution'. The extremes of the predictions about the eventual ubiquity and efficacy of information technology in teaching have proved to be chimerical, as any historian of technology would have predicted from the outset, especially when phrases like 'disruptive innovation' and 'fourth industrial revolution' are bandied about – a sure sign of an approaching storm of drivel (Edgerton, 2019, Reich, 2020). Declarations of online revolutions have been made so many times now that they have become shopworn; 'hip ideas ... and virtual words keep reappearing not because they are good, but because nobody wanted them' (Kernohan, 2021a). But, though one could argue, as Kernohan does, that interoperability and standards matter more than the latest gee-whizzery, still information technology has gradually changed the conduct of classroom teaching and especially the possibilities for classroom participation, for example through so-called flipped learning (Mazur, 2013, Şahin and Kurban, 2019). But it has usually done so at a much more mundane level, from technologies like electronic whiteboards and proprietary packages like Slido which allow remotely asked questions (and are excellent for the shy student), live polling and quizzes. (Only a few years ago, packages like this were the preserve of a few evangelists and were quite labour-intensive.) Equally, students are now given pretty well the full backup to lectures online, not just reading lists but the material for the course and the lectures themselves, recorded for posterity, as well as former exam papers. In some courses, it would in theory be possible not to turn up and still get at least a passing mark. In one way, this recreates the Oxbridge model of reading for a degree which allowed some students to simply read around, but with the big difference now being that the questions set allow much less room for original answers. (For pessimists, what is happening is uncomfortably close to spoonfeeding, a tendency that has only been reinforced by students increasingly carrying over and expecting school habits of learning. In other words, the system increasingly seems to militate against rewarding originality, providing too much of what students want and not enough of what they need.)

Even though the biggest leap forward of the last few decades – delivering courses online – may have lowered costs (though that is certainly contested (Reich, 2020), in fact for good courses costs seem to be about the same) the graduation rates of online higher education remain much lower than those of programmes taught in person. And online courses aren't a trivial teaching proposition either. To do them well requires much more work than is often advertised, as well as cultivating a range of what will soon become rudimentary skills that go beyond the usual line-up of video chat, virtual whiteboards, document collaboration, and screen recording and video production (skills of which many academics are still nervous). Even then, to really produce an online course that works requires an awful lot of interaction – even if it is remote – with students. (That is one of the reasons why blended learning still remains popular.)

Again, many online packages provide analytics which can track student progress and pinpoint class members having difficulties. That is to the good, surely, in so far as it reveals students who are struggling which can also form part of a more general stream of data which on study habits. But like all surveillance systems it is also open to abuse. Many systems are trying to use these data to reach the goal of 'personalised learning', a phrase first used as early as the 1960s but one that really came into its own in the first decade of the twenty-first century. Students are, in theory, able to pursue a curriculum at their own pace through algorithmic pathways (or adaptive tutors as they are often known) suited to them and theirs. The role of teachers on the course is to coach students when needed and to provide small group teaching where appropriate, in other words to do the higher-order tasks. Take-up of these systems has been slower than expected, not least because research shows that, on average, they don't seem to be notably more successful than ordinary tutoring, even for subjects like mathematics where one might imagine that they might have an advantage. Of course, evaluation of these systems is an immensely complicated business because they aren't all the same but the main takeaway seems to be that these systems show modest gains which are highly dependent on context.

Another gain from the use of information technology was meant to be that students would be able to call on their own peers to help them out with their learning through so-called connected communities. Again, this has proved a more difficult proposition in practice than in theory. Like personalised learning it requires the acquisition of computer skills that not all students necessarily have (like being able to create blogs) and it has not caught on at quite the scale its proponents wished for.

But, in case this might all sound too negative, one other gain from online learning has proved rather more substantive. That has been its uses for students with specific needs. The list of beneficiaries is a long one, in fact (Latchman, 2021). For example, there are mature students who are reskilling or upskilling and have work and caring responsibilities which prevent them from following a set timetable. There are disabled students, especially those with mobility issues, as well as students with illnesses which mean that they may have to shield. There are neurodiverse students who find social interaction challenging, as well as deaf and hard-of-hearing students who want to review work at their leisure. And so on. Taken together, these students form a sizeable constituency who are now much better served.

Whereas at one time, the technological new kid on the block was MOOCs, now it is AI. If history is any guide, the flashiest technological notions like this won't go far quickly, especially because AI is a lot of different approaches subsumed under one heading. That said, narrower outgrowths of AI sensu stricto or of just very large-scale computing like virtual sandboxes, writing tools (such as bartleby.write), immersion labs (especially useful for teaching languages), virtual teaching assistants (like 'Jill Watson' at Georgia Tech), mass simulations, augmented reality, and interactive holographic projections are now firmly on the cards alongside the growth of AI grading, much smarter software that can be tailored to individual needs, and virtual teaching tutors (Carey, 2020b). The range of off-the-shelf AI packages that are already available in the UK to deal with issues like the student experience (see Cook and Newman, 2022) shows that AI is already being adopted fairly rapidly. But how they will actually be used in an integrated fashion and to what extent is still a matter of debate.

Still, as a sign of things to come, many universities in the US have full-time 'instructional designers' who help academics map out courses and degree programmes. They also create learning modules, online exercises, virtual laboratories and assessments. At a minimum, like UK universities, US colleges have adopted so-called learning management systems like Canvas or Blackboard, various smartphone tutoring apps, virtual platforms that help faculty interact with students on campus and off, or, more recently, Voice Thread, a real-time, multimedia, cloud application. Quite a few also have chief innovation officers or some other similar job title. In the US, universities are collaborating on new teaching ideas in groups like the University Innovation Alliance and HAIL[18] – a coalition of academic innovation labs. Some universities like MIT have large funds devoted to encouraging faculty to experiment (Carey, 2016, 2020b).

What all this shows is that gradually, both to (supposedly) reduce costs and to provide better teaching, at least of positive knowledge, AI and very large-scale online teaching software will impinge on face-to-face university teaching. Before long, some adjunct teaching will likely be automated and it can't be too long before some universities decide to opt for subscription models for selected online courses.[19] In the US, for example, Boise State University is already piloting this notion for two online bachelor's degree programmes. It costs $425 a month for six credit hours or $525 for nine: for students, this makes it 30 per cent cheaper than would in-state, in-person tuition. Even an elite university like Georgia Institute of Technology is considering a subscription model which would include access to a worldwide network of mentors and advisers. If subscriber online models like these were to really catch on, it's not impossible to think of face-to-face teaching as becoming an increasingly elite pursuit – but then it already is to an extent. Again, it is possible to think of subscriptions being charged according to different levels of service.

My personal view is that teaching which requires multiple modes of delivery, which will include some online courses or courses with online components, will become the norm for many students erelong, the largely incremental pace of its take-up having been hastened by coronavirus (Lockee, 2021). Already in US colleges, nearly one-third of all undergraduates are enrolled in online classes, with 6.3 million students taking at least one distance education course and 15 per cent of undergraduate students learning exclusively online. Online course-taking has increased for 14 consecutive years, and there is no reason why it should suddenly slump (Carey, 2020b). In Singapore, prompted by a previous virus outbreak, training of faculty in online teaching (with retesting) is a mandated requirement for joining a university. Further, recent important research shows that the learning outcomes from online teaching can be as good as from face-to-face in certain context-dependent circumstances though the result depends heavily on what is meant by successful learning. Academically, at least, it is possible for students to do just as well in certain subjects, provided the course is well enough designed (Chirikov et al., 2020).

But there are limits. One of the main concerns is that online learning tends to be concentrated among the poorest communities. But there are others. Online learning assumes that teachers have the knowledge base to teach online effectively. Most, in fact, still use these technologies in old ways. It assumes too that charismatic technologies can replace charismatic teachers. They can't. It assumes that students have access to these technologies in the first place. Not all do. Quite often, it assumes that learning is a linear process. It's not. Very often, it requires complex communication and unstructured problem-solving for which software is still struggling to providing a substitute. It assumes that online will make mass education somehow easier. So far, there's only limited evidence for this. Finally, at the most mundane level, it assumes that the technology actually works. Anyone who has ever taught online knows that things can and do go wrong.

In other words, a lot of assumptions. … So, ignore the familiar hype of the pre-ordained extension of information technology and its corollary: when the actuality doesn't measure up it is obvious that not enough time has elapsed for the technology to get a grip, thereby leaving room for a second or even third cycle of hype (Reich, 2020). The lessons are clear: new technologies take a long time to be transformative, resistance to them is not necessarily conservative; it is not always clear what counts as a new technology; marginal changes often constitute better accounts of technological change than some grand technological leap; technologies in use are often not the same as the claims made for them; technologies can take a long time to become obsolescent; beware of Eurocentric accounts of technology but remember not to assume that this history is necessarily well understood itself; ignore 'grand sweep' ideas like a fourth industrial revolution; remember that very few people actually understand the technologies they are using but they know the right buttons to press (or when to right or left click on a mouse); don't forget the crucial role of repair and maintenance; and so on (Graham and Thrift, 2007, Edgerton, 2019).

In other words, digital reorientation of teaching will continue to be a challenge, and not just in terms of lecturer skills and lecturer time. It's all very well to talk glibly about an online revolution but the practice is a different matter which, even given extra impetus by Covid-19, will take time to have really far-reaching consequences for universities. It is not easily done piecemeal but equally trying to rearrange a whole educational system around information technology in one go has proved generally disastrous (Seldon, 2018). Still we can forecast some of the effects if there was a widespread take-up of online learning in universities. In many of them, campuses are likely to be rearranged around student hubs consisting of teaching development centres and drop-in spaces for students. Residential accommodation may decline markedly or even disappear. Some universities may do as has occurred in the US and sign away up to 70 per cent of future online tuition revenue to private for-profit companies which have the financial resources and the expertise needed to convert traditional courses to online (Carey, 2020b, Marcus, 2020), with the result that margins may well be thin, thus dictating the need for even greater volumes of students. And so on.

One irony which tends to be forgotten is that the UK led the way by founding the precursor of the distributed non-residential university and, indeed, online education, the Open University. It is a repository of considerable online knowledge and innovation which has boosted the lives of many, many people; but what is interesting is the way in which successive governments have sidelined this educational jewel. I have never been quite sure why.

Online or not, something needs to give teaching-wise. What is proving highly problematic for many academics is absolutely basic – increasing class sizes. It may not be ideal lecturing to more and larger classes – some now have overflow rooms from which students can watch the lecture remotely – but what drives many university teachers really mad is the increase in the scale of associated activities like marking. Try marking a mountain of essays or exam scripts to a deadline over and over again in ways which allow at least some attention beyond a few perfunctory comments. It's possible, of course. I can remember marking 600 to 700 A level scripts to a very tight timetable, for example (though I ended up having marking nightmares). But, after a while, these kinds of loads are soul-destroying. No wonder that many academics envy their American counterparts who have teaching assistants to do a lot of the grunt work (and to answer online queries). That doesn't usually happen in the British system, except for lab classes where postgraduates will be drafted in to act as instructors. It isn't just lecture sizes and marking, either. Tutorial groups that used to number four have been transformed into seminar groups which usually have eight to ten people and sometimes more. Even in Oxford, the famed one to one tutorial has become a rare specimen. (Coronavirus made matters worse. A few university faculties even revised their expectations of the ratio of teaching to research time upwards.) Just look at student–staff ratios, even at elite research universities. They vary from 10.4:1 at Oxford to as high as 15.9 at Exeter University, with most universities grouping around 13.5. (Some Australian research universities are up at over 16:1 which goes to show that the process of intensification can go further still.) Even more problematic is the fact that though these overall ratios have for some time now stayed fairly stable or even declined in research universities when taken in the large, thanks in part to an injection of teaching-only staff, there is some evidence that academics on research and teaching contracts in many research universities have found that their ratios have got worse (Wolf and Jenkins, 2021).

Unfortunately, as combative academic criticisms of each other's research have not exactly subsided but at least become more measured and more civil, criticism about their teaching from regulators and students has become much fiercer. There are the constant audits. Academics have to take what can often be quite difficult comments about their teaching and general levels of service from students. Not all students, of course. But it only takes a few who jot down not so pleasantries to ruin a day. Most students give honest and constructive feedback but a few seem to delight in a kind of I'm so cool negativity which stems in part from Generation Z's rather different attitude to expertise. It's particularly difficult nowadays because students not only mix up style and content (it's surprisingly easy to get better assessments of your course by turning up the performance dial) but also because, in step with the times, students increasingly tend to think that all their material should, in a certain sense, be entertaining. That can't always be the case, nor should it be. When you're laying the foundations, some things will be a slog, come what may, and some things will take a long time to penetrate. Learning is not like the TEDx talk which is intended to make difficult things look easy but misses all of the stops in between. It can be very hard work. Pity the poor academic who has to teach courses that are crucial but are already seen by students as 'difficult' before they start (like statistics for many doing social sciences, for example). And then there are the students who believe that it is their divine right to text or email at any time of the day and night and expect pretty well instant service. Many academics have horror stories along these lines.

Of course, academics do all manner of other activities than research and teaching. There is more and more administration to complete. There are more committees to sit on. There are all manner of internal projects that require staffing. And there is outreach: one of the good outcomes of the recent rounds of the Research Excellence Framework impact statements has been to show just how many and varied positive academic interventions in public life actually are.

Let me end this section with two of the main complaints that academics now have. One, perhaps the most serious, is the loss of autonomy at work. It is a truth pretty well universally acknowledged that happiness at work is bound up with a sense of autonomy – the ability a worker has to control their time and the authority they have to act on their own unique expertise. No doubt that is why academics tend to swear allegiance to their department before any other parts of the institution or the institution itself. But this autonomy has undoubtedly been eroded in universities, as it has been for many comparable professionals. The situation is more serious for academics than for some, perhaps, because they are creative workers who need time to conjure up something from nothing.

The mention of time brings me to another complaint. For many academics, time is increasingly hard to come by. There was a time when the university all but shut down over the summer vacation. A time when the university clubhouse might include one or two people who had imbibed and were snoozing the afternoon away (though certainly disapproved of, no one thought that they had to be fired). A time when coffee was more than a snatched moment. A time when email and texts didn't settle like snow, clogging up the day, and computers were that big building up the road. Those days are dead and buried. Academics have joined the general professionalised workforce in being expected to do more and more for no more in what is increasingly an industrialised setting. I have already pointed to an increased administrative load. Another point of tension is a greater teaching load. As

I have already highlighted, actual contact time has not only expanded in many cases but student growth also means more question-setting, a lot more marking, more advice to be handed out, and so on, while new teaching methods require increasing preparation, as Covid-19 has underlined. Then, there are a whole raft of different demands to fill in this or that form as part of an expanding audit economy, demands which to most academics feel like yet another horrid distraction (Strathern, 2002). Finally, the vacations, in which many academics did the bulk of their research, are being eroded. For example, the expansion in Master's courses means that teaching of one kind or another is becoming pretty well all year round.

A number of academics have another complaint. They write papers which argue that there is just too much pressure entirely. Lashuel (2020) is typical of the genre:

> Scientists are passionate about our work and tend to overvalue the satisfaction we get from aspects of our jobs: publishing our results, being recognized by our peers and hitting targets during our evaluations. It is not surprising that many of us work long hours and over weekends or holidays. We often forget or underestimate the toll that overworking ourselves, being constantly busy and ignoring our mental health takes on our students, team members, families and personal relationships. The lack of clarity about what is expected from faculty members and the requirements for promotion and career advancement further exacerbate the situation. This often provokes stress and anxiety and leads to the unrealistic pursuit of excellence and validation at high costs to faculty members, students, research and universities.

I'm in two minds about this kind of lament. There is a clear need to protect academics from themselves at times. They can end up with a work–life balance which is poisonous, hardly helped by the fact that universities have also loaded up academic schedules with more and more activities and fairly specific targets for research and teaching. Universities have at least recognised this toll on mental health and most now have the rudiments of various forms of intervention in academic welfare which can help when stress and anxiety becomes too great. However, at the same time, I am wary of going too far with this kind of refrain. Why? To begin with, because, come what may, becoming a successful academic is going to be stressful at times because of both internally and externally generated pressures. This isn't a 'snap out of it' argument. It simply cannot be got around. Then, because, taken to the limit, it can start to sound suspiciously like special pleading from people, some of whom, for all of the complaints, still have a relatively privileged life, one which contains a certain amount of autonomy, provides the wherewithal to follow an intellectual star, involves a working year which is still relatively loose-leafed, makes room in research universities for study leave (an unheard-of occurrence for most people), gives access to various kinds of research fellowships, and provides an opportunity, even in these days of flight shame, for all kinds of international travel. For the general public who, generally speaking, do not have self-directed jobs or sabbaticals, academic complaints can sometimes seem simply self-interested. (For example, to much of the public, the fact that university academics in the UK might be expected to produce, depending on the discipline involved, a modicum of good papers for the REF over a six- or seven-year period, while receiving what are still relatively long periods of time to conduct research – including even years off – does not seem an excessive burden, while enquiring if they are meeting this standard certainly does not seem like an outbreak of undue philistinism.)

One final point about academics. My complaint, I suppose. Perhaps precisely because of some of the characteristics I have already enumerated, they are rarely as active in the process of redesigning their institutions as might be expected. That's a pity. One of the frustrations that accompanies the actions of any person who tries to run a university is their colleagues' general indifference to becoming involved in any substantial redesign of the institution. Colleagues are happy to criticise from afar and to bemoan the declining influence of senate, the body that formerly ran the academic affairs of the university but now has much less influence because of the boost given to other centres of power like council and the senior management team. But they are rarely interested in doing more. They often claim that their voices will go unheard because of the influence of council or managers so there's no point. Sometimes that may indeed be true but it is also a self-fulfilling prophecy. The result of their hesitancy is clear enough: they cede the ground to exactly the tendencies they abhor since they provide no solutions of their own to the pressing tasks of reproduction that universities now face even though it's that future they need to command.

Contract research staff

Research isn't just about academics, of course. There is a much larger community involved in research. Research doesn't get done without three other vital groups of people: research staff, research support staff, and postgraduates.

Research staff have a contract which is purely to do research (though they do sometimes get involved in teaching). That might sound like nirvana but too often they get a pretty raw deal. They are usually young. They are usually on short-term contracts that depend on the length of a grant, which usually comes in at around two to three years. They are generally doing research framed, at least in the first instance, by someone else. And on completion of the contract there are far fewer job opportunities than candidates. Yet they are vital to the conduct and outcome of research. Full disclosure. I was one of them for five years. It was enjoyable work but the uncertain existence takes its toll after a while – you're not getting any younger and you're still in precarious employment. Of course, not all research staff are in the young and sometimes desperate category. Some are world-respected academics who head up large research groups themselves. But the majority are at the beginning of their careers. And they can be present in large numbers. (Take the case of Oxford. Oxford's research effort involves more than 1,900 academic staff, it is true, but also more than 5,800 research and research support staff, and more than 6,800 graduate research students. This is hardly surprising when external research grants and contracts continue to be the university's largest source of income. (In 2020–21, 40 per cent (£633.6 million) of the university's income came from external research sponsors.) Contract research staff often feel that their concerns – especially employment security – are neglected. In fact, over the years universities have tried hard to improve their lot, as the sign-up to the Vitae Researcher Development Concordat shows. Not hard enough, perhaps – but it isn't easy. There is no magic wand. A permanent job for everyone, when the flow of income from research is so uncertain, is a challenge. In Oxford and Cambridge, to add to their woes, there is also a particular problem over access to the collegiate life of the university. It is easy to feel excluded from what is going on if you can't be a member of a college, though some more senior research staff are. But at least Oxford and Cambridge are building large housing developments which are intended, in part, to address the problem of housing insecurity for contract research staff, research support staff, and postgraduates in cities which have very expensive housing markets.

Research support staff

Then there are the army of technicians and other research relevant staff. The group of workers consisting of lab, IT and other technicians fell, somewhat surprisingly, by around 16 per cent to just over 20,000 employees between 2005/06 and 2017/18, declining from 14 per cent to 10 per cent of the non-academic workforce (Wolf and Jenkins, 2021). They really are the unsung heroes of research though there have been more and more attempts to recognise their efforts, such as the Technician Commitment which aims to ensure recognition and visibility for technicians and the TALENT Consortium of universities, not least because one of the concerns for the future is that as research funding ramps up, a shortage of skilled technicians may hamper progress (Donald, 2021).

Technicians are crucial to the conduct of scientific research (and indeed teaching, getting lab classes ready, for example). Many of them are extraordinarily skilled. They are often the only people who can get a result from complex and temperamental equipment which can take years to learn to operate properly. I knew of one crystallographer who was famed for being able to get meaningful results from a particularly obdurate machine: academics were in awe of what she was able to achieve. I know others who were extraordinarily adept at radiocarbon dating using techniques like compound specific dating or at making the most out of new kinds of mass spectrometer such as the Super High Resolution Ion Microprobe. Again, the farther reaches of modern microscopy can require substantial amounts of skill to operate what are more and more complex machines.

It's a similar story when it comes to bioscience labs. Laboratories can take a long time to get up and running and they then need concentrated and continuous technical expertise to maintain. For example, starting up an anaerobic chamber, which is used to cultivate gut microbes that won't grow in the presence of oxygen, is a days-long process that requires ordering up gas canisters and generating a catalyst. Spaces like clean rooms involve donning protective suits, masks and gloves. After a person uses the lab, everything has to be cleaned with bleach and a decontaminant, and the laboratory will then be irradiated with ultraviolet light for three hours each night. And so on.

In some research universities with a large science presence, there will be several teams of technicians servicing numerous ongoing research projects. For example, a large biosciences laboratory will likely need a glass-washing operation, an engineering team to repair and maintain the machines, a fruit fly production facility, an animal facility, usually housing mice and zebra fish, cell services that nurture billions of cells, and experts on the myriad different kinds of microscopy. However, still, my favourite example of a bioscience service – one which took real skill to run, I might add – was the venom unit at the Liverpool School of Tropical Medicine which houses the largest and most diverse collection of tropical venomous snakes in the UK and leads pioneering research into improving the efficacy, affordability and safety of snakebite treatment. It was a wonder to visit.

Whatever else, these examples show just how central to research many support staff really are. But it's not just technicians. Think of the data analysts and research managers without whom many academics running laboratories would find it hard to win yet alone run grants. Or there is the army of librarians, of which, according to the Society of College, National and University Libraries (SCONUL), there are well over 10,000 spread around various UK higher education institutions. They are such an accepted part of the university furniture that their massive contribution to research as well as teaching is often overlooked.

Postgraduate students

Postgraduate students have come to take up a larger and larger proportion of student numbers in research universities. So, around a third of all students in Russell Group universities are now postgraduate students of one kind or another, rising to just over a half in universities like Oxford.

Typically, a postgraduate is thought of as studying for a PhD through a written dissertation. The idea of a written thesis to be presented – together with an accompanying disputation – appears as early as the seventeenth century but the modern form of the PhD dates from the early nineteenth century with the von Humboldt-inspired higher education reforms in Germany and the Napoleonic reform of higher education in France. The PhD was slow to catch on in the English-speaking world, however. Oxford was the first university in England to institute a research doctorate programme (the DPhil) in 1917, the first award being made only in 1919. The northern universities (Manchester, Leeds, Liverpool and Sheffield) all took steps to introduce them around this time too and the PhD was then fairly rapidly introduced at all universities around the UK (Simpson, 1983, 2009). Since the 1950s, PhD students have increased gradually in number in the UK, from the 4,815 PhD degrees granted in 1975/76 to 14,115 in 2000/01 to 21,685 in 2009/10 to 29,360 in 2018/19. Now, at any one time, there are around 100,000 doctoral students, around 40 per cent of whom come from overseas. 20 to 25 per cent of them are funded by UKRI and the rest by a panoply of means, mainly university-funded studentships (which account for 54.4 per cent of postgraduate research student funding), charities or self-funding. In all, around 10 per cent of postgraduate students are doing degrees by research (House, 2020).

Doctoral students are the lifeblood of research and they occupy an exceptionally important place in universities. But studying for a PhD is no easy thing. One recent survey suggested that the main concerns of doctoral students were: the difficulty of maintaining work/life balance; imposter syndrome; uncertain career prospects; and mental health (Cornell, 2020). Certainly, as two of these concerns imply, many students suffer some degree of stress, a combination of uncertainty about whether what they are doing is any good, concern about whether they're good enough to do it, uncertainty about their status and rights (many PhD students want to see themselves as apprentice faculty, not students), worries about things like meeting deadlines and their supervisors' opinions of their work, as well as the uncertainties of public presentations at professional meetings and the oral examination, both of which can be terrifying. There is no easy answer to many of these rites of passage. (I can still remember what I think was the first presentation I was involved in at which my co-author – who was presenting – dropped all of his cue cards as he was about to start the talk, as well as being involved in a public examination of a doctoral thesis in the Sorbonne which took place in a room which seemed to have been designed as a terror-inducing court of law with the candidate arraigned in front of a panel of four.[20]) On the whole, things are much better than they were – universities by themselves and in consortia now offer all kinds of support that just weren't there before, as well as better accommodation. But there is still much to do.

The slow but steady increase in PhD numbers is itself something of a problem. Even with a boost to research funding, there will likely never be enough academic jobs to employ all of those who want one. Only a very small percentage of PhD students progress to a career as a postdoctoral researcher and, in turn, only around 10 per cent of postdoctoral researchers go on to find permanent positions in academia (Brazil, 2021). Those who choose to continue as postdoctoral researchers are almost inevitably looking at years of fixed-term contracts. In 2018 nearly 67 per cent of UK postdoctoral researchers (33,000 in all) were in this position, having found a research job of some kind but then, with the odds against them, constantly seeking an academic job in their own country or overseas but not always finding one (or only finding an adjunct position) and getting older all the time. The mismatch between academic supply and demand is disillusioning for academic jobseekers, just as it was in the years of the Thatcher cuts. Judged simply on the basis of demand from universities, there are probably too many PhD students. The situation may not be as bad as in the US, where one of the Democratic presidential candidates, Bernie Sanders, made the proposal that in exchange for federal funding to reduce public college and university tuition to zero, at least 75 per cent of college courses would have to be taught by tenured or tenure-track professors. (Currently, that proportion is less than 40 per cent and still dropping.) But it deserves far more attention than it gets. Truth to tell, there probably ought to be some kind of constraints applied on numbers but there are all kinds of countervailing forces which militate against such an outcome: numbers of PhD students feature in some league tables, academic staff like to work with PhD students and take pains to find scholarships, and PhD students have slowly but surely become a part of the new mass teaching regime.

The UK may not have reached the US situation of 'adjunctopia' (Carey, 2020a) where the numbers of so-called 'contingent faculty' has reached very high levels but the trend is in the same direction. With some exceptions – there are people who are looking for part-time work – it is not a good one. In the UK, 13 per cent of academic staff are now paid by the hour. For part-time staff that number increases to 38 (HESA, 2020). But reversing out of this situation will not be easy to achieve. The problem is mainly financial. Funding models, combined with the ups and downs in student numbers on particular degree programmes and courses, militate against the obvious solution of more permanent contracts.

All this said, and contrary to a prevailing myth, by no means all PhD students nowadays are necessarily looking for academic jobs. They go on to all kinds of other careers in industry and elsewhere. Other countries' traditions show that the idea that a doctorate has to be a purely academic qualification is partly a construction – in Germany,[21] for example, having a PhD is an important qualification to do well in industry too. (It might be a good idea if that were true in the UK.) Whatever the case, British universities now take a lot of time to make sure that their PhD students are prepared for a wide range of career destinations, mounting all kinds of courses that prepare them for a world that is more random than they might like to know. Since the introduction of more formal training and a skills-based element to the PhD in the late 1980s, and Centres for Doctoral Training in the 1990s, the formal element of the PhD has become much better at preparing students for a wider variety of career outcomes.

Another development is the rise of new types of professional doctorate, usually taken later in life as an outgrowth of a career, for example, the engineering doctorate (EngD). Professional doctorates have grown rapidly in number. These are research degrees but the thesis element is generally shorter. Students must take a significant number of advanced courses and submit a professional portfolio demonstrating the use of new methods. The research is based in professional practice so that the links with the wider world (industry, government, schools, healthcare etc.) are much stronger. Many people now undertake an engineering or business doctorate later in their career. They do this as a means of extending their skills and focussing their career. These doctorates are usually part-time which can make them a challenging option when combined with a full-time job.

All this said, the majority of postgraduate students are doing Master's qualifications. Master's students have increased massively in number in the last few years in research universities – largely because of international students (53 per cent are from overseas) – and now almost two-thirds of postgraduate starters are doing a Master's degree (House, 2020). Indeed, it is often said that a Master's degree is becoming an entry level grade in some jobs and professions. Certainly, in many research universities it can often feel like a Master's is becoming the equivalent of the undergraduate degree honours year in a four-year degree scheme, hastened by the widespread adoption of the MSci degree at one point. No wonder given that they now account for nearly 15 per cent of all students.

Master's students have been a difficult proposition for research universities. They can feel neglected. Usually they are only around for a year and it is difficult for them to sink into the institution in that time. They also tend to feel that undergraduate facilities and entertainments don't fit their needs. They have grown beyond the freshers ball. But in the last ten years big strides have been made in how they are treated and in pedagogy. As well, what was a model in which a few taught courses were followed by a project or dissertation has mutated into something more likely to be tailored.

One criticism often made about the growth of Master's courses is that some of them are too utilitarian and do not chime with academic values. Though there is an element of truth in this criticism, it is universities who need to be held to account. It is easy enough to insert modules into these courses that would right the balance. Equally, I cannot see why it isn't possible to provide modules which will equip these students with the life skills that they are going to need for the future. These are of three kinds. To begin with, there is the ability to be a generalist – on the whole, it is generalists who run things. I well remember the head of one very large global firm telling me that they could always get quants and others with specific skills. What they couldn't get were generalists who know enough to see the whole picture. Then there's flexibility. Unexpected things constantly arise and students need the skills to be able to adjust rapidly and in good order. And finally, in an age of accelerating climate change, there is the absolutely essential quality of adaptability. Things are going to get much worse before they get better and students will need the skills to adjust. (I always thought that Master's students also ought to be taught a 'what you need to know that no one told you' course. That would include teaching these three qualities and others like how to do politics. If you're going to end up running something like a city or a corporation, you are going to need all these skills and more.)

Administrators

But those who work at the coalface of knowledge are only a part of the university staffing equation. Administrators have become a major force in universities too. That's no surprise. Large organisations necessarily require a lot of administration. In 2016/17 there were 212,835 non-academic staff in UK universities, of which 170,675 can fairly be described as administrators. This compares with 206,870 academic staff.

This latter figure shows the rub. Many academics think that there are too many administrators altogether and that too many of them are superfluous: sometimes, it has to be said, the same academics who think that administrative tasks are beneath them! Some have what amounts to a kind of below stairs attitude to administrators of the 'you wouldn't be here without me' variety legitimated by a narrative of administration as a burden imposed by malign outside forces, a narrative that becomes especially prevalent when things aren't going well and someone needs to be blamed. Indeed, some of the most serious bullying cases in universities have tended to arise from interactions between academics and administrators. Any growth in the number of administrators is regarded as a de facto bad thing, as a watering down of the university's purity, as a use of resources better spent on the academic enterprise, and as further proof, if proof were needed, of an insidious takeover by management intent on even further centralisation. David Graeber (2018) is typical of this patrician tendency. He espies all kinds of administrative jobs in universities that are what he calls 'bullshit jobs'. There is no real reason for them. They are parasitic. It is the same kind of contempt reserved by many people for 'bureaucrats' (Graeber, 2015).

But such characterisations are a bit too easy and they begin to break down when they are examined more closely. No university could survive without people to do the books, hire new employees, take minutes in committees, or organise the academic calendar and the allocation of teaching space. But there are many other jobs that often go unsung which are just as vital (which is not to say that it isn't worth making a regular examination of which administrative functions are still really necessary). The numbers of specialisms now needed to run a large university – the endless conveyor belt of new government initiatives, increasing student demands, student counselling, various audits, the need for expanded HR and finance functions, health and safety, larger communication departments, larger marketing departments (especially crucial as international students have become so vital to survival), larger fundraising departments, industry liaison departments, legal and governance matters, graduation ceremonies, examination boards, student recruitment, information technology and cybersecurity experts, teaching and learning support and especially educational developers – the list goes on and all of these different functions need staffing.

In other words, universities nowadays depend on a large penumbra of administrators to be able to persist. For example, research administrators are becoming a profession in their own right (with qualifications provided by Awards for Training and Higher Education). They are involved in all manner of research activities, including aiding with and submitting grant applications, making sure that grants are spent according to profile, liaising with grant-funding agencies, ensuring compliance with regulatory structures, maintaining a supply of consumables to laboratories, even making sure that power supplies are reliable, as well as enumerating numerous risk analyses, codes of conduct, dashboards, and all the other paraphernalia of audit.

As a result of the growth in their numbers and a search for greater acknowledgment, some research project and other administrators now fashion themselves as 'third space' higher education professionals (other examples might include mental health professionals, learning and other technologists, careers and employability advisors, impact managers, and employer engagement officers). Some of these professionals even want to be able to become involved in conducting their own research (to which, I suppose, the answer might be 'if it's world class research, we can talk').

Whilst acknowledging how vital administrators are to the safe and efficient running of universities, every vice-chancellor wonders whether they really need quite so many. The suspicion has to be that the expansion of administrative jobs is soaking up more and more overhead without a corresponding effect. Many consultants will have arrived at their doorstep ready and willing to make the administration more cost-efficient, though often without much sense of how these different jobs join up in what is often called an 'administrative lattice'. (That is why, although across-the-board cuts in administration can be and are made, there can come a point where they are self-defeating, or even dangerous.) Again, more and more administrative functions are being outsourced, a strategy which has its pluses and minuses (and also means that the extent of the outsourced workforce is often unknown). The Parallel Administrative State has its problems, then. And these problems may be increasing. For example, Wolf and Jenkins (2021) point to the way in which the stereotypes that academics hold about administrators are not entirely without grip. In particular, the number of highly paid 'managers and non-academic professionals' in universities increased by some 60 per cent over the 12 years from 2005/06 to 2017/18, with particularly strong growth in research universities, in part because senior management in research universities has given less scrutiny to the pay and conditions of this segment of the workforce (enabling an upward drift in pay and seniority) in contrast to academic posts where scrutiny tends to be greater, and in part because of greater centralisation (which can give greater job protection to those at the centre than academics). There are other issues too. The general tendency to greater specialisation of existing positions in the administrative division of labour coupled with the parallel tendency to add more and more new locations into it so as to tackle issues like the student experience, access, research culture or equality, diversity and inclusion has produced administrators who often have only a hazy idea of the generality of the university and who, in some cases, become almost evangelical advocates for their specialism and are, as a result, likely to argue single-mindedly for more personnel for 'their' patch.[22]

Whatever the specifics of the case, I can only say that I have always found administrators to be some of the most motivated and innovative people in a university. They had a sense of process which is vital in a duty of care organisation. And they often had serious strategic insights. When they do complicate things it is often because they are passing down diktats which come from without the organisation, not schemes to stop academics doing their job.

As a conclusion to this chapter, it is also worth pointing out – with some passion, I might add – all of the unheralded jobs in universities which are not administrative as such but without which the whole operation would come tumbling down. I am thinking here of the people who look after the grounds, provide security, clean the rooms, do the maintenance and repair, prepare and serve up food, and not infrequently provide both an important source of information and a shoulder to cry on for students.

They are almost never mentioned but they are utterly indispensable. They are often some of the people who are most loyal to the institution too. I am and continue to be leery of the trend for subcontracting out their jobs to save money. The search for savings can sometimes produce serious institutional losses.

3

So what is a 'university'? Part 2: Students, parents and other constituencies

Undergraduate students

Then, there are, of course, undergraduate students ... All kinds of rubbish has been talked about students over the last few years. For example, according to some, they've all turned into snowflakes. T'was always thus, one might say. In many ways, this is just the latest variant on the 'young people, I don't know what's got into them' theme.[1]

The motivations of most undergraduate students are pretty much as they always were. Heads down. Don't make a big fuss. Get on with it. Leave and get a job. Hope to have a moderately good time at university. Maybe indulge in some sexual activity along the way (though nowhere near as much as is sometimes made out (Hillman, 2021b)). Find out some interesting and useful things and every now and then come across a book or paper or a lecture that provides genuine intellectual inspiration. They're not the finished article and they know it. Marginson (2018, p. 17) puts it well when he discusses students' various and variable motives for study:

> Some love the subjects they study and find knowledge to be an end in itself. ... Some are intensively engaged in cultural or political action on campus. Some have a passion for the common good and imagine themselves working on global problems in the future. Many are simply 'finding themselves' while moving into adult life. Some want to please their families ... And, typically, students nurture more than one of these different higher education projects at the same time.

For international students, often dependent on parental savings from a lifetime of hard work, and therefore committed to paying back by producing a good performance, the family obligation characterisation often holds doubly true. For example, Chinese students, brought up in a different tradition which includes Confucian ideas of active learning, tend to work doubly hard. One study (Shostya, 2015) of business students in New York and Shanghai founds that, outside of classes, Chinese students spent an average of 9.6 hours per week reading and 22.3 hours a week in study. The comparable figures for

American students were 4.4 and 9.1 hours respectively. A British academic would probably find something not so different so far as Chinese and British students were concerned.

Many of the undergraduates I've met in the UK and overseas have been truly exceptional people. Not all, of course. This is the real world we're living in. But many of them. And they have shown real commitment to searching out new ways of doing things: to caring for the world in ways that previous generations did not; to negotiating difficult issues like ethnicity and race – hardly surprising given that their generation has grown up in a society in which ethnic pluralism has become a norm – and in trying to find new means of cooperation. Equally, many of them realise that they – and their children – are going to be fighting for their lives in a world grown hot, polluted, war-torn, and unlikely to show much in the way of pity or remorse, a world which has become sufficiently unequal and unfair that their life chances may well diminish when compared with their parents.[2] No wonder they want to do something about it. In some ways, one might argue that they ought to be creating more of a fuss.

Though there are many ways in which recent students are like previous cohorts, I don't want to give the impression that there are no differences. Of course, most still do all the usual student-y things though fewer drink (some because of religious strictures) and the vast majority, thank goodness, desist from stupid rituals like initiation ceremonies. But they are a more pressured and anxious group than they used to be. There is no condescension in making such a characterisation, one which arises from at least seven causes.

To begin with, many of them are in a competition that they have been in since birth, one that has only been exacerbated by teaching to the test. My childhood was never occupied by a constant round of extramural activities but many children nowadays seem to be caught up in precisely that. For all the best reasons, I'm sure, many middle-class parents have put them through life course callisthenics with the ultimate aim of going to a good university in mind. These callisthenics can make students both exceptionally broad in their experiences and yet still, somehow, rather narrow in their outlook. (Remember that in England in 1971, 94 per cent of primary schoolchildren were allowed to travel somewhere alone other than to and from school by their parents. By 2010, that percentage had fallen to a measly 7 per cent.) Equally, students continually have to show how good they are, to examination authorities, true, but most of all to their friends and indeed the wider world. In particular, we live in a time where it is increasingly unacceptable to be average. In the 1950s, 20 per cent of the UK population declared themselves as above average. Now that figure is 80 per cent. More generally, in many walks of life, the pressure is on to be a 'leader', something that it is patently impossible for everyone to be and which, in any case, is based on a model of leadership which is narrow and cramped (Cain, 2013).

Then, many more of them are financially insecure. My generation was lucky: they had free tuition and maintenance grants. Theirs has student loans and part-time jobs. Though the idea that it would be possible to provide free tuition for all the domestic students that now exist in England might be considered impractical, given the number of students currently attending university, and inequitable, given the class profile of university attendance, you can certainly see why the current situation involving tuition fees needing to be paid off and day-to-day maintenance needing to be found in order to live means that many students feel pressured by money issues. In turn, this feeds into a more general worldview, one in which financial insecurity combines with the possibility of accumulating lower net worth than previous generations to produce a sense of disappointed expectation. Unlike those who grew up in the 1960s, for example, for whom a future of, if not affluence, then at least security often seemed like a right, students now are confronted by a much more precarious existence – with the added bonus of climate change. Not surprisingly, given these circumstances, many contemporary students are serial overachievers, strivers who have negotiated countless examinations and CV-building activities. The net result is what can sometimes seem like numbing middle-class conformity brought on by a pinched version of what counts as success, one made up out of lots of education, lots of work, a mild form of insurgent bohemianism suited to the current establishment counterculture, and ultimately victory in the battle to secure what is regarded as a just share of the shrinking financial rewards that may be on offer:

> Modern society offers its citizens a remarkably homogeneous life experience. Half of young people go to university where they're all forced through systems of exams that tend to reward a very specific, specialised and often unquestioning kind of intelligence. Then, thanks to computers, the jobs available after university are increasingly indistinguishable. Our work culture rewards one principal attribute: the ability to bend your intelligence to unnatural extremes of concentration by sitting in front of a screen for hours every day. To do this we wear the increasingly ubiquitous uniform of jeans (or chinos) and a smart shirt, which is just as much a symbol of conformity as the bowler hats and briefcases of our ancestors. (Marriott, 2021c)

Third, they have grown up with the internet. This is Generation Z, born since the 1990s into a platformed world that is always on (Duffy, 2021, Katz et al., 2021), a world which in its mundanity has some worrying similarities to Adam Roberts' (2022) *The This*. That means that social media, in particular, are an integral part of how students now live. That produces a number of issues. One is that they live in a world of constant comparison and constant competition brought on by the advent of the internet. I used to worry about what my peers were doing and if it was better/more exciting/more socially central than me – it usually was – but I didn't have the benefit of a running commentary about this state of affairs complete with documentation and photographs to keep me pinioned in a state of permanent anxiety/envy/fear of missing out, yet alone the joy of being able to 'hear' everything nasty that was being said about me or of knowing that within easy and accessible reach it might be possible to find out so much about your life and thoughts that it is possible to talk about 'the public presence of our private lives' (Hayes, 2021, p. 18. It is difficult to find any kind of stable sense of self in this world. Again, and related, I wasn't bombarded by the kind of internet drivel which, for example, makes out that we can transform ourselves into stunningly successful people by making our private selves into a 'real you': it's that old prosperity church line – believe hard enough in yourself with enough passion and all will be OK. Yeah right. Not that everyone is taken in by the narrative of an authentic unbounded self, of course: cycling through different versions of the self in the way that some students do online, in a kind of psychic cosplay, is not to everybody's taste but many students tend to worry much more about 'who they are' even so. In other words, what can be said with some confidence is that extra momentum has clearly been added by social media to a tendency which was already underway before its advent, namely the fashioning of an autonomous, reflexive and constantly narrativised self and identity (Giddens, 1991) with all of its upsides (e.g. self-confidence) and downsides (e.g. narcissism). The reflexive self is most noticeable among American students who are already culturally primed to be more outgoing and to live their lives in public. But it is becoming true of supposedly repressed English students too. At one time, authors like John Fowles could liken the English structure of feeling to a vast cultural game of hide and seek. People did not declare themselves up front. Their inner life was private. That's no longer true. People tend to declare themselves constantly and unremittingly to whomsoever they consider to be their social circles, urged on by a self-esteem industry which is ever-present even though its intellectual foundations are dubious. This revving-up can be seen as a welcome breath of fresh air, of course. But it can also promote self-indulgence. It can lead to taking offence at the drop of a hat. It can mistake feeling strong emotion for being correct and attention for recognition. It can also result in misapprehending a declarative for an established fact, the result being that it can sometimes feel as though everyday life is in danger of becoming an always-on activist zone in which the Chinese Communist Party practice of regularly 'declaring your stance' becomes mandatory. Then, the internet has encouraged a more collaborative work style based on the modular team template adopted by the tech industry from a long line of forebears. Students are more likely to want to learn together rather than alone, a tendency that they will have already encountered in the widespread use of group assignments at school as well as on the internet. (This collaborative bent can also be seen in student activism which means that a 'leadership', understood in the conventional way, can often be difficult to locate.) The internet produces one other issue. Students tend to be more present-oriented, treat time more flexibly, and are more likely to jump from topic to topic. Thoughts are constantly interrupted. The internet produces a veritable bombardment of messages, entertainment and information which leave much less time for quiet reflection. In a TikTok/YouTube culture, it can seem as though the smallest space of time has to be filled with something. Even your daydreaming can be subcontracted to others. And the content that is available can be suspect too, to put it but mildly. Conspiracy theories and misinformation, graphic pornography, self-harm and suicide primers, violent videos and games are all freely available along with the usual run of news and gossip and music. This continuous bombardment of kinetic content – images, sounds, paths and directions – makes the practice of concentrated thinking somewhat more elusive for students. They are used to flitting from topic to topic. That tendency is complicated by another: the sheer profusion of content. Whereas in the 1960s it was still possible to talk about a canon, that becomes much more difficult to achieve in a world where there is so much content. For example, according to one source drawing on UNESCO data, the number of books published worldwide in 2019 reached as high as 2.2 million. Music has exploded too: 60,000 new tracks are uploaded on to Spotify every day (Page, 2020). Other sites like Bandcamp offer a similar kind of musical vista for set lists. This has academic consequences as well: when it comes to pretty well all areas of knowledge, but especially science, there is simply more to study, multiplying the division of labour and making synthesis ever harder to achieve.

Whether all this this means that students are less likely to engage in deep thought is a moot point but most academics have observed that there are changes in their study habits, in how they regard authorship and which sources they think are credible (which can often depend on what they think is most 'relevant' to them personally (Katz et al., 2021)). As Davies (2022, p. 26) points out, the old humanistic idea of an author, born out 'of transitions between spaces – library, lecture hall, seminar room, study – linked together by work with pen and paper' is being replaced by an 'interface between screen and keyboard' which dissolves everything 'into a unitary flow of "content"'. What counts as writing and learning are being redefined but to what extent we do not know.

Fourth, and hardly surprising considering some of the aforementioned causes, more students are the bearers of one mental health syndrome or another and especially various forms of anxiety and depression,[3] often amplified by the 'factory of unhappiness' (Berardi, 2009) that for many is their experience of social media. Many more students now declare conditions which in a previous era might have been considered tangential or simply a part of life's burden, the result of more and better understanding of mental health, a development that can only be counted as to the good. But this development has intertwined with broader cultural currents which are not always so positive, such as the contemporary tendency to medicalise vast numbers of pathologies (one which arises out of living in what has become a psychiatric culture (Rose, 2019) where patients want the comfort of precise diagnoses and doctors and psychiatrists are pressured into pretending that they are somehow omniscient), as well as the pressure to be 'happy' (and the associated tendency to think that if you're not there must be something wrong), to which can be added the rise of a generalised language of harm (in which, for example, words like 'healing' and 'trauma' have suffered from a degree of semantic creep sufficient to allow them to become a kind of boilerplate, able to be applied to almost any negative life event (O'Sullivan, 2021)) and the aforementioned ascent of the reflexive self which means that students too often tend to begin by thinking 'what is wrong with me?' as they struggle to perform an identity. For example, even before Covid-19, the numbers applying for mitigating circumstances with regard to examinations and similar events showed a steep rise. Some of these cases were serious and clearly deserved remedies like extra time to complete an examination. Other cases I'm not so sure about. Indeed, I wonder if they don't hamper some students' progress by providing them with a habit of laying off responsibility for their performance by appealing to something that sometimes can seem to be uncomfortably positioned between cutting-edge medicine and modern forms of folklore.

Fifth, students come from a culture in which everything has to be entertaining.[4] Boredom is out. Fast and easy to use is in. Slow and apparently inefficient learning is frowned upon – even though there is a large body of work that shows that 'learning is best done slowly to accumulate lasting knowledge, even when that means performing poorly on tests of immediate progress. That is, the most effective learning looks inefficient; it looks like falling behind' (Epstein, 2019, p. 118). The idea of an apprenticeship in which a slow progression from topic to topic builds a solid base has not been lost in research universities. But it is certainly under threat. Often, commentators argue that students can act as customers who somehow know it before they know it and all they need to do is need is stock up with something called 'knowledge'. But there is a problem. 'Knowledge'[5] is a much more difficult proposition than it may first appear. There are many kinds of knowledge and there are many different ways of acquiring it. The modern tendency is to make knowledge quicker to generate, circulate and consume. This has been anathema to universities. As I have already pointed out, thinking done in universities requires interruption, contemplation, and deferral. There is no quick fix. Though procedures and formulae that are going to be useful in work are certainly a part of most degrees, if that is all that a degree offers, then the degree is not from a research university. Degrees must offer slow learning and critical thinking, both of which, by the way, are components of what makes for happiness in later life (Willetts, 2017). They must also offer the habit of being able to search out a wide body of knowledge, not least because being an able generalist is ultimately a much more reliable path to success in life than being a specialist, including, it might be said, in business.

Sixth, and relatedly, they have lived through a period when the Americanisation of British popular culture stepped up a gear. Though the US's global dominance as a cultural exporter is now being challenged, still current British students have been exposed to a continuous American media diet in which me and we is composed from equal parts of: the legacy of American counterculture with its general bias to psychological explanations and individual self-actualisation (Malchow, 2011); the unfettered pursuit of individual prosperity and self-interest; hard work understood as not just a means but as an ethic (and building the ultimate resumé as proof of cleaving to this ethic); an identity that is nonconformist but in a conformist way; the confusion of attention with recognition; and public displays of moral earnestness and condemnation which might not have been thought of as out of place in Puritan times (Verhaege, 2014). Filtered through a politics which can seem not just polarised but factionalised (see the review by Edsall (2022) which suggests that Walter (2021) may not be quite as much of an exaggeration as critics have claimed), it clearly has some degree of grip as an internalised mindset. Though British popular culture is not in imminent danger of becoming a refried version of US culture – attitudes to the state, welfare and freedom are still very different – the main contours of current American popular culture have tended to seep into how domestic students (and not a few international students, I might add) understand the world rather more than might be considered comfortable. This is hardly a new complaint of course but, much as I might love the US, its extreme inequality and politics of mutual suspicion mean that it has become a low trust culture whose civic conversation is coming close to breaking down. This may not be the best time to emulate it.

Finally, what is a particularly interesting change in some contemporary students is their rapid recourse to moral censoriousness when it comes to matters of identity, a censoriousness which in some – some – ways is coming to recall the staid moral order of the 1950s and before in its imposition of strict and unrelenting standards of conduct and its dislike of moral relativism. That's a pity since the redistribution of dignity to include the marginalised and the parallel reconstruction of conscience and worthiness which many students are aiming for might well be seen as a more than worthy cause which can hardly be counted as a set of luxury beliefs. But, as Douthat (2021) notes, it can also mean that

> the categories of identity politics, originally embraced as liberative contrasts to older strictures, are increasingly used to structure a moral

order of their own: to define who defers to whom, who can make sexual advances to whom and when, who speaks for which group, who gets special respect and who gets special scrutiny, what vocabulary is enlightened and which words are newly suspect, and what kind of guild rules and bureaucratic norms preside.

A glib answer to the charge of such an unswerving, supercharged moral politesse, one which contains at least a grain of truth, is that, in the uncertain world that students currently face, an accomplishment like an all but transcendent sense of moral certainty provides an anchor in the storm. But there is more to it than that. As Marriott (2021a, p. 15) perceptively points out, and as the word accomplishment signals, perhaps it is also a matter of establishing some of the accoutrements of a new middle-class etiquette, a u and non-u code of the practice of identity that could become as demanding as the one used by eighteenth-century worthies to test their contemporaries:

> the precarious middle classes have always turned to complex social codes to distinguish themselves from the working class they fear falling into. Once upon a time this was a matter of using fish knives and not saying the word serviette. Today correct etiquette and vocabulary surrounding matters of race and gender are wielded by younger, educated members of the precarious middle class to differentiate themselves from the traditional working classes, who in some cases (plumbers, electricians) may be earning substantially more than they are.

Indeed, as Marriott (2021b, p. 17) subsequently points out: 'the mastery of complex linguistic codes surrounding matters of race and gender is an important way for people of my generation to display not only their moral but their intellectual superiority (it's hard to learn all the rules without attending university)'. It is no surprise that students have often been involved in the development of the various online courses mounted by universities (and also by the companies they sometimes contract like Marshall E-Learning ('Specialists in Inclusion, Diversity and Unconscious Bias')). They show institutions trading in a new culture of moral commandment through induction courses that ask what are too often rhetorical questions about what can be exceedingly complex issues, questions to which there can be, apparently, only one right answer[6] and which pass over the fact that diversity is itself diverse. This point provides a convenient way into the vexed and vexing issue of freedom of speech.

Freedom of speech

One thing hasn't changed. Just a few students are infected by what Romain Gary called 'mediocrity', a kind of vindictive self-righteousness – I'm right and you're not just wrong, you are positively evil. Secure in their certitude of being on the right side of a contest of faith, they would never be able to recognise, process or calibrate a Romain Gary aphorism like 'not even the most just causes are ever innocent'. Or the words of the American judge Learned Hand: 'The spirit of liberty is the spirit which is not too sure that it is right.' The idea that people might agree with a stance but have reservations is inexcusable: the subscription has to be to the whole package. The idea that all stereotypes are likely to be wrong to a greater or lesser degree is ruled out of court. And so on. Perhaps this level of sanctimony and general lack of empathy or forgiveness would not be so bad if that were all but it can be used by a few as an excuse for problematic behaviour: apprentice democrats can turn into apprentice totalitarians acting out middle-class privilege, just in a different way.[7] Social media has only amplified this tendency by encouraging pile-ons in which, too often, it seems like everyone else is a troll, everyone else is an extremist, but I am doing the Lord's work. (Even a few academics have got in on the act, dispatching tweets that wouldn't shame a pub punch-up.)

This tendency to evince absolute certitude is particularly problematic when it comes to the issue of free speech. Be in no doubt, free speech is integral to what a university is about, a position admirably encapsulated in the so-called Chicago principles which have now been adopted by some 70 American universities. Attempts to halt free expression of views by either right or left are a serious attack on what a university must be about (Sloterdijk, 2020).

Of course, it would be nice to think there would be no issues at all around free speech in universities. Why? Well, to begin with, because for universities it's the right thing to do: 'it is not the proper role of the university to attempt to shield individuals from ideas and opinions they find unwelcome, disagreeable, or even deeply offensive' (Chicago Principles, 2014). Then, because, at this political conjuncture, being wobbly on the principles of free speech opens the door to governments stepping in and policing what they consider to be free speech (which, strange as it may seem, tends to tally with their own views) (Zimmer, 2019). In a number of countries, as if to prove the point, legislation has now been enacted. In Australia a bill has been passed which will promote freedom of speech in universities. In the US various pieces of legislation have been passed by states, via various state governments.[8] In the UK, changes to the law are almost certain to be made over and above the relevant clauses of the 1986 Higher Education Act. Given the scale of the problem, you might think that there would be no need for actions quite as sweeping as the proposed Higher Education (Freedom of Speech) bill which allows

> the Office for Students to monitor and enforce freedom of speech measures at higher education institutions, [and] introduce a complaints

system and redress for breaches of free speech duties through the introduction of a statutory tort, extend duties on free speech to students' unions and create a role of director of freedom of speech and academic freedom at the OfS.

But that's what has happened. As a relevant body of law grows and as an accompanying bureaucracy establishes its remit so what constitutes free speech on campus will increasingly be defined by the state. You don't have to be a libertarian to think that the potential for this to end badly is definitely there. Whatever happens, university leaderships cannot lay off all responsibility for the outcome. They have too often opted for a quiet life in ways which have been interpreted by government and others as showing that universities are shaky on the principles of free speech. Not all leaderships have held out when things have got heated.

It's a pity because a number of surveys show that most students do understand, in theory at least, that free speech has to be free. But there is still a way to go to convince every student that this can sometimes mean that there will be people speaking on campus with whom they may profoundly disagree and whose views they may find offensive – but who must still be allowed to speak (which is no reason not to go along and disagree with them). One riposte often made to this stance is that unequal power relations make a mockery of the idea of free speech. To whit, some students (and some faculty members) feel that they are not accepted as equal members of the university community. Free speech is really just a cover for privileged people who have been made to feel uncomfortable about their unspoken privileges which are now being challenged, privileged people who need to be held accountable (Ben-Porath, 2018). Free speech 'is really freedom to belittle, oppress or harass' (Dickinson, 2022). Too often it is a means of disrespecting authentically forged identity – students have had quite enough of that on social media already, thank you. One doesn't have to entirely negate such a view to argue that this stance, when taken to an extreme, just ends up back with 'I am right and you are wrong' and no rejoinder can be tolerated.

Indeed, the general turn to identity politics, a turn which has been particularly strongly felt in universities, shows the rub. Meant to engrain ideas like fluid and amorphous identities, in some cases what looks suspiciously like the opposite has been achieved. The kind of strong social constructionism that was on the wane seems to have come surging back. Some activists seem to be keen to ground what were meant to be ungrounded identities so that they will become the equivalent of nations, fixed categories which can be walled off from each other rather than processes which allow of wider community (Garcia, 2021). Something like a cultural lockdown might well result from this economy of blame were it not for the fact that in everyday life people just get on with it. In a related vein, for all the talk of a postcolonial moment, it can sometimes seem as though what is being disseminated is a notion of the UK as an ideological colony of the US. To take just one example, the importation of US ideas on race and racism can lead to various anti-racism actions which are generalised from too little in the way of systematic evidence and too often arise from a distinctly American-style process of racialisation, a psychologisation of behaviour in which 'racism begins in the mind, and is therefore undone in the mind. All that is required is diligent mental labour' (Younis, 2022, p. 36). This stance places the blame for racism squarely on individual attitudes and then makes the mistake of assuming that a strong link can be found between these attitudes and behaviour.[9] A Universities UK report on racism in universities (UUK, 2020) produced a series of sensible recommendations but also included (in qualified form, it should be said) the use of psychosocial measures which have been shown in a large number of academic studies not to work or to work only very partially, such as many forms of anti-racist training which not only don't have grip but may even be counter-productive, actually entrenching bias (Atewologun, Cornish and Tresh, 2018, Green and Hagiwara, 2020, Martin, 2020). As Dobbin and Kalev (2018, p. 48) put it in their review of implicit bias training: 'That ... universities ... persist in offering [this] training to faculty and students, and even mandate it, ... is particularly surprising given that the research on the poor performance of training comes out of academia. Imagine university health centers continuing to prescribe vitamin C for the common cold.' Again, the adoption of off-the-shelf reporting software by a number of universities (one figure suggests as many as 60 per cent), software that enables students to anonymously accuse members of university teaching staff of 'racism, discrimination and micro-aggressions', threatens to combat something bad with something bad.[10] Hopefully, some clear social science research will emerge from universities[11] which gives a more detailed picture on which actions can be taken, actions which are both more soundly based and more effective than outsourced prescriptions which can import freight from other organisation's agendas, prescriptions which are often there simply to show that an organisation is doing something, initiated by a leadership which, in the heat of the moment, took the easiest path. It will likely show that serious change involves not panic buying but a slower constructive politics of crafting solidarity – as indeed a number of US commentators have concluded, 'putting bodies from different groups in the same room, on the same team and in the same neighborhood. That's national service programs. That's residential integration programs across all lines of difference. That's workplace diversity, equity and inclusion – permanent physical integration, not training' (Brooks, 2020b, p. 26). Of course, illiberal liberal attitudes aren't attached just to some students. They seem to be becoming more general. Some commentators would argue that this hyper-liberalism, a 'we're the dissenters/we're empowered to shout the loudest/you aren't allowed to dissent' tendency, which often deploys hurt subjective feelings as proof of concept, can be laid at the door of universities. I doubt that's the case, given that this kind of general approach has become something close to general currency in many other kinds of politics around the world (again, it would be good to see some proper research). But whatever the case, the inflationary spiral contained in this kind of illiberal liberal politics, one which tends to see more and more offence in more and more things, depends on practices which are visible, demonstrative and declarative, and tends to avoid the hard yards which are involved in building institutions which achieve more than symbolic change. It tends to believe in what might be thought of as an arithmetic of rights and deficits which, in its more extreme manifestations, can frame contrary views as forms of violence. It avoids complexity (for example, in the case of ethnicity, the growth of a large mixed-race community in the UK). It ignores success stories. It can divert attention from issues that cut across identities and especially the economic distress and entrenched income and wealth inequality that a large part of the population of whatever social grouping finds itself mired in, processes which have arisen out of a defective economic system that urgently needs fixing and an interlinked history of class and imperialism that goes back centuries now (Savage, 2021). And it passes by the views of all the people who don't want to shout but don't necessarily agree – as Burke famously put it 'pray do not imagine that those who make the noise are the only inhabitants of the field'.

There are other more subtle forms of suppression of free speech that arise out of the 'logic of the trial' (Wacquant, 2022a, p. 72) which both students, and just a few staff, are tempted by which ought to be anathema in a university, of all places. They involve wanting to write from a silo which provides absolute judgements, and with them the consolations of moral certainty, which produce an accompanying tendency to self-censorship among those fearful of being cast out.[12] In a world where having a 'bad' opinion makes you into a bad person who must do penance for their sins, there is pressure

> to *identify* with a community and to write as its representatives. In a way, this is the opposite of writing to reach other people. When we open a book or click on an article, the first thing we want to know is which group the writer belongs to. The group might be a political faction, an ethnicity or a sexuality, a literary clique. The answer makes reading a lot simpler. It tells us what to expect from the writer's work, and even what to think of it. Groups save us a lot of trouble by doing our thinking for us. (Packer, 2020, p. 1)

In other words, the message being sent out is 'stay in your lane' (Smith, 2019, p. 21), underlining Brooks' (2020a) point that belonging sometimes seems to have become more important than understanding. This pressure to belong,[13] which is often summarised as the tension between rightside norms and accuracy norms (Singal, 2019), is only increased by the trigger-happy world of social media which too often invites public shaming, social ridicule, cruelty, and ostracism if you get it 'wrong', by people who often seem only too happy to rush to judgement, who are exhilarated by their own outrage, who have become immune to complexity or ambiguity, who find themselves unable to grant forgiveness, as if no one ever changed their mind, and who are inured to the consequent loss of texture they have produced in everyday life. The imperative now is to *perform* divides, and in a way which is suitably devout. Why? It's the fear of landing on the wrong side of whatever group you feel you belong to and being not just condemned but morally condemned. It's the fear of being seen *not* to politicise a narrative. And it's the fear of being ostracised on and offline. In the face of this barrage of righteousness and coerced piety, more and more people are likely to self-censor rather than following a thought wherever it will lead without the comfort of certainty or back-up. Keep your head down. Wall yourselves in. Goodbye risk. Hello orthodoxy.

I am not saying, as some have, that a new McCarthyism or Maoism has installed itself in British university culture. It most certainly hasn't. But it is undoubtedly the case that a quick to condemn atmosphere can and does set limits to free expression and encourages so-called whisper networks – all of the people who feel, to come back to Burke, that they cannot express their opinion in public without fear of a censorious mob piling on. This would be an even more sinister development for universities. If you're too scared to speak out in the first place, if you're not even willing to express an opinion, except the one that all your peers do, their whole ethos is at risk. Certain areas of intellectual inquiry and certain viewpoints are likely to be treated as off limits. All kinds of interactions could be in danger of being compromised, simply because they won't take place.[14] Indeed, in the current atmosphere, even many vice-chancellors have felt constrained. 'You have to be so careful what you say' has become a common refrain among them.

OK, all of this is not the 'death throes of truth' (Sloterdijk, 2020). But it sure as heck doesn't help universities which are based on going where the question leads, not following the crowd. All those hear no evil cancel culture interventions like no-platforming (first adopted by the National Union of Students in the 1970s and still used sporadically (Smith, 2020)), and trigger warnings, intended to shelter a student from reliving some kind of trauma (which available evidence suggests have very little effect (see Flaherty, 2019)), may have their apologists, including in academe (e.g. Baer, 2019). But it seems to me that the danger is one of performing an intellectual health and safety culture which, in trying to produce spaces where you only have to hear what you want to hear, and see what you want to see, postpones a reckoning with a world where disagreement and strife are rampant. It would be nice to think of universities as havens in a heartless world and, to some extent, they can be. But they also have to prepare students for a world where things won't necessarily be easy and often are, well, heartless. Striking the right balance is always going to be hard but I don't think it does students any favours at all to be treated like intellectual invalids who need to be protected at all costs, even though that may be what some of them demand.

All of this said, I can't say that I am entirely convinced by periodic outbreaks of outrage about freedom of speech in universities from right-wing commentators who often have considerable access to the public debate (while claiming to be beleaguered). A few of them recall nothing so much as William F. Buckley Jr's (1951/1986) attack on Yale for disseminating the sin of 'collectivism'. For example, there are those on the right for whom the word 'critical' now acts like a red rag to a bull, as in critical legal studies, critical race theory, critical theory, etc.[15] Some organisations, like Education Watch, propose that students should report 'political bias'.

In other words, what is freedom of speech for some is censorship for others and there is no easy dividing line. In this situation, it is desperately important to call on evidence. Too often, it seems that mighty rhetorical sledgehammers are being broken out to crack nuts. For example, contrary to the amount of often frantic press attention given over to theatrical gestures like no-platforming, there have only been a very small number of instances of universities giving way on this principle. There is near to zero evidence that a rash of talks and meetings in universities are being closed down en masse: the OfS found, using its Prevent duty, that only 53 out of nearly 60,000 speaker events and speaker requests in universities were rejected in 2017/18, most of which had precious little to do with ideological difference, while students' unions – often portrayed as hotbeds of woke hotheads – found that of some 10,000 external speaker events that they oversaw in 2019/20, six were refused, four of which didn't take place because the necessary paperwork hadn't been filled out or the event was proposed to take place with insufficient notice (Dickinson, 2021a).[16] In other words,

> in higher education in the UK we have thousands of volunteer-run student societies organising hundreds of thousands of events every year featuring all sorts of external speakers. They're cheap, generally very well run, and provide immeasurable social, educational and mental health benefits for the people that run and take part in them. (Dickinson, 2020, p. 2)

Again, as I have already noted, a portrayal of students as denying the basic tenets of free speech is wide of the mark. A 2019 survey (Grant et al., 2019) found that 81 per cent of students both thought that freedom of expression was more important than ever and subscribed to a statement based on the

Chicago Principles, while 86 per cent were concerned that social media were enabling people to express intolerant views which prevented people from indulging in free discussion. Generally speaking, students thought that their universities handled the matter of freedom of speech and free expression well. That said, as these figures show, there was a minority of rebel-turned-into-enforcer 'activist' and 'libertarian' students who quite clearly felt that it was acceptable to take more drastic action in pursuit of their views. These are the students who tend to crop up in press reports. Indeed, for some of them, that is one of their aims. All this said, and acknowledging research that seems to show both an apparent hardening of student attitudes since this survey was carried out (Hillman, 2022) and a consequent increase in the chilling effect on those owning alternative beliefs as a result of a more liberal climate of opinion, it is important to record that, according to one recent survey of the general population, though attitudes to free speech vary according to people's beliefs (and people with poisonous racist views, holocaust deniers and those who advocate religiously inspired violence are persona non grata for most respondents[17]), university graduates are actually more likely to be in favour of free speech than non-graduates (Brabner, 2021).

But, whatever else is true, it is difficult to demur from the views of those who argue that students just need to learn to disagree better and that, as importantly, universities have a responsibility to teach this aspect of practical everyday morality from day one, as well as making their own processes more appropriate to the times. Some students (and even just a few of the academics who are, after all, meant to act as their mentors) are only respectful of and civil about the differences they agree with; they have swapped one kind of incivility for another. The nub of the problem of wanting to establish only one particular point of view as regnant is not disagreement as such but rather that, more often than not, absence of debate means that there can be no understanding of other views and therefore of one's own view (Fanshawe, 2021). The result is clear, in any case:

> individuals who express different views are demonised and subjected to vilification campaigns, often in public on social media or university forums. And both conservatives and progressives have been equally at fault on this score. If ideas are to be properly dissected, we shouldn't shut them down like this. We need to be better at listening to opposing views, identifying where points of real disagreement exist and where we share common ground. We need to be more humble about the fact that we might be wrong. (Spence, 2021, p. 15)

In other words, the case for formally teaching basic civic literacy to all students – and not just in an induction session or the like – seems to me to be incontrovertible (Daniels, 2021). Most students will probably never have been introduced to issues of freedom of speech at school, even though it is one of the cornerstones of democracy and responsible citizenship – and the foundation stone of universities. If schools won't do it then universities must.

Though the two issues are often confused, freedom of speech is a different issue from so-called decolonisation of the curriculum. There are genuine and legitimate questions to be asked about how disciplines, especially in the arts and humanities and social sciences, are taught so that the agency of the full range of actors is acknowledged,[18] so that particular spaces and times do not become the standard touchstones of narratives, and so that richer and more complex views of past and present can exist. This is an important project, initiated in large part by feminist and ethnic minority scholars, and through the advent of subdisciplines like global history, which are committed to writing fuller accounts of the world. Recognising the world's diversity is, after all, a crucial part of understanding it and teaching this diversity – whether in the past or present – is almost certain to make some people feel uncomfortable, come what may, given that it places new demands on how people think of and react to the world. New knowledge can often prove a bitter pill to swallow, in other words, and it can often appear to be 'political' if it challenges people's preconceptions. But this isn't political correctness. It's simply historians, geographers and anthropologists striving to produce and teach extended accounts of times and spaces that are more faithful to the historical and geographical record as, through the agency of concentrated research, we have come to understand it. They are adding more fullness into this record, not by taking things away but by putting more of them in (Bhambra and Holmwood, 2021). And the public understands this well enough. As Kernohan notes of a recent UPP/HEPI (2021a) survey:

> if you ask the public how it feels about 'decolonisation' you get 29 per cent who disagree with the idea … plus 16 per cent who don't have a clue what you are talking about and 33 per cent who don't feel they know enough either way.
>
> Flip that to asking about curricula 'allowing students to study about (sic) people, events, materials and subjects from around the world, and ensure that all groups are represented fairly and discussed in an even-handed way' and you get 65 per cent of the public in favour.

This doesn't mean that there are no challenges for universities. One is how to balance a need to include voices and places recognisable to a wide array of different student backgrounds with the equal need to include voices and places that many of them, from whatever background, have to work to recognise. Students are meant to be at university to explore the world, not just to keep to the bits they like. Another is the attitude of just a few academics and students on both left and right who want to use the questions raised by decolonisation to assert their own political currency in a way which can sometimes resemble the Chinese Academy of History's efforts to forge the 'correct outlook on history'. In particular, there is the presence on both left and right of what can sometimes seem like rampant chronocentrism, in which, for example, the course of history has to represent the make-up of the present or be found wanting, or in which historical actors can be judged and found to be in serious deficit if they don't meet today's exacting standards, be they concerned with moral probity as we now conceive it or be they taken to be unrepresentative of current social and cultural groupings as we now perceive them. This kind of easy ethnocentrism, a high-handed lording over history which does not see that, though the present may be moulded by the past, the past doesn't give it reciprocal rights to mould the past into the present, has been addressed by historians and anthropologists many, many times now since it produces a large number of dilemmas which cannot just be shoved to one side and which demand considerable rigour and, dare I say it, discipline. In particular, their efforts to think themselves into very different and often alien mindsets has produced large amounts of insight. But it is also uncomfortable in that it challenges the preconceptions held dear by all kinds of contemporary cultures, for example that distinct positions can be taken which allow of no porosity. Instead of the easy judgements of some iconoclasts and some traditionalists, then, a finer grain is needed. Ironically, tragically even, the problem is that too many academics and students don't seem to know about some of the finest work to have come out of universities, work which refuses easy cognitive shortcuts and which can consequently set them free from traps that are too often of their own making.

Of course, given the history of some universities as former adjuncts of empire and simultaneously as sources of historical, anthropological and geographical expertise, these issues are particularly strongly felt in their own backyard: universities have baggage and it can't just be ignored. That is as it should be. I am quite sure that for a time there will be a turbulent period involving some symbolic and material disruption, for the moment symbolised by that overused and not particularly helpful banner word, 'decolonial'. But a new settlement will emerge in time as the narrative of modernity and of different 'stages' of society slowly collapses (Savage, 2021), a settlement which is less prone to lazy differentiations and over-reactions of all kinds – by parties of all ideological stripes – and more agreeable to listening to how a past of empire, finance, metropole and periphery is still busily at work in the present. And what can universities do? They can help students through this period by giving them the means and the motive to think for themselves – it seems odd even to be making this point and it shows just how far things have slipped that universities have too often backed out of this domain. Back to the point about teaching civic literacy.

Parents

In the 1980s Julian Le Grand and colleagues came up with the idea of the middle-class welfare state. What might at first have appeared as a jarring juxtaposition of middle class with welfare state was purposely made, not just because the middle class had been a formative influence in the growth of the British welfare state but also because the 1980s probably registered a high-water mark in the distribution of middle-class perquisites. Since then a lot of those middle-class perks have disappeared. Pension tax relief severely eroded. Child benefit means tested. Services disappearing or being charged for. And, of course, tuition fees. Add to this a general squeeze on some middle-class incomes coupled with much greater precarity in some middle-class jobs and it is no wonder that large parts of the middle class feel beleaguered. Increasingly, many of even the better-off segments of the middle classes see themselves or their children as victims rather than winners.

Middle-class patience was tested further by rising inequality. When inequality hit a low in the 1970s in much of the Western world, there wasn't that much of a gap between what someone earned with or without a university degree. In the 1980s, however, as inequality increased sharply in Western countries, especially countries like the UK and the US, not only did the gap between white- and blue-collar pay start to widen but so did the gap between the middle class and the wealthiest 10 and 1 per cent. In what was increasingly a meritocratic system but one weighted to those who had the resources to boost their children's chances, getting a degree became more and more important for life chances, and, as student numbers increased and returns from higher education from some universities and courses began to decline, so getting a degree from a research university became not just a badge of honour but a necessary accoutrement for securing a good middle-class career.

It isn't just about austerity and the danger of loss of status, however. It's also a more general sense of grievance. Part of this sense of grievance comes from the feeling that middle-class children are having to try harder and harder just to stand still – even when the competition has been structured to make sure that they are the winners. At the end of all this educational investment their children's life chances may still be restricted in comparison with their parents, something that grates on both children and parents. Under these circumstances, restricting access to elite universities so as to allow others in is just about the final straw. There is increasing resentment, coupled with inevitable attempts to game the system. As Zaloom (2019) notes in a US study, as the small nuclear family has become a more and more dominant middle-class form, many middle-class families will do everything they can to give their children an educational edge and a future that can contain maximum possibility, including getting themselves into serious debt. For families like these, it can seem as though their children are being cheated out of the place at a 'good university' that they and their children's hard work deserves. It's a moral issue, in other words. What parents also don't want to see is their children deep in debt when they complete their course, even though whether student tuition fees count as debt in the normal sense is a moot point.[19]

Given the pressures, it is no surprise that middle-class parenting styles have changed. The US probably shows the most extreme manifestation of this phenomenon:

> permissive parenting was replaced by helicopter parenting. Middle- and upper-class parents who'd gone to public schools and spent their evenings playing kickball in the neighbourhood began elbowing their toddlers into fast-track preschools and spending evenings monitoring their homework and chauffeuring them to activities. American parents eventually increased their hands-on caregiving by about 12 hours a week, compared with the 1970s. Dutch, Spanish, Italian, Canadian and British parents ramped up their child care, too. (Doepke and Zilibotti, 2018, p. 26)

The old leisure class, focussed on spending its money on conspicuous consumption, has increasingly become what Currid-Halkett (2018) calls an aspirational class, based on competing in a fierce form of 'meritocracy' (it clearly isn't that since the investments made in education by the middle class obviously advantage them in demonstrating and accrediting merit), which necessitates spending more and more money on so-called 'inconspicuous consumption'. Among the different forms of inconspicuous consumption, investments in this class's children stand out, investments which will kit them out to be able to win prized and rare educational opportunities. In the US, the top 10 per cent now allocate almost four times as much spending to school and university as they did in 1996 (Rivera, 2015). From their earliest days, their children have to run on a treadmill to gain access to the best schools and then universities and that requires engaging private tutors, seeking out all kinds of juicy extramural activities, demonstrating powers of leadership, and gaining only the best placements. Social media makes things worse by providing a platform which means that these children are constantly having to compare themselves with others. No wonder that many middle-class US children are suffering from a permanent state of anxiety about keeping up with their peers as manifested in, for example, the increased use of antidepressants, counselling, and therapy. No institution now exists with the authority and public support to put these kinds of problems to bed. Parenting is in danger of becoming a substitute for this institutional vacuum, a kind of civil religion in which children are regarded as emotionally priceless 'friends' (Ganesh, 2019, Brooks, 2020a).

The UK isn't there yet but it is in danger of treading this same path, though at generally lower levels of expenditure and (hopefully) division. Investment in children's educational progression is increasing all the time. A middle-class educational arms race has developed as – understandably – parents try to do the best for their children. Take out the issue of private schools and there are still plenty of other investments to be made to further their offspring's educational advantage. Moving house to access better schools has become a commonplace, allowing middle-class parents to make a protected reserve of the best state schools. Private tutoring is becoming a near to must-have in many state schools. Children must participate in all kinds of extramural activities so that their curriculum vitae will stand out, usually as an extra cost. Internships have become increasingly important opportunities to hoard opportunities. More to the point, the tempo of this meritocratic competition is increasing. By the time these children get to university, investment in them has already been very substantial and it will likely continue with a postgraduate leg-up as parents indulge in what Zaloom (2019) calls 'social speculation'.

Getting into a top university is, of course, an unequal process, as is the process of hiring out of the other end (which still often relies on having been to a top university to reap the rewards). The middle class do win out and part of the reason is because of where they go to university (Tough, 2019). The trouble is that, even for those for whom the system actually works, its nature is such that they have become more and more anxious about the place of their children within it. They have to spend more and become more involved in order to give their children a leg-up and the children have to work harder. In other words, even when they are winning – and they still are – somehow it doesn't feel like it.

Whatever the case, no one can blame these largely middle-class parents for their changing attitudes to parenting. In many ways they are making a rational response to the situation they find themselves in: the presence of a competition that it is very difficult to step outside of. But the results have been problematic for research universities, many of which were already privilege-dependent, deriving social and economic status from the families that they serve. In the UK, research universities have effectively become positional goods. As more and more universities have joined the university fold, so their value has increased, leaving research universities as the destinations of choice for middle-class offspring.

The result is clear too. A few decades back no one would have included parents as a fixture in the life of universities. But that's what they have become. It is quite remarkable how things have changed in this regard. When I went to university, parents rarely involved themselves with their children's university education. My father was deeply involved with the mechanics of getting me into university (though he would never have thought of coming round with me to look at specific universities, not that this was a common habit at the time in any case); but after I finally got there I usually called my parents only once, maybe twice a week. I was pretty much on my own in term time.

Now, as middle-class parenting styles have changed, parents have become fully involved. They have often paid for extra tutoring, they come on the visits around universities (and go to sessions at open days that are specially laid on for them as well as talks during coming-up weekend); they don't just turn up to drop their children off but are often pretty common presences after that. They correspond with the university. They sometimes hover. I am not saying that this new kind of intensive and more prolonged parenting is necessarily wrong, by the way. But it is undoubtedly historically different. The transition to independent adulthood has been extended by what is sometimes called a period of emergent adulthood. That means that we are in a weird situation where students want to be treated as adults but at the same time they don't. It is increasingly accepted that universities should treat them as still being fledglings in certain situations. That can be difficult. Students are undoubtedly adults in law but parents very often want them to be treated as though they were still at school, and to be able to access school levels of services, or indeed better. Students want to be treated as adults too – until things go wrong, that is.

Take the vexed issue of mental health. Even before Covid-19, mental health services in universities were under severe pressure with more and more referrals (in just 2019, according to UCAS, there was a 20 per cent increase in students with a declared mental health condition entering universities), difficulties in making the necessary connections with the NHS, and the need to invest more and more in activities like counselling. I am not saying that universities have covered themselves in glory so far as this issue is concerned. Some of them haven't. But neither is the weight of heightened expectations easy to meet. In the public mind, one of the single biggest issues has been the rate of student suicide. But, according to 2017/20 ONS (2022) data, higher education students in England and Wales had a significantly lower suicide rate compared both with the relevant age cohorts and with the general population of similar ages. The overall suicide rate among higher education students (undergraduates account for the majority of the deaths but postgraduates register a small but significant number) was 3.9 deaths per 100,000 students in this period, compared with 12.5 deaths per 100,000 in the general population. The rate for female students was significantly lower than for male students. It is also worth noting that there has been a small decline in numbers of higher education suicides (though the small numbers year on year make it difficult to identify a trend). Yet to read the newspapers, you might think that universities were in a suicide crisis. This is not to say that student mental health (and especially suicide) isn't a problem, of course. It is. Nor is it to say that it is somehow bad that it is increasingly recognised as one. It isn't. Nor, again, is it to say that universities have no responsibility for students' welfare. They obviously do. The issue is rather that in the current situation no one is quite clear where this responsibility begins and ends and having a level-headed discussion about it is difficult. Significantly though, one of the key demands of parents and many students, now being implemented as policy in a number of universities, has been for parents to be able to be notified by universities of any mental health issues their 'child' might have at university if their offspring agrees by signing a release document in advance.

The frustration with this issue, as with others like racism and sexual misconduct in the student body, is that it often feels all but impossible to have a calm public conversation about what is realistically possible. These are all issues which require not only broad-based social change which cannot begin or end at the boundaries of a university but also serious systematic evidence. Yet any debate on them is hampered by the fact that they conform to one of Maslow's laws of cognitive bias: 'it is tempting, if the only tool you have is a hammer, to treat everything as if it were a nail'. Any sign of a purported lack of commitment is immediately treated as evidence of purposeful neglect of mental health, racism, or misogyny. (No wonder that universities are starting to subcontract investigations of some student grievance cases to law firms.) As liberal institutions, universities should lead the way on these issues but there are constraints on what they can do and other parties in the wider society have responsibilities too, discussion of which, in the heat of the 'debate', is simply being sidelined. I don't know of a negotiated way out of this dilemma at this point in time. It will likely be settled through the courts.

Other constituencies

Council

There are many other actors who are affected by universities. At one time, the university was run by two different groups of people. Through senate, academics did the academic stuff and, through council (or board of trustees or some such terminology), a group of people that included numbers of lay members (the terminology is revealing) who oversaw finance and business issues. In between sat the senior management team. Nowadays, though, the pendulum of influence has swung towards council. What is council? It is there to oversee the university's running. Across the UK, there are more than 3,000 members of these governing bodies, of whom 2,400 serve on higher education institutions in England. Typically, councils meet at least four times a year, with some meeting as often as eight or nine times. Council used to be quite a large body. Nowadays it is usually much smaller, somewhere between 22 and eight people with an average membership of 18.9, a majority of whom are external 'lay' members, but also including, again on average, five academics and two executive members. The majority of lay members are usually drawn from business and from the fund of the great and the good. Being a council member can be difficult. Most do not know much about universities and, at least to begin with, they can struggle under the barrage of acronyms, what may well seem like peculiar practices, and the sprawling nature of what universities now do (though I don't think it is a much more difficult task than being a non-exec in, say, a large government organisation). Many universities are now appointing an ex-vice-chancellor or an ex-head of a research council to council to provide an extra element of judgement, especially given that council has now been given – disastrously in my opinion – a degree of academic oversight.

One of the council's tasks is to provide what are usually the majority of the committee that appoints the vice-chancellor. Another is to keep tabs on the vice-chancellor. For the chair of council this can be a particularly difficult job, requiring a relationship with the vice-chancellor which is affable but at the same time keeps a distance. Sometimes a vice-chancellor really needs to go because of malfeasance or some such. This is usually pretty easy to sort out, even though it may be an unpleasant situation in the short term. Much more difficult to judge are the situations where a vice-chancellor has completed an initial five years and has done 60–70 per cent well. It is difficult not to renew their tenure but, equally, that is likely to condemn the university to a period of stasis which can be lethal in current conditions. Bravery is needed, then, but, going the other way, there is also a risk that the chair of council becomes too hands on and gets close to trying to run the university themselves. This happens every now and then and it can make for an explosive situation.

Alumni

Many people have now been students at university. They form, in aggregate, a very large constituency, in the hundreds of thousands for most universities. Many of them drop out of contact but far less than formerly because universities are making determined efforts to keep in touch with them, not least by setting up alumni chapters all around the world which vice-chancellors visit assiduously. Alumni often evince enormous pride in membership of the alumni body and many universities are trying to make them feel a continued sense of belonging through not just reunions but all kinds of other ventures. I fondly remember the annual Christmas party put on by the very active Warwick Hong Kong alumni chapter which was simultaneously a fund raiser.

Part of the effort to keep in touch with alumni is because it's the right thing to do. But part of it is also based on the prospect that they may become donors, either immediately or at a later date. And many do. The figures are nowhere near what would be found in US universities as yet. The US has had a tradition of giving to an alma mater over a much longer time period – and there are also, it has to be said, considerable tax advantages in doing so. But the figures are building and that's clearly a good thing, especially as it increases research universities' room for manoeuvre.

Donors

And so to donors. Gifts are now an important part of a university's income. In the case of Oxford and Cambridge, over a very long time period. This tendency has only been added to by the growth of development offices seeking out gifts and donations, in part to boost teaching and research, in part to substitute for lack of state funding, and in part to provide a measure of freedom. Few research universities can match Harvard's endowment, often reckoned to be the same size as Latvia's GDP. But all of them are trying to build their endowments and who can blame them?

Some academics get on their high horse about this. But universities have never been quite as far from the world of lucre as is often made out. From the earliest times, many have curried favour with the wealthy in search of cash and favours. For example, the early Oxford colleges performed all kinds of pirouettes to get their hands on money from sources which might not always be called respectable. Oxford put up welcome banners, prepared a feast and mounted a showcase of talent for the visit of Elizabeth I in 1566, partially as a bid to get money – and, by the way, it worked. Those who give now are often similarly feted, though perhaps not on quite the same scale. In any case, all research universities have gift committees which vet large gifts to guard against donors who have been accused of serious malfeasance (though what this means is a variable feast) or whose money seems to arise from suspect sources (again, on the evidence of some recent decisions at least, an elastic judgement which is legitimately open to public criticism).

Local communities

The most common complaint vice-chancellors get from local communities concerns student disruption of various kinds – loud parties, drunkenness, unkempt houses, general mess, unthoughtful parking, landlords buying up a string of houses which are rented out to students who never touch the gardens and leave a mound of litter when they leave, and so on. I was routinely buttonholed by disenchanted local residents at the university Christmas party for local residents and, in many cases, I can't say I blamed them. Sometimes it can feel to local communities as if they are under siege. Added to this is 'Saturday night syndrome'. In university towns and cities, 'students' often get the blame for rowdiness – though it usually turns out that they are a convenient object of blame for acts committed by young non-students.

All these symptoms have only been made worse by the rapid expansion of universities, producing 'studentification' of parts of many towns and cities as whole areas are all but given up to students. Residents may feel crowded out or just generally aggrieved; but there is, truth to tell, precious little that universities can do about it most of the time. Some universities, like Bristol, fund special police patrols in parts of the city with large student populations, responding to complaints from residents about antisocial behaviours. Universities can help set up organisations of local student landlords and give out lists of those that are recommended. They can implore students to behave well (and the vast majority do, by the way). They can help student unions to set up groups that both liaise with and try to contribute to local communities. But there is only so much they can do. Their control is mainly indirect.

All this said, all universities aspire to having a positive impact on their community. And they do. Recently, this influence has widened and has become a major part of university activity. Universities run hospitals, schools, arts centres, massive volunteering programmes, sports programmes. Staff run all manner of charitable programmes and other forms of outreach. Students are similarly active. So are alumni. The exact make-up of activity varies but one of the aspects of the modern university which is unabashedly to the good is the commitment to service by the institution, by staff and by students. This activity has grown substantially in recent years and has also internationalised so that a university's community may now span many countries. For example, universities help to run hospitals overseas, fund schools (I well remember a visit to an educational programme in an impoverished rural area outside Delhi), roll out mental health and environmental programmes ... the list is practically endless.

Business

Seemingly every year there is yet another enquiry led by someone or other important into the issue of universities and business. And seemingly every year pretty much the same recommendations are made. This conveyor belt of enquiries must mean something but I'm becoming increasingly hard pressed to know what. After all, it is a fact that, for some time now, universities have been a part of the machinery of economic growth. Though it is important to note that research universities primary function is not as engines of economic success, that has clearly become an important function, one which they cannot just shuck off, even if they wanted to. That has inevitably meant much closer relationships with business. As Callon (2021, p. 369) puts it, like it or not, 'those who loudly clamour that the values and norms of science cannot be reconciled with those of the markets have been proven wrong. The adjustments are made daily.'

According to the marketisation thesis, which tends to posit a single logic of action called 'market', universities have been completely taken over by the dictates of business, becoming caught up in the process of hollowing out of the British state by 'market' forces or, more accurately, by 'the deliberate reduction of popular expectations of public authority; the outsourcing of responsibility to technocratic, private and quasi-autonomous actors, weakening lines of control and accountability; and the hollowing-out of state capacities and authority to the benefit of frequently inept large-scale corporations' (Jones and Hameiri 2021, p. 239). Government has been replaced by governance, in other words. But, so far at least, it is not clear to me that universities have shared in this grisly fate, though they need to be constantly on guard as government, and certain kinds of corporations to which they increasingly outsource several of their functions, move ever closer. Universities certainly interact much more closely than in the past with corporate and other interests and in a host of ways as the categories of the recent Knowledge Exchange Framework (KEF) show only too well: research partnerships, intellectual property and commercialisation, economic regeneration, skills, enterprise and entrepreneurship, consultancy and contract research, and working with the public and third sector. In the US, this kind of engagement has been the case since the end of the nineteenth century. In other countries, it happened somewhat later but nearly all national governments now understand universities as key elements of economic growth poles, sometimes, it has to be said, by grossly exaggerating their powers. Add in all manner of government funding to universities meant to stimulate greater cooperation between business and universities and a raft of corporate funding and it is clear that an economic mode of existence has become more influential, a state of affairs that has been much decried – as a capitulation to the immediate and worldly, as economic serfdom, as the triumph of an economic logic, as a pathology of productivity, as an incursion by powers which threaten universities' neutrality (see, for example, Mirowski, 2011, Berman, 2012, McGettigan, 2013). The reality is rather more complicated.

Business certainly has more influence on universities than formerly, and in several ways. First, there is government. For the last 30 years at least, it's been sure that something else needs to be done to boost corporate engagement. So a series of policies has been rolled out, some good, some bad, most of them involving extra funding streams meant to promote closer business and university cooperation. The most recent of these is the innovation agency

Innovate UK's Industrial Strategy Challenge Fund (ISCF) which has been generally recognised as a success in that it has boosted investment in business support by bringing together business, universities and public institutions like councils to challenge and boost innovation in battery, quantum and other technologies via a combination of public funding and match funding from business.

Second, there is business influence through council. Many council members come from business and, not unnaturally, they tend to concentrate on those parts of the university which seem most business-relevant and on results that seem to fit business templates.

Third, there is influence coming from commissioning research. Universities actively search out money from business and indeed house businesses, not least as a result of the additions of entities like science parks. Some of the largest grants that they access are business-funded or have business components. Quite a few science academics routinely draw on these kinds of sources of funding but usually as part of a portfolio which takes in research monies from a number of sources rather than just business.

Fourth, business forms a constituency that universities are able to aid in various ways through operations like small business accelerators (often on those science parks), and the like.

Fifth, business forms a general lobby trying to influence universities, usually by attempting to influence government policy or via various intermediary organisations which bring actors in particular areas together in the name of economic development. It's true that there is a small but vocal lobby that demands more job-relevant (or, in the creepy parlance, 'oven-ready') training (often the businesses that have short-sightedly reduced their training budgets year on year, as too many British businesses have). That said, some of the larger employers which do still invest in training have more nuanced demands. Indeed, some have cooperated with universities in producing tailored degrees and providing bursaries for the students on them. When it is pointed out that these degrees need to be more than just job training, I have heard very few of these employers demur. You want employees who can go beyond the job.

Sixth, there is the rise of the business school to contend with. Not only have these schools inculcated more business-facing attitudes in universities, as well as ensuring that many university alumni now run businesses, but in most universities they also make a considerable surplus.

Seventh, universities themselves can incorporate and foster various kinds of profit-making businesses, from a conference business to multiple start-ups by both academics and students. The latter were at one time seen as a kind of saviour, especially of university finances which they were supposed to galvanise by producing a drug or another invention that would produce a financial bonanza; but now, though such discoveries do happen – rarely – a sense of proportion has settled in about likely fiscal outcomes. The same stricture applies to the ownership of intellectual property of various kinds from the make-up of contracts with business to a general chase after patents. Moderation makes more sense, given the likely costs and rewards. For example, research universities are much more selective about patents than they used to be.

So there are a lot of pressure points but they are usually partial. As a vice-chancellor, I have to say that I never felt unduly pressured by corporate behemoths. There are, of course, those who believe that even one contact with mammon is one contact too many. But given universities' size and reach, it seems to me to be incumbent on them to make some contribution to the national (and urban and regional) economy, as well as pick apart vital economic issues like productivity. Some North American universities already do this very effectively. I think of Waterloo with its extraordinary start-up operation and Stanford similarly. But British research universities aren't so far behind with the number of successful spin outs they generate (like Paragraf, Graphcore and Vaccitech) – the real problem is the volume of available investment, especially at later stages in a firm's development. For example, the amount of venture capital investment increased tenfold between 2010 and 2020 and has grown further since through organisations like the IP Group, Cambridge Innovation Capital, Northern Gritstone, Oxford Science Enterprises and Parkwalk, although it still lags the US. But it is as firms grow that the problems mount. In particular, their ability to access long-term equity capital is attenuated compared with the US. Again, a number of research universities have a permanent freestanding industrial operation which could go head-to-head with the best in the world. Warwick has this in the shape of the Warwick Manufacturing Group (WMG).[20] Sheffield has it in the shape of the Advanced Manufacturing Research Centre (AMRC). The point is that operations like these house a massive conglomeration of industrial research capacity, equipment, skills and ability to train students, apprentices and managers, both in the UK and overseas. They also tend to function as intermediaries between universities and business, since they have deep knowledge of what expertise there might be in the university which could be of use to a particular client. Not only does this help with turbocharging particular lines of innovation but it also takes some of the pressure off academics who feel that somehow their work has to be industrially relevant when it isn't, shouldn't be, and doesn't have to be.

To summarise, it is dangerous to generalise to too great a degree about the influence of business on universities. Not all businesses are termites busily undermining the foundations of universities. There are good and bad corporate links, good and bad contracts, good and bad expectations. What is equally clear is that for large research universities to carry out certain kinds of research makes it all but inevitable that they will call on business to some extent. It's true that a certain kind of business-driven economentality has become a habit of certain parts of the university. But it still often touches only certain functions and that is right and proper. That is not to say that vigilance is unnecessary. It is.

In particular, I harbour one worry that won't go away. That is that research is slowly but surely being industrialised (not marketised, or, at least, the two are not directly correlated). It has become almost received wisdom that research needs to take place in teams (or work groups). Much of the inspiration for this new orthodoxy comes from the tech industry (and how work relates to the internet), drawing on a long history of management ideas arising out of the practices of what I have called 'soft capitalism', practices concerned with how to get the best out of workers (which are therefore hardly neutral in their aims) which have been given a boost of late by other concerns such as inclusion. Though this orthodoxy may prove valid for certain kinds of research in certain disciplines, the idea that it can be applied wholesale to the pursuit of ideas strikes me as not only false but dangerous. *Thinking is an ecology.* There is no one model of thinking. Thinking cannot be reduced to one approach.

PART II

The contemporary British university system

4

A new Robbins? Recent changes in British universities

So, having got some sense of what research universities are about, it is now possible to survey what has happened to them, mainly over the last decade or so. That is what the next four chapters try to achieve by taking different perspectives on their recent history.

Research universities have changed and I doubt that many academics would argue that every one of the recent changes has been an unalloyed good. But this cannot be an argument against change per se. The research university as we know it now is only the latest in a long line of forms of university (Clark, 2009, Cole, 2009, Wolf, 2019), none of which were the land of Cockaigne that they have often been described as in retrospect by those commentators keen to show both a golden age and continuity of practice and values. Thus, in the UK the idea that universities should do research funded at scale by the state really only dates from the period after the Second World War although universities had certainly received some considerable state funding before that (British Academy, 2019). Again, the basic research apparatus of seminar, specialised journal paper and scholarly monograph, the doctorate and a structured career in research was, in the form that we would now recognise it, invented in the nineteenth and early twentieth centuries and it was not without its critics at the time (for example, see James (1918) decrying the diffusion of PhDs through the American university system). Even as late as 1869–70, there were only seven resident graduate students in the whole of the US Ivy League. When I first started at university, having a PhD was not an absolute necessity – there were still quite a few 'misters' among academic staff complements.

The point is that there have been many other forms of university than what in many countries of the world has become the default position for many, passionately defended as if it is somehow the only way of going on. There is no necessary reason why supposed fundamentals like the lecture or the seminar or indeed academic qualifications cannot be reinvented without the whole of the academic enterprise crumbling – which is not to say that care doesn't need to be taken in doing so. Witness just some of the major events of the last 60 years or so as an exemplar of how fast university systems can mutate and what becomes apparent is that a pretty constant rate of change has been maintained in British higher education since the 1960s. The Robbins Report in 1963 (Committee on Higher Education, 1963) and the major expansion of the university system it portended. The renaming of polytechnics as universities in 1992, abolishing the so-called 'binary divide' and nearly doubling overnight the number of university students. The Dearing Report, which recommended variable tuition fees, in 1997. The principle of tuition fees established in 1998 with students required to pay £1,000. Tuition fees of £3,000 introduced in 2004. The Browne Review of 2009 with its recommendation that the cap on tuition fees should be completely lifted. The increase in tuition fees to £9,000[1] and the removal of the student number cap in 2012/13. The scrapping of maintenance grants in 2016. The current fee of £9,250 in 2017 (now frozen until the end of this parliament). And, through all this period, a steady growth in international student numbers. As a starter for ten, against a background of these and other major events, I want to briefly sketch 12 of the main changes that have taken place in the higher education sector. Twelve is a lot but that only goes to show the sheer amount of change that has taken place.

The changes

The first and most obvious change is one of scale. In 1962/63, there were only 216,000 home and overseas students in the UK. By 2019/20 there were over 11 times more (Bolton, 2021b) Even given the expansion of the British population, this has still been a giant step and, with it, universities have increasingly become a part of the fabric of everyday life. Going to 'uni' (or at least some form of higher education) has become a life course expectation for many more people. But this expansion has not been a smooth one. Universities have tended to expand in fits and starts. There was the nineteenth-century expansion which produced the first wave of civic universities. There were the large investments in higher education that arose from the experience of war in the twentieth century, especially because of thinking on higher education reform in the UK led by writers like R.H. Tawney (Steele and Taylor, 2008). But the real acceleration in student numbers began with the 1963 publication of Lord Robbins wide-ranging report. As Halsey (1992, p. 5) pointed out, it was in some ways a quite conservative document, one which might best be seen as 'the last expression of Victorian expansionism'. But it became the touchstone for the great 1960s university expansion. It produced a raft of new universities and a large increase in domestic student numbers. It set the seal on expansion as both an end and a means which has typified the years since.

In the last few years, it has sometimes been made out that another great student expansion has taken place, almost a new Robbins period of student number growth. But that isn't quite true. Certainly, the 2000s were a period of rapid expansion, but if you look at aggregate UK student numbers from the more recent HESA statistics, there were 2,397,585 students in higher education in 2008/09 (1,860,425 undergraduates and 537,160 postgraduates) and 2,532,390 students in 2019/20[2] (1,889,475 undergraduates and 642,915 postgraduates) with not all that much variation in between.[3] (These figures conceal a sharper increase in undergraduate and postgraduate students in England and rather smaller increases in undergraduate and postgraduate students in Scotland, Wales and Northern Ireland and sharper increases in standard first degrees among undergraduates and in taught Master's degrees among postgraduate students.) But the figures don't mean that there has been no student number growth in the system. Rather, growth has mainly occurred lopsidedly in the distribution of students between different universities, enabled by government prompts (in England) which have provided a simulation of market competition (undergraduate students), and actual market competition (especially for international students whose numbers have increased markedly). Most research universities have grown student numbers, sometimes dramatically (Table 4.1). Some research universities have also grown through other means which do not fully show up in the figures. (For example, the official King's College student headcount is 31,300 but it is much larger again – nearer 45,000 – if you take in all the part-time, online and pre-university degree students it teaches.)

One thing that is definitely not correct: the idea that 50 per cent of young adults are going into higher education, Tony Blair's supposed target of 1999 (Brant, 2019). The actual figure for those applying to university in 2021, a boom year because of Covid-19 and a demographic bulge, was 43 per cent of 18-year-olds. (The UK Higher Education Initial Participation Rate, as it is called, on which the 50 per cent figure is based, is a projection of young adults from 17 up to the age of 30. Furthermore, it isn't just made up of university students but also includes those studying higher education in further education colleges, those studying higher technical qualifications rather than degrees, those studying part as well as full time, and those not expected to enter higher education until their 20s.)

Whatever the exact facts of the matter, and the presumably short-term impact of coronavirus in boosting student numbers even more (remembering that, because of demography, by one estimate, 350,000 extra full-time places will be needed by 2035), the student body has changed markedly. Most particularly, women have become the majority of the student population. They make up 57 per cent of all undergraduate students. Again, a considerable part of the student body now consists of postgraduates. There were 566,555 postgraduate students in 2017/18, a 16 per cent increase since 2008/09 (with a particularly strong increase in non-EU overseas students). Of this number, 356,996 were first-year starters. 65 per cent of postgraduate starters were studying for taught Master's degrees while doctoral and other research postgraduates accounted for 10 per cent of the cohort (House, 2020).

Table 4.1: English Russell Group universities

	Difference in UCAS acceptances 2010–2020	University total income (£000s), 2018/19	Research grant income from research councils, 2018/19 (£000s)	Tuition fee % of total income 2018/19
University of Birmingham	2,245	716,296	49,953	49.11
University of Bristol	3,210	706,891	65,136	40.85
University of Cambridge	590	2,192,053	216,629	14.61
Durham University	2,035	381,022	26,290	54.93
University of Exeter	4,025	449,278	35,543	55.18
Imperial College London	975	1,073,754	114,859	29.17
King's College London	3,815	901,965	47,823	43.66
University of Leeds	925	791,850	70,882	50.54
University of Liverpool	1,955	577,660	39,932	53.49
London School of Economics & Political Science	955	420,802	9,689	54.04
University of Manchester	1,985	1,097,182	149,273	44.02
Newcastle University	1,900	570,606	35,947	46.35
University of Nottingham	1,695	701,233	54,885	50.86
University of Oxford	505	2,450,135	162,031	14.44
Queen Mary, University of London	2,060	483,857	30,150	50.75
University of Sheffield	990	715,700	61,206	46.31
University of Southampton	845	594,310	48,023	42.91
University College London	5,115	1,487,079	154,000	37.99
University of Warwick	2,190	688,522	39,209	50.03
University of York	1,135	391,790	35,605	48.12

Source: UCAS, HESA, HESA, Kernohan (2021a).

Last, but not least, many more students come from overseas; in 2019/20, on HESA figures, 556,625 of them were enrolled. In other words, universities are now very different beasts from what many parents and grandparents of students often remember when they reminisce.

There has been a corresponding growth in staff numbers too. The total number of staff at UK higher education institutions is now 419,590 about half of whom are academic (teaching and/or research) and half of whom are administrators and other workers. Quite a large part of the academic staff growth has been fuelled by hiring non-UK nationals, especially from the EU. One notable development that has occurred in concert with the rise in academic staff numbers has been a greater heterogeneity of staff careers. A division of labour among academics has grown up. For example, whereas in the past the bulk of academic staff were on contracts which meant that they carried out teaching, research, and administration, a homage to the idea of the teacher-researcher, nowadays there are more teaching-only staff, more research-only staff, and more specialist staff like professors of practice and industrial professors. This division of labour may vary among research universities but the change has been dramatic. Thus, teaching-only staff increased at five times the rate of teacher-researcher roles between 2005/06 and 2018/19 with much of the increase concentrated in Russell Group universities (which, as a result, are now converging on the sector average from a lower base) for a series of reasons, many of them best characterised as 'residual decisions' (like the smoothing out of staffing profiles as student numbers have grown, managing costs, and providing teaching cover for vacancies, for example for academics who have been bought out to undertake research, when appointments have been delayed, and so on) (Wolf and Jenkins, 2021). Growth in research-only staff has also taken place too, though from a higher base. In this case, comparative research intensity has been the main cause. For example, at UCL, with its very large medical faculty, 16 per cent of academic staff are teaching only, 48 per cent are research only and 36 per cent are both teaching and research. As I have already pointed out in Chapter 2, there has also been something of a boom in the employment of administrators as well, to many academics' chagrin.

The second change follows on. What was a largely government-funded tertiary education system has become a diverse ecosystem with numerous providers, by no means all of which are universities sensu stricto. At last count, in 2022 there were 412 government-registered higher education providers in the UK (in 2018/19 453 providers were included in Unistats data, 444 in Graduate Outcomes data and 282 higher education providers returned Student, Staff, Finance, HE-BCI and Estates Management data). 165 returned a full set of data to the Higher Education Statistics Agency. In all, probably, around 140 institutions might be rightly counted as 'universities' in the conventional sense (this is the number of members of Universities UK). Much has been made of the greater involvement of the private sector in the university ecosystem. Certainly, there were a few more private institutions, institutions which are likely to increase in number, though not massively. Of these, the most important are the seven private universities in the UK with degree-awarding powers.[4] It is also important to note the role of the further education sector which increasingly teaches courses to degree level. Overseas students, industry, own companies, technology transfer and start-up companies, science parks, the European Union, trusts, endowments – all have played their financial part in providing funding streams that support this increasingly complex system and, in many of these cases, as we shall see, a very considerable part indeed.

The third change is that the constituent parts of the UK higher education system have begun to diverge quite markedly as the different devolved administrations increasingly go their own way. In Scotland, for example, the model that has so far been adopted can be interpreted as largely a continuation of the managed public system that existed in England before the advent of a more competitive student funding system (Scott, 2021), though, as Kernohan (2021a) points out, it has likely reached its limit in its current form. Overall, what this means is that there is much less in the way of student fee income from government, making Scottish universities even more dependent than their English counterparts on international students for succour. In part, this is because tuition is still free in Scotland for Scottish students though there is a debate about whether this prejudices access overall because it necessitates an unofficial soft cap on numbers (Blackburn, 2014), added to which there is a likely decline in domestic student numbers on current demographic trends by 2035 (Hewitt, 2020). Thus, Universities and Colleges Admissions Service (UCAS) figures show that only 55 per cent of university applications from Scotland resulted in an offered place last year. The equivalent figure for those based in England was 74 per cent. (EU students (from outside the UK) had a 65 per cent offer rate, 10 per cent higher than the Scottish figure, despite competing for the same Scottish government-funded places.) Again, Scottish government research funding has been declining though recently it has been given a small fillip. It might be wise to admit that no higher education system in the UK is without its problems!

The fourth change is what is best described as proliferation. Universities are expected to do more and more. They are expected to be prime economic movers in the nation and in their cities and regions and even 'anchor' them, provide major cultural services, fashion themselves as civic entities, bind the nation together, become prime movers in levelling up, provide means of stamping out harassment and sexual assault, make up for shortfalls in NHS provision of mental health services, plug gaps in the benefits system resulting from spiralling housing costs and the low maintenance loan, widen every kind of access, promote social mobility, largely pay for their own (increasingly onerous) regulation, and so on. Many of them have participated enthusiastically in taking on these responsibilities but the question that might well be asked is how far the elastic can be stretched before it snaps. In the case of research universities, in particular, one question that might be asked is whether the weight of the consequences of taking on extra responsibilities such as diverting staff time, producing cadres of administrators who can provide a constituency for diverting yet more resource, and producing even more ways in which universities can be measured (and then castigated), diverts research universities from what they are obviously good at. Look at what has happened with university education. Universities are being ordered around from pillar to post, expected to add more and more responsibilities to students, often via letters sent directly from the minister which can sometimes seem to demonstrate a less than full sense of what the financial consequences of the letter might be. A good example of this near-infantilisation is one of the latest DfE diktats which wants universities to help raise attainment in schools by actively working with and supporting local schools. Universities already do this to quite an extent but to make it into a formal responsibility seems an extraordinary progression, underlining that higher education is now being seen, by the DfE at least, as simply another rung in the schools system. It also begs the serious question of how universities are meant to afford this and other measures, especially given that there is what looks suspiciously like a pattern of government providing special funds for new higher education responsibilities which are subsequently withdrawn. As Dickinson (2021c) puts it:

> It may well be – as has been argued over almost all of these measures each time – that while the sector grows it can afford [them] and that local and tailored solutions are better than national programmes. ...
>
> It may well also be that this is a terrible, inequitable and chaotic way to distribute funding – and that not only do vice chancellors make terrible health bosses or disability service heads, there are plenty of examples of structures across Europe where these functions are run (better) (separately) alongside but not by universities, cooperatively; regionally or nationally.

The fifth change is that more centralised and managerial forms of governance have become common as universities have grown in scale and influence. This is hardly a new development – for example, the office of provost in US universities (a term which spread fast in British universities as a new cognomen for the deputy vice-chancellor) came about in large part because of the demands of running larger organisations. The idea that these scaled-up universities can now be run as though they are congregations of schoolmen is simply fantastical. Even universities like Oxford and Cambridge which are still loose federations of colleges and departments have had to take on centralised functions as they have grown in scale. But the growth of more centralised management has undoubtedly brought tensions with it. The rise of the administrative university and of a cadre of administrators much larger in number than in the past and more likely to wield some degree of power has, in combination with the increasing power of lay governing bodies and the rise of adjunct faculty, produced a model of the university which has become steadily more corporate and more distant (see Shattock and Horvath, 2019). It is not necessary to depict administrators as a kind of plague on the academic body or lay governing bodies as corporate stooges to be concerned that the ethos of universities is changing in ways which could cut across their ability to be worthy of the name. Wolf and Jenkins (2021) make the point that Oxford and Cambridge have a messy system of governance which is less managerial and more democratic than the norm but it does not seem to have served them badly. Indeed, there is some evidence that the inroads made into university and academic autonomy by government combined with some of the attempts to govern universities in a more business-like way may be retrograde in the sense that they produce diversions and digressions which subtract from any efficiency gains. Universities can be run in a business-like manner but that is not the same as saying that they are businesses, not only because they are not-for-profits but because their licence to operate is necessarily social and not just economic and their academic workforce cannot be treated as simply profit centres (ironically, a lesson that creative industries around the world sometimes seem to have learnt rather better than some universities).

The sixth change is much higher levels of auditing, from university managements, it is true, but most especially from the metrics imposed by both government and the rankings industry. The requirements of government through its various agencies have become increasingly onerous as universities have become caught up in a regulatory web of different agencies checking and cross-checking what universities are doing through the medium of audit – not just the big ones like the Research Excellence Framework (REF), which first furnished results in 1986, the Teaching Excellence Framework (TEF), which first provided results in 2017, and now the Knowledge Exchange Framework (KEF), which first provided results in 2021, but all of those other calls to judgement that never make the headlines – calls that seem to be launched without much in the way of thought about the extra burdens of time and money (and additional jobs) that they impose, yet alone whether they are actually effective. Meanwhile university league tables impose a permanent anxiety on the sector which clearly drives behaviour. Audits are redefining accountability, transparency, and good governance, reshaping the way universities and their individual staff have to operate, and undermining notions of professional autonomy, in ways which are not always healthy, especially when they make misleading distinctions (Strathern, 2002). As Mulhern (2020, p. 119) points out, it is not the use of quantitative data per se which are at fault here but rather the way in which they now form 'a threshold condition of relevance and admissibility'. To be relevant, information has to be countable, not least because these metrics are then able to be converted into financial allocations. But in the words of the well-known saying, not everything that can be counted counts.

The seventh change is the rise of technology in teaching. Universities are becoming the stamping ground of all manner of new information and communications technologies. Take teaching. On one account, universities will gradually become platforms providing courses and that will be that. Actual face-to-face teaching will slide out of existence as the online takes over. A whole new sub-genre of management books has become concerned with extolling the virtues of information technology-based learning, a familiar rhetorical move meant to imply inevitability that has its origins in the dot com boom of the 1990s. On another account, this time internally generated, universities need the push provided by new electronic pedagogy to become relevant again. As I have already pointed out, this technology has now been in place long enough for it to become clear that it is not an inevitable outcome that everyone and their dog will be taught online, as once seemed the endpoint of a MOOC-led 'avalanche' (Barber, 2013), not least because electronic courses, at least when done properly, are actually extremely labour-intensive and work much better for some constituencies than others (Reich, 2020). It is clearly becoming, slowly but surely, more influential without implying any necessary determinate endpoint. Coronavirus has changed the terms of the equation and though it may be that online learning, already a substantial force, will become a majority means of delivering higher education in a few non-research universities it is worth recalling that one recent survey found that, after the experience of online teaching during Covid-19, 90 per cent of students said they strongly or somewhat preferred in-person teaching where the content was also recorded (Student Futures Commission, 2022).

The eighth change has been growth in the scale of university research in the UK. English research universities have been the beneficiaries of a broadly stable research income from government in real terms since 2010 (Bolton, 2021a) as a result of the relative protection given to the UKRI budget (UK Research and Innovation is the main public competitive research funding body), and thereby the research and innovation budgets of the seven research councils, Innovate UK, and Research England as well as to a lesser extent from what has been a slowly declining QR, the quality-related block grant given to universities according to the results of the Research Excellence Framework competition run by Research England (currently set at about 64 per cent of every pound that the Research Councils (and cross-UKRI activities) spend between 2022/23 and 2024/25), the result of an acceptance in government, at least of a kind, that science and innovation are a long-term game. These state monies have been boosted by the presence of the Wellcome Trust, Cancer Research UK, the Leverhulme Trust, the Nuffield

Foundation, the Gates Foundation and other charitable funding sources and lately by disproportionate success in winning European Research Council and other European grants – indeed, the leading British research universities obtained between 13 and 23 per cent of their research funding from Europe before Brexit. The government's wise decision in December 2020 to agree in principle to stay in the €95 billion European research funding programme, Horizon Europe (the successor to Horizon 2020 and the world's largest multinational research funding programme) after Brexit has been welcomed – although the agreement looks to be under mortal threat because of political shenanigans. If this decision ever gets turned into reality it should provide the ability to continue to obtain European Research Council grants which are mainly reserved for fundamental discovery research and have become a much-respected academic gold standard, whether they be in the form of postgraduate starter or advanced grants.[5] The considerable increases in government research and development funding promised in 2020 (and the generally sensible R and D road map that accompanied them (HMG, 2020)[6]), when combined with this European move (or the 'Plan B' that may have to replace it), will certainly provide a real fillip for research, at least to judge from the most recent projected budget allocations to UKRI; but a way still has to be found out of what often seems like a perennial bind whereby overheads on grants are not fully supported, a pernicious practice which has once more reached an alarming scale[7] with the result that there is considerable university over-trading.

Of course, many researcher hearts beat a little faster when it was announced that the government wanted to increase total public research and development spending so as to reach an interim target of £22 billion a year by 2024/25. This ambition sits alongside a wider ambition to grow all-economy research and development to 2.4 per cent of GDP from its current 1.7 per cent, a figure that is very low by international standards. To put the scale of this latter aspiration into perspective, that requires total economy research and development spend in the UK to be lifted from £37 billion a year now to £68 billion in 2027, yet it is clearly necessary, not least given that competitors like the US and China are currently making massive investments in research that, absent this boost, will dwarf British spending. For a while, it looked like these two grand ambitions were likely to be honoured in the breach. (For example, UKRI received an 8.2 per cent cut in its 2021/22 budget compared with 2020/21, though it is still 7 per cent up in real terms on the 2017/18 settlement it received at its instigation.[8]) Short-sighted, one might think.[9] But the omens now look much more promising with the latest government announcement promising £20 billion by 2024/25 and £22 billion by 2026 (with the general direction of research being managed by a new Office for Science and Technology overseen by a National Science and Technology Council). Recent budget allocations to

UKRI foreshadow what should prove to be a real impact on research and innovation from these sums. For example, a London Economics (2017) Report on the economic impact of Russell Group universities, found that if about a third of the target of £22 billion of public investment was put into research and innovation at these universities, it would in turn deliver a return of more than £60 billion to the UK's economy (Stevens, 2021).

Whatever happens, the result of research funding given out to universities so far and universities own strategies is clear to see. Success. Take research. 6.5 per cent of world articles emanated from the UK in 2019 (and 6.8 per cent of field-weighted share), lagging behind only the US and China. Similarly, though one might think the results of 41 per cent of outputs deemed as 'world-leading' by assessment panels and 43 per cent judged 'internationally excellent' (up from 30 and 46 per cent in 2014) are more than a tad optimistic, the 2021 Research Excellence Framework suggests that many of these publications are of high quality. (But there are warning signs too – for example, not only is the UK's share of world publications falling but so is its share of highly cited UK global publications and its share of research and development spend and its share of researchers (Thompson, 2020). Although some of these falls are a relative effect resulting from the massive rise in the overall number of highly cited Chinese publications, still this must be a matter of some concern. Certainly, there is no room for complacency.)

The ninth change is the importance universities have gained as a component of the knowledge economy though their research and their role as suppliers of graduate labour. Though one might well be sceptical of some of the more inflated claims for the power of the knowledge economy, and of universities as drivers of economic growth, university research and skilled graduates are now integral to what economies are thought to be about. A recent study by Oxford Economics for Universities UK found that UK universities generated £95 billion for the country's economy and supported more than 940,000 jobs across the nation in 2014–15, an increase of 15 per cent in real terms since 2011–12, and more than 1 per cent of the country's workforce. The study also calculated that the gross value-added contribution of universities' own operations to the country's gross domestic product was £21.5 billion (or 1.2 per cent of GDP), 22 per cent greater than the contribution produced by the whole of the accountancy sector and almost 50 per cent more than the contribution of the advertising and market research industry.[10] Gross export earnings were reckoned to be some £12.4 billion in 2014/15. The UK higher education sector had an income of £35.7 billion in 2017/18. Just under 50 per cent of total income came from fees and health education contracts related to teaching (£17.7 billion), while direct UK government funding for teaching represented another 6.3 per cent. Income from research came to just over 22 per cent (£7.9 billion) of the total, and endowments and investments (2.4 per cent) and other income (19.4 per cent) accounted for the rest. Moving on from these bare figures, the research capacity of modern economies is an essential part of the supply chain of knowledge and innovation, particularly because the generation of high-end knowledge and innovation is increasingly concentrated in universities as companies, driven by the perverse incentives of shareholder capitalism, have withdrawn from research and development. Again, universities are linchpins of the collective intelligence of many national and regional economies, a crucial component of boosting these economies absorptive capacity. And again, universities are one of the central elements of the human capital plans of many nations (Goldin and Katz, 2008). They improve the competitiveness of economies since their graduates, by obtaining higher education qualifications, lead skills-based technological change and also provide an increase in the proportion of the workforce attaining high skill levels which leads directly to higher labour productivity. In other words, if the 'country needs institutions, public and private, better capable of generating widely shared growth' (Wolf, 2013, p. 11), then universities are clearly a positive component of that ambition. Becoming so important economically is, of course, a two-edged sword, but the sheer economic weight of the sector cannot be gainsaid.

But all this funding is built on teeter-totter foundations. The university system is very efficient, perhaps too efficient. For example, one recent study placed the UK higher education system third in the world in terms of 'output' but only 13th in terms of the 'resources' assigned to it (Universitas21, 2019). According to Statista, the UK invested a notoriously low percentage of public expenditure on higher education as a share of GDP in 2016 – around 0.5 per cent – but private expenditure, by contrast, was very high at 1.2 per cent. Consequently, expenditure on higher education per student was also high, ranking behind only Luxembourg and the US in 2017.

The tenth change is in international presence. In the 1960s, only 10 per cent of students in UK universities came from overseas. By 2019/20 there were over 538,615 overseas students (and coronavirus doesn't seem to have put a brake on this expansion). They have been an absolutely vital part of the reason why British universities are financially viable – as well as making a substantial contribution to the UK economy as a whole.[11]

On top of this inward movement, British universities have gone out into the world. Internationalisation is now a fact of life: universities have become more and more international and increasingly liable to compete (and cooperate) internationally. There is a blizzard of student exchange agreements and partnerships. There are more joint degrees between two or more universities. There are more international scholarship programmes. There are many more universities teaching overseas. 666,815 students are studying outside the UK for UK higher education qualifications.[12] Indeed, there are now more students studying for UK postgraduate qualifications wholly abroad, via transnational education, than there are non-UK students in the UK (House, 2020). There are more overseas branch campuses too – somewhere between 263 and 282 in total across the world, according to which definition is adopted, of which UK universities have a good number.[13] (Internationalisation of this kind went through a high point a few years back, with a rise in all kinds of overseas involvements. Then, as problems mounted with some overseas operations, and with a number of branch campus projects being aborted for different reasons, some good, some bad, a sense of proportion began to settle in.)

Research is following a similar internationalising tendency. The research university has become a system of research interaction which operates across the globe, as all manner of analyses from studies of co-citations to actual ethnographies of science show.[14] There are more international research agreements than ever. The boundaries of research universities have become more and more porous. Not only is there more collaboration between academics in universities in the UK but there is also more international collaboration. In the world as a whole, using Web of Science data, 21.3 per cent of the total scientific output of articles featured international co-authors, compared with 10.7 per cent in 2000 (Ribeiro et al., 2018). The US was the most connected, followed by England and Germany.[15] So far as research is concerned, British research universities are now firmly international entities, and they are becoming more international all the time. For example, 54 per cent of UK researchers' publications result from international collaboration, significantly higher than the OECD average of 31 per cent, while the UK's share of international collaboration has increased every year since 2010. In order, the UK's major publication collaborations are with the US, Germany, Italy, France, Australia, the Netherlands, Spain, Canada, Switzerland, Sweden, Belgium, Denmark, Japan and Brazil.

Whatever happens, it is clear that British higher education is now an international activity but one where the level of competition is increasing all the time.[16] US universities have been expanding overseas. Australian universities have been growing rapidly and are avid internationalisers. Canadian universities are committed to the goal of doubling numbers of international students within a decade and are becoming increasingly attractive to international students. Many European countries are involved in similar internationalisation strategies: teaching classes in English, concentrating research resources, sometimes, as in France and Denmark, through an explicit policy of amalgamation of universities, sometimes through new competitive regimes, as in Germany. More generally, Middle Eastern (Abu Dhabi (NYU), Dubai (Birmingham, Heriot-Watt) and Qatar (Education City)) and Southeast Asian countries like Malaysia (Nottingham) and China (Nottingham and Liverpool) have produced instant boosts to their reputation by luring overseas universities. Countries like India and Brazil are expected to begin to substantially expand their overseas capacity soon. And that is before we get to all the online options.[17] One thing is certain. Around the world this heightened level of activity means that there is more attention being paid by governments to universities as instruments of soft power and as key export sectors.

But the elephant in the room is China where the focus is firmly on better and better research as evidenced by a rapidly increasing share of global citations, on generating more international students, and on internationalisation more generally. Many Chinese universities have expanded at what sometimes seems like breakneck speed although the Chinese state has an explicit policy of concentrating its research resources in the top universities so as to make them more competitive, with the latest target being to concentrate on 147 universities that should become 'first-class' by 2030, all part of China's plan to become a global education power by 2035. Chinese universities committed to taking half a million overseas students by 2020, a target they have achieved. There has also been a push overseas. One Chinese university has set up in Malaysia, another may (problematically) set up in Budapest, and yet another in Oxford and this is to ignore the myriad cooperative agreements Chinese universities have with overseas universities for teaching and research.[18] In a display of confidence in their own worth, three well-known Chinese universities have even withdrawn from entering certain global league tables.

The eleventh change has been international too – Brexit. This prolonged ruction has had some large consequences for research universities. Taking students first, according to official statistics, there were 125,000 students from European Union countries at the UK's universities in 2016 – roughly 5.5 per cent of the total number of students. They brought in about £3.7 billion a year to the UK economy and it is estimated that 34,000 jobs depended on them. But the latest statistics show a sharp drop-off in the number of EU students wanting to come to UK universities. Around 200,000 UK students have benefited from the Erasmus programme – which entails spending a period of their study on the Continent but which has now been replaced by the so-called Turing Scheme which has a much wider international orbit and a wider educational constituency. Then there is research. About 15 per cent of total EU research grants ended up in UK universities. EU citizens made up almost one-fifth (over one-third in some subjects) of all academics working at UK universities. In universities with the greatest research power and funding, particularly those belonging to the Russell Group, this rose to a quarter. There hasn't been the catastrophic exodus of European undergraduate students from Russell Group universities that was first predicted but, worryingly, the proportion of new EU academics recruited by the Russell Group from universities has fallen and continues to decline. Again, whereas EU postgraduate student numbers rose by 11 per cent between 2008/09 and 2018/19, this percentage conceals a decline since the UK voted to leave the EU, by 2 per cent in both 2017/18 and 2018/19. The decline was particularly marked among postgraduate researchers, with 9 per cent fewer EU-domiciled starters in 2018/19 than in the previous year (House, 2020).

The final change, again international, follows on. Research universities have become geopolitical pawns as instanced by rising concern over the transfer of intellectual property and defence-related work occasioned by academics allowing Chinese researchers too close to nationally sensitive research topics.[19] This was bound to happen: 'New Cold War' tensions have mounted as the West has tried to face down Russia and China with the war in Ukraine producing serious levels of friction. It isn't unfair to say that universities and academics have sometimes been naïve, to be kind, when pursuing certain kinds of research and have sometimes overlooked the negative aspects of chasing certain research collaborations with China. But they have had good reason: until not so long ago, the government pushed them in that direction. Now there is a general retreat from cooperation and a chilling effect on that which already exists, hastened by the arrival of the National Security and Investment Act with its screening requirements (Brown, 2022) as well as Export Control Regulations, the Academic Technology Approval Scheme, and the likely introduction of mandatory reporting for UK universities of foreign donations and partnerships over £75,000 in the Higher Education (Freedom of Speech) Bill.

Given the cold war like tensions between some geopolitical actors, this was bound to happen. The problem is how to achieve a balance now where some kind of collaboration is still possible such that science doesn't just become a series of epistemic autarchies. China, for example, has become a superpower and it is basing part of its claim to that status on scientific and technological supremacy founded, in part, in its universities' research, as underlined by recent policy actions like gazetting 12 top Chinese universities as 'schools of future technology' (charged with producing 'the future leaders of innovation' and developing 'cutting-edge, revolutionary and disruptive technologies in the next ten to fifteen years') and looking to universities like Tsinghua to solve its semiconductor problems by establishing new integrated circuit schools and institutes and companies (though, as the case of Tsinghua Unigroup shows, things don't always go well). The Chinese understand very well that this means discovery as well as applied research, as does the current US government which is also pushing large amounts of funding into research, perhaps as much as $300 billion (of which a large proportion would go to various science agencies) if the relevant bill ever gets passed by both Houses. The danger, of course, is that geopolitical tensions will diminish the global scientific collaboration from which so many rewards have flowed just when it is most needed (Nature, 2021).

It's not just research, of course. The presence of more and more Chinese students in British universities is something of a two-edged sword. They are welcomed because they bring more diversity and a large slice of income but they also bring some specific problems, especially the ways in which the Chinese state monitors their students from afar in increasingly intrusive ways. Again, universities and university-related institutions can be accused of naïvety at times. For example, under understandable Covid-induced pressures to provide better remote teaching for international students, it still wasn't a wonderful idea for the generally excellent JISC (formerly the Joint Information Systems Committee), the digital solutions provider for UK higher education, to try to set up a remote access system with Alibaba or for so many UK higher education systems to use Alibaba solutions. A particular issue at the moment is obviously keeping Hong Kong students safe but many universities would be hard put to guarantee this.

The take-down?

It was bound to happen, I suppose. We live in an iconoclastic age when national institutions are often treated with scepticism and sometimes with downright contempt. One by one, institutions that once constituted the core of British life have succumbed. The monarchy, once thought of as Bagehot's dignified arm of the constitution, has become adjoined to the cheap thrill world of celebrity. No one is exactly in love with Parliament, the efficient arm of the constitution, after all the hoo-ha of expenses scandals, sex scandals, bullying scandals, and lockdown party scandals. (As for the actual machinery of government … it has produced gems like a 'hostile environment', outsourced health assessments, and a privatised probation service. Meanwhile local government struggles to maintain even basic services like child protection.) Other institutions that rivalled the monarchy as magnets for national sentiment have also lost their lustre. The Church of England may still be the established church but attendance at its places of worship has been in decline for many decades now. The BBC, once a monopoly public broadcaster, now competes for the nation's attention with Netflix and Amazon and Disney and Apple and … in what can seem like a digitalised cacophony. The defunded police no longer turn up to crimes like burglary in some parts of the country – you get a crime number after hanging about on the phone and that's about it. And as for online fraud … The NHS, during the coronavirus pandemic cemented in the nation's psyche as a source of pride, is already facing discontent again. Hardly surprising when you have to wait four hours or more in A and E and are then plonked on a trolley until a bed is finally found, when it can't even be guaranteed that an ambulance will arrive in a timely fashion, and when serious operations are routinely cancelled.

When it was research universities' turn in the grinder, it felt like a particularly brutal reckoning, however, because they had escaped intensive and concerted public scrutiny on quite such a scale for so long. It hurt. After all, in world terms it is as though a set of British research institutions had won Olympic medals over and over again every year for decades and were then criticised for not being good enough. The reckoning was only made worse because it took place at a time when, even more than usual, some people had not only come to think that they had the right to believe anything that they wanted to believe, a value that is absolutely orthogonal to that of universities, but that they could back their beliefs up with any old thing that they happened to find circulating on the internet (anti-vax, 5G, etc.), producing an epistemic excitability which is autocatalytic. This unruly public sphere was too often unruly for the wrong reasons. It delighted in cognitive shortcuts. It valued affect before fact – anger was intimately related to belief. It condemned other views out of hand. The rise of fake news, industrial-scale gaslighting, dark patterns, astroturfing, and so on only cemented these behaviours. The age of a kind of industrialised disillusion is also the age of maximum illusion. Yet the sector has been relatively supine in the face of this onslaught of fakery. Remarkably so. If there is one part of society which ought to be at odds. ... But universities stick to their last rather than intervening in any concerted way in this melee.

Now the university too has become a 'story'. Given momentum by the fallout from student number growth, the number of press articles has risen markedly: 'there were 7,193 stories about universities in the leading 16 national daily and Sunday newspapers in 2020, up from 4,644 five years before' (Bennett, 2021, p. 15). One of the peculiarities of the present moment is that so many media commentators seem to start from the premise that there must be something 'wrong' with British universities. Usually the criticism is prefaced by praise like 'British universities are one of the great British success stories', or similar, but it doesn't take long for it to become clear that this pronouncement is a hollow reed. Universities are, variously, elitist, monocultural, parochial, change-averse, money-grubbing, bloated, unaccountable – and, yes, defensive (there's a surprise!). A fairly typical *Times* editorial (2020), bemoaning universities' reliance on Chinese students and 'cack-handed' response to Covid-19 is typical in both content and tone:

> The likely bankruptcy of some institutions would be neither surprising nor particularly regretful. Too many are already in trouble, have been cavalier in adapting to straitened circumstances, have taken student numbers and ambitions for granted and have been selfish, if not plain arrogant, in bolstering the salaries of senior staff by unjustifiable amounts.

Equally typical is an opinion column in the same newspaper with its common complaint that 'many degrees are a waste of time and money' (Duncan, 2021) arguing, like the editorial, that the weakest universities should be allowed to go the wall. This is pretty mild stuff. Don't go on and read the opinions of some *Daily Mail* columnists! Why such dissatisfaction, even bitterness, with something so successful? Tall poppy syndrome? They're a bit up themselves? They've got too much money for their own good? They're full of left-wing ideologues? They didn't like their tutor at Oxbridge? The traditional English suspicion of intellectuals? Who knows?

If these were just the lock and load opinions of many media commentators, that would be one thing. But these opinions do have more general purchase among the public. One of the reasons that some segments of the public respect universities less than they did is that too often they are perceived as being more interested in accumulating lucre than learning. They are increasingly regarded as consumer industries offering up poor value for money to undergraduate students (and, as importantly, their parents) (Bennett, 2021). Then, they stand accused of too often pushing opinion dressed up as fact. In the eyes of many in the public, they seem to have gone low, becoming 'political', when they should have gone high.

It would be a tragedy if perceptions like these were maintained. Research universities stand for important things – no, that's not right, really important things. They represent, or should represent, exactly the virtues we are so sorely in need of at present: tolerance of other views certainly, for without that tolerance you can never reach out to the potential surplus that can be found in all forms of enquiry, a certain humility born out of the realisation that all knowledge (including the small moiety that each individual might have added) will likely be supplanted, a permanent restlessness which adds up to dissatisfaction with any epistemic status quo, and a dedication to seeking out the hard questions rather than the easy answers (Stengers, 2017). At their best, even given that some people clearly stand out, they are swarm institutions, with each academic a part of an epistemic collective. Universities are never paragons of these virtues, of course. Like all human institutions, they have always contained many of the same bents and prejudices as the societies around them. But, at their best, they embody a striving for the common good which is also, of course, the highest form of love for the world. I do not mean by this that they are somehow floating above the world. I mean that they are involved with it in a supercharged way. 'Disinterested' knowledge can mean 'knowledge that does not cultivate but despise(s) or appropriate(s) the emergence of common concerns' (Stengers, 2017). But 'disinterested' can also mean something very different – not being influenced by considerations of personal advantage but instead investigating something which adds to a common fund.

All this said, it's important not to overdo the sackcloth and ashes. The work of universities is still generally well thought of – even though they might not always be lauded as institutions. A look at any survey suggests that the general public still holds their work in relatively high esteem. The 2014 Public Attitudes to Science Survey, for example, shows both overwhelming support for science and for continuing research funding for science, as does the Wellcome Trust Monitor for health research. And, on the whole, survey after survey shows that it is research that is the most favourably perceived aspect of universities' work.

Even the institutions themselves come out reasonably favourably. A Universities UK/Britainthinks (2018) survey found that 48 per cent of the public were positive about universities and 31 per cent were neutral; but they also found that a large percentage of the public hadn't really considered universities' role at all (though, if prompted, research was regarded the most favourably) and, if they had, it was often in terms of employment prospects or student debt loads. But there was also a clear perception that they were increasingly seen as making decisions based purely on profit, not the public good. A more recent survey (UPP Foundation and HEPI, 2021) discovered that 43 per cent of people in England understood universities as a positive force compared to 11 per cent who believed them to be a negative. Overall, more people were of the opinion that universities were going in the right than the wrong direction.

Through the wringer

The year 2020 saw the coronavirus outbreak in full flood. Though universities coped reasonably well with the immediate practical concerns, coronavirus also saw many pigeons coming home to roost. Two weaknesses had become glaringly apparent, both the result of a dash for growth by some higher education institutions (which, also exposed some other institutions to difficulties in recruiting students). One was an over-reliance on overseas students as a source of income. The other – partly linked – was over-borrowing by some institutions which often included borrowing through private placements with restrictive and sometimes negative covenants: the UK higher education sector's debt trebled in a decade to some £12 billion pounds in 2018 (Gore, 2018). Neither strategy was inevitable but many research university leaderships, spooked by the growth spurts of their rivals had followed roughly the same path (when that was possible), and therefore found themselves in roughly the same boat. Now many research university managements were confronted with being in charge of universities premised on maintaining a large throughput of students. They had to feed the hopper.[20] For a short time, in among the stresses of trying to cope with Covid-19, as it looked as though domestic and especially international students might disappear from view, they had to face how vulnerable they had become.[21] (Let's not make too much of this. If you think of universities as having become a retail industry like any other – I don't but many now do – then universities were simply in the same boat as many other retailers faced with a potential lack of customers.) But, in the end, student demand didn't decline, it expanded. In 2021, 680,000 more students applied to British universities (incidentally giving the lie to those who argued that universities were a busted flush and that every 18-year-old deep down wanted to switch to an apprenticeship[22]). Universities, and research universities in particular, ended up with the opposite problem: too many students and all of the associated problems like accommodation shortages (with which the press made great sport, as though universities could simply turn on the accommodation tap), meaning that universities are now tightening recruitment.

Then there was the issue of online teaching. Covid-19 certainly improved the capacity of universities and their staff to carry out online teaching but there is not much evidence that students want to follow through with a wholly online offer (not least students who had been charged full tuition fees for what some might consider a substandard semi-online offer). Indeed, students still seem to hunger after face-to-face contact. A certain amount of blended learning may be acceptable but, when it comes to it, an online generation wants to interact with other people in the flesh. That does not preclude students opting for online in greater numbers in the longer term, of course, especially if that was to mean a reduced tuition fee. That would create a chain reaction of consequences. Hyper-elite research universities that are draped in endowments, like Oxford or Cambridge, will no doubt be able to weather any such storm. So should very large research universities, especially those who take the Arizona State University route and combine a more conventional university operation, an elite honours university within a university, and a large online presence. So too should a new generation of small arts and science universities which, in part, take their cue from US liberal arts and liberal science colleges like Pomona (1,670 students), Harvey Mudd (886 students) and Rose-Hulman (2,304 students).[23] But some universities may succumb or be swept into franchised online operations which only use their nameplate (raising the generic issue of whether the British model of shipping so many students away from home really makes such a lot of sense, financially or indeed pedagogically).

But remember one thing. In all the changes that will follow on from the coronavirus pandemic – some good, some bad – it is worth remembering one thing. *Research universities were the institutions with the solutions.* It has been their research on epidemiological modelling and new vaccines, as well as research on the historical experience of pandemics and on possible economic ways out, which has informed public policy. It has been their scientists that have produced the cures. It has been their medical schools that have provided new patient treatments and training. In other words, the value of these universities has been trebly underlined. Sometimes, they really can be the difference between life and death.

5

The hardy perennials

There are certain perennial and perennially important issues that have arisen out of this recent history of British higher education. They are persistent dilemmas which, because they are so important, have to be included in any survey. They continue to crop up and none of them show any sign of going away soon. They are: the balance of public and private funding, student access, funding teaching, league tables, funding research, research integrity and autonomy (or the lack of it). Best to tackle them up front now and then move on to an analysis of why research universities now find themselves in such a problematic state and, latterly, what they can do about it.

Public or private?

It could be plausibly argued that British research universities are one of the few national institutions that cannot be classed as failing. If there was a fire sale of the assets of UK plc, they would come out near the top. They are only tangentially a part of the British post-imperial malaise that seems to linger on to infinity. Rather, they are part of an international system which visibly rewards success and is a harsh taskmaster when failure occurs. Their record of achievement is pretty good, whether it's doing world-beating research, teaching students to a generally high standard, producing large amounts of export business, supplying industry with innovations, or even (though this can be a double-edged sword) becoming big business. Some research universities have a turnover over the £1 billion or even £2 billion mark. A number would be in the FTSE 250 by some measures. According to Corver (2019), for example, if universities were added to the main FTSE groupings on a competitive revenue basis, higher education would actually be the largest industrial sector. But they are not particularly high on the list of government priorities. Indeed, on a bad day, it can feel as though what scant attention is paid to them by government is focussed chiefly on their supposed failings in serving students. As Seldon (2018, p. 2) puts it:

> The painful truth is that we have become unloved by Ministers, Whitehall officials, the commentariat and the media. Barely anybody in No. 10, the Treasury or the Department for Education has much time for us. Newspaper editors and leader writers don't get us, and struggle to name any Vice-Chancellor or the causes we espouse.

Why? Several reasons, nearly all of them arising from a lack of the kind of debate that informs rather than polarises. Three of these debates come to mind. To begin with, are universities private or public institutions?

This particular debate takes place mainly through the medium of vice-chancellor salaries. We had to come to it somewhere in a book like this, I suppose, so better to do it earlier than later. Vice-chancellor salaries have become a cut-through, a shorthand for what is wrong. It is all but impossible to have a balanced conversation about vice-chancellor remuneration. Given the nature of the institutions as public goods, there should be salary moderation but, that said, vice-chancellors head up large and extremely complex international organisations which have to face in many directions at once and which rely on multiple sources of income, by no means all of it public. In the sector as a whole, about 80 per cent of funding comes from government (including indirect funding from government in the shape of domestic student tuition fees.). You would never know this from the debate on vice-chancellor salaries where universities are nearly always characterised as simply and unproblematically a part of the public sector, rather than as not-for-profits acting for the common good and using differential proportions of government funding. The point is underlined by the fact that a large research literature exists on the topic of vice-chancellor salaries which is almost never referenced (e.g. Gschwandtner and McManus, 2018, Lucey, Urquhart and Zhang, 2020). Opinions are more fun.

As I have pointed out, research universities rely on a mix of public and private funding. (The exact proportion attributed to public and private depends mainly on the stance taken on tuition fees. Public funding across all universities, including tuition fees, teaching grants and research grants. may average out at about 80 per cent of their income but if you count tuition fees as loans taken out by students as private citizens then the figure reduces to about 28 per cent. However, these loans will not be fully paid off in many instances and the ultimate cost to the public sector is currently thought to be around 54 per cent of the face value of loans made to full-time undergraduates. So the figure for private funding is much smaller.) However, some research universities receive considerably less of their funding from government and a few like Oxford and Cambridge significantly less. But politicians often act as though they are entirely public sector entities – like a larger version of schools. Again, the public tends to think that they are public sector entities (though they may also think that they increasingly display the grasping tendencies characteristic of some big businesses). Business thinks universities are public entities which should help them out since they're paying all that tax (well, some of them anyway). Quite a few academics are convinced that universities are an open and shut case of 'neoliberalisation', in the process of moving from their former role as glowing public resources to becoming feral moments in the search for a quick buck, greedy vice-chancellors at the helm. And so on.

It is interesting to compare universities with some other 'private' sector companies which obtain a good proportion of public funding through a multitude of public sector contracts but (and it is a big but) often make large profits from them (Watson, 2009) – defence companies, various large service providers, large infrastructure companies, even private equity firms acting as agents for what used to be public sector responsibilities like healthcare and care homes. They receive very little of the opprobrium that universities get heaped upon them – at least until things go wrong. They are considered to be private, even though many of them are providing key public services from cleaning hospitals through to guarding gaols.[1] However, perhaps a better analogue might be arm's length government public corporations like the Met Office and the Ordnance Survey which generate a large proportion of their income from outside government. Again, these institutions have generally received very little in the way of opprobrium – comparatively. So why universities? Mainly, I am sure, because they bear the stain of middle-class angst because so many middle-class people are now involved in them through their own experiences, or those of their children, in clearly consequential ways.

To return to vice-chancellor pay, vice-chancellors are paid far less than in any large private sector organisation of comparable size. That's a stone cold fact. Still, their salaries (and expenses) have become a political football. There seems to be no way of having a grown-up debate about the right level of pay for those who lead universities (Oswald, 2017). That's a pity because all kinds of questions need answering and they are susceptible to rational analysis and debate.[2] If universities are largely publicly-funded institutions, then some vice-chancellors pay looks high. If they are privately funded to a significant degree then it doesn't. If vice-chancellors exist in an international labour market, which is at least suggested by the number of vice-chancellors of research universities who come from overseas institutions, their pay doesn't look particularly high. If they don't, then it does. And so on.

There are other debates that need to be had too. In particular, there is the matter of student welfare I raised in Chapter 3. How much is it appropriate for universities to contribute? Again, we need a proper debate, this time about boundaries. Universities have real and genuine responsibilities to students without a doubt, some of them statutory, many about operating in good conscience. And, added to that, the students are paying. But responsibility has to stop somewhere. A proper discussion needs to be had about duty of care. So universities have a statutory duty of care but presumably it is not the same as the duty of care that is extended to schoolchildren. After all, students have reached the age of majority. Generally speaking, in common law a university has a duty of 'reasonable care'. In the context of universities, that means delivering educational and pastoral services to the standard of an 'ordinarily competent institution' and, through the services it provides, acting reasonably to protect the health, safety and welfare of its students. But that's where agreement ends, not least because many of the issues of what is a fair, just and reasonable level of service and appropriateness have never been fully tested in the courts, and because issues of statutory and contractual responsibilities also arise.

Issues like sexual harassment, rape, racism, mental health and bullying all understandably stir up passions, producing some genuine moral dilemmas and posing some important questions, for example over the extent of welfare services a university can provide from a finite budget (for example, counselling services), over the fact that responsibilities for issues like various kinds of harassment and assault and mental health are also the province of government agencies who, it might be argued, are far better fitted to the task but are not pulling their weight, over the degree to which a university should be able to burrow into its members everyday interactions in order to police behavioural boundaries (making plenty of room for misunderstandings as well as producing a myriad of opportunities for reputational damage by doing too little or too much or by issuing apologies that go horribly awry), and, of course, over the efficacy of their own complaint procedures (Ahmed, 2021). To listen to some accounts, universities are private sector grinches or worse, skimping on student welfare and intent on squeezing the last pound out of the student pocket. They should be responsible for pretty well anything that happens to a student, wherever it happens. But students are adults. Or, then again, maybe they're not. It is generally agreed that the hinge to independent adulthood has changed to around the mid-20s or even later, a thesis that can be illustrated by the fact that in the UK the average age of new parents is now reckoned to be as late as 33 for men and 30 for women, while for first marriage it is 33 for men and 31 for women. (Meanwhile, the average age of a first-time home-buyer has pushed back all the way to 34.) (Marriott, 2021d)). Certainly, it can sometimes seem as if students want to have it both ways, to be treated like they are schoolchildren when they see fit but otherwise to be treated like the wisest of counsel. T'was always thus, one might say. But one of the results of the drifting adulthood boundary is that it can seem like there is a lot more thus around at the moment.

Last but not least, universities have real and genuine responsibilities to their academic and other staff. Again an out-front debate is needed. How far should these responsibilities go in what are now very large organisations which necessarily have to work in ways which are going to be more impersonal? Scale of operation, much more explicit job responsibilities, job specialisation, workload monitoring, the pressures of audit in its several forms, loss of job autonomy, the rise of adjunct faculty and postgraduate teachers (most of whom do not have access to the graduate teaching assistantships that a few Russell Group universities have instituted), the loss of collegiality that has come from the downgrading of senate, all of these have eroded that feeling of community that typified universities and they have produced many quandaries and grievances. It may well be that the terms and conditions of academic life have been subject to attrition as academics have moved from the clerisy into the laity (Halsey, 1992) or, put another way, from higher aims to hired hands (Khurana, 2007). Perhaps that is the price that had to be paid for creating so many academic and other jobs with such stretched resources. The only way to bring back a genuine rather than ersatz sense of community would, I suspect, be for research universities to get smaller again. That seems pretty unlikely for all kinds of reasons, even if student number controls were to be reimposed in some form. We need alternatives. And so we return to Halsey. What is the degree to which it is possible to marry a research university with mass education?

Access

When I was 17, I took a year out. Fresh out of A levels – which I had done less than well in – I had to resit to get the grades necessary to get into university (and even then I only just scraped in!) So I signed up to work in a phosphorous factory a couple of miles away from home (in a sign of the times, it's now the site of a marina). It was a dangerous place but the result was that the wages were much better than the average. I wasn't working on the front line where people really did get killed. I was in the stores. But I learnt an enormous amount that year, from how to weigh train wagons and their loads as they rolled by on the weighbridge to what and where various obscure pieces of kit could be found. What I really learnt most about, however, were cultures that I had very little experience of.[3] This experience served me well and has made me a big fan of certain kinds of gap years.

It's a cliché used to distraction now but I really was the first person in my family to have gone to university. Based on their intelligence, both my parents could easily have gone – it just wasn't something their segment of the middle class could afford or even aspired to at this time.[4] University just wasn't on the cards. And a few years earlier I doubt that there would have been the number of places for me to gain entry into university either.

But I had the luck to live in a time when social mobility was increasing for certain sections of the population. Though there has been some small improvement since then, it is still the case that those from poorer backgrounds are twice as likely to end up in working-class jobs as those from more privileged backgrounds, that those that do make it into professional jobs progress at a slower rate (Social Mobility Commission, 2021) and that the distribution of wealth is becoming more unequal, being reminiscent of Britain before the First World War (Savage, 2021). (The gap between the wealth of an average household in the top decile and in the fifth decile increased by some 50 per cent between 2006/08 and 2016/18 and has got no better since (Leslie and Shah, 2021).) Perhaps one of the single most shocking facts I know is that a boy born into the working class in England today has little more chance of making it into the middle class than in the year 1900, while a 40-year-old man is actually more likely to be in the same social class as his father than would have been the case a generation ago. Given such an austere background, in which the working class is systematically excluded, economically and politically, while it is hard to argue that returns to higher education (or at least some higher education) are insubstantial or that access to university (or at least some universities) doesn't boost individual chances of becoming socially mobile – they obviously do – it isn't obvious that greater access to higher education has shifted relative life chances overall. Relative social mobility hasn't changed much, stymied especially by lack of expansion of jobs at the top of the hierarchy of employment that might free things up. If you start at the top your likelihood of staying there is much greater than for someone starting at the bottom getting to the top. Though a good part of the period from 1900 has included a substantial expansion of university places (Bukodi and Goldthorpe, 2018, Mandler, 2020, Wolf, 2019), it hasn't made a vast difference to degree of social closure. (Indeed some data for the US (Price and Edwards, 2020) suggests that for many getting a degree may not necessarily be a passport to upward social mobility any more. Rather, it is a defence against downward social mobility. The same situation may perhaps apply in the UK too.)

That's not to say that enhanced access to university doesn't have good effects, especially when located among a number of other policies (Blanchard and Rodrik, 2019). It's not just moving deckchairs on the *Titanic*. So an assessment of government policies on social mobility from 1997 to 2017 (Social Mobility Commission, 2017) considered the progress made in addressing all of the different forms of educational inequality. One of the only two areas rated as making any significant progress was higher education. (As just one example, from 2013 to 2022 the number of students going into higher education from the UK's lowest-participation neighbourhoods has increased by over 50 per cent according to UCAS figures.) But, given the scale of the problem, access policies are at best a sticking plaster over the wounds of the British class/educational system and the different starting points, neighbourhoods and parenting styles it engenders: achievement gaps open up early and they tend to persist. (In any case all of the talk now is about 'tearing up' the 50 per cent target in favour of more technical education, forgetting that the target wasn't about university entrance only (and, by the way, was never explicitly signed up to by subsequent governments).)

All is not doom, however. It does not do to detract from the real and welcome progress over the last few years in promoting access to universities and this progress is certainly not to be disparaged. For example, recent actions by universities have boosted the numbers of children from disadvantaged areas. Since 2009, they are 52 per cent more likely to go to highly selective universities. In 2021 20.9 per cent of pupils eligible for free school meals were accepted on to a university or college course, up from 13 per cent in 2012. Even from a low base and against a background of gradually increasing numbers of places in these universities, these are impressive statistics. Again, so far as research universities are concerned, the number of students from state schools has been steadily increasing (though in the unusual circumstances dictated by Covid-19 where grades were inflated, some research universities registered a slowdown in the rate of increase as the number of applicants from wealthier backgrounds increased at a greater rate than those from less well-off backgrounds. Oxford and Cambridge did not, however. In 2020, nearly 69 per cent of the school-leaving undergraduates starting at Oxford and 70 per cent starting at Cambridge hailed from state schools).

However, most attention has been fixed on students from ethnic minority backgrounds and it is their progress that has been the most impressive. In 2017, 26.2 per cent of all the students studying at UK universities were from these backgrounds. By 2021 that figure had increased to 28 per cent with a particularly marked increase (from 24 to 27 per cent) in those on taught Master's programmes. The number of black students who accepted places at selective institutions in 2021, in particular those in the Russell Group of leading research universities, rose by 19 per cent over 2020, from 3,775 to just under 4,500, according to UCAS figures. Becoming more specific, in 2020 young black people from state schools, like nearly all minority ethnic groups, were now more likely to go to university than young white people from state schools, by 47.5 per cent to 32.5 per cent, having had the biggest entry rate increase out of all ethnic groups from only 21.6 per cent in 2006, a trend that continued in 2021. This was in contrast to young white people who had the slowest entry rate increase. (GOV.UK, 2021). (Meanwhile, 71.7 per cent of Chinese young people got a higher education place in the UK, as did 53.1 per cent of Asian young people (who can now be found 'dominating entry to many medical schools' (Scott, 2021, p. 83), and 39 per cent of mixed heritage young people.) But in research universities the picture was not quite as favourable. Thus, in 2020 23.7 per cent of cent of English and Welsh Russell Group undergraduates were from an ethnic minority compared with 26.9 per cent at all UK universities (19.4 per cent of the overall proportion of the population of 18- to 24-year-olds were from an ethnic minority). Put another way, of those who enrolled in a UK university, 24 per cent of white British students attended a Russell Group institution, more than most but not all minority ethnic groups. (Black African and Pakistani students show the largest differential between high university attendance and low enrolment in Russell Group universities.) Again, fewer young black people were going to Russell Group universities compared to white young people, although more black students are going absolutely rather than relatively and some Russell Group universities like Queen Mary have excellent records. Clearly, research universities still have work to do incorporating some ethnic groups,[5] though it is worth underlining that considerable progress is being made in individual universities. For example, according to its Annual Admissions report, of English and Welsh undergraduates who won a place to study at Oxford in 2020, 23.6 per cent were from minority ethnic backgrounds, up from 15.8 per cent five years ago.

But, without taking away in any way from the scale of the task of washing away the stain of racism, these figures also point to another major access issue: white youths from disadvantaged backgrounds. Like black and other minority ethnic pupils, white pupils are not a homogenous group. Whereas 45 per cent of white British pupils attend university after leaving school, in recent decades, the aggregate performance of ethnic minority pupils has overtaken white British pupils as the performance of minority ethnic pupils has picked up and as white British pupils from disadvantaged areas continue to lag behind (Kirby and Cullinane, 2016). Indeed, in each and every year from 2007 to 2020, of 18-year-olds at state school who had secured a place at university, white pupils had the lowest entry rate into higher education (defined as college or university)[6] although those that do go had generally higher attainment than most (but not all) minorities. A recent Department for Education annual statistics report argued, 'male white British free school meal pupils are the least likely of all the main ethnic groups to progress to higher education by age 19' and these pupils are especially concentrated into former industrial towns and cities in the north and the midlands, and into certain coastal towns: there is a definite place effect. Across all pupils eligible for free school meals, used as an index of relative poverty, 26 per cent went on to university by the age of 19. But for white pupils on free school meals the figure was 16 per cent (and only 13 per cent for boys). (In comparison, 59 per cent of pupils from black African families on free school meals went to university as did 32 per cent of black Caribbean pupils eligible for free school meals (Millward, 2021).) Of course, the case of poor white pupils can be used in racially charged ways by some commentators, but facts like these suggest that there is an issue here which cannot just be set aside.[7]

Another aspect of access is educational attainment at university. To begin with, ethnic minority students and students from less well-off backgrounds are more likely to drop out of university. The highest overall non-continuation rate at 15.5 per cent is found among Black students, a pattern that holds true even in STEM subjects. Again, among 2017/18 domestic graduates at UK universities, white students were 13.4 per cent more likely to get first-class or upper second-class degrees than students from black, Asian and other minority ethnic backgrounds. The so-called award gap between white and black students was even wider, at 21 per cent. White students outperformed students of all other ethnicities in England even when taking into account their previous qualifications. Worrying figures that clearly need action, not least because the award gap then influences what jobs people get or their chances of going on into graduate study (Cramer, 2021). The latest figures also show a 10 per cent gap in degree attainment between those from the poorest and most well-off areas which again shows a correlation with minority ethnic populations (HEFCE, 2018). It seems that the most potent causes of the award gaps – which are multiple – are now well known and what is really needed is sustained attention to gradually eliminate them.

Then, there are actual outcomes after leaving university. Much ink has been spilled concerning the different labour market outcomes of each ethnic group. Labour market inequalities have tended to persist since the 1970s, particularly disadvantaging men and women in Bangladeshi, black Caribbean and Pakistani groups (although the study by Karlsen, Nazroo and Smith (2020) stops at 2011). But all is not gloom when it comes to graduates. For example, so far as earnings are concerned, Britton, Dearden and Waltmann (2021) find that average returns to undergraduate degrees at age 30 tend to be positive, irrespective of socio-economic or ethnic group. Returns are particularly high for privately-educated graduates: their median earnings are the highest of all groups. Interestingly, that result apart, returns vary relatively little by socio-economic group. Ethnicity is another matter. There are particularly high returns for South Asian students, especially women. Returns for Black women are lower than for White women and they are particularly low for Black Caribbean women:

> Subject choice explains little of the variation in returns by socio-economic status, but a substantial amount of the variation in returns by ethnicity: Asian students systematically choose more lucrative subjects than White British students. Conversely, institution choices can partly explain why private school students get higher returns from university than those who attended state schools; however, institution choices do not explain much of the variation in returns by ethnicity. (Britton, Dearden and Waltmann, 2021, p. 3)

Still, so far as actual earnings are concerned, although earnings differences between graduates and non-graduates are smaller than between graduates and non-graduates, still graduate men from all non-White ethnic groups earn less than White British graduates. But, even given problematic facts like these, it is difficult to deny that a multi-ethnic middle class is a growing presence, especially as a result of the growing presence of Indian and Chinese graduates. And some part of this development can be sheeted home to increasing representation in universities.

One more aspect of access is the difficulties of categorisation. So far as access by particular ethnic groups is concerned, universities will continue to have to walk through this minefield, come what may. Think only of the broad brush category of 'Asian-American', often used by American universities in their admissions process, and the way that it mixes all kinds of completely different student backgrounds and experiences together in ways which are actively misleading in a number of cases and sometimes downright unjust when they assume, for example, that all potential students with a Chinese background are somehow privileged (for a brilliant piece of reportage, see Kang, 2019). In the UK, the category of 'Asian' similarly mixes up groups with very different educational outcomes, as does 'BAME', now falling out of use, 'BIPOC' which has never received much use in the UK, or the many other terms currently in play (Kim, 2020). Or think of the difficulties of treating students of mixed ethnicity fairly, even though they may well be one of the largest 'minority ethnic' groups in the UK at around 6 per cent of the population (Nandi and Platt, cited in Economist, 2020, Adekoya, 2021). Again, think of the way in which the spatial categories most commonly used in contextual admissions can exhibit the so-called ecological fallacy in which the average characteristics of individuals living in a given area do not necessarily reflect the characteristics of specific individuals and can include some students who are from well-off backgrounds and exclude some students who are from badly-off backgrounds.

The starkness of some of these figures underlines the need for a university to be a haven for all the talents, regardless of background. An elite research university even more so. Indeed, at least since the work of the economist Alfred Marshall and before, strong arguments have been made for access of the working class – and, in the end, that's still one of the central issues – to university. For example, it is sobering to realise just how far back in time practical steps were taken at Oxford to allow more access to 'poor students' (Halsey, 1992). But ... there are limits. These limits are a mix of both the political – how far are politicians and vice-chancellors willing to go to guarantee equal access to elite universities which have only become ever more attractive to the middle class as positional goods as yet more of the population access higher education? – and the cultural – how is it possible to surmount the ingrained British middle-class suspicions that more must necessarily mean worse, that the only good things are things it's difficult for other people to access?[8]

There is no easy solution. Universities have become a part of a quasi-meritocracy (whose aim might be described, as it was by R.H. Tawney, as existing to create a greater equality of opportunity to become unequal) which functions like an iron cage, a social structure in which a degree at an elite university is one of the basic stepping stones to success in life.[9] Research universities may shout loudly about inclusivity but they know full well that they are also part of a chain of educational inequality which is why, in some senses, they are so attractive to many applicants. Getting more people into them from less privileged and more ethnically diverse backgrounds doesn't really solve the issue. It brings a more diverse group of people (where 'diversity' primarily means race not class) into the fold of what has now become an international elite but in what has become a more unequal world. As in the US, it may take some of the sharp edges off the composition of the elite but it does not produce really fundamental change (Khan, 2016). Look only at Oxford and Cambridge which, in a classic instance of the process of elite capture (Taiwo, 2022), are in the process of switching from producing an old white British elite focussed on academic prowess to a diverse international elite focussed on achievement, just like Harvard, Yale and other US Ivy League universities. This matters. Given their disproportionate access to resources, Oxford and Cambridge are making decisions which affect the UK even though the absolute numbers of students involved may be small.

Ever since one of the real heroes of the British university system, the quite extraordinary Michael Young,[10] first coined the term 'meritocracy' in 1958, universities (and especially research universities) have become an increasingly identifiable part of a mass higher education system which acts to reward 'talent' in such a way as to exclude and diminish those judged without it through the mechanism of competitive qualifications. The familiar criticisms of this system have become louder of late (e.g. Markovits, 2019, Sandel, 2020, Goodhart, 2020) but the problem is not just that the system runs on flawed premises. It is also that research universities are one of the cogs in the machine, one of the means through which both advancement and advantage is gained, disbursed and perpetuated.

I admit to being defeated by this issue. Yes, hand needs to be valued in the same way as head. Yes, more students from less well-off and more diverse backgrounds need to be admitted. Yes, some areas of the country are massively privileged compared with others and there needs to be some rebalancing. But these are all salves at best on a wound which arises from a social structure based around accumulating and protecting wealth in which some universities – especially Oxford and Cambridge – are *still* stuck in an increasingly uneasy alliance with a ramshackle English class and status system which has remained remarkably stable over a long period of time, constantly adapting to new circumstances like the internationalisation and 'diversification' of elites in ways which ensure that the same old social groups still come out on top, the result of a system which, in its essence, has roots in the seventeenth century (Anderson, 2020, 2021, Savage, 2021). There is no reason to think that it can't continue to adapt.

What is clear, above all, is that even if it isn't complicit, higher education, by itself, could never compensate for unequal opportunities, most of which have been inflicted long before anyone becomes a university student, by an unequal system for which they cannot be held more than marginally responsible. Probably all it can do is make a dent in their worst effects. So the debate around 'access' to university is obviously important. Universities can offer some salve for the hidden injuries of class, especially as it intersects with certain ethnicities, but this compensation will probably always be somewhat limited, given that the middle class has so many advantages and that targets like the latest OfS one which aims to eliminate the socio-economic gap in access to higher-tariff providers in England within a generation will likely run into more and more kinds of friction. So long as the parameters of a system continue to focus on attracting 'students of the highest intellectual potential, irrespective of social, racial, religious and financial considerations' (Cambridge Admissions Policy), given the voluminous evidence on the various biases in outcomes that such a meritocratic policy currently engenders, there will probably always be issues. But, at the same time, I am also leery of losing the meaning behind that phrase. After all, universities are not simply social policy machines. As Goldthorpe (2020) puts it: 'More people than ever have a chance to realise their academic potential. We're a better educated nation now. And that's what I think education ought to be about, rather than an instrument to achieve social mobility, which is taking it out of its proper sphere.' But if you are going to make universities into social policy machines, then perhaps its best to do it wholeheartedly. Rather than continuing to tinker at the edges with contextual admissions and the like (which, truth to tell, would require very large reductions in tariffs to have an impact (Boliver, Gorard and Siddiqui, 2019)), I would much prefer that research universities either began to craft classes – the American system where a well-rounded class is gradually built up, composed of many different backgrounds and skills, in such a way that well-off students effectively pay for those who do not have the money – or introduce quotas for particular disadvantaged groups, recommendations that were made by the IPPR Commission that reported in 2013 – or even think about lotteries (subject to minimum tariffs). I am well aware of the furore this would cause from a middle class that, not without some cause, feels under siege but it seems to me to not only a fairer way of proceeding but would also no longer place so much of an onus on to individuals if they are unsuccessful in gaining entrance to an institution.

There is one more aspect of access I want to point to, the intergenerational argument. It is possible to argue that the contract between the generations has been broken in modern Britain:

> We know that the bulge of post-War baby boomers in many advanced Western countries will grow old and will reach a point when they want to command a lot of resources without working to generate

them anymore. We know that the environment is changing fast and avoiding or, more likely now, adapting to these changes is going to be very expensive. We also know that we are currently seeing a massive increase in public debt which will have to be paid for out of our taxes then. There are good reasons why the next generation may not be as much better off as we like to think. (Willetts, 2009, p. 142)

In order to restore some degree of intergenerational equity, action needs to be taken which will rebuild the bridge to the future by investing in future goods. Some writers want to argue that universities are giant engines for sucking in government subsidy. That is not the case. Nearly all of the public money that goes into universities consists of investment into future goods. It is an intergenerational investment, a way of booking a place in the future for the next generations. The investments in more students going to university will pay back massively, even excluding the effects on their lives, such as better health and mental wellbeing. (David Willetts (2017) argues this particularly well.) Meanwhile, the investments in research will enhance their understanding of the world, provide lifelines of all kinds, and give their lives a richer warp and weft too.

Funding teaching

And so to perhaps the most controversial aspect of the English system, the imposition of tuition fees. As Kernohan (2021) points out, though they were meant to be a means of promoting price competition between universities educational offers, tuition fees have, in effect, become a voucher system with a quality baseline set by a regulator, access and finance determined by two quangos (the Office for Students and the Student Loan Company), and student choices informed, in theory at least, by a range of sources like the Teaching Excellence and Student Outcomes Framework (TEF), plus a state-run comparison engine, Discover Uni, and league tables like those of *The Times* and the *Guardian* which, in effect, chiefly measure teaching and the student experience. This system has all kinds of idiosyncrasies. For example, the cost of the degree the voucher represents can't be fully known until the end of the 30-year repayment window for each student cohort. In other words, the system started out somewhere but has ended up somewhere else completely. In particular, it has proved expensive so far as the Treasury is concerned, especially since 2018, when tuition fees were reframed in government finances, existing partly as a financial asset in the national accounts, because some loans will be repaid, and partly as government expenditure, as some of the loans will never be paid back in full. They are not seen as an investment, then, though they are not really a debt in any conventional sense, more perhaps a kind of tax.[11]

I should start by saying that I have no objection to tuition fees per se. Though there is an obvious attraction to the idea of universal free education, it brings with it numerous problems. The much-expanded higher education system we have now, one which has produced more social equity, would be put under threat. To begin with, free tuition leads almost inevitably to a student number cap of some form. Equally, free tuition is regressive, strongly favouring the middle class (though, as Scott (2021) points out in certain forms tuition fees can favour the middle class too). Free tuition will also lead to a bite on university budgets as clearly as night follows day. And, as domestic student numbers increase because of the demographic bulge, free tuition will become progressively less affordable. There is empirical proof of the validity of these propositions: the Scottish experience of continuing with free tuition shows up many of these limitations in one form or another.[12] Then, where does free tuition end? Given that Master's courses are becoming a sine qua non of career advancement, should they be included too? What other aspects of higher education should be free? That said, the government's latest attempts to provide a degree of lifetime education, long espoused by so many, through policies like the Lifetime Skills Guarantee and the mooted Lifelong Loan Entitlement, is one excellent way of at least beginning to solve conundrums like these, as well as the unequal funding of university and further education students.

But there is another line of attack, often but not exclusively from the right. That is that some degrees just aren't worth it. To begin with, students are paying tuition fees but just not getting value for money. We need to get rid of 'Mickey Mouse' courses that don't provide a payoff. Some students would be better suited to following other educational opportunities, especially vocational education. The problem here is threefold. One is that identifying 'Mickey Mouse' courses on value for money or any other basis is much – much – more difficult than it first seems. Often, such courses exist only in the eye of the beholder. Another is that value for money cannot be measured simply by the salary you get after completing higher education. On that basis, everyone would be becoming bankers or accountants. Low pay does not mean that a job isn't valuable. But, as importantly, it also needs to be noted that there is no proof that arts students, who are often identified as the worst examples, do notably worse in the employment or salary stakes than STEM students. For example, those taking arts, humanities and social science degrees end up being employed in eight out of the ten fastest-growing sectors of the economy more often than do their STEM graduate counterparts. And, again, STEM graduates have only a single percentage point advantage in finding a job within a year of graduating than do humanities graduates (British Academy, 2020a). Clearly, arts, humanities and social science graduates have skills that employers want. Lastly, most of the expansion in student places in the last few years has been in business and medicine (including nursing) while numbers doing humanities courses have been declining, so it is difficult to argue that the country has been swamped with these supposed ne'er do wells.

There is another issue which is often linked to this plaint: record numbers of students may be graduating from universities and colleges but many of them are not getting graduate-level jobs. They should do apprenticeships or similar instead. Laying aside the instrumentalism of statements like these, the lack of understanding that the UK is now a full-on service economy (Bell, 2022), and the surge currently taking place in university admissions which suggests that many school pupils still consider university a good prospect, or certainly better than the alternatives, there is good evidence that graduates going into non-graduate jobs have a positive effect. They can act to stimulate the organisations that they are in. Be that as it may, what is clear is that right at the heart of today's high-participation higher education systems there is a paradox (Marginson, 2018). While these systems have undoubtedly made educated human capabilities more widespread, the opportunities to use those capabilities seem to be shrinking as societies become more unequal. Some newly minted graduates are being shunted into jobs that will give their talents limited scope.[13] But this is partly a function of the way that the British economy runs.

One other issue is often linked in too. It is a matter of record that companies do not feel that they can get enough staff with the appropriate skills. These kinds of surveys of industry can be taken with a pinch of salt but they do foreshadow a more serious problem. Many jobs may flick out of existence in the next decades as automation of middle-class jobs becomes a reality (Brynjolfsson and McAfee, 2014). Ironically, many commentators argue that an education system that teaches students to think creatively, exactly as a liberal arts education is supposed to do, may be the only way to steal a march on the march of the robots (e.g. Zakaria, 2015). The alternative could be a world in which '0.1 per cent own the machines, the rest of the 1 per cent manage their operation, and the 99 per cent either do the remaining scraps of unautomatable work, or are unemployed' (Lanchester, 2015, p. 7).

Under current circumstances, directing more people into vocational education of one kind or another, the main educational alternative which is on offer now (and ignoring the fact that the main destinations of students are business, law and medicine degrees, which are vocational on a number of measures), may prove self-defeating. It will almost certainly strengthen class segregation unless it is linked to a radical change in cultural attitudes of which there are only fitful signs. Writers like Sandel (2020) and Goodhart (2020) are certainly correct when they say that there is a cultural bias in favour of head over hand or heart in many Western countries, including the UK. But cutting back on university places in favour of vocational education alternatives like apprenticeships isn't necessarily going to solve it. The risk is it may strengthen it by making the available university places even more sought after.

None of this, of course, is meant to disparage vocational education which has been scandalously under-funded, to the detriment of many young working-class people. Like social care, further education colleges have been in the 'we should do something about it' category for far too long. Many further education colleges in England are now in serious financial difficulties. It is therefore good to see government policy turning this way – at last. But I don't see why a choice then has to be made into one between funding higher and vocational education, an either/or, rob Peter to pay Paul strategy. Both systems should be properly funded, not least because they now interdigitate to a much greater degree than previously. The same higher education institutions can be involved in both higher and vocational education. Equally, a number of vocational institutions offer degree courses.

All this said, there are things that are undoubtedly wrong with the current teaching funding system, some of which have been solved by the government's long-delayed response to the Augar review and some of which haven't. The interest rate has been uncomfortably high and this had become a political problem. But the new system is not progressive in the sense that mid-earners end up paying more as a per cent of their income than high earners, a tendency that has only been exacerbated by the decision to extend the loan repayment period from 30 to 40 years. The student loan repayment threshold has been lowered from £27,925 to £25,000, which will certainly affect numbers of students but will not, truth to tell, make a substantial difference to the public finances. There will be a national scholarship scheme to soften some of the blows for less well-off students. There will be a modest increase to the teaching grant to foster government priorities like producing more STEM students which will soften the blow of the tuition fee being frozen for universities. And so on. However, the really glaring omission continues: maintenance grants which go to support living expenses. In what is effectively a voucher system, what are now severely occluded maintenance grants, recast as means-tested loans, are the real issue for many students, especially those from less well-off backgrounds for whom inflation is a particularly severe problem, not least because grants have continued in the devolved administrations. If the government response to Augar does nothing else, it makes it plain that a major overhaul of the tuition fee system is long overdue.

I personally favour giving every post-secondary school child a learning account which they could spend as they wished on educational opportunities through the course of their life. Though government is leaning in this direction with its Lifelong Loan Entitlement (which is likely to begin in 2025), I can't see such an entitlement being funded to the degree necessary but it is nice to dream.[14]

Funding research

So to another hardy perennial: how to fund research in universities. And there is a lot of funding to consider coming from numerous sources. In all, Hutton (2021) calculates that UK universities received some £9.1 billion in research funding in 2019, funding disbursed by government, business, charitable foundations and other sources. It is a bit of a dog's breakfast, though I'm not necessarily against dog's breakfasts if they work. The problems is that this one only partially does. Ramshackle may be in danger of becoming a shackle.

The ins and outs of research and development policy require a book in themselves and this one is already quite long enough (see British Academy, 2019 for the history and Chandler et al., 2021 for a resumé of recent research and development policy initiatives). To simplify, but not too much, in England research funding is probably best understood as being delivered in three packages (Forth and Jones, 2020). To begin with, UKRI through Research England (the research part of what was formerly HEFCE) distributes a block grant to English universities via a quality-related (QR) stream of funding allocated through a formula based on research excellence as measured by the six- or seven-yearly Research Excellence Framework (REF).[15] The total funding was £1,095 million in 2019/20. It's a vitally important source of funding because it provides a stable income for universities over a number of years based on their research quality, one which also gives them some freedom and flexibility in how the money is spent and, in particular, allows them to sponsor discovery research which may seem risky but which pays dividends later.

The next package is more complex. It mainly consists of research funding that is competitively won by individual researchers or consortia of researchers for specific research and innovation projects. Funding for these projects is the primary responsibility of the seven Research Councils. Until 2018, these were independent entities. But they have now been incorporated, together with Research England and Innovate UK, into a single research organisation – UKRI. Crucially, within this larger organisation, the research councils can still own to some degree of autonomy as the representatives of clusters of particular academic disciplines. Their budgets fund project-based support via proposals submitted competitively by university researchers. They may be a response to open calls which don't outline in any great detail the research area being supported (usually known as 'investigator-led' or 'responsive mode'). Alternatively, the research councils may specify the goals of the research they want carried out or the general problem areas they wish to see pursued (usually known as 'challenge-led' research). The funds available for this kind of research can sometimes come from outside the research and innovation budgets of the research councils, using instruments like the Industrial Strategy Challenge Fund and the now sadly reduced Global Challenges Research Fund.

In addition to project-based funding, some funding is also distributed to individual researchers, in the form of research fellowships. The funding for these fellowships is often thought to be the province of government,[16] but it is bulked out by private sector and charitable sources, and to a very considerable degree by universities themselves.

A recent addition to the research funding landscape is a British version of DARPA (Defense Advanced Research Projects Agency), ARIA (the Advanced Research and Invention Agency), which will exist outside UKRI with some £800 million of funding over four years. It will have no chosen single research focus and, somewhat ironically, will exist, at least in part, as a way of minimising government bureaucracy. Indeed, it is designed to be immune from ministerial interference, even to the extent of a ten-year moratorium before it can be abolished. The obvious question is why the situation demands a special institution to address unnecessary government bureaucracy (as well as why it will be outside freedom of information legislation) (Kingman, 2021).

The UK's competitive research funding scene is complemented by a number of large research charities – especially medical charities like the Wellcome Trust, Cancer Research UK, and the British Heart Foundation but also including other major research charities like the Leverhulme Trust. These organisations' support is necessarily connected to their charitable aims and they interpret these to include considerable amounts of discovery science. In particular, the Wellcome Trust is an important actor in the UK research landscape. Its support for research in the biosciences and on major health challenges is at the same scale as some of the largest research councils. In 2019/20, it had a grant portfolio of £5.1 billion.

Another major funding source also needs to be considered in this competitive package, even though its future is now past. That is the EU. In the past, the EU's research and innovation programme – Horizon 2021 (now replaced by Horizon Europe) – contributed about €0.9 billion a year to the UK's overall research and development effort, of which 63 per cent went to universities. On 2014/15 figures, that represents 'about 12 per cent of university research income compared to 47 per cent from the Research Councils and other government bodies, 17 per cent from charity, and 6 per cent from industry' (Forth and Jones, 2020, p. 35). You can see why the leadership of research universities were sceptical of Brexit and welcomed the government's post-Brexit decision to subscribe to Horizon Europe.

So we come to the third package. It is now widely accepted that the cost of research carried out in universities (including over half of the cost of postgraduate research students) is not fully recovered from these two packages of funding: the average grant currently only covers some 71 per cent of the full economic cost resulting in a deficit reckoned to be at least £4.6 billion (Stevens, 2022). So the remainder has to be drawn down from other sources of income, a cost that only becomes bigger the more research contracts a university wins. The largest of these sources – and the most problematic – is the surplus generated by fees from students, both domestic and, much more importantly, international. The Augar review (2019) (which was only tangentially about research universities though its recommendations were hardly favourable to them) spent a lot of time working out that domestic undergraduate students were caught up in the cross-subsidy to research. But, currently at least, the bulk of the subsidy comes from international students. Hillman (2020) finds a shortfall in research funding amounting to some £4.3 billion across the UK and £3.7 billion in England and Northern Ireland. Drawing on an analysis of TRAC data (which no one suggests is perfect but it's all that there is), he calculates that the gap has been filled mainly by cross-subsidies from international student fees – with each UK international student paying an average of £5,100 more than it costs to educate them.[17] (One of the ironies of the current geopolitical situation is that Chinese students are, in effect, propping up UK research allowing it to produce a substantial amount of intellectual property that otherwise wouldn't exist.)

In other words, research in universities is being paid for by a *triple* not a dual support system, one comprising contributions of a roughly similar amount from the block grant, from overheads on project funding provided by government and other bodies, and from the surplus garnered from overseas students (Forth and Jones, 2020). Any decline in one or other of these contributions would have serious implications for the others in terms of research universities' ability to do research. Put another way, the system has fragilities which are not incidental but baked in.

However, there is some good news on the horizon. As I have already pointed out, the government has stated an ambition to increase its total research and development expenditure to 2.4 per cent of GDP (from 1.7 per cent in 2016) by 2027 so as to catch up with the OECD average. Whether this happens or not, the fact is that the government has committed to increasing R&D expenditure to £22 billion a year by 2024/25. But under current conditions that could mean that universities would have to gather in even more money from overseas students to make up the shortfall in overheads of around 25 pence in the pound. Unless the government and other funders commit to a 100 per cent overhead on grants, that is going to require a massive leap in numbers to somewhere around 600,000 students at a minimum (Johnson, 2020). And this could well happen. UCAS (2022) already predicts that the volume of international undergraduate overseas applicants will increase by 46 per cent from 2021 to 2026, from around 144,000 to 208,500, mainly from China and India, with the majority of interest being shown in the most selective (research-intensive) universities.

Johnson (2020) argues that the government needs to 'double-down' by wholeheartedly supporting a leap in numbers through policies like a four-year post-study work visa to replace the current two-year visa. (I do not see an increase in overseas student numbers on this scale being welcomed with open arms by the parts of the university sector trying hard not to unbalance their operations, a point I will return to.)

Research integrity

Boring through the timbers of research universities is another research issue which can no longer be swept under the carpet, namely research integrity. The increasing scale and international reach of the research enterprise worldwide has brought with it issues that no doubt existed before but have become much more visible and – possibly – more widespread (Ritchie, 2020). Above all, research is about cleaving to hard-won standards. Vice-chancellors sign a letter to the research councils each year in which, in effect, they guarantee the trustworthiness of their academics' research but, truth to tell, much of the time they are doing this largely as an act of faith based on trust in a kind of honour system in research, the system of peer review. But like all honour systems it can be abused and indeed it has been, at least since Newton accused Leibniz of plagiarism over the invention of calculus and got his mates at the Royal Society to come out with the right (or, rather, maliciously wrong) answer. This was an early – and spectacular – example of a lack of what is now called research integrity.

Now, in a system which is much larger and much more complex, research integrity has become a multifaceted problem and one with adverse effects not just for individuals but for institutions too – consider the enormous $112.5 million fine levied on Duke University by the US federal government to settle allegations that researchers submitted applications and reports containing falsified data in order to win over two dozen grants from the National Institutes of Health and the Environmental Protection Agency (Kaplan, 2019).

Research integrity has become ever more important in a time when science is no longer trusted in quite the way that it was. As science has become just another institution in the eyes of many members of the public, any slips have to be dealt with rapidly and efficiently. Not only has public trust declined but the contours of research integrity have changed too. We are heading into a period of real uncertainty and it will be easy to get the balance wrong. Why? Because the conduct of science itself has changed as science has become a larger and more global enterprise. Derek de Solla Price famously observed in 1961 that, of all scientists who ever lived, 90 per cent of them were alive then. It probably wasn't true at the time. It probably is now. There were 7.8 million full-time equivalent researchers in the world in 2013, representing a growth of 21 per cent since 2007. Researchers accounted for 0.1 per cent of the global population. The number of PhDs granted has been doubling every 18 years (Gastfriend, 2015). Between 2008 and 2014, the number of scientific articles catalogued in the Science Citation Index of the Web of Science grew by 23 per cent from 1,029,471 to 1,270,425 (Bornmann and Mutz, 2014, Unesco, 2015). Roughly speaking, the number of scientific papers published has been doubling every nine years (Gastfriend, 2015). That is bound to mean more problems.

But it's not just the scale of the research enterprise. It's also the fact that research has become more international. When things go wrong, the reverberations increasingly work across jurisdictions. A good recent example was the case in China where human embryos were being gene-edited by He Jiankui. It soon transpired that he had connections to Stanford and another north-eastern US university. Though these proved to be negligible, neither Stanford nor the other university seemed to have had much if any knowledge of them.

To point to just a few of what are multiple changes as the scale and reach of scientific endeavour has increased. To begin with, scientific cultures have changed. For example, many scientific papers now have numerous authors making it much more difficult to attribute responsibility. One sign of this is that so-called hyperauthorship – papers with more than 1,000 authors – is growing as research globalises, being found especially in work on particle physics, global epidemiology, astronomy, and climate change. The number of these papers has doubled over the last five years to 1,315 papers (Chawla, 2019). Equally, quite a lot of science is produced by large research teams which have their own dynamic and problems, including the vexed question of attribution, especially as more people are getting attributed than formerly.

Even more problematic is the question of the reliability of results. In medicine, as one example, it is easy to say that scientists should mask (or, in the parlance, 'blind') studies, randomise, work out appropriate sample sizes, and draw up rules for data handling that can often be quite a difficult task (Landis, Amara and Asadullah, 2012). But, in fact, reproducibility in medicine has often proved surprisingly hard to achieve even when it is being aimed for as more than one study has demonstrated (e.g. Errington et al., 2021), while ethnography shows that in some cases there are good practical reasons why particular experimental protocols are not always followed (Nelson, 2021). Replicability of data remains a stubborn problem in other areas of science too.

Then there is the more general issue of error. Errors are so varied that whole books have been written on the topic. But there is some good news. For example, the availability of data for all to inspect is becoming much more common. The datasets on which papers are based are now available to be accessed in many of the best journals, allowing for reanalyses so that any errors can be found and corrected at a later date – many journals now routinely publish corrections and there are also many more retractions. That said, by one reckoning from the Committee on Publication Ethics, very large numbers of papers still have errors of one kind or another that need correcting.

Many other issues also intrude. Take the issue of inference. It is at least questionable whether certain inferential statistical methods are appropriate at all (e.g. Amrhein, Greenland and McShane, 2019, Amrhein, Trafimow and Greenland, 2019). There are other more general inferential issues too, such as publication bias, low statistical power and hypothesising after results are known.

Another issue is the quality of experimental design which platforms like DataExplained are starting to show up (Schweinsberg et al., 2021). In medical research, for example, a field in which it's worth remembering that the phrase 'evidence-based medicine' only dates from the early 1990s, many commentators have pointed out that huge amounts of money are still being spent every year on research that is seriously flawed through the use of faulty or inappropriate designs, unrepresentative samples, small samples, incorrect methods of analysis, data misuse, and suspect interpretations.

Then there are the more malign issues such as the hacking of university computer systems by foreign powers. This practice has now reached an extraordinary level of intensity, showing how science has once again become mixed up with national security, as illustrated by increasing concerns about the presence of Chinese American and Chinese nationals in the US system (where over-reaction also seems to be a constant danger) as well as concerns about academics in the UK whose research grants may have become tainted by close association with the Chinese military-industrial complex. This is all before we get to 'normal' ransomware attacks.

There are all kinds of other issues too. Gender and ethnicity now figure constantly as flashpoints in research conduct and analysis. Animal research is a moral minefield, especially as attitudes to animals have become much less utilitarian. (Is it OK to give cancer to animals? Many people, probably most, would say no.) There are issues like the ownership of ancient bones and whether and in what circumstances they should be returned (and to whom). There are issues of collecting fossils in the Global South without involving local palaeontologists (so-called paleontological colonialism). There are issues of working with specimens of new species that may have been acquired outside the CITES regulations by poachers (Nuwer, 2019). (Who would ever have thought that a paper announcing a new species of tarantula would have caused such a stir, except that the spider was likely sourced second-hand from collectors who had bought it from poachers in Malaysia?) The list goes on and on.

Attention is increasingly paid to all these issues. It has to be. If the public lose confidence in the conduct of research, everyone loses. Certainly, it is at least questionable whether peer review is an entirely adequate system anymore although many journals are attempting to make it even more transparent by, for example, publishing referee comments. That said, no one is clear what should replace it. But there are plenty of green shoots too. In medicine, for example, there is a litany of different initiatives that have sought to improve standards such as the COCHRANE collaboration, which aimed to provide unbiased summaries of research topics, and the EQUATOR network, aimed at improving medical research and the way it is reported, as well as all manner of recommendations for activities like randomised controlled trials, protocols for clinical trials, observational research, systematic reviews, and animal studies. Then there is the attention to research papers coming from what are often self-appointed arbiters using artificial intelligence to point out problems of various kinds, a practice which is becoming more common but courts the danger of producing false accusations even when the results are surrounded with caveats. So the new UK Committee on Research Integrity is to be welcomed as an arbiter of good practice, adding to the firepower already provided by the UK Research Integrity Office and UUK's Research Integrity Concordat.

Pensions

Like many other sectors, universities are beset by the issue of pensions. Particularly bothersome has been the issue of academic and related staff moving from a generous defined benefit system to a defined contribution system. This has been a particular problem for research universities since they are the universities whose scheme – the Universities Superannuation Scheme (USS) which is the largest private sector pension scheme in the UK – is most affected, a scheme which has a particularly unpleasant sting in the tail in that if any member university goes bust the others have to pick up their pension tab.

There is no satisfactory answer, I'm afraid. On the one side are universities worried about their financial position. So far as they are concerned, they have added as much to their budgets for pensions as they can. They are not far wrong, by the way. On the other side, there are aggrieved academic staff who believed that the pension was one of the benefits of the job they could count on and now they find that their pension is going to be reduced and will cost more to get. They are not wrong either. Perhaps something could be sorted out but there aren't just two people in this relationship. Two other actors also have a say. First, there is the Universities Superannuation Scheme (USS) which covers most but not all universities, and especially research universities. This is a one of the largest pension funds in the UK but, basically, it doesn't think it has enough money to fund the scheme into the future, a stance that is contested, it has to be said. It has constantly forecasted a shortfall and the shortfall has tended to get steadily bigger at each valuation. (The break point for many was an estimated shortfall of between £14.9 billion and £17.9 billion in 2020 which would have meant a combined member and employer contribution rate of 42.1 per cent in order to fund the same level of benefits in the future as are being built up now. It must have known that this was an impossible figure to recover. Certainly, the forecast seemed to infuriate just about everyone.) How much of this shortfall is down to market conditions at the time of the valuation and how much is the result of USS's investment strategy is a moot point but certainly companies like Aon have challenged the projected size of the deficit which has come down dramatically to £1.6 billion in the 2022 valuation. Then, there is the pension regulator who has powers to bring the pension fund into line and can insist – or threaten to insist – on a time period when it must come back to equilibrium. The regulator often seems to act in a shadowy fashion which means that its pronouncements can be used as an all-purpose threat.

Everyone blames everyone else. The result is an utterly debilitating stalemate consisting of a strike in response to the university employers' latest offer, an uneasy truce as a result of a compromise that satisfies precisely no one, new forecasts of the deficit leading on to what is usually an even worse valuation than last time, plus hints that the regulator is really going to get nasty so something must be done, a new employers' offer, a strike, and so on, and on. Seemingly for ever.

That said, for various reasons the latest round of conflict, which has added bitterness because academics feel some acknowledgment of their undoubted efforts during Covid-19 is deserved, has produced some movement from employers which could actually prove to be very important in the longer term. The proposed additional covenants concerning debt monitoring, the pari passu principle, and new rules on leaving the USS might produce a greater level of university financial responsibility (which in some cases might be no bad thing) but at a cost of making investment more expensive, and likely slowing it down, as well as producing much greater USS involvement in university financial affairs than may be healthy.

League tables

Starting some 15 years ago, world university league tables have already become a permanent fixture in the university landscape, joining national rankings which were introduced much earlier.[18] I don't have much to say about these tables because so much has been said already (see Brink, 2018 for a summary of the voluminous literature). Most people in universities express a greater or lesser degree of scepticism about them – while accepting the plaudits when their university does well! They are undoubtedly taken seriously by universities, most particularly because they are taken seriously by those outside the sector, and especially by parents and students, and because they can be shown to have modest effects on applicant behaviour. (One paper found that when their rank worsens, universities experience small but statistically significant reductions in the number of applications received as well as in the average tariff score of applicants and accepted applicants (Broecke, 2015).) Many universities have strategies for maximising their performance in the tables, therefore, and some even set up special sections of the administration to put their shoulder to the league table wheel. However, they do this in the sure knowledge that league tables are inherently unreliable except within very broad bands. For example, no serious statistician would accept the jumps in a university's position from year to year that are sometimes evident in the tables as either credible or as evidence of evidence: universities are large organisations that take a long time to show progress.

It is true that some league tables have got gradually better over the years, having reacted to some of these criticisms. I think, in particular, of the Times Higher World Rankings. But most league tables continue to rely on a relatively small number of indicators which contain goodness knows how many cross-correlations with the other variables in the table, fairly arbitrary allocation of weightings to each indicator, failure to differentiate between inputs and outputs, comparison of dissimilar institutions with different missions, and too little attempt at calibration with the evidence from more rigorous peer review exercises like the REF. At the very least, they should conform to the ten principles of good practice set out by Waltman, Wouters and van Eck (2017) and include indicators that really do matter. (For example, universities should lobby for degrees of academic freedom to be included as a measure in the major league tables. After all, a university that restricts thinking – or has its thinking restricted – to particular channels cannot lay claim to being able to ask the best questions. There is no excuse not to do this anymore since the advent of the Academic Freedom Index, a collaborative project by the Global Public Policy Institute, the Friedrich-Alexander-Universität Erlangen-Nürnberg, the Scholars at Risk Network, and the V-Dem Institute.) But it is inevitable that league tables of whatever stripe will call forth appeals to the referee such as 'Researchers at many institutions, such as mine, miss out on opportunities owing to their placing' (Gadd, 2020, 2021a). It's in the nature of the beast that some institutions will be aggrieved and there is, of course, a cynical response to criticisms of league tables like this which is that they are often made by institutions that don't fare so well in them. But that just is too easy. It's the whole set of practices around league tables that matters and the fact is that they do lead behaviour, though to an indeterminate degree. Part of the reason for the increase in first-class degrees has clearly been league tables, for instance.

League tables undoubtedly work best when they are about one clearly identifiable activity. Perhaps the most reliable data on research quality originate from the Research Excellence Framework. Though it is true that the REF was not intended to be a ranking exercise (Gadd, 2021b), still if you have to have one, then this is probably the best one there is. Some academics have negative attitudes towards the REF, seeing it as an untoward imposition (even though in surveys they will then often remark that it has had no impact on their own research). But one of the most powerful reasons for retaining the REF is that it provides the closest we are ever likely to get to genuine evidence on research quality, through its emphasis on peer review and the fact that it appeals to genuine academic norms, even though 'impact' seems to be doing a good job of trying to muscle them out of the way in the overweighting it now gets. It is true that its results inevitably appear as league tables which allow universities to make all kinds of, shall we say, optimistic claims. But this by-product is not the largest of crimes. If the REF is excised it will be replaced with much less worthy acts of comparison, believe me. The idea that it is an onerous imposition on academics shows an almost extraordinary naïvety in this regard, as well as what seems like an attitude that somehow or other academics should exist above the fray which will likely be interpreted as arrogance by those whose lives are run by far more demanding indicators. Yes, all kinds of games are played with the results and any ranking derived from the REF must be taken with a pinch of salt (surely it would be better to go back to grouped outcomes which don't rely on tiny numerical differences between institutions). But the data is about as reliable as we are ever likely to get in showing where the best research is concentrated.

Autonomy – or the lack of it

And so we come, finally, to that hardiest of the perennials. All discussions of universities seemingly must fix on the vexed topic of autonomy. Numerous studies suggest that autonomy is an important element in any university systems' degree of success. As if to underline the point, a number of countries in Europe are giving their universities more autonomy as they try to rouse them from slumber just at the point that UK universities – often praised by overseas commentators for their high degree of autonomy – are becoming less autonomous.

Some people tend to be naïve about autonomy. They think it means that universities should be able to do pretty much as they like without interference from the state or any other actor. But it is a difficult to think of a point in recent history where such a state of affairs has either existed or, truth to tell, been possible. Universities and the state have nearly always been intertwined in some form or another and, as the university system has grown and government has put more and more money into university coffers, so state influence has inevitably become stronger (Wolf, 2019). In other words, it's not a question of denying the state any influence – in their modern form 'universities have always been creatures of the state' (Wolf, 2019, p. 30) – but a question of *what kind of influence*. After all, even in 1971 it was already being argued that 'the central government is now almost completely the universities' paymaster' (Halsey and Trow, 1971, p. 85) and by 2000 Gombrich was arguing that state policy towards universities was so dirigiste that it amounted to de facto nationalisation.

Better to argue that a look back at the history of universities shows much of both what is good and bad has come from state involvement in its various forms. Indeed, it is difficult to separate out the history of British research universities from the history of government intervention. Some of the greatest triumphs (and some of the greatest failures) of British research universities have arisen from government[19] intervention. Left to themselves, it is not at all clear that universities would have made many changes at all.

That said, generally speaking, until recently the relationship between state and universities has been an arm's length one. Probably the first signs of an entente more or less cordiale arose from the setting up of the University Grants Committee (UGC) in 1919 (an idea first proposed by R.B. Haldane in 1904) and the Medical Research Council in 1920. The UGC was funded directly from the Treasury until 1963, as a 'buffer' which meant both that the government didn't have to assume direct responsibility for universities and that universities were safeguarded from too much political interference (Halsey and Trow, 1971, p. 62). But the system could not hold and with the transfer of universities to the Department of Education and Science in the late 1960s, the writing was on the wall. Universities were increasingly being funded directly by the state – boosted by the post-Robbins growth of students, the increasing ascendancy of sciences, medicine and the social sciences, and a vision of the UK as a science and technology superpower – and their autonomy was inevitably going to come under pressure as a centralised and centrally funded university system was put in place. Of course, it wasn't only about the distribution of finance. It was also about the distribution of power. Money was the symptom. Halsey and others stressed the need for 'financial pluralism' so that the state could not lord it over universities but, ironically, for some research universities which have now reached quite substantial levels of financial pluralism, this hasn't guaranteed them a matching degree of independence. Indeed, one could argue that the reverse has occurred.

Halsey and Trow (1971) outlined five different accounts of autonomy, based on differing levels of claims on universities made by the state. They are still relevant. One is the classically liberal position. Government should have no involvement in university planning or direction. Universities should rely largely on endowments and fees. Another is a left position which argues that universities have become the agents of state capitalism and support specific class interests. They have been captured and are now not much more than hacks. A third position might be called the Franciscan model, the one which Halsey ultimately favoured. Academics would retreat back into being small hermetic communities of scholars who have withdrawn from the world – with the downside, it might be added, of rather less in the way of salary. In Truscot's (1945, p. 69) words, this would be a 'society for the pursuit of truth' that could waylay the spiritual crisis of universities beholden to too many masters. A fourth position might be deemed realist. Hands of some kind will be laid on universities by the state so let's get the best deal. Finally, there is what might be called the efficiency and accountability position. The challenge is all about trying to make universities work with maximum efficiency and transparency. That will make them better, surely?

Of course, as Halsey (1992) also pointed out some years ago, autonomy could be interpreted as the last gasp of a model of scholarly independence now being consigned to the dustbin of history, a decorative rather than an operational notion. All of the paraphernalia like the royal charter, the academic senate, external examining of students by academics for academics, and true intermediary bodies like the old University Grants Committee, all of these vestiges of other times, were to count for nothing in the brave new world of what he called 'bureaucratic professionalism'.

But it is a fact that university autonomy as concept and practice is there for purposes other than simple academic self-interest and most especially to promote the freedom to think freely and concentratedly. In particular, the kinds of knowledge that research universities produce is best generated at a distance from any interested party which might skew its findings or try to interfere in how it is interpreted. But, not surprisingly, as they have become more important, many more parties become more interested and would like to have their say. For example, politicians tend to want quite a lot of control over universities. They nearly always recite the mantra of university autonomy and some of them undoubtedly mean it. But even the best of them find it hard to resist at least a bit of a nudge or even quite a big push if they have favourite bugbears or want headlines, or if the media is pressing them to 'do something', or if their job is under threat in a reshuffle and they need headlines that play to their base. And an increasing role for government seems obvious to many politicians anyway. Government is usually universities' biggest funder (though, in the case of research universities, not always as big as people think) and universities need to be held accountable for that funding in one way or another. Equally, it is obvious to them that universities make important contributions to the business of economic growth in urban and regional economies which increasingly rely on knowledge and innovation from state-backed research, as well as a supply of high-end skills.[20]

The clear and present danger is that decisions on the trajectory of what ought to be a freethinking mode of enquiry are likely to come under increasing government control with all that entails. Shorn of the essential element of research, which is to go where the question takes you, however difficult, unexpected or downright controversial that may be, research would gradually be corralled into what was considered useful to government and what priorities government saw fit to set out for the future. It would also hold the risk of censorship of topics government didn't like or found uncomfortable, as well as the risk that academics self-censored for fear of giving offence. That said, the problem is that it is very easy to get on a high horse about all this but much more difficult to say where the horse should actually fetch up. After all, government funds most research and it clearly should have some say in how the money is spent. The question is rather how much of a say is appropriate, and at what remove?

In the past the holy writ of the so-called 'Haldane principle' was meant to mark out that remove. Not surprisingly, its history is a little less holy than is often made out in standard accounts where it is often portrayed as the result of a Manichean struggle between the values of a visionary academe and a Gradgrind state around a single science policy animated by a single principle (Edgerton, 2009, British Academy, 2019). It would be more accurate to say that the principle has involved a constant struggle to promote science or, more accurately, particular versions of science, mutating as they were filtered through various different science policies. First established by Haldane's machinery of government report of 1918, the principle is straightforward enough but, in truth, it was mainly an invention of the 1960s. Willetts (2010) put it well in a ministerial statement.

> 'The Haldane principle means that decisions on individual research proposals are best taken by researchers themselves through peer review. This involves evaluating the quality, excellence and likely impact of science and research programmes. Prioritisation of an individual research council's spending within its allocation is not a decision for Ministers ... There are areas where Ministers should have no input: Ministers should not decide which individual projects should be funded nor which researchers should receive the money. This has been crucial to the international success of British science.'

Further, 'Overall, excellence is and must remain the driver of funding decisions, and it is only by funding excellent research that the maximum benefits will be secured for the nation.' But, in the Higher Education and Research Act of 2017 setting up UKRI, this latter sentence was somewhat ominously omitted from consideration. And actions before and since then suggest that more and more funding is being placed in special pots which reflect current government economic and other priorities and that what counts as excellence is being qualified as a result.

The Office for Students

As I have pointed out already, the principle of arm's length interaction between universities and government has been typified in the UK, so far as research is concerned, by the setting up of buffers like the old University Grants Committee (UGC) which existed from 1919 to 1989, which was followed briefly by the Universities Funding Council (UFC) and then by the Higher Education Funding Council for England (HEFCE) which existed from 1992 to 2018 and by separate funding councils for Scotland and Wales. Most recently, it has been enshrined in the Higher Education and Research Act of 2017 which set up the Office for Students (OfS) and merged the research councils and the research part of the HEFCE into a new body, UK Research and Innovation (UKRI), which would follow 'the principle that decisions on individual research proposals are best taken following an evaluation of the quality and likely impact of the proposals (such as a peer review process)'. (This is not quite the same as the Haldane principle, of course.)

Allowing for what is a chequered policy history, these intermediary bodies have enabled budgets to be set and government fiats to be negotiated rather than simply imposed. This is important. In some other countries, academics are civil servants, universities are expected to enrol any student who hits the national standard, any new courses have to be signed off by government, representatives of government sit on the equivalent of council, ministers meddle in which academics get grants, and even term dates are set from afar. But there is ample evidence that a greater degree of autonomy produces better organisational performance, better ability to improve quality, and better ability to attract additional funding (Estermann, 2015).[21]

Of course, some care needs to be taken when arguing that autonomy is being eroded in UK universities. University academics are prone to crying wolf about university autonomy when what they really mean is that things are happening that they don't like or that external scrutiny of universities is somehow invalid (Hillman, 2017). In the UK, it is also true that universities still have some freedom of manoeuvre. As Hillman points out, their powers over admissions are enshrined in law, Vice-chancellors can set staff terms and conditions free from government interference, and institutions can open or close any course they like.

But this time it's different, as the saying goes. I really don't think that it occurred to most vice-chancellors – I am the first to admit that it didn't occur to me – that tuition fees would become a means of exerting more rather than less state control. (Foolishly, no doubt, I saw them as meaning less.) But gradually and remorselessly that is what has happened. Hillman (2017) argued that the increase in tuition fees and total removal of the cap on student numbers in 2015/16 had actually increased organisational autonomy. But it certainly didn't feel like that at the time. Martin Wolf (2016, p. 18) may have been exaggerating to a degree with his famous phrase 'Make no mistake, this is a fully-fledged government takeover of the UK's university sector.' But not as much as all that.

The move of the student activities of universities into the Department for Education only underlined these kinds of concerns. Notoriously, the Department has never had what Robbins (1963, p. 249) called a 'feeling for the reins' of universities. As he went on to point out:

> it must always be remembered that the business of the main institutions of higher learning is not only education: it is also the advancement and preservation of knowledge. There can be no doubt of the vital importance of research; and, as we have argued at length earlier, ... it is essential that much research should be domiciled in institutions of higher education. Research, interpreted in a large sense, has parity of importance with teaching; indeed the latter loses vitality if the former is absent. If therefore the solution of the problem of responsibility is to turn on the existence of organic connexions, we should argue that the organic connexion of the universities with other forms of organised research is even closer than their connexion with the work of the schools, important though that is, and that it was the connexion with research that was most suitably recognised in the allocation of ministerial responsibility. (ibid., p. 249)

But not much thought was given to what such a move might have meant for research. The changes were all driven by an imputed need for student choice. With the founding of the Office for Students as a formal sector regulator on 1 January 2018, the chains of state control were tightened still further. Many vice-chancellors will tell you in private how concerned they are by this institution's powers and general attitude. It is meant to be an independent risk-based regulator but for a lot of the time it doesn't act like one. Its actions have often seemed arbitrary so far as the sector is concerned. Witness the fact that the sector has been threatened with fines some 55 times since the passage of the Higher Education and Research Act in 2017 (though only a small number have actually been issued) (Kernohan, 2022). At the same time it can often seem too submissive when it comes to government intentions. Cynics might accuse it of becoming simply a creature of government, its purpose being to maintain a regulatory bureaucracy and to transmit what are, in effect, orders from the Department for Education[22] (that is when ministers bother to use an intermediary at all – letters have been known to fly directly from the relevant Minister to vice-chancellors of a Friday containing yet another diktat).

In other words, this latest sector body isn't an intermediary in the way that typified its predecessors, most particularly because it covers such a large spectrum of responsibilities. As the white paper that introduced OfS into the public domain states, 'the OfS will have oversight of the sustainability, efficiency and health of the higher education sector, and as part of its role will monitor the sustainability of individual institutions'. In essence, it will manage the UK's higher education system by 'controlling entry into the sector; promoting choice and competition; providing data, analysis and information to the secretary of state; developing, publishing and operating a risk-based regulatory framework; helping widen access for disadvantaged students; assessing quality; monitoring financial sustainability, efficiency and governance; being responsible for the Prevent programme against extremism'; and, last but certainly not least, acting as the principal regulator for providers that are charities, though the OfS's interpretation of this fact is somewhat different from the norm (Synge, 2021). Yet the campaign by universities, including research universities, against instituting such an over-reaching body often seemed half-hearted, even careless. They did not seem to believe in one of their most important principles.

Interestingly, the OfS must 'have regard to' to 'the need to protect the institutional autonomy of English higher education providers', defined in the 2017 Higher Education Research Act as a general duty amongst others where institutional autonomy is defined as:

(a) the freedom of English higher education providers within the law to conduct their day-to-day management in an effective and competent way,
(b) the freedom of English higher education providers
    - to determine the content of particular courses and the manner in which they are taught, supervised and assessed,
    - to determine the criteria for the selection, appointment and dismissal of academic staff and apply those criteria in particular cases, and
    - to determine the criteria for the admission of students and apply those criteria in particular cases, and
(c) the freedom within the law of academic staff at English higher education providers
    - to question and test received wisdom, and
    - to put forward new ideas and controversial or unpopular opinions, without placing themselves in jeopardy of losing their jobs or privileges they may have at the providers.

But, as an OfS manager (Lapworth, 2018) points out, this definition is 'in tension' with some of OfS's other general duties. For OfS 'institutional autonomy is only one of a number of considerations informing whether we need to intervene'. Intervention will mainly take place when any risk to students is found: 'the greater the risk to students, the less right a provider has to institutional autonomy'. But it clearly encompasses other issues as well. For example, in the interests of students, intervening in vice-chancellor pay is justified on the grounds of value for money. The problem is obvious enough. Pretty well any intervention can be justified by appeal to the impact on students or value for money. Conceivably, there might even be instances where the risk to students would warrant intervening in the academic freedom clause.

But has it all been worth it? So far, the results of the 2018 regulatory system which replaced HEFCE with the OfS and Research England can seem close to nugatory. One might argue, as Kernohan (2022, p. 1) does, that the OfS, for all of the noise, has had relatively little impact.

> What was the state of the higher education sector before the advent of the Office for Students? Overall student satisfaction in England has been at above 80 per cent since we started to measure it in 2005 – it reached a peak of nearly 85 per cent in 2015 and has then declined in a stately manner since the advent of the new regulatory regime.
>
> The world-class research seen in REF 2021 was primarily conducted in the times before HERA. The bulk of the growth in 'grade inflation' and in conditional unconditional offers occurred after the demise of HEFCE. Most of the heavy lifting in widening access was done even before 2010. We could go on.
>
> This crude comparison is unfair to OfS for two reasons – the regulator administers a larger and more diverse sector than ever before (though, to be scrupulously accurate, the overwhelming volume of provision is still in the old HEFCE sector), and the new regime has weathered a major pandemic and a geopolitical upheaval that have had far reaching consequences for data time series of all types.
>
> But – to be frank – was the sector really that awful on 31 December 2018? (Kernohan, 2022)

As a footnote, little or no thought seems to have been given to the impact of OfS on research. I think it was probably assumed that any cross-infections, so to speak, between the business of the OfS in the DfE and UKRI in BEIS would be minimal and could be picked up by UKRI. So far as I know, UKRI has tended to be passive, assuming that developments on the educational side of the house have little to do with research. That isn't so. Many of them directly affect academics' ability to carry out research by taking up more and more time and effort, especially when coupled with UKRI's evolving tendency to put funding in set pots, which leaves relatively less funding for the freestanding and free-range research which is such a vital element of universities' ethos.[23]

So why bother with intermediaries?

And now we have the logical endpoint of this trajectory of greater and greater control. Just skip the intermediary. The government will issue orders. The OfS will carry them out. The desire for stronger lines of accountability over universities means that the notion of a supposedly arm's length intermediary body like the OfS seems more and more brittle. The OfS increasingly looks like it is becoming simply a delivery body for government.

Covid-19 has been particularly instructive. Universities have been subject to all kinds of actions and expectations which they have found difficult to fulfil. Universities have spent millions out of uncertain budgets, staff have been stretched and many are not surprisingly exhausted, students are out of pocket, and many of them are only just coping. Government has offered little in the way of recompense. I know of few research university vice-chancellors who have felt fully supported in this difficult period and I know of some who have felt undermined by what have sometimes seemed like 'if things are difficult, blame the universities' moves.

In other words, the reaction to Covid-19 just adds to the evidence that, for government now, autonomy is something to be hauled on stage only when it wants to look the other way. Yet the criticism of this loss of university control can't all be placed at the government's door. It's not all the OfS's and the Department for Education's fault. The sector keeps presenting government with open goals. The Office of Students is there now because the sector provided no real sense of where it wanted to go and what it wanted to do. The OfS is a monument to uncertain university leadership as well as state ambition. The sector was largely reactive to government initiatives rather than actively initiating its own. On a whole series of issues – grade inflation, conditional offers, mental health, harassment, post-qualification admissions, transferable credits – the sector prevaricated or looked the other way for far too long and then had to acquiesce to government prodding. On others, truth to tell, it just hoped they'd go away. On others still, like competition, it often participated willingly, even to the extent of leaving institutions that were adversely affected to swim – or sink – by themselves. It's not a happy story.

So why autonomy?

In the face of this onslaught of command and control under the guise of risk-driven accountability, and their own apparent passivity, research universities' claim that they must have autonomy can sound increasingly hollow. After all, you might argue universities are not the only homes of intellectuals. Intellectual life does not necessarily need an institutional carapace to thrive.

Hillman (2017) argues that there are three downsides to granting autonomy to universities. Most importantly, politicians do not feel that they have sufficient levers to respond to the economy. Then, there is a danger of uniformity fostered by lack of competition from new entrants, as well as the danger of prompting homogeneous behaviours. Finally, there is a danger of 'excessive hierarchy'. In other words, to summarise his argument,

> running an independent institution with hundreds of millions of pounds in income from multiple sources should never mean running an institution closed to the eyes of the outside world. Moreover, while accountability should come from robust internal governance procedures, on the really big things it should also come from outside, including from official bodies. (Hillman, 2017, p. 6)

The problem is that Hillman's not unreasonable prescriptions can impinge on the mission of research universities in untoward ways. Too much government interference in the name of the economy could lead to these universities becoming simply job-training machines and economic crutches. Uniformity of response is what has actually been promoted by many government policies, not the reverse. And there is no real alternative to 'hierarchy' when it comes to research universities. Some universities are better at research than others and it would be foolish to pretend otherwise. Indeed, one could argue that the inevitable result of worldwide competition – I know of no research institution 'closed to the eyes of the outside world' – will be some kind of hierarchy.

So, assuming that autonomy is not simply a backward-looking relic of an 'old power' producer cartel (Grant, 2021), there are three main reasons why – [it] is important. The first is that our general understanding of the natural and social world is bound up in the free thinking associated with unlearning. That doesn't mean just reducing confusions and misconceptions about what the world might be like. It also means producing actual new accounts. At this moment in time, these new accounts are particularly crucial. We are now attempting to understand the planet in a very different way. No longer is it a 'stable Earth that is the décor of human history'. Now it is becoming a misplaced Earth which is 'active on the stage of a common drama' (Latour, 2016, pp. 1–2), a change that we can almost talk of in terms of a rediscovery.

This kind of understanding is something much more than is covered by words like 'innovation' and 'creativity'. Innovation and creativity were only used sparingly as words until the 1950s or 1960s but they are now in such frantic circulation that they have become words that mean less and less as they are used more and more. Like it or not, universities have played their part in the normalisation of these terms. From the early 1950s until the 1980s,

Godin (2015, 2019) argues that innovation was understood primarily as a process. Theoretical research in university laboratories provided the initial foundation; applications of this research were then developed; and, from there, they became commercialised products. Innovation was thought of as a packaged, predictable research product and government funding directly corresponded to the rise of this understanding of the word. Now its meaning has broadened and is often applied to all and sundry as simply implying something new (Green, 2013). But innovation was not always framed as an economic term. It dates back at least to the Middle Ages. Then, the central (and better) meaning of innovation was renewal. For this renewal to take place it is necessary for people to choose to understand and do things differently, to make choices outside of the norm. (That is much closer to what Latour is getting at and what universities are best placed to achieve.) 'Creativity' followed a somewhat similar path towards blandness. Bolstered by business and the military, Shapin (2020) finds that it has now become a signifier of divergent thinking of pretty well any kind, its identity eroded by constant and constantly widening circulation. Universities had their part in this ascension too, not least through the use of the term in business schools:

> politicians, executives, educators, urban theorists and economists see it as the engine of economic progress and look for ways to have more of it. ... There are academic and professional organisations devoted to the study and promotion of creativity; there are encyclopaedias and handbooks surveying creativity research; and there are endless paper and online guides to creativity – or how, at least, to convince others that you have it. (Shapin, 2020, p. 7)

Then, a second reason. Research universities are also in the business of producing subjects that can work on their understanding, not just take it as a given. Their academics and students don't just fall in line with the nostrums of the day. They chart their own independent course. Perhaps this is a means of keeping in touch with the university tradition which argued that universities were there to imbue 'character' and cultivate 'good judgement'. That said, I seriously doubt that the total package of character that was envisaged by many past writers is still possible in an age when so many universities have enormous student bodies whose identity is forged, at least in part, by individualistic ideas. But it is important that those aspects of the student experience that do emphasise character and good judgement do not go by the board – or are revived. We need such people, especially as our world tips over into a period of planetary change that is likely to be comparable with the onset of the last Ice Age, but in reverse.

But there is one other reason why universities need to have autonomy. They are public goods, goods held in common (Horgan, 2020). But what is meant by that oh so innocuous-sounding phrase is, of course, a moveable feast. Generally speaking, a public good is defined as a service or good that is provided in common and without profit for every member of a society. It is therefore non-rivalrous and non-exclusionary. In turn, a public is defined, in large part, by its having access to such goods. But there are genuine problems with that definition when it comes to both higher education and research. The situation is complex.

Presumably, higher education grants access to the public goods of knowledge and expertise. There is no in principle economic reason why knowledge and expertise cannot be supplied as a public good: that is presumably why governments pay towards universities' operations. However, the supply of this particular public good is not necessarily held in common. As an empirical fact, higher education and research is often based on excludability and is rivalrous, even though, at least in the UK, universities are normally not for profits (that said, within that category there is a wide range of possibility: New York University's strapline, for example, is 'a private university for the public good'). Again, much of the knowledge universities produce circulates in the hands of private organisations who make money through having rights over it, whether that be an informational conglomerate or a publishing company. This is why the issue of open access is so important (Smits and Pells, 2022). There is a considerable way to go to get to true open access – if you are a member of the public without a university connection you will still find it difficult to access the bulk of journal articles. All that said, the march of open access also shows that things can change so that the results of research more properly resemble a public good. A good deal of progress has been made via a range of innovations from pre-print servers, through the requirement by public funders that any research that they fund is publicly available to publisher agreements that use subscription models and by the rise of open access books. In the past, university researchers often tended to hunker down with their work so that it circulated only in narrow cliques but, given that the general public pays for a large proportion of research out of its taxes, it is surely right that they ought to be able to access the knowledge that results. (Whether the idea of prestige journals needs to disappear entirely which some open access proponents have argued for, with all papers being published openly in a kind of publishing scrum, is a matter for future argument (though I would be willing to bet that if it ever came about other means of giving some papers prestige would evolve).) Then, finally, there is knowledge which is actually generated by the public. Through the rise of citizen science, nowadays the public can have a hand in generating and sometimes analysing data, for example. Citizen science has been an immensely important development in that it allows all kinds of people to not only participate but actively contribute to the business of research (Gabrys, 2016). It is simply remarkable to see how many people want to be allied with scientific projects, whether they be working on transcribing nineteenth-century weather observations from maritime logbooks, scanning for new stars or meteorites, recording the densities of particular birds and insects, joining in open source mapping, recording Covid-19 symptoms, or becoming a part of the effort to defeat coronavirus by transcribing lab notes. (I will have more to say on this issue in the last chapter.[24])

There is also the issue of which publics the public good argument applies to. It may not be the public as a whole. As Kennedy (2011) has argued, making arguments concerning why more university resources should be devoted to some publics rather than others – for example, particular ethnic minorities – is often quite difficult and can be seen by some other publics as an implicit politicisation of the university. There is no explicit method for determining which publics a university should serve, especially differentially. But what is clear is that to be worthy of the name universities must pass some kind of public benefit test, one which must recognise that they serve many different publics, not just a few privileged ones. Universities are run for the benefit of myriad publics who are now not just national but international in nature – staff, students, alumni, donors, companies, government, local and global communities of concerned citizens, the list goes on – and they have to try to balance off the needs of all of them via an expanded collegiality which is still a work in progress.

One more public good issue. Universities also need to communicate the knowledge they generate to the public. In a sense, that is a public good in its own right. It is undoubtedly the case that universities have become far, far better at this aspect of their activity. There are now numerous successful professors of research communication, for example, as instanced by television luminaries like Jim Al-Khalili, Brian Cox, Bettany Hughes, David Olusoga, Alice Roberts and Michael Wood. Since around the 2000s there has been a sea change in the communication of research led by specialised television and radio programmes, podcasts, websites and associated email newsletters like *The Conversation*, as well as by enterprising academics who simply enjoy reaching out. It's also worth remembering that academics continue to produce books for the general market, many of which have sold very well, and contribute to all kinds of outlets like Substack. For better or worse, there are even branches of science which have become entwined with celebrity like ancient DNA. This point about communication is one to which I will return: a university education no longer stops at students. Nor should it.

To summarise, universities are charities, one of whose goals is to act as a public good. This does not mean that they have to be entirely publicly funded. Indeed, without privately sourced funds many research universities would be dead in the water. But they would also be dead in the water without public funds. The truth is that, for-profit operations apart (and we can debate whether most of these are universities, except in name), universities are public–private hybrids with some being more public and others being more private. The real question is how much responsibility they owe to the taxpayer for the public funds they take and how much they should be able to operate on their own account.

The clear and present danger is the obvious one: 'universities will be rendered "mere outliers of Whitehall", made narrow and cramped by a government seemingly intent on turning universities into schools' (Jenkins, 2019, p. 17). Which brings me on to the final part of this chapter and a perennial that is becoming hardier year by year: the generalised dissatisfaction that many academics and other staff in research universities feel with both their lot and with what has become of universities as this so-called 'schoolification' takes place.

Dissatisfaction

As I have pointed out already, there seems to be growing dissatisfaction on pretty well all sides with universities. The media just know that something is agley. The government is sure there is something wrong that needs sorting. Parents and students often feel short-changed. And as for university academics …

Of course, academics have always liked a good grumble about work, just like anyone else. Indeed, they may well be better at it than most professions. But what is happening now is something else altogether. Of course, there is widespread dissatisfaction over stagnating pay and especially pension cuts. Autonomy has declined too. Academics still have considerable flexibility in how they achieve their goals and in setting their work schedules more generally but not as much as before. (Some also feel stuck on a treadmill until retirement though that is not exactly an uncommon feeling in the world of work.) Job insecurity has increased. Tenure is now a pretty well meaningless word: if financial exigencies so dictate, tenure counts for very little. And workloads have become increasingly onerous. When I talk to senior academics who have left for industry one of the first things they remark upon is that their workload has decreased. But for academics there is one other thing. They have increasingly found themselves stranded from research by the demands of student growth. For research universities there is an undoubted tension between the mass student experience and what might be called the staff experience. This is not, as it is sometimes painted, about a producer cabal which is short-changing student 'consumers'. It is simply that good research becomes more difficult to achieve when, in the case of academics on research and teaching contracts (as well as many teaching only academics striving to find a full-time position by eking out time for research), time is short and teaching and other loads are heavy and getting heavier. Time, time, time. What most academics wanting to follow a research trajectory long for is the time to think and do their work. This is often painted in the press as though it is all about honing a citation score at the expense of the students. Or about lounging about over long breaks in that famed farmhouse in Tuscany (a standing academic joke). Or about spending their life working on things of no use to beast nor man. Those selfish academics! Those lazy academics! Those dilettante academics! No, they're just doing what they're supposed to do. Finding out things. That requires concentrated runs of time to think. That is a basic, perhaps the basic, requirement of being a research university academic. But the helter-skelter growth of the sector can feel like it is turning academics into drones when their self-image necessarily has to be that of a creative professional – because they are creative professionals.

For many of those academics who have lived through the last few years of expansion, the future therefore looks increasingly bleak. There has been an accompanying rise in 'quit lit' and in hashtags like #leavingacademia, accompanied by talk of 'the great resignation' lapping up on university shores, all registering more and more dissatisfaction with academic life. All this said, much of the quit lit tends to comes from those who have been unable to gain any kind of career stability and it is a sad fact that, as universities have expanded, there are more of these people around than formerly because, even with the expansion in student numbers in many universities, there is more supply than demand for academic and academic-related jobs. Limited contract positions have proliferated in something that looks more and more like a classical dual labour market. That said, this is not a new phenomenon. Even in 1997/98, Gombrich (2000) noted that a large proportion of academic staff were on fixed-term contracts, a figure that has only grown since.[25] (Among academic staff in 2018/19, 72,750, or 34 per cent of the whole, were employed on fixed-term contracts. Of full-time academic staff, 25 per cent were employed on fixed-term contracts in 2018/19. In contrast, 50 per cent of part-time academic staff were working on fixed-term contracts (HESA, 2020).) That said, though it will be no consolation to those who are stuck in the wrong part of this academic dual labour market, it has not gone as far as in countries like Australia and the US (Wolf and Jenkins, 2021).

It is, of course, possible to overdo the sackcloth and ashes. From some perspectives at least, universities are better places to work than they were. Certainly, they provide many more academic and other jobs than formerly, even given that many of these extra jobs can be precarious and can be poorly remunerated. (That said, not every academic is badly paid.[26]) The position of women academics is better than it was: the proportion of women academics is steadily increasing age cohort by age cohort. (That said, there is still a gender gap in pay and a disproportionate number of women academic staff are concentrated in part-time jobs.) Promotion is, generally speaking, on something much closer to merit against what are usually explicit and understandable standards. Much more is done about bullying than in the days when, for example, heads of department sometimes ran their departments like mini-dictators. Younger faculty get massively more help and support than in the past, as well as access to all manner of research fellowships that simply never existed before. Though difficult to measure, it is possible – one can say no more – that more really mind-bending research is getting done.

In other words, care needs to be taken. If you do have a permanent position, life isn't that bad. You will still get quite a lot of individual autonomy, including so far as research is concerned. You will still get a relatively long 'vacation' time in which to do that research (though that has been seriously eroded by the increase in the number of Master's students). You will still get the opportunity to apply for research fellowships that can give you the concerted time to do research, as well as the possibility of buy-outs from grants. In research universities, you may well have access to study leave every few years. These are not terms and conditions that most taxpayers have or can access. And if you really don't like the UK system, you can at least entertain the option of moving overseas where, if you're seen as talented, you will likely receive a welcome.

By the way, I'm not saying that because other people don't have these job conditions, academics shouldn't have them. And I am certainly not saying that all is well. It isn't. It really isn't. And many academics would certainly agree. So the recent strikes over pensions in 2018, in 2019/20 and in 2021/22 were partly about pensions, a decline in pay and conditions, and general precarity but underlying them was and is a structure of feeling which reflects a more general concern about the way in which the sector has been driven. They were as much a howl of protest over the state of universities more generally, over the downsides of 'marketisation' and 'schoolification', and over a perceived absence of recognition from management which arises out of the feeling of asymmetry that pertains when an academic is expected to put a lot extra into their job but seems to get less and less back in return. In particular, as many universities have got larger, so the distance between them and their institution has increased. Whereas at one time academics felt that they were part of the institution, their sense of belonging has been eroded. The problem for universities is that – unlike in the case of many other workforces – talented academics can go elsewhere. If they have no voice, they can exit – most especially because many of them have come to our research universities from overseas in the first place.

UCL is a good yardstick of this issue. It was a great university which had a very specific ethos and a collegial feel. It has been driven hard to expand and the result is that pre-Covid-19 it increased its undergraduate student numbers from 12,643 in 2008/09 to 23,527 in 2021/22 and its graduate student numbers from 8,492 to 24,357. But, though the accusation that UCL has become too big has been rejected by management, there has been a determined fightback by some members of the UCL academic community who feel that the collegial university that they knew is being pulled out from underneath them. I don't think this was just a backward-looking gambit. Dissident UCL academics fundamentally disagreed with the strategic direction that the university was taking. Rightly or wrongly, they thought that UCL's status as an elite university was threatened by a likely drop in student intake standards. They were concerned by a likely increase in time spent teaching as a result of student number growth. They disliked the idea of a non-Bloomsbury location for the new campus at Stratford East. Most importantly, they believed that there was no necessary correlation between size and excellence. None of these are unreasonable complaints. Unsurprisingly perhaps, their protests proved to be in vain but the visitor assigned to look at the case noted a 'loss of trust and morale among a significant number [of academic staff]'.

6

The Australianisation of British higher education

So what are the proximate causes of all this dissatisfaction? I have lived through a time when universities were still given quite a lot of freedom. There were reasons for this but most particularly they didn't matter as much as they do now to government and business. Universities were still quite small and, by and large, they taught and were a part of the 'establishment', a social complex who knew that 'people like us' were likely to do the right thing for people like us. Then, no one really thought that universities were a major economic sector in their own right or that they might be a key determinant of a country's economic success. Again, universities educated only a relatively small number of people and touched the lives of many people hardly at all. Universities tended to fly beneath the radar a lot of the time, quietly confident that they were doing the right thing with the right stuff. That doesn't mean that there was no politicking about how they were funded or what they should be doing. Government reviews kept coming. Haggling over funding was sometimes as fierce as now. But it still seemed like the state would act as a shelter in the storm if needs be.

Then came Margaret Thatcher. With her, shall we say, robust views, universities needed to measure up like any other institution. The storm was the shelter. Universities budgets were cut, sometimes drastically. Between 1981 and 1983, for example, university budgets were cut by 15 per cent, and there were further cuts in subsequent years. Some universities fared far worse with, famously, Salford (44 per cent), Aston (31 per cent) and Stirling (27 per cent) being singled out for particularly rough treatment.[1]

By the end of the 1980s, the unit of resource, the sum that universities got from government for each student, had reduced significantly. Universities were on their uppers. There was widespread demoralisation:

> The position of the academics in relation to state funding, salary levels, research facilities, staff–student ratios, public respect and indeed every dimension of professional status, had deteriorated by the end of the 1980s to the point where both domestic and foreign observers regarded the British higher education system as in crisis. (Halsey, 1995, p. 2)

It is difficult to understand university management support for the introduction of tuition fees in 1998, or the subsequent increases, without harking back to those grim days. They had scarred the whole psychology of vice-chancellors of the time. Uppermost in the minds of many of them was never, ever going back to that period of resource hunger – under any circumstances. That resolve was only compounded by their suspicion of any government promises to up spending on universities. Bitter experience showed that, in the competition for funds, universities tended to lose out to government departments with cases which looked much more electorally threatening – schools, the NHS, the police, and so on. So a brief spending boost would be followed by yet another decline. At the same time, general cost pressures were increasing, not just from pensions but from many other angles as well. In other words, vice-chancellors were caught in a financial vice and they were looking for ways out.

One thing Tony Blair understood was that universities were valuable. Another thing he understood was that resources were over-stretched. Academic salaries had slipped. People more generally rarely understood how bad things had got. And, at the same time, Blair wanted to get more students into university. And, indeed, more and more students were going to university which meant that the pressures on the Exchequer were growing year by year. The idea that it would be possible to keep funding what were mainly middle-class students out of the general taxation pot seemed less and less tenable.

But there was a solution – of sorts. Over in Australia, income-contingent loans had been introduced in 1989. The invention of Professor Bruce Chapman at ANU, they coupled loan repayment amounts to a debtor's actual income. Students are charged tuition, but the obligation to pay is deferred until the debtors' income rises above a given threshold. They have become became a model for higher education funding in many parts of the world (currently nine countries use them). But there were big differences which were not taken on board between what transpired in England and what happens in Australia. The Australian scheme charges more for particular kinds of degree. The Australian scheme charges lower fees, on the whole. And the Australian situation has another advantage. England has a system whereby most students leave home to go to university. In Australia, it is the opposite. Most students stay home. So many Australian students don't have quite the same burden of maintenance to afford.

And so vice-chancellors were willing to enter the compact on tuition fees, even given the very considerable grief they had to go through and the undoubted reservations that some of them undoubtedly had, because it meant more money and what looked like more freedom . The public–private equation would be rebalanced and universities would be able to follow their own stars. Basically, the attitude was that tuition fees were the only way of getting more money. For a while, this did indeed look to be the case. The introduction of tuition fees in 1998 by Labour undoubtedly produced more cash on the barrel. Not as much as would have been liked, of course. And far more for the universities without large research overheads who could and did charge the same fees. Even so, more money.

Then came the jump-the-shark moment, the 2012 increase in tuition fees to £9,000 (now £9,250). Elements of the coalition government in England had always wanted to introduce a market into full-time undergraduate higher education both so that universities would become more business-like and to increase the diversity of providers. With the advent of such high tuition fees, the government did exactly that. Indeed, the move succeeded beyond what were probably its wildest dreams. The reforms themselves, coupled with strong underlying demand from 18-year-olds and seemingly ever-growing international recruitment (especially from China), pushed the competitive revenues of universities to around £20 billion for the first time in 2019/20, up from a mere £2 billion prior to 2012 (Corver, 2019). Many universities in England and Wales are now dominated by these student-generated revenues. This change, as well as the huge growth of the overall market, has propelled many universities into a world of big business, based on a volume model. In the worst interpretation, universities have stepped into the shoes of mass retail and a world full of traps for the unwary. Big traps. Universities living on the supposition that the revenues will just keep on coming which have too few weeks of cash to hand. Universities whose supply chains are vulnerable. Universities that have accumulated too much debt and especially off-balance sheet obligations that spice up returns at the cost of more financial risk and only show up in a crisis. Universities that in running the gauntlet of high operational gearing are locked into fixed costs that leave limited room to cut expenses in the face of any sudden collapse in revenues. In my opinion, universities, as not-for-profits, should run what is often called in the parlance an 'inefficient' balance sheet with little gearing, plenty of cash, and a large overdraft facility. Some do but you might be surprised by how many don't.

These developments were interpreted in various ways. On the right, they were seen as the fruits of bracing competition overturning years of complacent or just plain bad management, and as evidence that running a university like a business brings with it badly needed discipline. Any criticisms were interpreted as the predictable moaning of people who belonged to an over-privileged 'producer cabal'. British research universities were on to a cushy number, coddled by government subsidies, but now they were having to shape up or ship out. If they couldn't hack it, they would have to go to the wall.

On the left, universities were often understood as having caught a bad dose of neoliberalitis from the market. Unfortunately, 'neoliberal' has been a standard term of criticism for some time now, a cognitive shortcut used freely and indiscriminately like confetti to signal 'bad'. The result is that it is a debased currency able to be used as an all-purpose universal explanation which, knowing no bounds, answers everything and nothing, a nostrum which tends to take many different strands of behaviour and argues that they all amount to the same thing. As Storper (2016, p. 248) puts it:

> By failing to master theories of liberalism, much of the neo-liberalism literature attributes virtually all deregulation, laissez-faire, tolerance of inequality, cronyism, and oligarchic behaviour as outgrowths of liberalism, ... or as Ferguson (2010: 171) puts it, 'a sloppy synonym for capitalism itself, or as a kind of shorthand for the world economy and its inequalities'.

So far as universities are concerned, the critique of universities as being taken over by economic imperatives is hardly a new one. It arises in about 1895 in the US and has been a constant ever since, spreading out to other parts of the world as a ritual academic complaint. In book form, it goes back at least to Veblen (Cole, 2009, Teichgraeber, 2015) who in 1918 contrasted the good European university interested only in the disinterested pursuit of knowledge with the evils of American universities run by business people (Teichgraeber, 2015). Since then universities have changed, most especially because of the rise of big science research. They have become the main redoubts of science and medicine in the UK, replacing, to a considerable extent, corporate research and research in specialised government institutions (Berman, 2012). In turn, corporate interests have come to hold greater sway in university research than before, since they fund a considerable amount of research. The actual extent of the influence that they exert on universities is difficult to gauge not least because, as Mirowski (2011, p. 88) points out, 'the commercialization of science turns out to be a stubbornly heterogeneous phenomenon' but it has certainly increased, especially because of the industrialisation of certain kinds of research.

In certain senses, the neoliberal critique of universities is only the latest form of the Veblen narrative (Thrift, 2016). The trouble is that while there is certainly something in this critique – few people would deny that a certain 'economentality' (Mitchell, 2015) has taken hold of universities or that the humanist values that some of the more elite universities subscribed to have been watered down (Nussbaum, 2010, Brown, 2015), values that were more easily subscribed to when universities were small, elite institutions – it is hardly the whole story (Thrift, 2016). After all, universities are not entirely innocent entities. They themselves are a part of the unfolding history of rationalisation and commodification rather than a breed set apart (Clark, 2009). The history of British universities is itself set within a particularly odd form of arrested capitalism with which its research universities have sometimes been bound up, one which combines an economy with an addiction to rentier capitalism and economic liberalism (Christophers, 2022) with a state with an unwritten constitution, a state which has constantly outflanked any really substantial changes to its nature through a form of democracy which still has some roots in 1688 and a bureaucracy which, even now, retains at least a whiff of colonialism (Anderson, 2020, 2021, Savage, 2021).[2] More recently, it is also set within an international context within which transnational educational indicators with a distinctly economic flavour based on acquisition of skills and thus jobs and thus pay have become influential in governments of all stripes. In particular, the work of the OECD Director of Education and Skills, Andreas Schleicher, has taken on importance out of all proportion as he has helped to create a new educational orthodoxy. Not only is this orthodoxy almost entirely instrumental but it specifically treats university education as simply being the next step on from school education in an odyssey to create 'motivated, dedicated learners and prepare them to overcome the unforeseen challenges of tomorrow'. Simple cognitive skills can be taught through an automated pedagogy leaving time to teach problem-solving and decision-making skills via new means of communication and collaboration. Though Schleicher would take pains to deny it, this stance seems perilously close to the standard Silicon Valley playbook.

Risky business?

Even so, there are a number of ways in which what has happened in and to universities does not conform to stereotypes on either right or left. To begin with, there are the contra-indicators. For example, it would be difficult to make the case that the British state has become inured to issues of equity in the university sector. The record of intervention may be patchy but it is undoubtedly there. Politicians of all stripes are genuinely and laudably concerned to open up universities to a much wider range of potential students. They may have done this with means – like tuition fees – that are disliked but some would argue that it is only through these fees that the expansion in student numbers has been made possible which has allowed at least some levelling-up to occur. Then, there are the dubious ad hominem arguments. For example, blame it all on the vice-chancellors. According to this argument, university leaders have adopted a business mindset lock, stock and barrel and sold the whole university enterprise down the river. But not only does this kind of explanation over-estimate university leaders' influence but it also avoids having to talk about what has been a much messier business in which some business practices have been adopted but by no means all.

I suggest that a much better explanation of recent developments in research universities is provided by the intersection of a series of processes: financialisation, nationalisation, and growth.

Financialisation is the process whereby financial elites attain greater influence over the economy by inventing and exploiting new financial markets, instruments and institutions. As many commentators have pointed out (e.g. Leyshon and Thrift, 2007), financialisation has transformed the functioning of the economic system at both the macro and micro levels, especially in supercharged rentier economies like that of the UK. Universities were already substantial financial entities.[3] As they have grown, borrowed more, and become ever more financially complex, they have come under the influence of the process of financialisation. Private equity, private placements and variants like special purpose vehicles have become increasingly common in higher education, often replete with scary covenants and accompanying dangers of default and insolvency.

But financialisation and the accompanying danger of over-gearing is a partial influence, not least because universities follow a rather peculiar financial model which is not typical of business at large. Each year they have to juggle various budgetary pots in order to hit an annual financial target which is often not too far above break even. Business people who become involved with universities are often amazed by this process and by the level of skill required to achieve it: they rely on much larger margins which give them a lot more financial slack and freedom of manoeuvre. Then, university budgets often mainly consist of wage bills. Once more, this limits freedom of manoeuvre since it takes very little slippage to affect people's job security. Then again, very little of a university budget can be transferred between headings. A lot of it is, in effect, hypothecated for research or teaching or buildings and is not fungible. Quite a bit of it is necessarily loss-making. Many other activities are structurally under-funded: research does not run at full economic cost, for example, and much science teaching requires topping up too. Only a few pots of money (international student fees, QR from the REF, various private sources of income, endowments) hold out any hope of allowing genuine freedom of manoeuvre. Oh, and finally, if the budget was out of kilter for too long, rest assured that the council would fire the hapless vice-chancellor who had allowed it to get in such a state and get a new one.

One of the consequences of greater financialisation has been greater borrowing. All research universities borrow and it was a sensible way to fund some projects, especially in an age of low interest rates. But just because you can borrow doesn't always mean you should. I don't think that there is much doubt that some research universities will turn out to have over-borrowed to find the resources to construct new student and other facilities. Others have covenants on loans and placements which imply expanding student numbers to keep up with the repayments. If students then don't turn up for whatever reason, this would have serious effects and especially the need to trim staff numbers, given how much of university budgets is devoted to payroll. Again, when research universities have used bullet loans to raise money, the issue becomes whether they will be in a position to pay back the principal when it becomes due. That might be a long way in the future but it will still need to be repaid. For Oxford and Cambridge this is never likely to be a problem. But for other universities who haven't found a mechanism to put the money aside over time, who knows?

The second process is government. Over several cycles, since the introduction of tuition fees, the government has been keen to introduce competition between universities in what it is prone to call a market. The outcome is certainly not the 'martial law' (Sloterdijk, 2020) of the ideal of a free market, whatever that might be. There are comparatively few players so competition is bounded, student fees are limited by fiat so that a price mechanism only exists in theory, consumers cannot judge the value of the product until long after it has been consumed, and, though there are instances of provider failure and a redistribution of students to other institutions as a result of this marketised system, realistically the major providers like research universities are very unlikely to be allowed to fail. Neither does the outcome quite meet the criteria for a functioning quasi-market, that is a public sector institutional structure which is able to reap the supposed efficiency gains of markets without sacrificing the equity benefits of systems of public administration and financing. There are some private players, for example. Then, Hillman (2017) argues that the plan was never to create a market in any case. But it has to be said that many politicians of whatever stripe perceived the changes as marketisation and matched them to their ideological templates willy-nilly.

I want to understand this process of installing a sort of market in another way – as a form of nationalisation by other means: that is, forcing universities to ape a kind of market but using this move as a means of interfering ever more in their running. Nationalisation, you say? Surely not. But there are different kinds of nationalisation. One is when the government places industries into public ownership of various kinds to gain more control over them. But there is another type, which is when a government rings a sector with rules meant to promote and enforce market-like disciplines via incentives, market-facing regulation and enforcement of those rules via regulations – forced marketisation – which also and at the same time through those regulations bring it under greater government control. This is what I call market nationalisation. In this new forced market the rules and regulations multiply like knitting. For anyone who thinks that markets cannot be produced by governments, just look at the National Audit Office's (2017) utterly transactional – and unutterably depressing – *The Higher Education Market*. It's not like a market. It will be like a market. It is a market:

> We are deliberately thinking of higher education as a market, and as a market, it has a number of points of failure. Young people are taking

out substantial loans to pay for courses without much effective help and advice, and the institutions concerned are under very little competitive pressure to provide best value. If this was a regulated financial market we would be raising the question of mis-selling. The Department is taking action to address some of these issues, but there is a lot that remains to be done. (Morse, 2017, p. 11)

The National Audit Office pretty well takes it for granted that higher education should be a market and that it should march to the dictates of value for money and competition. What needs sorting out by government is the price of the commodity, the degree of competition, the issue of mis-selling, and other associated market imperfections. Then students can pick and choose and go home happy consumers. So far as modern economics is concerned, it's a curiously old-fashioned, even naïve, notion of both market and competition, with very little basis in reality, though unfortunately one that still holds sway in certain quarters.

Voluminous research shows that markets of the kind the National Audit Office proposes as an article of faith do not just come into being. They have to be fostered by incentives, by rules and regulations and by formulations. There is no such thing as a 'free' market, a single logic of action, as numerous empirical economists, economic sociologists and anthropologists have shown in empirical study after empirical study (e.g. Callon, 2021). So far as public services are concerned, market nationalisation usually comes in two forms. To begin with public goods like higher education are opened up to more and more competition from private sources. Though this is clearly happening in higher education through the founding of some new private providers (though probably less than the government hoped for) it is not the nub of the issue. More importantly, existing higher education bodies are hedged around with rules and regulations and targets which move them in the direction of competition with each other. Crucially, the government keeps control over this hybrid of government and market through various regulatory bodies like the Competition Commission and most especially, in the case of the UK, the Office for Students, which serve to ensure that competition is enshrined as a principle in its own right and oversee the disbursement of government funding on that basis.

But this is not the former arm's length arrangement. Whereas the old HEFCE used to be an intermediary and, to some extent at least, a buffer, on all manner of issues, the OfS, as I have already pointed out, seems more like a cog in a machine for transmitting (too many) government diktats. Indeed on latest evidence, it looks suspiciously like it is even going to get into the business of manpower planning by moving some of the £1.3 billion of direct government funds allocated to high cost subjects, access for disadvantaged students, and the like towards mainly technological disciplines that merit high industrial priority in by now time-honoured fashion. There is little evidence that this works, considerable disagreement about what might represent an industrial priority subject (the usual blah about 'slashing' subjects like media studies managed to avoid mentioning that the entertainment and media industry is one of the UK's largest industries, likely to be worth £76 billion by 2021) and a lot of evidence from places like Australia that reallocation like this only marginally affects student preferences. Added to that is the subject-level TEF which was mooted for so long but which has now, thankfully, been all but taken off the agenda. The TEF is constantly advertised as just another piece of information to aid student choice (even though the Pearce Report found that it was just about the last thing students looked at and instead emphasised the TEF as a mechanism of teaching quality enhancement) but few people believe that the idea of it as a financial driver won't stay on the table in some form.

The third process is growth. This is the subject of the next section. Suffice it to say that many universities, especially research universities, have grown substantially over the last decade, usually on the back of increased student numbers. Growth is a self-defining process. Large organisations tend to become more complex. They tend to have more stakeholders. They tend to add all kinds of new functions. They tend to require different means of management. Whether this makes them more business-like is a moot point, however. It depends on the solutions that they put in place. In universities, some of these have been gleaned from business, often through intermediaries like management consultants, but by no means all. And, most importantly, growth is not some kind of business panacea: indeed, it can serve to underline the by now overly familiar Warren Buffett aphorism 'when the tide goes out, you discover who's been swimming naked'.

Growth and more growth

Australia has a vibrant and important higher education sector. It has three main characteristics. The first is student number growth. Australian universities have increased their numbers of domestic students, in part because research income was (bizarrely) linked to number of students (though this has recently changed). As for overseas students, they have dramatically increased numbers – especially of Chinese students – as Australian universities have become a major export sector, the third after coal and iron ore. In many university systems around the world, international students have become the main answer to university funding gaps. Australia is at the extreme. International students average 25 per cent of the student body and can be as much as 40 per cent per cent at individual universities. Australian universities have walked to the end of the international student plank. Any downturn, even a minor one, in international student numbers is bound to result in financial problems. Even before the pandemic, a fall-off in Indian students produced quite severe problems for a short time. But the fear has always been that Chinese students might stop coming. That hasn't happened as yet to the prematurely gloomy extent forecasted as a result of geopolitics and Covid-19. But it would only take the Chinese government to move from suggesting that Chinese students should think twice about going to Australia as a part of their programme of sanctions against the country to actively stopping them from doing so for the financial base of Australian universities to come under severe pressure.

The second characteristic follows on. Size. The top eight Australian research universities have large or even very large student complements – four are above the 60,000 mark, one is above 50,000 and the other three hover around 25,000. Many of them are conglomerates with multiple campuses, extensive overseas operations, and very large numbers of disciplines and programmes. Size has some advantages, of course. It means more academics doing more research (though not as many as might be thought due to the extensive use of adjunct staff). But it can also make these universities unwieldy, lacking in focus and particularly exposed to government funding cutbacks.

The third characteristic follows. It is institutional similarity. Glyn Davis (2017) has written an important book about Australian higher education. In it he worries that Australian universities have all followed much the same model – the idea of a comprehensive metropolitan public university – with the upshot that they are now vulnerable to disruption.

To underline this point, Davis contrasts this model with the one found in the UK where there is more institutional diversity and so less need to be concerned that disruptive forces will sweep higher education institutions away. But is there more diversity in the UK? Really? It certainly used to be the case that British universities followed a number of quite different models. But that has been changing. There are still universities which continue to plough a different furrow, especially the smaller arts universities. Some interesting new universities are also being added to the roster. But my sense is that, so far as research universities are concerned at least, the majority are coming to resemble one another at quite some rate – just as has happened in Australia – as a result of the student numbers competition taking place between them. Right at a time when the government has argued that more diversity of approach is needed in the sector and has used sort of market forces to push this agenda, why might this be?

Two main reasons come to mind, both of which arise from an emphasis on institutional growth. The first of these is UK research universities reliance on overseas students. Like Australian universities, UK universities are now heavily dependent on these students for institutional income because it is income which actually makes a surplus. The financial projections for fees paid by international students in 2018/19 were equivalent to 15 per cent of total income. The proportion of income from overseas students has risen markedly with some research universities like Imperial (24 per cent), UCL (19.6 per cent) and King's (18.4 per cent) being particularly notable. Out of the 458,490 international students studying in UK higher education institutions, currently around 200,000 international students study at Russell Group universities.

Overseas students bring many benefits, not least, as we have seen, income to supplement research income, but they also bring undoubted risks, not least because universities become dependent on a relatively small number of countries for the bulk of these students (Johnson et al., 2022). The predominant overseas student nationality is Chinese. According to HESA, there were 104,240 first-year Chinese enrolments in UK universities in 2019/20. UCAS figures show that the number of Chinese students accepted on university courses increased by an extraordinary 22 per cent in 2019/20, in part the result of the deterioration in US–China relations and the consequent difficulty Chinese students had in securing US visas, and though applicant numbers dipped slightly in 2020/21 they increased again in 2022. All told, the Chinese embassy in the UK reckons that there were 216,000 undergraduate and postgraduate students studying in the UK in 2021, a 90 per cent increase from 2011/12 (Bolton, 2021b). Across the Russell Group, one in every ten students is now of Chinese origin, and they provide about a fifth of all tuition fee income, some £1.3 billion per year. Certain research universities – UCL, Manchester, Liverpool, Sheffield and Birmingham, among them – seem to have got perilously close to treating Chinese students as the goose that will continually lay the golden egg.

Universities are trying to diversify. For example, in 2020/21 the number of first-year students from India rose by 27 per cent to 53,000, with growing numbers thought to be attracted by government changes to post-study work visas. In all 84,555 Indian students are studying in the UK with applicant numbers increasing again in 2022. The number of Nigerian students tripled between 2019/20 and 2020/21 to 21,305 with applicant numbers also again increasing in 2022.[4] Part of the reason for these increases is no doubt the result of the pattern of Covid-19 travel restrictions in other countries but it is difficult to argue that international student demand is doing anything other than holding up at present.

There are other issues that cannot just be gainsaid either. Though the denials are loud and clear there is bound to be a temptation to squeeze UK students out of some institutions and courses since there is a clear imperative to take on higher paying international students. Again, some courses now contain more international than domestic students and this has led to pedagogic challenges in some cases. As has already been pointed out, international students are likely to continue to increase.

The second reason why growth is now emphasised is that the funding model universities are pursuing for domestic undergraduate students, based on tuition fees and a sort-of market, and on an unconstrained market in international students, is one that, rather like the Australian model on which it is partially based,[5] tends to force them towards homogeneity by producing a feedback loop that benefits more growth. It single-mindedly rewards increasing volume of students with more income (though, in the case of domestic students in research universities, very little in the way of margin and in many cases losses). As universities get more students, so they need more facilities and services to serve them, which means attracting more students to pay for the expansion of the facilities which, it is thought, make these universities more attractive to students. And so it goes on. Growth has its own dynamic.

As universities get bigger, they change. More and more people rely on them. It becomes more difficult to back out of the growth model and accordingly more difficult to take the risk of striking out on an unusual course. This growth dynamic is reinforced by classical follow-my-leader behaviour. Most vice-chancellors of research universities have seemed to want to go the same way so far as student numbers are concerned, partly out of fear that they will somehow be 'overtaken', and, to an extent, this affects strategy. I can remember one former vice-chancellor telling me that they just didn't want to be head of the smallest Russell Group university. It was as simple as that. So, through such cognitive shortcuts, we arrive at an age of supersizing. Research universities have been growing and growing and growing student numbers. Is this a sensible strategy or just a way of making every research university obese?

The net result is clear in any case. This is a time where the emphasis is on teaching rather than research. It can sometimes seem as though most of the important policy shots are being called by the Office for Students (aka the Department for Education) rather than UKRI in BEIS. Because of the influx of student funding, the proportion of income from research as opposed to teaching has declined in many research universities. Of course, research is still very important in research universities. It would be absurd to argue otherwise. But it has lost some of its sense of priority as their leaders' attention has increasingly focussed on students and teaching, with corresponding negative effects on the amount of time put by for research. The coronavirus pandemic only emphasised this shift with at least one research university temporarily changing the teaching time expected from some of its academic staff to include a greater proportion of time spent on teaching, and cancelling research leave.

It should be said straightaway that there are some good reasons for the emphasis on student growth in many research universities. Supplying more and more people with an excellent university education at home and overseas is an unalloyed good, surely? And there is the access point too, of course. Elite universities are being opened up to a wider range of students as they search for more numbers. In particular, more students from disadvantaged backgrounds are going to get an excellent education. That's good too, surely? More and better facilities for students. More and larger departments and more academics. More ability to borrow. More ability to subsidise research. More research, even as more staff are appointed. More ability to do lots of things. In other words, growing student numbers undoubtedly has some immediately attractive effects for research universities but I am less sure that they make much sense in the longer term, even as a student offer.

The undergraduate student warehousing model carries quite a few risks, some of them problematic. In particular, competition means that some research universities risk losing their elite student body status. It becomes more difficult to claim to be attracting elite students when, for example, an average A level offer is declining. Absent the fortunate few who can simply take their pick of the excellent students, some British research universities have had to take students with lower A level scores as they grow, while praying that other research universities are taking students with even lower tariffs so that they still look good relatively. After all, only around 12.9 per cent of students aged 16 to 18 achieved old-style three As or A★ at A level. (Pre-coronavirus, I was seeing research universities in clearing that I never expected to see there at all. Some had become involved in unconditional offers and conditional unconditional offers, and the like, often driven to these measures by other competitor institutions that had started using these distinctly iffy practices.)

There are student welfare and pedagogic risks too. Greater scale means that an institution almost inevitably becomes more impersonal and its student services more distant and more likely to have holes in them, as a review found in the case of a student at Edinburgh University who committed suicide: 'staff and systems were under-resourced and struggling to cope with an increase in overall student numbers, in particular numbers suffering from and disclosing mental health issues' (Weale and Baldwin, 2021). Students find it difficult to relate to larger and larger communities, increasing stresses and strains. Then, class sizes often become larger and larger, facilities like lecture theatres and teaching laboratories become over-stretched and there are more adjuncts. It is hard to believe that in the 1960s the ratio of staff to students hovered around 1:7.8 to 1:7.9,[6] down from 1:10 between the wars (Halsey, 1971)! Now (on figures which are admittedly suspect, complex, and open to wide interpretation (Finn, 2022)) it's still 1:10 or 11 for the top universities like Oxford and Cambridge but, as I have already pointed out, most research universities are at 1:13, 14 or 15 (and probably even higher since student number data doesn't include certain kinds of student). Admittedly these figures have held constant for a while now (mainly thanks to an injection of teaching-only staff which has concealed the increasing loads put on those on research and teaching contracts in some research universities) but I doubt that it is possible to reproduce teaching at this kind of scale which can give undergraduate students the face-to-face experience that they used to get. No one has to argue that this was a perfect set-up to see that something is being lost as research universities follow much the same teaching path as other universities (and, as a result, become vulnerable to the gradual spread of electronic pedagogy which will make it even harder to differentiate themselves). At the same time, faculty research time is attenuated as the load of marking and examining grows. Essay and project marking in the large, answering numerous emails and management queries, administering courses, multiple committee meetings … the list goes on. Commentators will rightly say that this is just like many other parts of the economy, so stop moaning. But the difficulty is that teaching is only one part of the job.

I should lay my cards on the table at this point. I don't know what an ideal size for a university is. After all, it's worth remembering that at one time in the 1950s it was thought that the 'natural size' for a university was about 3,000 (Laslett, 1967). But my sense is that somewhere above the low to mid 20,000s – the same size as Oxford and Cambridge – students start to become the majority preoccupation of a research university. Of course, there are successful research universities which have far larger numbers of students (Sydney, Melbourne, NYU, ASU, Ohio State) but usually they have all kinds of ways that they mitigate the effects of scale from honours classes to large, almost independent schools which act as universities within universities. But what we are getting now in the UK is often something much closer to student depositories and many research universities have become more alike as a consequence. Would you want to be a student holed up in a university with 50,000 or so of your compatriots, going to classes that might number in the hundreds, in some cases commuting in from far away because accommodation is at a premium, inevitably knowing only a scattering of your compatriots? Well, many clearly do. But, if I'm frank, I think you would probably be better off looking for a smaller university (not least because a sense of belonging has been identified as one of the keys to good student mental health and that sense is much harder to build in larger universities). Take just the case of the University of Bristol, one of the very best research universities. In 2012/13 Bristol had the equivalent of 18,000 full-time students on undergraduate and postgraduate courses. By 2018/19 it had 25,957, and by 2020/21 29,356. It intended to keep on growing, adding a new site that will house some 3,000 more students, partly through borrowing. It is still one of the hardest universities to get into. But this kind of growth threatens that status. Unsurprisingly, class sizes have increased. There has been a lack of study and accommodation spaces. It is getting hard to argue that, as it says in the university's marketing, 'Bristol is small enough to feel warm and friendly'. This is an experience that has been repeated many times elsewhere among Russell Group universities with UCAS figures for the admittedly unusual year of 2020[7] showing pretty well every Russell Group university pre the Covid-19 boom taking on more undergraduates between 2019 and 2020, in some cases very considerably more (for example, UCL showed a climb of 3,030, Manchester 2,215, Exeter 1,285, Sheffield 1,270 and King's 1,130).

Equally, universities become more impersonal for staff too. Who really wants to be part of a giant impersonal combine? Again, it is not at all clear that better research automatically arises from the scale now on offer – sometimes it is better to concentrate on just a few things done exceptionally well. Then it may be that quality staff will become increasingly hard to find. Not surprisingly, one of the first questions most high-grade research and teaching staff ask around the world when they are offered a job is 'what is the teaching load?' Added to this, scale has, in some instances, simply expanded the ranks of temporary and adjunct staff whose allegiance and commitment is bound to be conflicted by the search for a permanent position.

Then, there is the obvious point that I have already foreshadowed that a number of UK universities seem to have been, in effect, chasing turnover over margin or, in order to make a surplus, allowing investment on students to lag just behind income – or just hoping that they can make it to the next year, for all the talk of strategy. None of these are immensely attractive options. The immediate bottom line may look good but this is not a viable financial model over the long term and it also carries considerable risks, not least from domestic student demographics (though these are now looking favourable again), from general vulnerability to a slump in overseas student numbers, and from technological disruption. The point about margin versus turnover is an obvious one, number one in every beginner's business textbook as that old saw 'revenues are vanity, profit is sanity' or, in another form, as 'no margin, no mission'. It was always drummed into me never to confuse the two. But something else was drummed into me too: a lesson from retail. Ultimately, it is the relationship between gross margin and inventory turnover rate that is important. As margin declines, the rate of sales must increase to maintain a constant level of gross profit. If a store can sell inventory faster without decreasing margins, then there is more gross profit available to pay expenses and make a profit. If it can't, this is a downhill path. I suspect that this is what is happening in a number of universities and it doesn't end well.

Further, so far as domestic students are concerned, a funding model based on growth is massively exposed to government priorities. Indeed, the unit of resource has fallen in real terms since 2015 putting pressure on many university budgets. The government has now decided to freeze the tuition fee at £9,250 until the end of the current parliament. But inflation has already inexorably reduced the real value of the fee. According to Hudson and Mansfield (2020), the 2012 university tuition fee of £9,000 per student was worth £7,855 in real terms in 2020. After inflation, and taking into account the small rise to £9,250 in 2017, it would be worth only £7,100 in 2025 and probably less given where inflation is currently heading. According to the latest Russell Group figures submitted to a consultation on higher education funding, the situation could well be worse than this. The average shortfall per student is now £1,750 more than is received in tuition fees and teaching grants with the deficit per student widening to as much as £4,000 by the end of the freeze.

One more risk. Why bother with going to university if you end up in something that increasingly looks like fee-paying mass education which could be done more cheaply at a distance without losing benefits which look increasingly nebulous? You can go online. Or you can turn to the Australian model. In Australian universities, most domestic undergraduate students live at home. Perhaps this is a solution the university sector needs to explore further, even though it will threaten many interests (from real estate to ancillary services) and cause problems for some universities which are a long way from large population clusters. Or you can go overseas. UK research universities live in a globalised world in which students are by no means constrained to the UK for their higher education choices. They can look abroad if they so wish. Although the numbers are still small, they are growing. Thus, in 2019/20, according to the Fulbright Commission, 10,765 British students were studying in the US, many of them with substantial scholarships (which they may well need, given the fees at US Ivy League universities[8]). In other words, students who either have better-off parents or have access to scholarships (or both) can choose to exit from the UK higher education system as a viable strategy in a way that would have been all but impossible in the past and more will no doubt do so, especially given that state school intake has risen from 55.4 per cent to 68.7 per cent at Oxford and from 62.3 per cent to 70 per cent at Cambridge between 2015 and 2020 (Griffiths, 2021).

The only salve envisaged by some universities seems to be the prospect of yet more student number growth on the horizon, so the issue of growth will not go away. Indeed, there may be more demand, and not just from the short-term domestic undergraduate boost prompted by the pandemic and favourable demography. Take just the case of domestic students in the UK. In 2022 there were nearly 67.9 million people. By 2035, according to the latest available estimates, there will be 72.4 million with nearly all of the growth taking place in England in larger cities. That is a large relative increase arising from a combination of immigration and a boom in births which, after a downturn in numbers, is now beginning to make its impact felt on universities. According to Bekhradnia and Beech's (2019) calculations, by 2030 the UK could see an additional 50,000 undergraduate students entering higher education because of the demographic bulge arising from the fact that the number of 18-year-olds in England is set to rise by 23 per cent by 2030. Higher participation rates minus a Brexit effect could mean that an extra 300,000 students will enter higher education by 2030. So right away we can see a much stronger demand for higher education forthcoming in England, even taking into account the fact that there will likely be another demographic dip after 2030 (Bennett, 2021) though this dip discounts the prospect of any further rise in the participation rate and the prospect of even more international students.[9] Indeed, looking further ahead again, the situation may become even more pressing. By one estimate, the UK population could be over 75 million by 2065. Population is growing rapidly in some other parts of the world too, and especially in Africa and India. That could mean even more growth in international students than I have already noted is forecasted. In other words, after the coronavirus boom, the temptations of growth will likely continue.

More generally, there are two strategic points that need to be made. To begin with, the UK has to face up to the fact that it has too many research universities which are finding it difficult to remain internationally competitive in the current situation because they operate at too small a scale research- rather than student-wise. Research scale really does mean something. There are remarkably few universities in the Times Higher world top 100 with a turnover of less than £1 billion. But, and this is the second (and crucial) point, there is growth and there is growth. *The best research universities have grown this large on the back of their research income, not student income.* Indeed, many of the top universities in the world would count as quite small in student number terms – of the top 12 universities in the world, none has more than 22,000 students and two have fewer than 10,000 – but they have what are often massive research incomes. Growing student numbers is, at least in some cases, likely to be an admission of research defeat. Indeed, as Table 4.1 shows, some large by turnover Russell Group universities have quite small research incomes comparatively speaking.

Of course, it is often argued that for most UK research universities only through a boost in student numbers is it possible to pay for all of the research that they are undertaking. You need 'critical mass', especially to do cross-disciplinary research. It's a valid argument. The number of staff will increase as students are added and with it – if they're good – 'research power'. But, as I've already pointed out, there are also arguments to be put against the proposition. For a start, quantity doesn't necessarily mean quality. Plenty of universities with relatively small student numbers have enormous research enterprises. Then, the larger an organisation is in student terms, the more difficult it is to keep it focussed on research. Further consequences surface from a push for growth arising out of the involvement of other stakeholders who have their own imperatives. It is worth examining these separately.

The consequences of the growth machine

For research universities, what market nationalisation has unleashed, as indeed it was meant to, is a modest increase in domestic undergraduate student numbers which has been coupled with a boom in international student numbers. As I have pointed out, one consequence of this two-handed growth is that student concerns have become uppermost in the minds of universities, including many research universities. There are simply more students, and they are paying. But research universities used to have two missions – to do the very best research they can and to act as places of learning. When these missions get out of joint, morale plummets. And in many research universities, that is what has happened or is in danger of happening. To recover morale requires many things but, in particular, it requires restoring a sense of pride to the academic enterprise as an academic enterprise.

For many research universities, growth has therefore proved a problematic harvest. Yes, they have become more prominent actors. But growth also means all manner of other actors have taken an interest in them. Four actors come to mind. To begin with, there is government. Government was bound to take a greater interest in research universities, of course. Who can blame them? Universities are becoming economic and cultural battleships and ministers and civil servants want a degree of control over the fleet, whatever they say about valuing university autonomy. Given the amount of taxpayers' money now tied up in universities it was hardly going to be otherwise. And precisely because universities now span so many activities, it can sometimes seem as though practically everyone in or around government now has a view on them. (Even the former deputy governor of the Bank of England had a go with an untypically stereotypical example of the 'I know what we should do about universities' genre (Haldane, 2018).) But it's not just government.

There is a second actor that has jumped on stage: a large wodge of the private sector has become involved in growth. Of course, the private sector has been involved in the activities of universities for many decades now but growth has given their involvement a turbo boost. A few examples will suffice to make the case. To begin with, the university construction boom has attracted all manner of construction companies. Universities are now a major construction market. Volume has doubled in real terms since 2012, as universities have invested in new facilities to tempt and retain increasingly footloose students. If associated residential development is taken into account as well, the universities construction market was worth £6bn in 2018 (Rawlinson, 2019). Universities may have reached 'peak campus' in the sense that, after they've built the student study centre, the new library, the new sports centre and the extra lecture spaces, there's only so much left to do, though decarbonisation work may offset some of the decline. Private educational companies like Laureate and Pearson have gone into alliance with some universities. For example, King's College, London runs online Master's courses with Pearson and in three years of recruitment has reached 5,000 students. Companies like Springer (through Springer Nature), Wiley, Sage and Elsevier have substantial interests in journal publishing, publishing just over 3,000, 2,786 and about 2,500 journals respectively (Herb, 2019). They have often reached agreements with learned societies to run what were formerly in-house journals. Each of these companies is mutating into something more like data management corporations. Elsevier, for example, has an impact database, Scopus, an institutional benchmarking arm, using its data and research information systems like PURE, reference management tools like Mendeley, and social networking and news coverage. It is moving rapidly into open access, especially through SSRN, and is intent on also capturing audio files, blogs, software, datasets, expert opinions, and so on through Altmetrics. Elsevier is aiming for a presence in every academic and institutional transaction as a ubiquitous operating system which can provide information and metrics on almost any aspect of academic life (Herb, 2019). In other words, the publication, curation, and evaluation of science is no longer solely in university hands. Headhunters have massively expanded their university operations, often setting up specialised higher education practices, with the result that job hiring for senior management posts and many senior academic positions, and increasingly for more junior positions too, is no longer entirely in university hands either. Consultants, often with their own higher education practices, are routinely used by universities with the result that university management decisions are often intertwined with advice from consultants. The result? Even university management is no longer solely in university hands. Workforce training companies have sprung up that train segments of the university workforces like administrators. Student education agents have expanded, helping to recruit more and more overseas undergraduate and postgraduate students. Currently, worldwide there are 354 of them on the British Council list. Specialist higher education policy think tanks like the excellent HEPI and more generalist think tanks like IPPR or Policy Exchange, as well as a kaleidoscopic mix of other 'thought leaders' have all had their say on universities too. Opinion and news operations like Times Higher and important policy outfits like WonkHE and Research Fortnight also flourish. This myriad of operations are all praiseworthy but they are also symptomatic.

By itself, the presence of all these different partners in growth need not be a cause for concern. They can and do add weight to the sector in a number of cases. But what is a cause for concern is that some of their operations are pulling universities into making decisions based as much on their imperatives as those of universities. For example, the growth in students has led to the flourishing of private student accommodation. It is a peculiar characteristic of the British system that four out of five students live away from home and rent is a large part of each student's finances. Some raw figures (Jones and Blakey, 2021): there are now some 627,000 student beds in the UK overall conforming to the so-called national codes of which 52 per cent are to be found in university-provided accommodation and 48 per cent in private sector purpose-built student accommodation. (Another 32,491 more private sector purpose-built accommodation beds came online in 2019/20.) Then there are around 551,000 students living in houses of multiple accommodation (HMOs). This means that in all about 1.2 million students are renting housing (and that consequently 28 per cent live in university-provided accommodation, 27 per cent in private sector purpose-built accommodation; and 45 per cent in HMOs.) In other words, student housing is now preponderantly supplied by the private sector and increasingly functions as an asset class in its own right. Of course, many private landlords have cashed in on the student expansion and especially the revenue opportunities provided by buy-to-let and HMOs. But what is more noticeable has been the presence of other, larger players and especially property development companies like UPP (University Partnerships Programme), CRM Students, Unite, Blackstone (IQ Student Accommodation) and APG (Scape Living)[10] and, more recently, owners of larger HMOs, all attracted by a reliable income stream and average annual rents of £6,777 (compared with university rents of £5,864). There are numerous attractions for property developers in building student accommodation, not least that the planning system does not oblige them to contribute to affordable housing, as they must with other types of development, as a result of which the education-themed real estate sector, as it is called, is now worth an estimated £50 billion.

The result is that an increasing proportion of student accommodation is now concentrated into the hands of relatively few private property companies. Take the example of Unite, founded in Bristol in 1991 and now the UK's largest student accommodation provider, having recently bought Liberty Living for £1.4 billion. The combined group boasts 75,000 beds (with 5,000 more in the pipeline) in 173 buildings across 27 UK towns and cities and a portfolio valuation of £5.2 billion. It operates all its properties and either rents rooms directly to students or to about 60 universities. Unite has been selling properties in cities such as Plymouth and Huddersfield, where there are lower-ranked universities and a glut of properties, and concentrating on high and mid-ranked universities, many of which are still increasing their numbers at between 2 and 5 per cent a year. Meanwhile, in a sign of the times, one of the world's largest real estate investors, the private equity firm Blackstone, has re-entered the market. It has bought the third largest student housing group iQ from Goldman Sachs. iQ owns and operates 67 student housing blocks comprising more than 28,000 beds in 27 UK cities, mainly cities which contain Russell Group universities and, of course, London.

Another student housing development is the continuing rise of large HMOs for the student market. They can offer up large accommodation blocks to potential investors, many of them from overseas, which provide a novel investment opportunity with higher-than-average returns.[11] Often what is on offer are individual units with as long as 250-year leases, yet another sign of a not-so-nascent student housing asset class:

> Developers hunt for an alternative source of financing to the banks, and retail investors hunt for high returns on their savings. Demand from parents for 'safety', 'luxury' and campus proximity *facilitates* that demand, and permitted development routes (which allow for swift conversion of offices into student accommodation of the cheapest type – 20m² studios rather than the 37m² flats you'd have to build if it was "proper" housing) *smooths* it. Even if a council has thought about this in their local plan, the regs mean they can't stop it. (Dickinson, 2019)

I leave it to the reader to judge whether these new property actors are symbiotes or parasites. Some are, some aren't. But the fact is that they are now an integral part of a university sector fabric in which 'we've ended up in a situation where people believe that it's their god-given right to use the student maintenance system as a way to make vast profits, even during a pandemic' (Dickinson, 2021, p. 3). It is not possible to throw the money changers out of the temple. Yet their growth has produced substantial issues of student equity:

> well-off students are hived away in gated, low risk high profit blocks with careers services and extra counsellors. In fact, in plenty we've seen, the rent rises as you go up the building – students pay more simply for being at a higher altitude ... Those from families on middle incomes struggle away in dangerous HMO properties and "investment opportunity" blocks that offer the illusion of luxury to them and their parents but offer nothing of the sort. Meanwhile, if they can find a course locally, poorer students commute in and end up with worse outcomes than everyone else. (Dickinson, 2019, p. 3)

A third actor has a vested interest in growth too. Cities have increasingly come to rely on universities as ways of regenerating their fabric and economy Student and ancillary university spending now fuels a substantial part of many urban economies. All manner of jobs are supported by the university itself – universities and hospitals are often the largest employers in a city – and by its supply chain. A while back, universities ritually produced reports on how many jobs and how much spending was being generated by their presence. Now the case is proved.

Then, there is one final actor to contend with: many of those employed in research universities themselves. The number includes all of those PhDs now being produced in universities – 24,850 in 2017/18, up by something like 20 per cent in ten years – who need to end up somewhere. Many of them want a UK academic position, and the expansion of the sector has given more of them that opportunity, even though the expansion has often been in teaching-only posts and term-limited research contract positions. Any shrinkage will hit them first. They are invested in growth even if they don't know it, especially because, to an extent at least, growth has brought with it not only more jobs but more academic job mobility and more promotion opportunities – there are simply more options available. The same stricture applies to the cadre of administrators, simply through the fact that more jobs and job opportunities become available through new locations in the division of labour. Many people have been attracted into the cadre from outside it (and they bring new business practices with them).

I could go on but hopefully the point is made. The growth of the sector has produced numerous stakeholders, most of whom have a vested interest in – growth, growth and more growth.

The problem of leadership

Leadership of universities is always going to be an issue. Universities are large, diverse organisations which have many different missions and goals. Their leaders do not always agree. Even research universities can have different priorities. The 2018 strike is a case in point. To the despair of some of their colleagues, a small number of Russell Group vice-chancellors visited the picket lines and talked about alternative solutions. However sympathetic and well-intentioned, such actions were bound to be interpreted as employer weakness and they did not go down well with colleagues who had kept to the party line and were the butt of some pretty unpleasant stuff as a result. They left a lingering legacy of distrust in the Russell Group for quite some time.

This might be regarded as simply a local spat but it is illustrative of wider concerns about coherent research university leadership. Sitting somewhere near the top of the pile is the fact that British research universities often have very little idea about what they want (more money aside). Their leadership spends a good deal of their time gaming government proposals to seek various kinds of short-term advantage. Tactics not strategy. Then, add into the mix the fact that government (in whichever jurisdiction) does not see universities as a big problem in the first place. Add to that the empirical fact – at least on recent evidence – that the more government tells universities what to do, the more government feels inclined to tell them what to do. It's not a happy picture, any way you look at it.

There are three issues here. To begin with, there is the organisational leadership of the sector as a whole. This is split between Universities UK (an institution originally founded in 1918) and a series of other inter-organisational entities representing various 'mission groups'. Universities UK is now such a broad church that it is in danger of losing its faith. It represents very different kinds of institutions, many of which have little in common with each other except for finessing government policy in their favour. It is no longer fit for purpose, 'hopelessly ill-equipped to deal with the world of 2019' (Seldon, 2019, p. 3).

The organisation that represents many of the research universities is the Russell Group, founded in 1994. But Russell Group universities have always been members of UUK as well. Both UUK and the Russell Group represent the sector to government and other stakeholders. There are tensions between the two groups and these have tended to become more apparent as the UUK membership has got steadily larger and more diverse. Making a convincing case for joint action becomes more and more difficult (though at moments of crisis – where its members all share the same urgent problems – it is generally agreed that it does a good job. Covid-19 is an obvious example).

The Russell Group, meanwhile, is pinioned to the sector. Members will often talk gravely about their responsibilities to the whole sector – as though it needs their protection – but it might just as well be said that the Russell Group now needs protection from the rest of the sector. (Equally, the other members of the Russell Group are pinioned to Oxford and Cambridge. They well know that if Oxford and Cambridge left the group it would be a serious reputational problem.) The Russell Group should be more effective but too often it seems captured by its fear of being left on the outside by government (no more cups of tea with ministers) and by a lack of cohesion on strategy and indeed what would count as a strategy in the first place. A simple first step might be for Russell Group members to become solely members of the Russell Group and leave UUK. Taken by itself, though, this is not a solution. The Russell Group needs buttressing so that it has real force. It needs to mutate from a membership organisation to a leadership organisation which has real structure, a shared outlook about the future of research universities, and serious means of delivering that future through mechanisms dedicated to the purpose. At the moment, its institutional structure is still that of a membership association. It needs to become more than that. Equally, whomsoever leads the Russell Group needs to be a full-time CEO, not one of the member universities' vice-chancellors, someone who has had real powers ceded to them to lead, someone with genuine strategic foresight – which means that the Russell Group actually sets out to go somewhere according to a real strategy – and someone who owns the kind of public presence and gravitas that comes from a long history of fighting the good fight. Above all, someone needs to start forcefully saying 'no' to government and start fighting for a future for research universities which is more than the sum of reactions to individual policy initiatives.

Then there is individual leadership of research universities. Vice-chancellors are hampered by the fact that their primary allegiance is to their institution and as competition between institutions becomes more intense so it becomes more difficult to get agreement between them. In my experience, the Russell Group spent most of its time concerned with what government and government agencies were doing and finessing whatever the latest initiatives were. It did very little in the way of strategic thinking and what strategic thinking it did do was often less fulsome than might be expected from an organisation of leading universities full of imaginative and informed staff and a set of vice-chancellors who individually had a massive amount to offer. Some business was effectively parked under 'too awkward' because it would be likely to offend one or other institution. As a result, quite often the only coherent point of view was the lowest common denominator. The Russell Group knew what the government wanted. But it wasn't clear what the Russell Group wanted (except more money, of course). Worst of all, the government knew this. It wasn't afeared.

Having such a dependent relationship with government meant that a series of quasi-capitulations followed. For example, the Teaching Excellence Framework – widely regarded as damaging by many research universities because it ignored precisely the things that mattered in their teaching and, in particular, the actual content of courses and the quality of the actual teaching itself. They could have boycotted it or run their own parallel exercise based on actual teaching quality – that's right, observing teaching and considering the actual content of courses, a solution which was briefly on offer in the HEFCE years but neither of which the TEF does.[12] Instead they gradually succumbed and soon, inevitably, some of them were boasting that they'd won a gold star. So, give in. Then the Office for Students – widely regarded as a direct threat to autonomy by research universities, not least because it is gradually extending its jurisdiction into the postgraduate sphere. Some letters sent behind the scenes. But, given the scale of the threat to autonomy, in effect, this is a give in too.

Now, the situation is dangerously close to a point of no return. Those letters to the government or the OfS expressing concerns about threats to autonomy are too late. University leaders have ceded the power to say 'no' which might at least have given them some respect in Whitehall. On just about every issue which involves government intrusion, with governments of whatever political stripe, they have ultimately gone with the flow. The reasons are numerous but they boil down to an inability to take any serious collective action on matters of principle as opposed to immediate pragmatics. The occasions on which research universities say a resounding 'you've got to be kidding' to government have been exceptionally rare. Not surprisingly, the result is that government regards the sector as a bit of a soft touch. Having been able to impose its will so often, the government has gotten into the habit of doing so without much in the way of let or hindrance. The irony is that, as universities have become more and more important actors on the national stage, they have actually gained quite a lot of power, if only they knew it.

The fight is not lost. Of course not. But lack of concerted inter-institutional leadership means that the threat to the sector has moved from moderate to severe. We need figures who don't just fight back but galvanise the debate. But, with a few exceptions, vice-chancellors have not led the public debate. Anthony Seldon, one of the vice-chancellors who was game enough to take on this role, has made this point over and over again – and he is surely right. Being in the public eye is not always enjoyable, to put it but mildly, not least because reporting inaccuracies and personal attacks are too often a part of the package. But it is the only way to fight for universities. 'I'll just have a word with ...' hasn't worked. No one is suggesting that every vice-chancellor needs to become a contemporary version of Miguel de Unamuno, the famous rector of the University of Salamanca who, in the 1920s and 1930s, stood up for liberalism against all-comers, left or right. But a bit more pluck might come in handy at this juncture:

> how many Vice-Chancellors have taken part in BBC Question Time, Any Questions? or any mainstream national news panel programme where broad views are required? Broadcast producers are desperate for senior figures who are above the political party fray. ... Of course, these appearances are challenging and carry risk. They require lengthy preparation. But they are a platform to raise the profile of the sector. (Bennett, 2021, p. 25)

Finally, consider the fact that the sector has scored some gaping own goals which have only bolstered government intervention. Look at some of the issues of the last few years that the sector should have been able to sort by itself but didn't, as a result giving the government the space to step in: degree inflation, conditional offers, degree classification, transferable credits, the admissions timetable, even though it's much exaggerated, no-platforming. Each of these issues has been a running sore for a number of years but no one has cleaned house. Everyone knew that the rising number of first-class degrees was untenable and was based as much on pressure to keep up with other institutions so as not to be left behind in the league tables as it was on any increase in quality. How could anyone defend the number of firsts awarded increasing from just 7 per cent in 1994/95 to 15.7 per cent of degrees in 2010/11 to 37.9 per cent in 2020/21? (In total, 84.4 per cent achieved a first or 2.1 in 2020/21 compared with 67 per cent ten years ago.) Many research universities participated in this absurd bonfire.[13] Yet nothing was done to usher in a grade point average scheme or some other solution. Instead the action now finally taking place to moderate firsts depended on government prodding. Or what about the rise of conditional and then unconditional conditional offers? Introduced in 2012, by 2018/19 the situation had reached absurd levels with 37.7 per cent of applicants having received unconditional offers, a situation amplified by the rise of the unconditional conditional offer wherein a university – quite extraordinarily – guarantees a student a place regardless of A-level results but only on the condition that they put the institution as their first option. In 2018 57 per cent of those holding an unconditional offer dropped three or more grades at A level. In 2018 18-year-olds were more than 30 times more likely to receive at least one offer with an unconditional component than 18-year-olds in 2013 (OfS, 2019) and these trends continued until these offers were quite rightly banned for the 2022 entry. After all, unconditional and unconditional conditional offers could be interpreted as a direct attack on the schooling system by universities, even by Russell Group research universities which had participated in a body which was meant to help improve A levels. Many other issues that needed joint attention received it after the horse had bolted and often in such a way that it looked to the public as though the sector was dragging its feet even though individual institutions were often doing exceptionally good work.

The upshot of all this is clear, in any case. Government has been given almost free rein to step in. And who can blame them, given the issues that have lain on the table either unresolved or avoided? In turn, as government extends its grip, universities are being turned into schools. They are being put in their place. With each step, government gets closer to making degrees into just the next qualification on the ladder of education, one step closer to that job you always wanted, on a course in which you'll get a readout on what salary you should be able to expect. Nothing wrong with that, you may say. And it gets one step closer to putting universities literally in their place, as civic institutions serving their local community. Nothing wrong with that, you may also say. But it leaves research universities in an uncomfortable position if that's the case. As Robbins pointed out, they were never ever meant to be simply extensions to the school system: the next step on. Their education was meant to be a part of something more. There is an ugly word for this whole process – 'schoolification'. But research universities aren't schools. To make them into schools is to defeat their purpose. They were never ever meant to be simply civic universities either, serving their local community (though that can be an important function), unless, that is, you count their community as the whole world.

And as for research, that was about 'curiosity' and gaining access to thinking that will allow us to discover that world anew, day after day, year after year. These kinds of words and phrases sound bloated and slightly pompous now, loaded down with freight from a bygone age, but I can't help feeling that the best part of the impulse underlying them still stands examination, however frayed it may be by time and circumstance. Indeed as the Anthropocene bites back, they take on renewed meaning.

A number of vice-chancellors were and are deeply concerned about what is happening but they are now trapped like flies in amber. As student numbers have grown, as the university system becomes just another step in the school system, it will be difficult to beat a retreat from a government and bureaucracy that doesn't really understand what all the fuss is about and anyway is prone to seeing universities as a hotbed of the anti-Brexity, the leaning to the left, the over-the-top politically correct and, in general, as the defenders of a 'liberal elite'. The sector

> has allowed itself all too often to be positioned negatively in public debate and in the media. It risks being seen as protecting and perpetuating the interests of an educated metropolitan elite, when in fact the sector is much more diverse and at its best reflects the whole of the nation and the wider interests of the local communities that it serves. But the value that the sector offers is not cutting through. (Hudson and Mansfield, 2020, p. 40)

Life could get tougher still. Government argues, not entirely unfairly it has to be said, that universities largely escaped the austerity regime of the 2010s so a few cuts to tuition fees are neither here nor there. They will also argue, again not entirely unfairly, that, in any case, a research funding bonanza is coming their way. (However, the danger is that most of this bonanza will be funnelled to applied research that supports innovation that, in turn, supports particular economic clusters around the country: consequently, discovery research will be given its due but probably only a small one.) And they will argue, once again not entirely unfairly, that too much emphasis has been placed on universities to the detriment of technical and vocational education.

A coming financial crisis?

One more issue, already foreshadowed. British research universities' financial model makes less and less sense. It relies mainly on the fees from overseas, and specifically Chinese students, to make up shortfalls, not only in research but also increasingly in teaching domestic students. If Chinese students stop coming in large numbers or even plateau, financial problems will arise, not least, as I've already pointed out, because the fees of Chinese and other overseas students must bail out the shortfall in overheads on research. But, as the domestic tuition fee gradually diminishes in value, they must subsidise domestic students too. Indeed, by one estimate, publicly-funded teaching is already in deficit to the tune of half a billion pounds. In 2021, not only at Oxford and Cambridge but also at UCL (Adams, 2021), there was no course where the domestic undergraduate tuition fee covered the cost of providing the course and many other research universities have now joined this list. (Indeed, as if to underline the point, an enquiry by the Russell Group (2020) into the OfS data for higher education institutions in England generally showed that laboratory-based subjects like chemistry, physics and engineering faced average deficits of £1,848 per student per year in 2019/20. The deficits for medical and dental provision were higher still, as much as £2,094 per student. Even classroom-based courses like those in the social sciences and humanities were operating at a loss of some £974 per student. The latest figures show a further decline which is resulting in a number of Russell Group universities putting a ceiling on the number of domestic students they will take, simply because they can't afford to take more, at a time when these numbers are rising. This is hardly surprising. So far as teaching is concerned, a university's teaching income model can be stretched by adding more students at a lower margin (producing larger classes and lots more marking, no doubt to the joy of the academics concerned). It can be stretched by increasingly asking postgraduate students and contract researchers to take up the teaching strain by acting as adjuncts. And it can be stretched a little further by pursuing more online and blended learning. But each of these strategies has limits. Margins can only be cut so far. Casualising the teaching workforce has limits (and can be deemed unethical). Space to teach more students is limited. Adding a lot more online learning – which done well isn't low cost anyway – runs the risk of encroaching on the preserve of non-research universities, some of whom do it just as well, and, anyway, more face-to-face teaching has been one of the factors that has given research universities an edge.

Research costs are also rising as inflation bites and, combined with the fact that overseas student fees now have to subsidise a broader range of activity, they are likely to lead to research universities having to think seriously about how much research they can really afford to do. In a sign of the times. one Scottish research university has already decided not to target further growth in research.

Then there are all of the other rising costs – pensions, of course, but also the loans that need paying off, the financing of yet more buildings that are in the pipeline or planned and which are costing more and more to build because of inflation and the need to somehow afford a wider range of student services. The list goes on.

Lastly, as the cost of construction indicates, there is also above-average cost inflation to cope with which is not only hitting costs but also income. This could be very serious. For example, Corver (2021) calculates that if inflation were to rise to 1970s levels then the £9,250 fee for a full-time undergraduate in England would decline in value to 'around £2,000, less than a quarter of 2012 resource' by the end of the 2020s. That would mean teaching four students with the money universities had for one in 2012. Something's got to give.

Indeed, there are signs that for some universities it already is. Though, pre-coronavirus, some research universities like Oxford, Cambridge, Imperial, UCL and Warwick reported good surpluses in their 2017/18 accounts, others reported large deficits, not least because of the impact of a recovery plan for the Universities Superannuation Scheme (USS). According to the Higher Education Statistics Agency, 42 out of 165 higher education providers had an operational deficit, including significant deficits at research universities like Cardiff and Reading. Again, 64 out of 247 higher education providers forecast that at the end of 2020/21 their cash balance would likely fall below 30 days of net liquidity at some point over the next two years and 10 institutions have already been placed under 'enhanced financial monitoring' by the Office for Students (with a further 13 providers being 'engaged with') while the proportion of providers with an in-year deficit, after adjusting for pension deficits, increased from 5 per cent in 2015/16 to 32 per cent in 2019/20 (National Audit Office, 2022, see also Committee of Public Accounts, 2022).

Things could all unravel quite quickly for some research universities as all kinds of chickens start to come home to roost. For example, should UKRI be providing research grants to a university which it knows to be in a problematic financial situation? In a normal milieu, questions would be asked of the UKRI Board about whether this was intelligent contracting yet alone a good use of public money. Again, can UKRI be sure that QR is always being spent in line with its purposes and not being used to prop up the general budget of universities in stretched financial circumstances?

It's not as if all of this hasn't been foreseen. For example, each year, the loss of the Chinese student market comes top on many risk registers. The mitigation is usually to 'diversify' But year after year very little of major significance actually seems to happen. Now all kinds of other risks are surfacing.

It's a bit frightening.

7

On vice-chancelloring – a footnote

So does one cope with all of the changes and leadership challenges I have outlined in previous chapters? One of the key university leaders is the vice-chancellor. In previous chapters, I have sometimes been critical of the stances taken by university leadership. However, that does not mean that I think that being a vice-chancellor/university president is an easy job and that they're all a load of wasters. It isn't and they aren't. Leadership of a university is just as trying as it always was but with added zest resulting from the intermixture of so many different, and sometimes conflicting, priorities: universities now serve many constituencies. As I have already pointed out, universities have taken on more and more functions and are in danger of becoming all things and none. But the fact is that they have to be made to run as if they are a single entity. So the vice-chancellor must wear more and more hats and expect to switch rapidly from one to another – and expect more and more criticism, or so it can sometimes seem.

Indeed, on a bad day, it can sometimes feel as though no one likes vice-chancellors. They can be the subject of all kinds of righteous wrath. Their academic staff think that they have sold out to Mammon, trying to run universities like businesses, and, moreover, trying to ape business-style salaries. The more radical students are sure – rock solid sure – that they run 'neoliberal' or 'entrepreneurial' organisations which are in it only to strip the shirts off their backs, oh and that their organisation is institutionally racist and sexist to boot, drawing upon the sins of a colonial and gendered past to produce a biased present. Businesses think they are run by people who would never be able to make it in business, poor approximations of the right business stuff. Government thinks that they are sclerotic and need a good kick up the rear. Oh, and they need to buckle under to more government oversight – for their own good, of course. Local communities, meanwhile, are often sick of all the students living in their area, forgetting to take the bins in, holding loud parties, and making parking impossible. Need I go on? The problem is that too often it can seem as if there are only two alternatives on offer. In the blue corner, there are all the people who think universities need to snap out of it. What they need is a concentrated dose of competition, both with each other and with new, mainly private entrants. In the red corner, are all the people who believe that universities are being shelled by concerted neoliberal attacks. What they need is to go back to the future. Neither side ends up in a particularly attractive place.

Both offer solutions which tend to be mirrors of each other. And they know, just know, that they are right.

On a bad day, it can also feel like most everyone thinks that they could be a vice-chancellor. At the extreme, I met a few academic staff at Oxford who didn't even think the job was necessary, except as a kind of symbolic figurehead (which it had been for a good part of Oxford's history). And there are still a number of academic staff who think that the job is a doddle. There are government ministers who know it's a doddle. Their knowledge of universities is often (but not always) quite sketchy. They have a tendency to think of university leaders – not without some justification, it has to be said – as a gang of people acting like a group of hungry chicks in a nest, constantly asking for resource, always complaining that they don't have enough. Why, thinks the minister, can't they get it together and stop asking for more? Then there are the over-confident business people. For some of them, it's obvious that they could smarten universities up, make them more business-like and whip those pesky academics into shape. There are the general commentariat who are sometimes prone to off-the-cuff comments and whose comments about vice-chancellors seem to be more off-the-cuff than usual. Then there are the parents who feel that the university isn't giving their children value for money. And, lastly, there are, of course, all of the experts on Twitter with their sublime confidence in their own opinions.

Given this degree of opprobrium, why would anyone want to take on the job? In this chapter, I will try to explain both why and what they have to do.[1] On the whole, most vice-chancellors are doing a difficult job in difficult circumstances in the best way that they can and very often producing the goods.[2]

All that said, vice-chancelloring is a very peculiar job. Almost no one explains what it entails but everyone seems to think they know what it is, at least to judge from the number of commentators willing to make definitive judgements. I could cavil about some of these judgements, to put it but mildly, but it might be more appropriate to give some sense of the task to hand. Then, knowing something about it instead of feeding off prejudice and half-remembered conversations, we can come back to whether vice-chancellors are doing the job well or badly.

You might think that the barrage of criticism of vice-chancellors I have just set out would make anyone hesitate before taking the job. The answer, in short order, is that, for all the flak, it is a privilege.[3] Universities are key future-shaping institutions and who doesn't want to help to shape the future? As importantly, by and large, they do good, not harm. Leading them can be done with something approximating to a clear conscience. They may not be paragons of virtue but, generally speaking, they produce limited emissions and they are working hard to lessen their carbon footprint. They aren't tainted by corruption or dodgy accounting. Few have any connections with oligarchs. They don't work through offshore financial centres.

What do vice-chancellors do?

So, having got such a plum job, what does a vice-chancellor actually do? The answer is lots of things. Being a vice-chancellor is an exceptionally diverse activity. That is actually one of its joys. All kinds of things can and do turn up in a day. As the cliché has it, the unexpected is the expected.

Let's start with a favourite cliché about university management, one which is actually pretty accurate. You will sit in and chair a lot of committees, often quite a few in a week, both in term time and out. They will cover topics as diverse as finance, building projects, and awarding honorary degrees. Contrary to the stereotype, committees are usually interesting and can be fun. Chairing committees is a learned skill in itself but enough has been written about it now that I need say little more. The big committee that you chair is senate, the main representative academic body, usually four to six times a year. Sometimes it can be fiery. But it certainly has more of a sense of occasion than other university committees which often deal with humdrum but still important business. The other big committee, chaired by the head of council, is council itself. Though you don't chair it, you will have a major role in explaining decisions and addressing agenda items.

Then there are the meetings. There are the usual managerial meetings familiar to anyone in a large organisation. There are lots of these but this is where delegation is so important. You need to be able to trust people to get on with things and, generally speaking, you can. There are regular senior management team meetings, usually once a week. There are away days that allow the management team to keep an eye on the strategic prize. And there are all the meetings which people book in order to see you, on a myriad of issues, from academic staff who are threatening to leave to aggrieved parents who feel that their progeny has been unjustly treated.

Then there is your role representing the university. That means setting a tone. To begin with, you will give a large number of speeches, certainly more than one a week, sometimes in a run of three or four. Giving a good speech is a great skill. It only comes naturally to a few people. Everyone else has to work at it. I was never a great extempore speaker – some people are – but with a script in front of me I could usually produce something like the goods. I wrote quite a few of the speeches myself but I was lucky to have the services of an executive assistant who would often do first drafts. I still found that, however good these drafts were, I needed to add my own touches to give a convincing performance.

As part of representing the university you will travel overseas. You need to be out there to find opportunities that you can bring back home and you need to be constantly raising the institution's profile. Be prepared for the media and the students to spend large amounts of time decrying your 'jet-set lifestyle', scrutinising your expense claims, and abominating your general levels of personal indulgence which this travelling must go to show. Don't just ignore the complaints. After all, carbon emissions are a genuine issue. But if you are restricting travel that should be the reason why, not the other stuff.

You will meet a lot of people, from delegations from other universities to distressed parents, from heads of research councils to heads of visiting delegations from overseas, from ministers out and about on fieldwork to actual and potential donors. You will, of course, take time to meet students. (I used to have informal dinners every few weeks in term time at which I could glean opinions and moods.)

You will make sure that you visit each department every year. This is a crucial means of gaining feedback. Some of the feedback will be robust but this is also an opportunity to combat misconceptions, scotch rumours, and allay fears. You will find that departments are very different in tone. Some tend to be quite moany – it's almost a tradition. Others are lovely to be with.

You will go to the various meetings of your trade associations like UUK and the Russell Group. You will go mainly to pick up straws in the wind. You will want to interrogate ministers and the various luminaries that will be at these meetings and take the temperature of the sector – which institutions seem to be in trouble, which vice-chancellors are struggling, which policies are being formulated. These meetings are almost always in London. Given the shape of the British polity, you will spend a lot of your time circulating through Whitehall, Parliament and other relevant institutions like the Wellcome Trust.

You will spend quite a bit of time wining and dining actual and potential donors. Most of them will prove to be a pleasure to be with: I still fondly remember my time as point with James Martin at Oxford who set up the Oxford Martin School. Only a very few potential donors play along and then, after much effort, provide little in the way of sustenance. Most people are sincere and genuinely want to give. Your task is to find out what they want to give to and then match it to the university's plans. (By the way, you will also be a major donor.)

You will conduct graduation ceremonies. In most universities, that means giving a speech and conducting the ceremony. As universities have grown, there are more and more of these occasions (often stretching two a day over many days in both summer and winter) involving more and more students (a typical Warwick ceremony would graduate around 400 students in an hour and a half), so many that some of them are now conducted by the deputy vice-chancellor. (By the way, this is nothing compared with some larger universities: one Australian university I know does 80.) Many of my vice-chancellor colleagues considered them to be great fun – people are there to celebrate achievement, after all. And they are undoubtedly joyous occasions. But I found them stressful too. You are on the spot in what is often a hot and sweaty room wearing hot and heavy gowns (the ceremonies in summer nearly always seem to coincide with very hot weather) and you are worried that something will go wrong – and be captured on the graduation video. Of course, sometimes it does. Most commonly, a student falls over parading across the stage. Sometimes a student lingers too long, wanting to engage you in a conversation. Or the person reading out the students' names gets the rhythm wrong – too fast or too slow are both a problem – so that the students start to arrive to shake hands and be congratulated on graduating either too fast or too slowly causing either a car crash or congestion. Or the honorary graduate gives a speech which is way, way too long. That actually happened once. I still bear the scars.

I was very lucky at Warwick in that the ceremonies were always incredibly professionally organised – it was a matter of great pride to get things right, especially last-minute reworking of the lists of candidates when a student didn't show so that there were no gaps in the running order. Inevitably every now and then things would still go askew. But it was always a great feeling to get to the end of the ceremony intact knowing that the people there had enjoyed it – or at least the bit of it with their child or sibling or friend in.

You will represent the university at many other occasions. In particular, you will eat a lot. Dinners are a ritual you'd better get used to. Everyone tells you that every now and then you will be sat next to someone boring but I never found this to be the case. And sometimes you will sit next to somebody absolutely fascinating.

Then there are the formal university occasions like the annual graduation dinner. Puritans argue that these occasions are redundant but they are often crucial means of binding supporters together. Guests feel part of a community. The university gains kudos and an opportunity to bruit its achievements abroad and, in particular, show off staff and student achievements.

There are also all the dinners around and about the university or, much more rarely now, in the vice-chancellor's residence. Many people argue that having a residence on or near campus is just an expensive indulgence and many vice-chancellors now eschew them or have radically downsized, helped in their decision by changes in taxation rules. But people appreciate the personal touch and the message it sends about the kind of university they are involved with in a way that being invited to some impersonal university dining room most certainly does not. Living above the shop, so to speak, can have its downsides, of course. You will be close to the action and visibly on call. But that is no bad thing either. Living away from the university sends its own messages about your degree of involvement in the life of the institution.

Then there are the occasions for administrative and other staff, usually thank you events of various kinds, or awards nights. These can be extraordinarily good-hearted affairs and extraordinarily enjoyable too. But remember to leave at ten o'clock sharp before the partying starts to really rev up.

There are all the other events that you need to be present at too. Coming-up weekend is one in which you will be expected to make speeches to parents. Clearing is another. Though most research universities are only in clearing in a limited way and there's not much you can do personally, this is a crucial event in the university's life.

Finally, you may try to find the time to keep publishing, partly because you still love research and partly so that your academic colleagues don't think you're a hack – something that some of them are only too willing to believe, by the way. Universities used to be more like partnerships in this regard in that you needed to both be a manager and also continue to practise, however patchily. But it's hard work being a player manager (Augar and Palmer, 2002) and the practice is gradually dying out. However, without this imprimatur your credibility can be put under threat. In the eyes of many academic staff you will be 'just' a manager.

A typical day can sometimes be 14 hours or more. Physical stamina is a must. You will be working evenings and very often weekends. You will only take a very brief annual holiday. You will always be on show and you will always be on call if there is a crisis. You will check your phone, email, texts and WhatsApp groups constantly for any adverse news, as well as coping with the hum of business as usual. I made a tally of some of my countable activities and found, for example, that, excluding graduation ceremonies, I delivered somewhere between 54 and 87 speeches in any year, about half internally and half externally. I made somewhere between ten and 16 overseas visits each year (not all of them paid for by the university, by any means). I have no idea how many meetings I chaired or attended – a lot is all I can say.

If there is a risk involved in all this constant and unremitting activity, it is that it is easy to become distracted and lose focus as the press of events unfolds. There is always something to do. There is never enough time. It is easy to sink into a comfort zone of thinking you're doing something because you're doing something.

One other thing. How long should you carry on doing this? The average tenure of a vice-chancellor is currently around eight years (a Russell Group university vice-chancellor is likely to serve for longer) (Hillman, 2022a) but some go shorter – some, indeed, have no choice but to go shorter. Others go longer – up to 15 years or even longer than that. The challenge for these extended stayers is whether they have anything more to offer after a particular period of time or whether they just start doing the same thing over and over again. Certainly, there is a commonly held view that ten years is the right length of time in one university. Another option is to extend your career by moving to another university. This has become a much more common alternative as the number of universities has multiplied and as 'vice-chancellor' has become a career grade. But this development has also occurred because vice-chancellors are being appointed at a younger age. In the 1970s nearly all vice-chancellors were appointed in or around their 50s to retirement (Halsey and Trow, 1971). That's no longer the case. By the time vice-chancellors have finished their first term of ten years, they may still only have reached their mid-50s so they have to find another job – hopefully at a better university – unless they have kept their research record up and so can return to an academic position. A number of vice-chancellors taking up this option of a second go round have come from overseas, showing once again that to be a vice-chancellor is increasingly to be part of an international labour market and, additionally, that the administrative system is becoming increasingly Americanised.

Leaving can be difficult. An institution has taken up your life. It feels to you as though you have forged a permanent allegiance. You haven't. You will get invited back to unveil a portrait that will then be hung in the rogues gallery of previous vice-chancellors when the dust has settled.[4] Very often councils will have chosen a successor who you are duty bound to think will lead the university into an abyss of mediocrity – the most serious sin any research university vice-chancellor can commit – and they will then of course do the opposite. (That said, it is not uncommon for councils to appoint polar opposites to the previous incumbent with the result that some research universities' leadership styles and trajectories can resemble a kind of switchback.)

What are a vice-chancellor's main aims? Well, of course, they vary. But some are undoubtedly the same. First and foremost, you will try to keep the university financially viable. It is no good decrying this aim as though it is a mark of Cain. Without a balanced bottom line, there are no jobs and there is no investment. For the staff who believe that money is just a fiction (and there actually are some, believe it or not), all this seems tiresome or even traitorous. But vice-chancellors are hemmed in by financial constraints on their ability to operate which a business would find difficult to countenance. University finances are tightly – very tightly – constrained. This is hardly surprising – not only do universities routinely pursue activities that are unprofitable which they then need to finance through surplus-generating activities but they also need to build and rebuild mundane things like research laboratories and halls of residence (Weisbrod, Ballou and Asch, 2008). Again, most funding is hypothecated. It cannot be vired. That is why vice-chancellors are so keen on the income from overseas students, from commercial ventures, from business schools, and from donations – they can actually do something with at least some of the money. Usually that means cross-subsidising their other activities but every now and then it can mean setting out on new projects.

In other words, universities have become a kind of business but it is a business with margins that would horrify any normal business manager. This is not a business most business people would necessarily find easy to run, pace the myth retailed by some commentators that vice-chancellors are really only substandard administrators who could never run a whelk stall and get paid well for not being very good at their job. Universities are more complex structures than most businesses and their finances are often permanently on the edge – one of my chairs of council once said that making the yearly budget balance was like landing a helicopter on a pound coin. That's also why university budget deficits are so problematic – even a relatively small deficit is often hard to recover from, especially if there are unexpected events in year that soak up money. It's why taking in more international students has always been such a temptation. It's a quick fix when the budget looks iffy. It's why cross-subsidy is necessary in a university, something which often riles heads of department who are producing a large surplus and want to spend it on new hires and projects, not have it taken away to keep other departments going. It's why university departments are usually disbarred from running large deficits for any length of time: in the long run, that creates permanent structural impediments to progress that keep mounting up and can threaten the institution. Sometimes, if the deficit is large enough and shows no sign of resolution, drastic action may have to be taken.

Second, you will try to keep the university on an even reputational keel, doing well in the various audits that now infest the sector as well as a miscellany of league tables. These league tables are the vice-chancellor's curse. Just as businesses have quarterly reports, universities have league tables – more and more and more league tables – cropping up through the year. I used to hate them. They made me extremely nervous – I knew my council members would be checking them out. You would suddenly get to the week in the year when league table X reports its results knowing that they would produce either an emotional high or a low, while also knowing that in most cases the result, however carefully compiled, was bound to be questionable. For example, in the space of a year it simply isn't possible for institutions to go bounding up and plummeting down these tables in the way that they often do. Nevertheless, league tables have real impacts – some parents use them as a proxy piece of information when choosing institutions, for example – so they are important come what may. Some colleagues go for the breezy approach in the face of this fact – the more league tables the better – but there is a distinct hierarchy of league tables so this doesn't really work. In this hierarchy, for research universities the REF is the main game in town. It is the one league table result which research university vice-chancellors must secure if they want to feel secure.

Third, you will try to initiate a strategy that will make the university more successful. That is something that is easy to say but hard to do. It is possible to shift a university's position though it is certainly not easy. The truth of the matter is that most vice-chancellors do not shift their university's overall position much if at all. Many of them seem to console themselves with growing student numbers and what might be termed conspicuous building syndrome, as though more fancy buildings must equal better.

Fourth, you will try to keep the university's work in the public eye in a positive way. This is a two-edged sword, of course. Universities weren't immune from public comment in the past but, as they have expanded their activities, grown into powerful economic actors, and taken on more and more students, so they have become a larger and larger target of criticism. Social media storms are just the icing on the cake, so to speak. Universities now often have large communications departments which are there to register, communicate and interpret the presence of both favourable and adverse events and issue responses.

Fifth, universities are long-term institutions but most of the incentives are increasingly short term. As a vice-chancellor, you are committed to shepherding into the future an institution that is meant to be around for a long time. You are a steward. This is one of the single most important facts about taking on the job. At least once in your tenure you should at least attempt to lay down a project that will only come to fruition over the long term. It should be something that will start out small but grow large, something that will help to characterise the university in the future and add to its weight over time.

Last, but not least, you must make the institution even more intellectually excellent. If you haven't done this, you should take your bat and ball and go home.

Is all of this too much for one person to handle? Of course. That's why seeking out a great senior management team is so important – I was very lucky in this regard to be able to turn to a deputy vice-chancellor, pro-vice-chancellors and deans, and a chief operating officer and chief financial officer who offered the inspiration and hard work that you so badly need. Even so, I do wonder if the vice-chancellor's constantly expanding role doesn't challenge the bounds of possibility. For example, take the issue of producing more public visibility. Most vice-chancellors are probably best described as adequate to the task occupying a spectrum from workmanlike to inspiring with most bunching somewhere in the middle. But some of the issues that need to be tackled now require real rhetorical skills. I have often thought that it might be worth thinking about having an official university spokesperson with a high enough profile to put these kinds of issues across to the public. Oxford and Cambridge already have public orators whose job it is to act as the voice of the university on particular public occasions. Perhaps an expanded version of these positions would be appropriate.

Leading a research university

You have been appointed as a vice-chancellor of a research university. Likely, you will have made a promise to instigate a strategy that will see your newly adopted university power its way onwards and upwards. But, if you stop believing all the publicity declaring that the university you have just become head of is a major global player and just look at the bald statistics, your likelihood of achieving that promise probably looks pretty remote. As I have already pointed out, moving a university's position in terms of quality of research, and in accompanying public esteem, is exceptionally difficult. It requires a remorseless focus on standards and that is always going to create waves in an institution. Truth to tell, for all the rhetoric most research universities will stay roughly where they were when their vice-chancellors started their tenure.

In some cases, that's at the top of the heap. Some universities are so successful that their reputation carries them forward, come what may. I think of Oxford, which I was privileged to be a part of for a few years. Oxford is a great research institution, both extraordinary and extraordinarily enjoyable to be a member of, and there is no reason to think that it is suddenly going to fall off its perch. It has advantages that most universities could never match – from rich alumni to revenues from Oxford University Press (which made a profit of £85.6 million in 2020, a considerable amount of which was passed to the university). In the US, Princeton, Harvard and Yale have the same sorts of advantages. It's a bit like the Premier League. Money explains a lot of the variance. But it doesn't explain all of it. Oxford also has a very distinct spirit, as does Cambridge, one which transmits itself around the world as stellar research, what seems like a closeted culture, and a bank of common images, held even by those who didn't attend the university at all. (To get some sense of this global cultural influence, consider only 'Second Farewell to Cambridge', the famous Chinese poem by Xu Zhimo, written in 1928 after his final visit to the university. It is now quite widely read in Chinese literature courses and has been set to music numerous times (most recently as a Mandopop song, one of many renditions in various styles). Or consider all of the books by Americans on Oxford (of which by far the most entertaining – because it isn't just a hagiography – is *A Garden of Paper Flowers* (Ehrenreich, 1994)).) Of course, not all leading research universities around the world are monetarily and reputationally rich. But most are.

But most research universities aren't like Oxford and Cambridge. Their resources are limited. Their histories are of interest only to them and their alumni. Their room to succeed is constricted. Still, within a tight envelope, it is possible to make some waves. However, in order to progress even a few places up the hierarchy can often require what may seem like draconian measures. After all, each increment will be more difficult than the last and requires even more effort. So how can some degree of success be achieved (given that success is no easy thing to frame or measure)?

After all, every university is different, rather more different than they may appear from the outside: even the newest universities can have quite distinct cultures. So it is appropriate to provide a few words on Warwick where I was a vice-chancellor. As these things go, it was an unusual institution. It was poorly resourced compared with most of its competitors. It had no large endowment. It had no reserves of any consequence. It had nothing to fall back on except its reputation as an innovator, its academic attainments, and its ability to generate extra resource. But it had consistently managed to punch above its weight by taking the attitude – the only one possible if it was going to be successful – that it always needed to come out fighting. It tried to leverage its resources so that they had the maximum impact. It was very careful with money, only borrowing for income-generating projects. It was constantly trying to cut costs and generate new business ideas (the registrar called this strategy save half, make half), famously offending a choleric E.P. Thompson (1970) who edited *Warwick University Ltd* and resigned in protest at what he saw as crass commercialisation. It was always trying to add income streams. It realised that it had to innovate continuously (really innovate, not just do what everyone else was doing) to stay one step ahead: if it stopped, it sank. It always looked hungrily for new opportunities to pounce on. It was blessed with an extremely effective administration which both knew what it was doing and did it. It purposely cultivated a chip on the shoulder attitude. But all of this effort was put towards one goal and one goal only – being academically excellent.

It wasn't all uphill, of course. Warwick had some major assets as a result of its chequered history. One asset was some really excellent departments, for example mathematics. Then it had the Warwick Manufacturing Group (WMG). Led by the indomitable Lord Bhattacharyya, WMG went from strength to strength and I was lucky that, during my time, it hit a peak. WMG was in tune with the times, to be sure, with its emphasis on working with industry, but it was much more than just another university–industry outfit. WMG had global reach. Then, the university had a large number of university-related companies (16 in all, including Unitemps and jobs.ac.uk) that brought in substantial funding. The additional revenue from these companies (though comparatively small) gave the university considerably more room for financial manoeuvre than many, as well as pointing to the main lesson of portfolio management theory: distribute risk. And, it had one more asset – land, enough land for many decades of expansion with which it could parlay its future.

Warwick wasn't a civic university. There was already a civic university nearby in any case – Coventry. Another one wasn't needed. The university was in the region but not captured by it. Many books and reports sing the praises of the so-called civic university (e.g. Brink, 2018) but that wasn't Warwick, even though it produced extraordinary service for the West Midlands and for Coventry and not just in terms of an industrial boost. For example, WMG had set up two secondary schools. Warwick Arts Centre was a cultural dynamo. And so on. But, first and foremost, it believed that a research university was there to help a city or region by being a great research university.

The biggest single danger that Warwick faced was that, as it has become more successful, it might start to act like a normal university. Complacency was a constant danger. Warwick might decide that it had made it and start doing the same thing as some others, just hugging the shore. Warwick might decide to dial down its appetite for risk when its whole history has been premised on taking risks. Warwick might decide to adopt a large university mindset when the mindset of a small university punching above its weight is what had served it so well. Or Warwick might decide to jettison its distinctive administrative model which regularly moved administrators from one part of the university to another so that they were able to generate a broad skillset and a genuine sense of ownership.

No one ever said that producing a successful research university is an easy task. There are many reasons why. To begin with, most large research institutions suffer from a degree of inertia, especially if they are moderately good, in which case they will often over-estimate their qualities. 'What's the point of doing this? We're already doing pretty well' is a common plaint. Then, making a marked difference takes time. Any strategy worth its salt will take five to seven years to show real signs of life which means that it can be knocked off course by unexpected events. Equally, all strategies hit bleak spots when it doesn't look as though the strategy is going to work out. (I still remember when one year the *Times Higher* produced a new global ranking which placed Warwick outside the top 200 universities.) Getting through this valley of death can be challenging. Then again, rolling out a strategy requires the consent and often the active support of the institution. For a vice-chancellor, the support of council is particularly vital and that requires a good relationship with, as well as constant cultivation of, members of council in order to ward off the heebie-jeebies that arise when a council member talks to a neighbour or a member of a Council in another university who asks why your university seems to be down there with the fishes. The support of academics and administrators and all of the other staff is also vital and that means, above all, trying to make the university into a good place to work.

Of course, mistakes are inevitable – I certainly made quite a few – but ambitious strategies can work. These are some of the rules that I followed. Some of them are pretty tough but the truth of the matter is that this is what you have been signed up to do. You are there to assure the future of the university and protect the jobs of its members when you can. You are there to make sure that the university you lead is better going out than coming in. Some of what is here will feel elitist. It is. There is no getting away from this. But, realistically, given the scale of the competition and the enormous resources that some of its competitors could muster, it was the only way that Warwick could prosper.

Most important of all, set standards and then keep to them, come what may. Always, always act to the standard. That might seem obvious, but it can be extremely difficult to achieve. The whole university has to be involved. It's not just a matter of research and teaching standards. Every part of the university has to act in concert. Every part of the university has to get better. Academics and grounds staff are in it together. Meals at formal occasions need to be memorable. Graduation ceremonies need to sparkle. Entrance tariffs need to have an edge. The ability to spot those who are becoming eminent to whom honorary degrees can be awarded needs to be honed. And so on. Everything must reflect everything else. Resistance to this level of challenge is inevitable. But because of Warwick's history it was more amenable than most institutions would be to stepping up.

Make at least two innovations a year. Don't be frightened if some fail. It's the price of success. But be sure that council members understand this or they will start reading from small signs to the big picture.

Don't go grand. The institution needs to have or get a chip on its shoulder. I was lucky here. The good thing about Warwick was that it already had this sense of being given the short end of the stick. It thought that its quality wasn't acknowledged often enough in comparison with older universities.

Always appoint better. People are the crucial element of any research university so new academic appointments need to be better or have the potential to be better than their predecessors. (You would have thought that this was obvious but appointment panels have been known to appoint a person who they know is not optimal, for a variety of reasons. For example, a department needs someone to teach in the new academic year and time is running out.)

Wherever possible, make room for new academic talent. In particular, initiatives like Fellowship schemes can make a real difference and also act as a way of finding the research stars of the future.

Try to spot new opportunities in advance. That means being constantly out there, speaking at conferences, talking to your academic staff about the novel research that they are doing so that you are informed (and enthused), and generally horizon-scanning. If you get it right, you can catch a wave. For example, Warwick was able to catch the big data wave.

Institute a strong strategy. The strategy needs to be ambitious and detailed. It needs to contain real challenges and scary targets that are right at the edge of what's actually possible. For example, one goal of the original

Warwick strategy was to be top 50 in the world in ten years. That was a real stretch but it focussed minds and, in my last year, Warwick got to the top 50 in the *Times Higher* league table – at 50. Skin of the teeth!

Stick to the strategy. Some vice-chancellors let it lapse after a few years, either because of events or because they claim it worked by pulling out examples of some things that did.

Go for quality not quantity. It is much better to be smaller and better than larger and mediocre. Remember Caltech, Princeton, Brown. Also, there is the issue of when you run out of really excellent researchers. They are not an infinite resource. Departments don't necessarily have to be bigger to be better.

Only borrow on income-earning propositions. Some universities have been known to borrow for propositions that have no means of producing income and therefore paying off the loan.

Take up any credible opportunity to diversify income. British research universities have been frighteningly dependent on international students for margin. Warwick, having been blasted by cuts in the 1980s, never forgot the over-dependence lesson and always looked for new ventures that might produce a broader portfolio of income-earning activities. Equally, it tried to get a balanced portfolio of international students.

When looking for international students, use agents sparingly. Warwick had a network of its own recruiters and got much higher quality students as a result. For example, in India just one person made a difference because of her network of contacts in Indian society.

Don't do what everyone else is doing. The sector suffers from follow-my-leader behaviour so it isn't particularly difficult to do something bold. But this requires courage, and that can be in short supply. But, if you are going to get ahead, it's no good just honing existing systems and making small increments.

Think about how many departments are appropriate. Undoubtedly, there are virtues in being a comprehensive university. But there are also drawbacks. You almost certainly can't afford for every department to be brilliant. Many comprehensive universities are on a treadmill where 90 per cent of departments are working well but the remaining 10 per cent need help to succeed. By the time you've got those 10 per cent back on track another 10 per cent appear to be in need of attention.

Hope you never hear the word 'consolidation' from a member of your management team. Consolidation is the kiss of death at this point in history.

Say thank you – a lot. Quite rightly, people want to feel appreciated. You have the means to do this and in multiple ways. Use it.

Last, but definitely not least, remember that you're there to do good. There is the research that the university's academics do, much of which has direct benefit for human welfare. There is the terrific teaching. There are all the economic and cultural outputs. There is the mass of volunteering that staff and students sign up to. A university is something you can genuinely be proud of, an institution that generally makes things better not worse.

Summary

My senior management team and I were employed to make the university more successful. Sometimes we made mistakes but, generally speaking, I think we did that. Mainly, we took appropriate actions that made the university better. Sometimes, there were difficult decisions to be made which I am sure left some people bruised and forlorn. Obviously, I regret that. But these decisions meant that more people were employed than would otherwise been the case. They resulted in better research. They gave alumni's degrees more visibility and more clout. And they enhanced Warwick's global reputation.

But were they the right actions to take so far as higher education more generally is concerned? Of that I am less sure. In a system in which the state sort of wants universities to sort of compete, vice-chancellors are structurally set against each other. They can't step off the treadmill. Now, I certainly don't believe that competition is always an awful thing. To begin with, it can pay dividends. Then, if the public is paying towards an institution, they have a right to see it perform. But though the frenzy of competition unleashed in the 2010s may have rewarded some institutions, I am less sure that it has advantaged research universities in general. Some of it has almost certainly been a distraction. Some of it may have been actively damaging: research universities take an awful long time to build up but they are easily scuppered by what are often rushed and careless policy initiatives. Then, there is the issue of how far competition should be allowed to go. After all, higher education is 'not the kind of "market" that works simply by driving out all of the competition' (Watson, 2009, p. 121) And, finally, competition leaves open a question that still needs to be answered: is a university 'a scholarly retreat, a national investment or a finishing school for the aspiring rich?' (Jenkins, 2019, p. 23). After all, on one reading, 'a good university is still the nearest a secular society gets to a sacred institution' (ibid., p. 23).

One of my concerns is that vice-chancellors of the future will be drawn from a population which has more limited horizons because that is all they have known. They will have no qualms about signing up to a system that runs without due regard to the long term. If that happens, then a receding baseline is all but inevitable. Attempts to 'professionalise' governance so that it more nearly resembles business norms won't help either. For example, recent talk about professionalising management is mainly code for making universities into something which is more convenient for external stakeholders to direct, accelerating the 'decline of donnish dominion' (Halsey, 1992) and cramping horizons by imposing what, for all of the protestations, are very similar models of what a university is and should be. Can you imagine a new generation of vice-chancellors arguing, as Joan Didion did with respect to the University of California of the 1960s, that its universities represented 'California's highest, most articulate idea of itself, the most coherent – perhaps the only coherent – expression of the California possibility' (Pelfrey, 1984, p. 3) or that 'the challenge to the University of California today is nothing less than to help bring forth the civilization of the future' (ibid.)? Or, on this side of the Atlantic, can you imagine a new generation of vice-chancellors recovering some of the impulses behind the new universities of the 1960s, universities which managed to achieve often quite different things while also being funded by the state (Taylor and Pellew, 2020)? Or, going farther back in time to 1935, can you imagine a new generation of vice-chancellors falling in with Alfred North Whitehead who argued that 'the task of a university is the creation of a future, so far as rational thought ... can appreciate the issue. The future is big with every possibility of achievement and of tragedy'? (Whitehead, 1968, p. 171). I'm not sure I can.

But the fact is that there isn't much in the way of constructive opposition to a new settlement. With some notable exceptions, academics are often remarkably uninterested in the specifics of these issues. Sure, they are willing to moan about the generalities and indulge in what Collini (2017) calls 'mere hand-wringing' but imagination of alternatives is pretty minimal most of the time, truth to tell. Academics all but refuse to participate in designing new kinds of university or university system, leaving universities to be run by the managers they are so suspicious of, in the name of an alienation which guarantees exactly that. That is a real and genuine tragedy for everyone. There is no real counter-agenda which takes reimagining the research university as its cause. We don't just need critique. We need alternatives.

There are three reasons why academics hang back, I think. One is that many academics are so busy – and, yes, so obsessed – that they will not give up the time to follow what may look to some of them like a quixotic quest. The second, is that academics may think that the fight is already over. A managerial coup d'etat has taken place. That might be correct – or it could be a convenient reason for inaction. Third, there is no counter-force, either singly or as a coalition. The major learned societies have generally been remarkably quiescent (they get a considerable amount of their money from government which makes for an obvious conflict of interest). The union concentrates on the bread and butter issues and rarely offers any signposts to the future. The Council for the Defence of British Universities has struggled to attain effective levels of membership when it should not have had to. Academic members of council often stay quiet. And so on.

It's a pity.

PART III
The research university of the future

8

So what is a research university?

Let me summarise the argument of this book so far. The problem in UK higher education is that, like the British natural environment, British research universities are the victims of a receding baseline. Things that we would never have envisaged are coming true, things that we all cleaved to have gone extinct, things that were threats have become realities. But we have all got so used to the situation that we are becoming inured to it. We are in danger of becoming the educational equivalent of that night-time blizzard of moths which used to smear the car windscreen when the headlights were on which we can now only tell our children about. This is not to say that all is doom. To the contrary. The basics of British research universities are still very, very strong. But the threat is there, unfortunately.

Of course, there are many reasons for the current situation and not least student number growth[1] but I am increasingly of the view that research universities keep offering the same answers to questions that are no longer being asked, to use the famous phrase that Peter Drucker deployed to explain why organisations fail. In the face of many substantial changes, from the acceleration of online education to the rise of for-profit higher education, from the continuing problems of student finance to the not so gradual encroachment of government, from the relative disinterest in discovery research to erosion of research time, these are difficult times for UK research universities. But in the face of these provocations they tend to keep on repeating the same old, same old answers which act as a salve but do little to stop various other institutions setting the agenda by simply ignoring these answers because they were never interested in the questions universities thought they'd want to ask.

Why this bit of a mess? Five reasons. One is that the research universities keep being included with all universities. The case needs to be made unashamedly for why they are different and cannot be part of the pack, while still retaining strong links with the overall higher education ecosystem. So long as the argument persists that all universities are the same, just laid out along a spectrum, a policy which creates sameness while aiming for difference, these universities will find themselves assimilated to a run of institutions that governments feel are theirs to do with as they will, using the spur of more competition and the whip of government funding. Government will always be able to claim that the majority of the sector are behind a particular initiative.

Second, get out ahead of the problems. There have been and are things wrong with universities in this country and they are mostly well-known. But they have been left to government to fix. The result? University autonomy can look like an increasingly thin reed. And, especially in a time of culture wars which have polarised opinion of whatever political stripe (but have also left large segments of the population out of the loop just looking on bemusedly), it wouldn't be beyond the bounds of credibility for the erosion of university autonomy to become an attack on academic freedom. That would be really serious. Grant (2021) argues that academic freedom is simply another index of academic entitlement. Tell that to the academics in other countries who are being fired, sacked, jailed, harassed, tortured or even killed for promoting ideas that their prevailing regime doesn't like. (Luckily, the Council for the Defence of British Universities (CDBU, 2021) has produced a well-argued paper (which includes a sample ordinance) that pithily lays out the case for restating why academic freedom is important.)

Third, the great research universities need to start protecting each other. When there are problems in other universities, colleagues rarely ride to the rescue or even offer much in the way of support. They might offer a bit of sympathy (and not a bit of schadenfreude) but that's about it. When they are meant to stick together, it is always easy for government to peel off a few. It is just embarrassing that George Soros has had to offer $1 billion to form a global university network that can begin to defend the open liberal values that universities rely on when rich institutions like Harvard, Yale, Oxford and Cambridge could find room in their capacious budgets for all manner of defences. That they seem to do so little shows either a certain lack of foresight or a high degree of institutional insularity, or both.

Fourth, many research universities have not practised strategic differentiation. In the longer term, the most successful universities will be those which have genuinely original strategies and not just ghost strategies based on achieving a few indicators, usually based on relativities with like institutions. The strength of research universities will come from a unity that is forged from difference, making them both less fragile and more innovative as a bloc.

Fifth, we need to reboot the narrative of what research universities are for. They need to have their own agenda and this can't just be 'teaching and research are really important'. Or 'look at what we're doing for the economy'. These are long-term institutions. Real anchors. There needs to be some sense of mission, in other words. And mission there is. The next 100 years are going to be very difficult. Climate change will bite in increasingly frightening ways. At its worst, heat will build with some parts of the world becoming unliveable. Extreme climatic events will multiply. Sea levels will rise. Topsoil will run out, one of the many signs of an unsustainable agricultural system built on pointless animal death. Oceans will suppurate, their inhabitants hunted to extinction, their waters no longer able to soak up carbon dioxide. Forests and many other natural resources will continue to decline. Pollution of all kinds will continue to grow. The frequency of pandemics will rise. Population is slated to continue to increase, though more slowly. Cities will balloon and face the danger of implosion. In the face of all these changes, there will be enormous shifts of population, a process that has already started. Many people will likely starve. Wars will be fought over basic resources like food and water. Abuse of the planet will reach a crescendo and human beings place in its ecology will need to be rethought.

Universities are where many of the solutions to this scary but not necessarily apocalyptic future are likely to be born (Barnett, 2018). As the problems mount up, science will be one of the only ways out. Equally, new kinds of medicine will be desperately needed. But that won't be enough. Political systems will need to be rethought so that they support new kinds of more inclusive citizenship – inclusive of the planet as well as many more kinds of people. Cities will have to be to be completely redesigned. Economic systems will have to be reworked so that they take less out and put more in. Our place in the world will need to be resignified. And so on. Making universities into conventional short-term organisations when they are meant to be there to scan the far horizons will leave the world adrift in this storm of events.

No doubt this will sound to some like yet more candyfloss from universities grown too big for their boots. So be it. The narrative that is rolled out by research universities at the moment is too modest for its own good. If you don't think you're important, why should anyone else?

What is a university for?

So, against this sombre background, what are research universities for? Whatever they were for, the continuing addition of new activities has produced a kind of fog which doesn't so much smother as confuse intentions. Any rethinking needs to be done against the difficult background I have outlined in previous chapters as well. The best that can be said is that the system has tacked reasonably skilfully with the ups and downs of government policy on tuition fees and allied issues and will survive. But it is difficult to find many who believe that the current outcome is entirely satisfactory, whether they be the most convinced free marketeer or the most committed public sector enthusiast. The university system and the research university itself needs to be redesigned. We need to turn the page.

But, as universities have become larger and more complex so the problem of applying simple one-note solutions to the problem of what a university is have only multiplied. Complexity is a fact which cannot be navigated around – it has to be faced. But, that said, there is now a pressing need to rework the university so that it doesn't become an increasingly hollow drum, all things to all people and pleasing none. Against this background, it seems obvious that the idea of the university as originally conceived of by Newman in religious terms or by von Humboldt in statist terms needs more than a mild makeover (Barnett and Peters, 2018, Peters and Barnett, 2018). Of course, it is debateable whether any university could be or ever was gathered around just one idea of its existence. But one thing is now a matter of fact: the universities of today are generally large, heterogeneous and multifaceted. The question that needs to be posed is whether they and the systems they exist in have genuine *design* limitations as a result (Crow and Dabars, 2015). I am sure that they do. But how might the idea(s) of a research university be reworked so it doesn't just equate to a post hoc justification of what is already there?

Before we do that, it's worth revisiting that old chestnut of a question one more time: 'what is a university for?' and, most especially, what counts as the central mission (or missions) of research universities in a time when their heterogeneity has become a watchword? To carry out world-changing research? To conduct great teaching? To become civic universities, serving their communities in manifold ways? To become economic powerhouses for cities and regions? To become key exporters. To act as cultural nodes. To disseminate soft power? To act as international crossroads? Or, most controversially, to provide a means of inculcating a new mindset that will allow the world to breathe? I'm not sure that I know the answer but I am sure that we have too many answers at the moment, most of which look suspiciously like post hoc rationalisations. Maybe that's the way of the world but surely research universities ought to know better. After all, knowing better is meant to be their stock in trade.

Duties

Quite often, universities will include as an almost obligatory moment in their strategies a 'statement of values' which will frame a university as if it must be a system of beliefs that sweats a civilisational mission through every pore (Viveiros de Castro, 2011). Yet these statements often ring curiously hollow. They can seem far removed from the actual business of the university and more often they act as a convenient justification for what they're doing anyway. Of course, practices vary. In some elite institutions which regard themselves as inheritors of the tradition, statements of values, conducted in a high moral tone, may still be the general currency of the common room. But, in most higher education institutions, statements of values are often only thin threads of justification to be wheeled out when a situation requires them.

Universities are important institutions, of that there is no doubt. Like the Church, universities tend to think of themselves as inheritors of a tradition even though they have constantly innovated to endure as long-term institutions. Even new institutions often play to what Crow and Dabars (2015) call 'filopietism', literally in the case of practices like graduation ceremonies and the like which are assumed to bestow prestige by appealing to history. But asking that they justify themselves by appeals to universal and essentially hieratic and quasi-sacerdotal forms of value reduces what are now many different modes of existence to a spurious unity which cannot hold – it is doubtful that any human institution has ever been 'single-mindedly concentrated on a single function' (Halsey, 1992, p. 42). Rather, they represent

> an almost perfect model of the complexity of the relations between a value and an institution that harbours it: sometimes they coincide, sometimes not at all; sometimes everything has to be reformed, at the risk of a scandalous transformation; sometimes the reforms turn out to consist in dangerous innovations and even betrayals. (Latour, 2013, p. 44)

Instead of values, then, I suggest that universities need to stand tall by emphasising the duties or obligations that they fulfil. There are modest, practical ways of proceeding which might more readily fit with a putative honour code based on academic life as it really is lived. For example, terms like dialogue and judgement and connection might signify one practical means of proceeding. Another might be signified by terms like curiosity, unlearning, growing knowledge, inspiring new generations. A third might use terms like 'sharing' and 'held in common' and 'care of the possible'. These duties aren't grand moral mountains. They are something smaller, understood less as acts of purity and heroic altruism and more as something achievable which depends on the deployment of a certain kind of honour. In using such a term, I mean to signify that honour does not have to be the competition for status that it is sometimes understood as but rather a means of forging respect out of an honour code which relies on a regime of justification that acts as an index of worth (Appiah, 2010). Instead of a point, a vector. Instead of moral perfection, an aspiration to virtue. In other words, universities could be founded in duties embedded through an implicit code of honour which does not have to be written down as a vacuous mission statement. It seems to me that this honour code is what needs to be reinstated in the lives of universities (Tuchman, 2009). And there are ways of doing that. One of the most moving moments in any graduation ceremony is when new medical graduates stand to recite the Hippocratic oath or nowadays the Declaration of Geneva. They actually perform their honour code.

The notion of duty or obligation that is there in honour is hardly a new one. It has a long history going back to at least Cicero (1991) and is found in the work of many philosophers, for example in Kant's writings on perfect and imperfect duty. But of late it has fallen out of favour. In one account, it is not in tune with the times. It sounds stuffy and conformist, concerned with slavish adherence to laws of one kind or another. But, in another account the notion can be considered as central as a practical emendation of value.[2] The notion of duty as that which is owed could be recast. It would no longer be subjectivist but rather it would be concerned with the cultivation of new types of potential, powers which are not framed in terms of fully realised beliefs but instead espouse an incompleteness where 'becoming and relationship prevail … over being and substance' (Viveiros de Castro, 2011, p. 47) – which is, of course, exactly how unlearning works. Then the university is understood as a place where we call into question what we know and a sense of the world that has become naturalised over time, a place where the tradition is meant to be one of breaking with tradition, not in order to pronounce one path as leading to salvation and the other to perdition, but in order to catalyse invention.

Nothing could be more important at the present time. As I have pointed out, we are engaged in a kind of rediscovery of what the world is like, spurred on by multiple planetary crises, a rediscovery that involves 'migration to another planet, one that we could rightly call "ours" [this will require] more ingenuity, infinitely more technical and scientific innovations, and a level of mobilization and institutional innovation several orders of magnitude greater than sending a few cosmonauts to Mars' (Latour, 2016, p. 2), not least because it will also require a wholesale change of mindset so that we include the planet and its beings as a part of the family and not just resources to be used up as we see fit, the very stance that has brought us to this sorry pass. Landing on this new planet means resurrecting the Humboldtian university. But the von Humboldt in question will be Alexander, not Willem (though he was no slouch either), and the idea of a natural history as if everything mattered (Latour, 2016). It is time to recast research universities as what Latour (2016, p. 8) calls 'neo-Humboldtian'. After all,

> Soon, eight billion people will need help in landing on a territory … which is totally new to everybody. It will require of each member of the public an amazing effort to adjust, to inquire about the right way to survive there, to propose changes in lifestyles, to resist conflicts over land appropriations and to entirely retrofit goals, morality and values.

Every university discipline has something important to contribute to this great migration to a new planet. It's not just the sciences. For example, the arts and humanities are an enormous archive of different ways to be human, different cultural sensitivities, and different ways of understanding what counts as agency. Likewise for what I have called elsewhere the mid-latitude disciplines, archaeology, anthropology and geography, which, as a matter of course, have to understand the planet and its peoples as multiple combinations of practices, practices which can be altered.

What duties might universities then have? No doubt there are many contenders but I want to concentrate on just the four that I think are the most important at this time. Others will no doubt want to add more – civic responsibilities, economic wellbeing, social mobility, EDI – but I want to stick with a core set of duties which are not general social responsibilities but are specific to universities.

Let's start with the most obvious duty – *research*. Research – unlearning – must be the central duty for research universities and for at least four reasons. To begin with, universities are now one of the only concerted producers of genuinely disruptive knowledge and interpretations in the world as corporations and other actors withdraw from discovery research, seeing it as a cost rather than an investment. As almost the only arks of this kind of knowledge generation, they bear a heavy responsibility, not least because of the pressing problems that the world faces which they are now an integral part of solving, from new diseases to the growing perils of climate change. Then, second, because that fundamental of academic life, curiosity, is at the heart of what a research university does. Without that constant and unremitting questioning, a university is nothing. This doesn't have to mean that university research is closed off from 'the real world'. Indeed, nowadays at least, academics are positively encouraged to intervene in it and the stream of innovations coming out of universities, either singly or in concert with business and other actors, gives the lie to sceptics.[3] But neither does it mean making discovery research into an orphan, set to one side. The restlessness and slower gestation time of discovery research is vital. The alternative is to sink into fast, mechanist explanations which only ask questions which can be answered, not least because they assume a universe that is essentially passive. One more reason. Universities have become one of the few repositories of long-term deliberative wisdom in a time when long-term deliberative wisdom has become an imperative in the face of a planet that we have come to realise, as Stengers (2008, np) points out, 'is something that does not demand a response from us, that is utterly deaf to our repentances', a planet that completely exceeds us even as we have become akin to a natural force. In an era in which several existential threats don't just loom on the horizon but lower over us – not just climate change and the resultant heatworld but also general scarcity of basics like water, roiling pandemics, even artificial intelligence running out of control – perhaps. In the absence of other institutions willing or able to take up the baton, universities have moved from commentators to the side of these issues to being centrally involved in them as 'the environmental crisis questions the seeming self-evidence or coherence of such basic conceptions' (Clark, 2015, p. 20) as the human or the environment. Universities have become temporal and spatial arbitrageurs, trying to knit the planet together into new survivable combinations. Then, a final reason. Universities have become one of the only institutions that keep watch over the long term. T'was always thus, one might say, but the responsibility is heavier than has been laid upon them heretofore: at this point in time at least, their research has become a matter of survival. Research universities are becoming akin to planetary watchkeepers who must espouse a kind of biophilia. One might think that a mission like this would require excessively burdensome biblical values but it might be more accurate to argue that it requires a variant of eudaimonism, traditionally understood as a bias towards human flourishing, but oriented now towards care for the planet and planetary flourishing rather than just human flourishing – the university of life.[4] That demands constancy certainly, a commitment to accuracy, of course, a rage against simplicity of explanation, naturally, but, most of all, the kind of adventurousness in research and general enquiry that Stengers has repeatedly lauded as representative of the best science,[5] 'the creation of a situation enabling what the scientists question to put their questions at risk' (Stengers, 2012, np).

To achieve this imperative of rich and uncertain 'de-scription' (Schmidgen, 2015) of the world we live in will require a number of actions. One will be *stimulating more cooperation between universities*. Research universities are often set against each other in various competitions. But they need to cooperate more, and more extensively. Individual universities, even the most eminent, simply do not have the resources to tackle many of the kinds of questions now being posed by themselves. In particular, it is important to build on the groundswell of international cooperation between academics that has become the norm, over and above the large projects like CERN or ITER or the use of the range of telescopes sponsored by governments and universities. These projects are being joined by the growth of explicit global research priorities made by most research-intensive universities of any note which are often tied in with burgeoning inter-university cooperative networks of various kinds. But there is a lot more to do, even given that a base of shared projects now exists and is growing daily. In *Finches of Mars*, Brian Aldiss (2013, p. 7) foresees a future in which 'the universities of the … world [have] linked themselves together under a charter which in essence represented a great company of the wise, the UU (for United Universities)', an organisation which, among other things, has colonised Mars. This is a pipedream, to put it but mildly! In any case, we do not always have to go grand to do grandiose things. But larger 'moonshot' projects can serve to bind research universities together – while acknowledging that the differences between these institutions will always persist – and some of them could be of extraordinary consequence. With a trillion dollars to hand, Hooper (2021) lists some of them: eradicating malaria, tuberculosis and HIV, a resilient international energy grid that would enable renewable energy to flow globally, and a sustainable moon base or a successor to the Large Hadron Collider or the James Webb telescope. After all, as Hooper points out, $1 trillion is only equivalent to five times the personal wealth of Jeff Bezos, 1/162 of the combined wealth of the world's richest 1 per cent and two-thirds of the money the world's private equity firms hold in 'dry powder' (the cash that they have not yet invested). Again, it is less than 20 per cent of what world governments spend each year on subsidising fossil fuel industries, or the amount that the US spends every year and a half on its military.

Another will be *enhancing mechanisms of trust*. If universities are to be trusted, their house needs to be, and must be seen to be, in good order. A whole series of issues have arisen around the conduct of research, a number of which I highlighted in a previous chapter. Many of these issues are procedural – such as the need to prove that experimental results are replicable, unbiased and transparent – a sine qua non which has proved to be somewhat less qua non than had been assumed and now requires urgent remediation. There are other issues as well. But solutions are being put in place. Replicability is being addressed by a system of so-called 'registered reports' in which academics preregister their hypotheses before carrying out a study and scientific journals agree to publish the study on the strength of the methods rather than the results (Chivers, 2020). So far as bias is concerned, guards are being put in place to prevent manipulation of the peer review process and citation abuses like so-called coercive citation, wherein a few referees try to get their own work inserted into papers they are reviewing in untoward ways, and excessive self-citation, something that because of the rise of citation databases is now fairly easy to pick up (Van Noorden, 2020). When mistakes occur, most journals now issue retractions and corrections in a timely manner. Again, to enhance transparency, referee reports are increasingly being published as a part of a publication, allowing readers to appreciate the back and forth between author and referees.

Another set of trust issues are concerned with ensuring that there is a level playing field for all researchers. That means moving away from the overbearing, and sometimes misogynist, behaviour of some research supervisors and research team leaders. (Bodies like the Wellcome Trust are now attempting to put better behaviours in place.) It means producing a balanced workforce, not something found in all academic disciplines. While a large amount of work has been done by both universities and disciplines to correct what are undoubted biases of gender and ethnicity, any action is bound to involve some degree of historical hangover as actions work their way up the age cohorts.

The second duty is inspiring the population by *transmitting what I have already called unlearning through teaching and mentoring* (while at the same time imparting some of the practical skills that will be needed to survive in the coming heatworld). In the past, such a duty would often have been framed as producing a better, more rounded citizenry but that would have meant reaching only a small cohort of students from like-minded backgrounds producing like-minded moments called 'character'. Now research universities have extended the boundaries of their intakes to take in more students from different backgrounds. They have also realised that there is a job to be done to shift the scandalous levels of inequality that these institutions certainly haven't initiated but have helped to perpetuate since the majority of students from low-income families never apply to them in the first place and are concentrated in other higher education institutions by default – the so-called 'undermatching' issue.

What does teaching character look like under circumstances where there is a more diverse and much larger student body? Most universities have produced rather weak responses. There are expectations of behaviour enshrined in student contracts and discipline processes. There are moments when ethical issues get scrappily and very unsatisfactorily discussed. There are public-spirited acts that are rightly encouraged and rewarded. But that is usually about it. Unlike in the US there is rarely any kind of core curriculum – contested as they may be – or any other means of binding students together by discussing (and disagreeing about) common issues early on, and almost no mention of civics teaching more generally.

That's a pity. Unlearning involves not just seeking out new questions but also trying to mould the right temperament to ask them. Perhaps the foremost need is to cultivate patience. Another essential need is to cultivate public-spiritedness: those with strong views must recognise that they share a community with fellow citizens whose competing views are just as intense. 'Both patience and public spirit entail caring not just what happens, but also how it happens' (Wiener, 2019). Appealing to patience in a world where many issues need urgent solutions may seem like a paradox. It is not. Equally, trying to teach public-spiritedness may sometimes seem like a lost cause. But we have a duty to try to instil it. Students naturally tend to want to be involved. We need to teach them good involvement – involvement that is non-violent, understands that people who have alternative points of view aren't necessarily evil, and that cultivates resilience and creativity but also humility. I have seen the opposite of these traits in students in my time but I have also seen many instances of students who have understood that changing the world means making a new compact, one that allows the acquisition of knowledge to be regarded as not just a career boost or another technological instrument but as a lifeline.

Universities have been places where people can meet and discuss their differences – and often agree to disagree – in a safe space committed to the values of the enlightenment, often in a formative period in their lives. Though most of them were originally set up to take on this mantle, it was always assumed that this would occur on a much smaller and face-to-face scale, not least because small scale doesn't only make instruction stickier but also allows students to teach things to each other in depth: interaction between people of different cultures and faiths can produce a quality greater than the sum of its parts. The best universities still do this. They refuse to simply pressure and programme (Delbanco, 2012). They try to cultivate an open-minded sense of purpose. Scale makes it harder, without a doubt. Still, there are many sterling examples of attempts by research universities to produce this sense of purpose in these changed circumstances, from volunteering programmes through business start-up programmes through to much more ambitious international programmes, meant to relieve poverty and hardship. Encouragingly, many of these programmes have been student-generated. Equally, many universities are trying to increase the practical element of their courses in such a way that they can reproduce small group interaction and learning in other ways. Witness the way in which some universities are trying to refocus the teaching of engineering so as to make it into a process of thinking and making in which the 'and' is removed through project-based learning or other universities that are mounting humanities courses which include a heavy practical element. Yet others are considering how to produce degrees which involve the student in constructing their own curriculum so that they can follow through on a practical issue like climate change, not least in their own university backyards.[6] Others still are trying to do all of these things and also introduce a substantial locational variation into courses so that students sample different parts of the world as a part of the course in order to understand different understandings. This is an age of experimentation aided precisely by online developments which can sometimes seem threatening but which, when used appropriately, can expand what can be achieved.

However, there has to be more to it than just reaching out to students, important though that no doubt is. Research universities must be seen as spaces of learning that are not confined to the lecture hall and seminar room or screen and to those students who have been accepted into the university in any year. The third duty, in other words, is to greatly *enhance communication* so that much wider publics can be included. Pedagogy has to join the frontline. That means that universities need to become more dramaturgical, and in several dimensions, to build a nexus between research and public engagement which is a vital part of what they are. This will no doubt sound like a strange quality to paint as a duty. But to the extent that universities are about thinking together in ways which are inevitably fictive in so far as they require a projection of the imagination into the future, it is not. So many of the issues that universities are concerned with, which require the world to show up differently so as to make people think anew, need heightened levels of communication, and different kinds of communication, so that they become more likely to press on the interests of the various publics that flicker into and out of existence (Amin and Thrift, 2013). At present, while many university academics have become involved in all kinds of experiments in heightened communication and shared experience, in rewilding how we see the world so that we are able to appreciate its magical qualities, universities themselves do far too little to produce concerted communication in this way. Endless press releases from the media office and summary booklets highlighting an institution's research achievements mainly act as a booster for institutional priorities. University research needs to feel like it belongs to the public and not just alumni and donors by providing all manner of channels of access and participation. The pandemic has shown that there can be a genuine demand for much more knowledge than universities currently issue. The population at large contains all kinds of unrequited intellectual longings which can be transformed into gold, aided no doubt by the fact that more and more people have a degree but by no means restricted to this audience.

Of course, there are communities which are already receptive (Oreskes, 2019). Four come to mind. One is professionals who need relevant information. In medical research that could be people like doctors but also nurses and midwives. Another community consists of people who have daily contact with arenas like the land and the oceans which gives them heightened sensitivity to change and a pressing need to understand what is going on, like farmers and fishers. A third community consists of people who have educated themselves on particular topics, often to very high standards, a phenomenon found in numerous fields, from environmental science to history. Then, finally, there is the aforementioned citizen science. Citizen science, a phrase first coined in the mid-1990s, though its origins lie much earlier in the bird counts of the early twentieth century, is now an extraordinary enterprise, aided by the advent of desktop computers, GPS, home weather stations, and smartphones (Irwin, 2018). Each year around 700 new projects are launched, from crowdsourced citizen science, in which lay people contribute data or computing power, to citizen science in which lay people are actively involved in a project, contributing research and ideas of their own. Some projects are enormous, for example many of those to do with climate and weather (like Rainfall Records which has rescued more than five million rainfall measurements dating back to 1836), or astronomy (including a number of projects searching – successfully – for new exoplanets) or ecology. (Many ecological projects now involve special apps like eBird, arising out of the Cornell University Lab of Ornithology international network which has registered over one billion bird observations and BirdNET an associated birdsong identifier or Cicada Safari which tracked the 2021 swarm in the US, allowing the insects to be mapped and their time of emergence recorded.) Others may be smaller scale but require citizens with considerable expertise, like the night-time underwater photographers who have been enlisted to photograph larval fish or the repairers being surveyed for The Big Repair. Others draw on the expertise that citizens have that professionals often lack, for example the knowledge of combat and arms that some English civil war re-enactors have amassed. Of course, citizen science has its limits. People will sign up en masse for a short period of time but only a few will want to subscribe to a deeper engagement. It is, after all, a time-consuming activity. But, for all the pitfalls, like ensuring that data quality persists, citizen science is a real advance (and it is heartening to find that UKRI has now provided funding for some citizen science projects). One estimate suggests that the global reserve of people which can be drawn in is about 1.7 million at any one time.

Many more communities and potential communities exist, ready and waiting to interact. Take just the extraordinary example of March Mammal Madness (Hinde et al., 2021) which draws a large and diverse audience (including approximately 1 per cent of US high school students in 2019) into mammalian biology through a broad range of media but particularly a simulated tournament. 'Outreach' is entirely the wrong word for a project like this, which has to be much more all-encompassing than simple extension. Here are potential epistemic communities. But too many of them stutter because they are carried out by individual institutions when they should be a common preserve. Perhaps the most obvious topic – climate change – shows the rub. Stoknes (2015) points out that communication by universities and other institutions about climate change has been remiss, at least if judged by results. Surveys show that, until the advent of a new generation of climate change protestors in the last few years, citizens cared more about the issue 25 years ago.

But it is possible for research universities to mount subtle, concerted and, above all, positive campaigns that will help to change opinions on issues like climate change, based on an archive of enunciation and performance which runs across the arts and humanities in an almost seamless fashion, an archive which is intent on conjuring up redemptive feelings which can be converted into positive actions and can help people to make free with their own projects by drawing on the multiple kinaesthetic insights of performance studies and its consequent ability to present and dramatise issues in new ways as well as the battery of different arts and crafts that allow us to experience the different milieux of the world differently, from music to painting, from film to games, from dance to drawing (Thrift, 2009, Masschelein, 2019). Currently, universities as a corporate body sometimes hold off from this work as somehow 'too political'. That is not an attitude that can last as the portents of disaster mount up.

A genuine research communication strategy would have to be much more ambitious, then. It would flood every media channel. It would democratise parts of research by continuing to embrace citizen science. It would make data available as a matter of course.⁷ It would produce more apps like e-bird. It wouldn't just proselytise. Rather, it would lay out the current state of knowledge, the stumbling blocks and roadblocks implicit in particular courses of action, and the dangers of different courses of inaction. Research universities need to think much more seriously about this prospect but as a bloc. The online journal, *The Conversation*, shows that they can work together but that is just the start. Research universities need to dramatically expand their orbit to encompass new publics. It's true that the very notion of a public has been corrupted – by platforms that encourage anger rather than debate, by package-deal ethics by easy cognitive shortcuts which construct spurious certainties, by the ability to give an immediate response rather than stopping to think. Universities need to fight back, no longer functioning as an expert vanguard dispensing knowledge and expertise or as intermediaries who know their place but rather functioning as a means of producing creative energies in the public at large so that a new kind of critical commons is produced.

To begin with, I cannot see why the research universities – combined as one – couldn't provide a serious fact-checking service. The facts would have to be well-specified but juries of academics could certainly scrutinise the evidence and come to provisional conclusions which could be updated as new information becomes available. It would be like a hybrid between Wikipedia and projects like the *Stanford Encyclopaedia of Philosophy*, in that it would provide authoritative accounts and judgements on major issues. It would not give instant responses but rather provisional judgements which recognise a variety of views. One model could be the IPCC Climate Change reports. Research universities also need to understand the need to inform policymaking, perhaps through founding a think tank of their own. And they need to privilege slow thinking in the midst of the press of events. One journalism venture, Tortoise, already does this in interesting ways so there are existing templates.

Another issue is scaling up communication. I am quite sure that there ought to be a permanent university research television/internet channel, for example, which extends much further than periodic documentaries and YouTube. What about the beleaguered BBC 4 becoming this? After all, many of its presenters are academics. For the spoken word, we need to join up all the excellent work that currently goes on. There ought to be a central repository of podcasts or, at the very least, a system of accreditation. There ought to be a central global repository of citizen science projects to which citizens could sign up, an expanded Zooniverse or SciStarter which would also allow citizens to gain qualifications, as ASU (Arizona State University) does. There ought to be a dedicated research university radio channel. Radio 4 has already shown the demand for informed material from commentators like Melvyn Bragg and Laurie Taylor and I have already mentioned accomplished science communicators like Jim Al-Khalili, Brian Cox and Alice Roberts, as well as the large numbers of history communicators such as David Olusoga, Bettany Hughes, Michael Wood and Lucy Worsley. And in the online world, there are just so many – so many – opportunities for new platforms. Why not a research university platform?

This recasting of university communication leads on to the fourth and final duty: the *sharing of not only knowledge but action*. By a process somewhere between design and osmosis, research universities have become increasingly involved in service to the community since the Second World War. That service takes place across many registers. I am not sure that even now many people in research universities themselves realise just how extensive this service is. Whenever I hear an academic being cynical about the world, or read authors who think universities somehow lack enough social responsibility (e.g. Grant, 2021), I can direct them to their own backyard where staff and students are busy at work on a myriad of projects, mainly but not only small scale, mostly but by no means only charitable, which cover an extraordinary variety of reachings out into the world, from teaching in schools around the world to science outreach, from running hospitals overseas to giving basic health advice, from providing legal aid to pursuing human rights, from religious and other conciliation services to ecumenical pursuits, from the whole gamut of arts and cultural and sporting activities to producing film and video, from ecological and environmental projects like environmental remediation and species conservation to battling pollution. The list goes on and on. This work is different in kind from the officially sponsored initiatives that place universities centre stage as urban and regional economic actors, important though they may be. It is more low key in nature but my guess is that it is just as effective. In other words, universities have become, in part unwittingly, a mainstay of civil society in a way that they never were before. This can only be to the good. It provides new connections, new relays, and in a way which gives the lie to the raddled idea of an ivory tower (Shapin, 2012). More to the point, it provides an introit to new ways of upping the research university ante which it is hard to disagree with.

And the general theme of these four duties? I have already touched on it. We are entering what could be a new Dark Age as climate and biosphere change bites. Though they are meant to be long-term institutions, research universities could end up as just another casualty of a coming barbarism. So let's go large and think about them as experiments in how to make a common future, but this time by reaching out to not only students but the whole population. Surely research universities could position themselves as something more. After all, something more must be their guiding ethos.

And this brings me finally to the subject of indigenous knowledge. Science has produced many boons for humanity. But some of the technologies that have arisen within its orbit have contributed to our current unsustainable state, not improved or ameliorated it. Science, especially in its fast, mechanised version which still sometimes – even now – sees the universe as a passive backdrop to human thought, has not always been an innocent party and it cannot shuffle off all responsibility for how its products are used. Of course, there are things that universities can do themselves to contribute to general sustainability and new kinds of ecologies – and they are doing so. Most universities are hurrying to make their often enormous environmental footprints nature-positive, for example, though the task will be a difficult and challenging one, as the University of Oxford's ambitious Environmental Sustainability Strategy shows only too well, not least because even this strategy will only take it one third of the way towards biodiversity net gain and because mitigation can involve so many different options (Bull et al., 2022). But actions like these, commendable as they might be, do not signal that epistemic flaws in the actual conduct of science can suddenly be solved. One source for thinking about ways in which science can change to help the transition to a new planet is provided by indigenous science. Indigenous peoples tend to live in/think of the world in a different more reciprocal and perspectival way. And this extends to how they do knowledge. The result is clear. In many cases, indigenous communities have amassed knowledge that has allowed them to coexist with and nurture their environments over hundreds and sometimes even thousands of years. For example, indigenously-managed lands tend to have far more intact biodiversity than other lands, even those that have been purposely set aside for conservation. Of course, it is possible to exaggerate indigenous knowledge, trying to make it into something it isn't, a kind of general all-purpose saviour which has all the answers. But in its respect for coexistence with the planet resulting from understanding the universe as active right from the off, it now chimes with many developments in science, acts as an inspiration in certain ways by rattling science's self-inflicted cages, and demonstrates that there is more than one pathway that can produce enlightenment (Poskett, 2022).

A loss of research excellence?

Before I move on to some potential solutions to research universities' woes, I want to mention one further issue: research excellence. This may seem like a strange choice. After all, in many ways, British research universities may well be at or near the top of their research game. But here's why I think this might become an issue.

In the end, much of what research universities have to distinguish themselves with is their high standards of research and there has to be a concern that these standards might be adversely affected by dilemmas which are becoming more and more pressing. I am genuinely in two minds about drawing attention to this issue (and indeed whether there even is one) but it does need airing.

Too much

Most particularly, there is the content of research itself. A lot has been written about the decline of scholarship, the deadening hand of management, the pressure cooker of aspiring to do good research, the decline of the monograph, and so on. But there is precious little work that really shows whether these developments have made any difference to the *quality* of research (howsoever measured). Oft times, we seem to be casting around in the dark for guidance. So what do we know?

To begin with, the conduct of research is changing. It is becoming larger scale, multi-authored, and more procedural. The days of single authors may not be numbered but they are certainly threatened in many parts of academe. More and more papers are being produced by what is, in effect, a research machine. Instead of standing on the shoulders of giants, standing on the shoulders of crowds. Between 1726 and 2009, for example, Jinha (2010) estimated that the cumulative total of papers reached over 50 million with a doubling time of 24 years.[8] But is this profusion producing better results? It is undoubtedly covering more topics, and these topics are being covered by academics from a much wider set of backgrounds (Kozlowski et al., 2022). It clearly does some things better – when it involves enquiry that covers many locations, for example, or utilises new technologies and methodologies. But is the *quality* of research stemming from the change to full-on mass production good, better or worse?

Recent work suggests that more doesn't necessarily mean better and that more is producing not only a glut but also adding substantially to academic tasks like refereeing (Bauerlein et al., 2010).[9] There are some straws in the wind. For example, medical research has often been accused of over-production. As Altman (1994, p. 59) famously wrote, 'We need less research, better research, and research done for the right reasons'. Again, over-production may be part of a more general problem of declining research productivity. In the US, on some measures, for parts of the economy where it is possible to document all research and development, 'research effort is rising substantially while research productivity is declining sharply' (Bloom, Van Reenen and Williams, 2019, p. 1), one result being that it seems to be getting more expensive to get to good ideas (Bloom et al., 2017). In other words, more researchers seem to be needed to get to significant results (Bloom et al., 2020). General declines in research productivity may be being offset by increased research effort – or not. Part of this fall may be because of a decline in discovery research spending, or because of a decline in academic productivity (perhaps linked to team working), or because of a decline in business research and development productivity, or all three. Truth to tell, we just don't know. Someone needs to do some more research!

Part of the reason for this state of affairs may also be that getting research published is no longer the challenge it was. In these days of online and open access, there are more and more journals – I would say too many – and many of them are willing to publish a large amount of what comes along. The result? Three million journal articles were published in 2018 from about 33,100 active scholarly peer-reviewed English-language journals (plus a further 9,400 non-English-language journals).[10] It is impossible to tell exactly how many of these articles will ever be cited.

There is some partially good news. Recent research (Van Noorden, 2017) on the core group of 12,000 or so journals in the Web of Science found that zero-citation papers are much less prevalent than is often believed. Fewer than 10 per cent of scientific articles are likely to remain uncited and this proportion is declining over time.[11] The true figure may be lower, because large numbers of papers that the database records as uncited have actually been cited elsewhere. Again, just because a paper goes uncited doesn't mean it is never read. That doesn't necessarily mean that there is less low-quality research to be concerned about: many more thousands of journals are not indexed by the Web of Science. In other words, there may be a problem of too much low-quality research, as evidenced by, for example, the rise of so-called predatory journals that have questionable publication practices. But it would be dangerous to just assume it. Again more research is needed!

The problem of pressure to publish only adds to concerns. Most research university promotion committees do take some notice of volume, it's true, but, folk theories aside, there isn't any overwhelming evidence that academics are disproportionately rewarded for publishing large numbers of papers. It is quality that committees mostly look out for. True, a certain volume of papers may be necessary to get into a committee's line of sight but high citation tends to come chiefly from publishing papers that lay the foundations for new lines of research. Of course, some academics may think the opposite, which might induce a slipshod tendency. As Nelson (2021, p. 191) pithily puts it 'Scientists are rewarded for getting things published, not for getting things right, and so they tend to favour speed and ease over robustness'. But, to the extent that this is true (and I think one needs to be very careful not to exaggerate what is a common stereotype which needs a lot of unpacking), it is important to take care in depicting even such academics' work as simply a land grab. Things are more complicated than that. More research is needed!

That said, and for whatever reason, as a flood of papers has appeared it has made it almost impossible to keep up, leading to constant fear of missing out. No wonder that a raft of different software tools have appeared that trawl databases for papers on topics specified by their users, some of them like

ResearchGate linked to social networks. 'Feed fatigue' has become a feature of academic life. When a database like Google Scholar has an estimated 400 million papers on its books and a preprint server service like arXiv gives access to over two million papers (not to mention Sci-Hub, a popular but controversial website that hosts pirated copies of scientific papers), software tools are pretty well the only way to go (Matthews, 2021).

Research culture

An allied concern. Research culture. Critics will tell you that just about everything about the current conduct of research is wrong: in a sign of the times, the latest international review of the Research Excellence Framework is concerned with research culture. It has become almost sacred writ that the REF must become part of an attempt to 'create a positive culture which recognises all contributions to research' (Speech by the Minister of Science, 2020), one which recognises that the 'criteria by which we judge excellence in research are too narrow' (UKRI, 2022). But the criticisms of research culture spread more widely than just the conduct of the REF. The criticisms are multifarious. First off, there is what counts as research itself. In tune with the collaborative spirit of the age, some researchers and funding agencies believe that research needs to be redefined so that the process of research output is accompanied by acknowledging and buttressing a whole raft of other skills which can make the quality of research 'better' such as teamwork, collegiality, synthesis, replication, and curating, each of which in their own way go to acknowledge the many contributors and contributions that have to be made to attain a finished piece of work in some, though not all, fields (this part of the debate often tends to concentrate on big science to the exclusion of fields like the arts and humanities, the social sciences, and pure mathematics and almost never tackles the issue of where to stop when, for example, some of those occupying supporting roles no longer seem to want to see them that way). Second, to return to a previous point, there is the common complaint that there is too much emphasis on quantity rather than quality (this part of the debate tends to ignore the fact that assessment exercises like the REF have tended to become less demanding of quantity over time).

> While most researchers feel that their sector is producing high-quality outputs, they also report deep concerns about how sustainable the culture is in the long term ... a complex network of incentives from government, funders and institutions ... seem to focus on quantity of outputs, and narrow concepts of 'impact', rather than on real quality. The upshot is that they feel intense pressure to publish, with too little value placed on how results are achieved and the human costs. They

accept competition as a necessary part of working in research, but think that it is often becoming aggressive and harmful. (Wellcome, 2019, p. 3)

Moving on, the current research culture has equality and diversity issues. Research is beset by racism and just about every other ism as well. The net result in many (though not all fields) is citational and just about every other kind of injustice (Kozlowski et al., 2022). So, for example, promotion and similar needs to be overhauled so that it no longer biases against particular groups of academics. Third, research involves a blizzard of bullying and harassment, some of it racist or sexist (Wellcome, 2019, Russell Group, 2021). I can't think of anyone who would want to deny the presence of bullying and harassment in research but it is exceptionally difficult to know its scale and extent or how higher education performs compared with other sectors. Surveys carried out so far tend to be self-selecting and what counts as bullying and harassment is often imperfectly specified. (Just from my own experience, different people can have very – very – different views of what counts as bullying. A few people want to put words of criticism with which they disagree into this category. Equally, a few people seem to bear unacceptable behaviour long beyond what most would regard as the point of no return.) Then, one final and all too familiar issue. Researcher terms of employment often make researchers feel nugatory, moving from one contract to another, constantly having to look for the next opportunity, feeling that they lack any bargaining power, concerned that they are perceived as second-class citizens whose rights have been trampled on.

What is interesting is why issues like these, many of which have arisen many, many times before, should have gained so much traction at this point. There are simple practicalities, of course. For example, the problems of short-term contracts and job insecurity have been commented on (and, to an extent, acted upon) many times now. (So apart from the pressure applied by a number of national organisations, most universities have schemes in place that are meant to shave the worst edges off these issues like bridging schemes, though the short-term nature of a lot of research funding makes it difficult to achieve what many researchers crave most, that is much more in the way of permanence.) However, the greater part is a zeitgeist which manifests as at least three practices. First, as the contemporary emphasis on equality, diversity and inclusion which, for example, reveals itself in mentions of being decolonial on many grant proposals. Second, as a profound suspicion of, even hostility towards, individual genius in a time in which everyone can be marked as special in some way and every achievement has to be marked as a triumph of team-led collaboration. (This is a business management idea originally arising out of the Hawthorne studies of the 1920s and 1930s on group performance – though its roots can be traced even earlier in the work of writers like Ringelmann and Moede – one refreshed and made popular in its contemporary 'collab' form by the tech industry in the 1990s and found now in many other spheres even including popular music where in place of the individual songwriter the tin pan alley tradition of industrial production involving multiple writers of a song has broadened out into a standard industrialised way of producing music which includes acknowledging the efforts of multiple songwriters but also large numbers of other individuals acting as a team.) And third as the swash of the idea of innovation communities, and its side-shoots like democratising innovation, open innovation and the like, business ideas which became current in the 2000s that have washed up on the shores of academe.

And part of it also seems to be existential: a sense that competitiveness in research has run out of control and what were jobs that gave many rewards, even with all their downsides, increasingly resemble a treadmill which isolates rather than brings researchers together. In particular, there is a general feeling that research is not a meritocracy (as it should be, presumably). Certain people are favoured. They get the goodies while other people struggle. For example, there is compelling evidence that women and ethnic minorities working in prominent fields tend to get fewer citations than white, male peers, that white applicants are more successful than minorities in grant applications and that men tend to receive more funding than women. Many of the complaints about competitiveness and bias may well be valid but to a degree which is still sometimes uncertain. It is hard to disagree that evidence badly needs to be sought 'to improve the efficiency, effectiveness, fairness and impact of research' (Wellcome, 2019, p. 3) but on the basis of systematic and carefully framed studies which don't start by already knowing the answers.

Not surprisingly, the result of all this concern spills over into research assessment where some familiar themes are currently being repeated once more with feeling (Nature, 2022). There is the cost of assessment. For example, the 2014 Research Excellence Framework cost about £246 million, the bulk of which was borne by universities. Again, the criteria for promotion and other forms of individual assessment need to be broadened to include activities such as teamwork, mentorship, replication, and curating. Equally, so it is said, in the disciplines to which it applies, publications, curriculum vitae, incentives like prizes and even fellowships need to move from being largely based around the idea of individual genius to being based around a form of industrial production by collaborative teams made up of many different contributors, in the process recognising more diverse outputs than final publications. (For example, UKRI has launched a publication platform called Octopus[12] which is intended to distribute credit more broadly by unpacking the process of discovery into eight components and assigning it accordingly, as well as working with other funding organisations to foster the use of narrative curriculum vitae in funding applications, while others have run a 'hidden REF' which distributes credit to those individuals and groups in hidden, 'non-REFable' roles, nominated by their colleagues for recognition for the work they do.) The presence of quantitative indicators of research success is also under examination yet again – even though the Willsdon report (Willsdon, 2015) did a perfectly good job of summarising the pros and cons of quantitative metrics and best practice some time ago – again on the grounds that they imperfectly summarise a researcher's contribution (Wang and Barabasi, 2021). Different methods of evaluation of research and different means of granting research funding – like a lottery – are on the list too.[13]

No one doubts that a good part of this research culture and assessment reform agenda, one which intersects in its concerns with issues like co-design and 'open science', needs to happen in the cause of a more welcoming research culture. But that still leaves a problem that cannot just be circumvented. That is that, at the end of the day, it has to be accepted that some academic researchers are just better at research than others – more inventive, more creative, more entrepreneurial, more focussed, more adept at winning grants, what have you – and that any research institution is going to want to seek these people out. Not everyone is going to get the research prizes and those institutions that opt out of attracting and retaining these researchers are going to be at a disadvantage. Let's put it another way. Weber (cited in Clark, 2009, p. 466) argued that to succeed as an academic, one's work needs to demonstrate some degree of 'inspiration'. 'But this inspiration does not allow itself to be compelled ... Inspiration does not replace work. And work for its part cannot replace or compel inspiration.' That means, like it or not, some degree of judgement about whether people are excelling at inspiration and work. And that, in turn, means that, like it or not, a good part of that judgement of research[14] is going to continue to be about peer-reviewed publication (in whatever form that takes) as proof of both inspiration and work – as indeed the Declaration on Research Assessment (DORA) recognises when it declares that 'the peer-reviewed research paper will remain a central research output that informs research assessment'. I can't see a way around this. So, quantitative publication indicators can only point in the direction of achievement (and can be misleading) but as part of a broader portfolio of evidence they can provide guidance without necessarily leading to what Osterloh and Frey (2014) call a 'taste for rankings' overshadowing a 'taste for science'. Both the Leiden Manifesto and the DORA recognise the need for breadth and balance in making judgements and that must mean using a broad evidence base which calls on both quantitative and qualitative judgements which do not 'cede decision-making to the numbers' or to opinions flavoured with too much rhetoric (Hicks et al., 2015, p. 430). In particular, any quantitative judgements need to be field-sensitive, adjust for age, take account of the vagaries of different data sources, and be based on a suite of indicators, but, used correctly, they 'can provide crucial information that would be difficult to gather or understand by means of individual expertise' (Hicks et al., 2015).[15] The same strictures apply in different forms to many qualitative judgements. For example, the current vogue for narrative curriculum vitae comes with its own problems and susceptibilities to abuse, some of which are serious.

Some complainants seem to want to go further. They come close to arguing that in pursuit of a kinder research culture all pressure is illegitimate, all quantitative indicators should be scrapped in favour of purely narrative accounts of research careers and publication should become, if not an optional choice, just one of many indicators in a world of all but forced collegiality in which authorship should be seen as just one of many qualities, no more or less important than, say, sharing open data.

Some care needs to be taken here. Though some academics seem intent on depicting life in a university as a 'psychological hell' (Fleming, 2021) on earth, it provides quite a range of privileges even now and it would be difficult to persuade the public that these don't need to be earned. So, to take just one example, the REF is an inherently unequal exercise. It judges the quality of people's research, after all. Quite rightly, its terms have gradually become more and more focused on quality rather than quantity. But, absent the obvious issues of maternity/paternity leave, serious illness, gradual loss of productivity during a career, disability, and so on, surely there are some minimum research standards of quality and quantity that ought to be met if you're an active research academic in a research university.[16] (Not least because of the ghostly army of many other academics who would love nothing better than the privilege of standing in the shoes of academics in these universities whose research activity has lapsed.)

One of the issues that is often skated over in all of this is what would actually constitute better research. We do know many things about the conduct of research already. For example, that whereas large teams develop science, small teams are more likely to disrupt it, that, in many (though not all) cases, cultivating diversity in a team is a real boon and that researchers who continuously co-author papers across time – so called 'super-tie collaborators' – are likely to be more successful (Wang and Barabasi, 2021). But there are some other pretty fundamental issues that have been very rarely addressed. How many people are doing really pathbreaking research? How many people are doing great confirmatory research (which can often turn up unexpected results)? How many people are adding just a sliver of knowledge or none to speak of but may be making a major contribution to the dynamics of a team? How can we judge people who may be producing work which is simply too good or too much at odds with accepted paradigms to be appreciated and comes into its majority many decades later? Or, what about the John Rawls syndrome? (Famously, Rawls took 21 years to produce that milestone work of philosophy, *A Theory of Justice*, and he produced little else in the meantime. Are there other Rawls-like figures out there that we're missing? Or are the likely candidates never going to finish whatever it is they're working on, or aren't really working on much at all?) Or, more generally, how would we ever know if research is better now than in the past – or worse – and why? Have we substituted quantity for quality and, if so, to what degree? Indeed, how might we even begin to judge this? And all this before we get to research teams where some of the same questions recur plus the issue of team productivity in its many guises, especially given that UKRI and other funders, sometimes seem to be getting dangerously close to mandating this form of thinking as the favoured one. For any system of research, these are all crucial concerns but there is surprisingly little work that addresses them head on, even research commissioned by grant-funding agencies who you would think would want answers to questions that are central to their existence. That is why the setting up of the Research on Research Institute is important and not just an exercise in academic navel-gazing. Policy on research needs to be research-led.

On a good day, I think that the efforts to change research culture can only be a boon. Take just science. As a matter of historical record, what counts as a scientist or indeed science has changed over time, partly in tune with the prevailing culture, and there is no reason to think that it won't continue to change, not least as those coming up in the current culture have been socialised into collaboration as a way of thinking and not just organisation. Science is increasingly, as Halsey had it all those years ago, a 'professionalized bureaucracy' (although industrialised professionalised bureaucracy might be closer to the truth now) carried out in teams by people with many different kinds of skills. Why shouldn't the kind of research being produced be skewed in line with this set-up, producing new possibilities of new? Why shouldn't standards change around what is good research, research which chimes with these new ways of working? Why shouldn't publication take on new more inclusive forms? Think of just the shifting nature of what has counted as both the machinery of scientific innovation and what counts as objectivity through the ages. According to this outlook, not only will there be no decline in standards but there could be a kind of renaissance. New organisations of science can produce much better research and be more humane to boot.

Whatever the case, I think the issue of research excellence needs pointing to, even if it will – I'm absolutely 100 per cent sure – be misconstrued by some as managerialism or elitism or such like. (Perhaps that's why publications like the latest UKRI (2022) research strategy hardly mention the excellence word). After all, notwithstanding all the legitimate doubts and concerns about equality of opportunity – and there are many – and about judgements of excellence that are suspect or that are too often honoured in the breach, a fundamental pillar of research universities is that they are a meritocracy.

Because this meritocracy is undeniably imperfect or more distributed than is sometimes thought does not mean that the ideal is invalidated, though it surely needs work.

And there are good reasons to continue to make the case for excellence. Now, more than ever, we must have the very best research. Of course, there are many kinds of very best research done in very many different ways. But anything less than the very best, howsoever it is interpreted, is a disservice to a world that is crumbling beneath our feet, a world that is now in a state of emergency which is only going to grow worse by the year.

Discovery research

Another concern. Discovery research. Of course, discovery research is valuable in itself. It is not some useless gewgaw but rather a means for humanity to aim for the stars by transforming its perception of the world it inhabits. But even in instrumental terms it has immense value. Much of the literature tends to focus on applied research. But all the evidence suggests that many substantive new industrial sectors will grow out of discovery research – those Nobels again – not applied research and that cutting back on it is damaging economically as well as intellectually. Three concerns predominate. One is hypothecation. A research strategy that blocks out more and more funds for hypothecated purposes can bypass as well as boost discovery research and end up winning the battle but losing the war. Another is assuming that the major problem is translation of research into actual products. The government has wisely committed to a big boost to research funding. But if the extra monies are allocated to yet more applied research, there is an issue. There is nothing wrong with more money being committed to developments like the new Treasury-funded Future Fund (to be administered by British Patient Capital) which will give boosts to fast-growing firms working on (hopefully) game-changing technologies, or to Innovate UK, but without discovery research there will soon be nothing to develop. The pipeline would stop flowing. There are some worrying signs. REF-related QR funding declined by 14 per cent in real terms between 2010/11 and 2020/21 though the latest UKRI settlement looks like it will halt this trend. The balance of funding between QR and Research Council funding has fallen from 80 pence in the pound in 2007, to 64 pence in the pound in 2021/22 (Stevens, 2022). Meanwhile research council funds have stayed pretty well flat over the last few years (and, though that is now changing, for some research councils it is not by much) while translational funding has received more of the share of the cake and is about to receive another boost. Meanwhile, Horizon Europe funding, some of which goes to discovery research through the European Research Council, lay ready to be doled out to 46 UK scientists who were successful in its first round but has now been withdrawn (though the government has promised to substitute funding), as, in a stupid act of self-harm, the EU has now blocked access to its funding, using Horizon Europe as a political pawn. (It is interesting to consider how similar in character any British 'Plan B' replacement will be.) Finally, there is the issue of picking research winners. In moderation, there is nothing wrong with such a strategy. But it has its downsides. For example, funders in practically every country tend to pick much the same often over-hyped areas of research – hydrogen, batteries, life sciences, big data and artificial intelligence, cybersecurity, space – on which to concentrate although it is by no means clear that these are where the real action is or will be. Meanwhile, other areas which may well form the core of extraordinary new advances are crowded out. Certainly, a number of economists have pointed out that there has been no industrial advance that has led to really major increases in productivity for 50 years or more (e.g. Gordon, 2016) but I'd be willing to bet that the next one will come out of left field from university discovery research.

In the wrong place

Moving on, government is considering making research funding an explicit tool of regional policy, enthusiastically supported by the universities who think that they will benefit (Mckenzie, 2021) who will have already noted the avowed propensity of funders like UKRI and Wellcome to want to alter the balance and range of institutions they fund. Given regional disparities, it might seem difficult to object to such a strategy, especially given that the government has committed to increasing the level of research funding to the OECD average of 2.4 per cent of GDP by 2027, making it possible for there to be no losers, just relative winners. After all, the UK regions and subregions that contain London, Oxford and Cambridge account for 46 per cent of public and charitable research and development in the UK, but only 31 per cent of business research and development and 21 per cent of the population (Forth and Jones, 2020). Again, of the series of major capital investments made in research infrastructure between 2007 and 2014, 71 per cent went into London, the East and South East of England and the need for continuing revenue funding to support these investments will lock in geographical imbalances in R&D for many years more (Forth and Jones, 2020).

Game over, you might think. UKRI already has a Strength in Places Fund (as well as other instruments that can be used in a similar fashion like Knowledge Transfer Partnerships and the Higher Education Innovation Fund) and at least one research council has reinstated 'regional engagement' advisors. There are other likely boosts too like the UK Shared Prosperity Fund which will act as a replacement for the EU structural funds. More locational rebalancing will come as part of the 'levelling-up' innovation agenda. Thus,

> by 2030, domestic public investment in R&D outside the Greater South East will increase by at least 40 per cent, and over the Spending Review period by at least one third. This additional government funding will seek to leverage at least twice as much private sector investment over the long term to stimulate innovation and productivity growth. (HMG, 2022, p. 3)

This policy will apply to the funds of UKRI and the National Institute of Health Research (NIHR). In addition, £100 million will be spent on three new innovation accelerators in Manchester, the West Midlands and Glasgow which will apparently become the nuclei of new Silicon Valleys. Why not keep going? The levelling-up policy could be applied to QR. Why not devote all of the increase in public R&D investment arising from the 2.4 per cent of GDP target wholly to projects outside London and the South East (Fraser, Blagden and Holloway, 2021)?

This kind of research funding reprofiling seems obvious to many commentators. So 'the West Midlands and the northwest, ... have good universities and generate more than their fair share of private sector research funding with precious little help from the government. They should get more' (Duncan, 2021).[17] It's not that far from there to loading all research funding according to place, though, to be fair, I can find no commentators who have seriously argued for this option[18] and indeed the government's reprofiling is more modest than might be first thought.

But there are some important objections to the tendency to level up research funding. First off, the level of geographic research concentration in the UK is actually *less* than in other major research countries. The UK is *not* concentrated relative to these countries. Indeed,

> The combined R&D expenditure in London's universities falls behind the equivalent investment for each of the US top ten cities. Even after adding together university R&D spend in Cambridge, Edinburgh, London, Manchester and Oxford, the total is about the same as in Houston, Texas. These five great UK cities include some of the world's most famous and highly respected universities whose combined research spending is around half that in either Los Angeles or Boston. (Chaytor, Gottlieb and Reid, 2021, p. 22)

Second, you might no longer be funding so much of the very best research, which often tends to be concentrated in the universities of London and the South East, and by robbing Peter to pay Paul (the Royal Society's concern) you might compound the declining economic productivity problem rather than give productivity a boost, and pose yet another economic threat to the national interest in a time when really excellent research may be one of the only ways out of the binds the UK has made for itself (Hillman, 2022a). Third, you might also find that research investment made on the basis of levelling up makes somewhat less difference than assumed, given that what literature there is has been largely based on correlations rather than causality. Perhaps it would be more appropriate to focus on the impact of research rather than level of investment (Chaytor, Gottlieb and Reid, 2021). Finally, what is particularly interesting is how often commentators mention the negative aspects of the Matthew Effect according to which to them that hath shall be given more. For example, a valid criticism might be that concentrations of excellence may block off good young researchers with unorthodox solutions who work outside of the core institutions. The issue is that although the Matthew Effect may well be a problem in terms of immediate economic development it is not at all clear that it is a problem in terms of building research excellence. It cannot be airily dismissed. (Who cares if the UK gets 'fewer Nobel laureates' argues Duncan (2021), completely ignoring the fact that Nobels are awarded for founding new strands of scientific enquiry, many of which have changed not just our worldview – though that really ought to be enough – but have founded new economic pathways – like graphene or laser physics or quantum systems or many of the breakthroughs in semiconductors or genome editing or lithium-ion batteries or DNA repair or immunity to viruses.)

Truth to tell, we have no real calculus with which to settle these issues but one thing is certain – unproblematically funding research by location rather than via excellence is not quite as simple a solution as it may seem.

9

Redesigning the research university

So what to do? The process of design – or rather redesign – of universities and university systems doesn't have to be seen as a benighted rebirth of central planning or as a playing field for consultancies. Design is not an alien concept to universities and university systems. For example, pretty well each and every system of higher education has been the subject of intervention in its functioning on a large enough scale to earn the description of design. Clark Kerr's design of the California State system is often cited. In the UK, the university system has been the subject of successive government reports which have led to redesign, often on an epic scale. The same stricture applies in many other countries where there has often been wholesale top-down change. Europe, for example, has seen the growth of a number of super-universities or clusters with eight identified in 2012, 12 in 2013, 14 in 2014 and one more in 2015,[1] of which the most notable example is found in France where the merger of some 20 higher education and research institutions into the new Paris-Saclay federal university has already led to it becoming the 14th best university in the world in the Shanghai Jiao Tong league table (Cassasus, 2020).

Equally, the work of institutional design of individual universities has been a constant work in progress. It can consist of something as simple as changes in committee structure or the addition of a new school or department. Or it can be of wider consequence, as in the vogue for wholesale administrative reorganisation that was current for a few years – which mainly failed. Or it can mean recasting inter-institutional relations.

In what follows, I therefore offer up a series of policies – at several scales – which might act as a basis for moving forward. They suggest intentions primarily to stimulate debate by broadening its current rather cramped confines.

Redesigning the university system

To begin with, the university system needs changing. Against a background in which still more research funding will probably be placed into special pots, where the scale of the research enterprise will likely continue to grow – and with it a bias towards research done in large teams – and where research will probably continue to become more and more international, even against the current geopolitical background, here is what I would like to see happening.

For policy

Replace the Office for Students with a proper intermediary body, one that intermediates and doesn't just pass along orders along from government or is simply bypassed by ministers. At the same time, stop it from creeping up on research policy. For example, take away from it any responsibility for postgraduate research students who are researchers as much as they are students and make sure that it does not get involved in vetting overseas research grants and contracts for whatever reason, as has been proposed in one amendment to the Higher Education (Freedom of Speech) Bill.

Revive the idea, made as far back as 1967 by Peter Laslett, of a cadre of nominated 'national universities' (perhaps, as set out below, made up of a number of research universities which have coalesced in one way or another) at which the very best research is carried out. One possible terminus for some of these national universities might be, as Laslett also suggested, that they become entirely or mainly postgraduate, hastened by the fact that postgraduate qualifications continue to become more important as a labour market differentiator. (In particular, because of schoolification, a Master's degree is becoming a vital means of differentiation and an entry ticket to many of the best jobs.) In effect, this is already happening in some universities, by default. Even in Oxford and Cambridge, postgraduate students now number half or more of the student complement, and they are increasing year on year. (It is not entirely fantastical to think of these two universities as running an undergraduate operation which looks increasingly like a heritage part of the institution, deeply embedded in the hearts of the nation but off to one side of the bulk of what the university is doing.)

Move research universities – or the new breed of national universities that I have argued for – from the DfE back to BEIS, under the aegis of a single minister. I'm sure there must have been research university vice-chancellors who were content with the move of responsibility for higher education back to the DfE in 2016 after its sojourn in DIUS, BIS and BEIS but many feared what might happen in a direct oversight culture – and they were right. At the same time, allow BEIS to initiate individual agreements with each research university. Through an instrument akin to the framework agreements (now being reworked) made with its arm's length bodies (ALBs), the civil service is already well used to tailored forms of interaction. Indeed, government departments like BEIS often have more ALBs than the total number of research universities. Such agreements would also be an excellent way of producing more diversity of approach since they could allow for a degree of autonomy and promote strategic diversity while recognising the claims of the state.

Increase the overhead on grants to 100 per cent. Even though this might mean less research getting done, it would mean that research universities would be doing that research on a sound financial footing. The issue is particularly pressing because of the injection of new research funding from government which, under current circumstances, could cause problems for some research universities as they scrabble to fund the missing overhead for more grants by loading up with yet more international students. If those students don't turn up there will be a research funding gap which, for some, could be unbridgeable. Alternatively, at least acknowledge the amount of funding research universities put into research by giving them a proportional say in funding decisions and how they are handled. At the moment UKRI and its research councils and many charities are spending other people's money by default and expecting them to compete for it.

Find institutional mechanisms which will husband investment so that it can be used to invest in longer-term institutions like universities (Mazzucato, 2020). Governments around the world have increasingly turned to sovereign wealth funds as a means of husbanding such resources, including education. Indeed, the first instances of sovereign funds were created by the state of Texas in the last half of the nineteenth century precisely to fund public education: the Permanent School Fund was created in 1854 to benefit primary and secondary schools, with the Permanent University Fund following on in 1876 and specifically intended to benefit universities. Other governments have tried half-way houses such as the Australian Future Fund, founded in 2006, part of which is devoted to medical research and innovation. The prevailing opinion seems to be that a British sovereign wealth fund might be a step too far but there may be other options. One oft-made suggestion would be to order the national accounts in a different way so that investment goods like research become visible and then commit to increasing the proportion of national spending on these goods by a certain percentage every year.

Instigate a determined campaign to rid universities of that perennial government habit of making bureaucratic demands on them that continually increase costs, for example by insisting that any new demand is balanced by the deletion of an older one. This is, of course, a common political promise but it is hardly ever kept. Perhaps this time it could be. I hate to think how much of university budgets is soaked up by regulatory and other governmental transaction costs.

For teaching

The residential model of undergraduate learning long applied in many universities should at least be questioned. In 1963 the Robbins Committee welcomed 'the widespread and deeply held conviction in all of the universities of the role that university residence can play in university education' (p. 15) but that was when halls of residence were seen as part of an attempt to create what Halsey and Trow (1971) called the 'domesticity' of a small, elite university. In such universities, living in residence was regarded as an education in itself, 'creating community and offering opportunities to enculturate undergraduates, affecting them even more effectively than any formal teaching' (Whyte, 2019, p. 46). As Albert Sloman put in in the 1960s, it would do 'most students good to get away from their families' since it would provide an 'experience of living' to sit alongside 'an opportunity for learning' (cited in Taylor and Pellew, 2020, p. 4). Those days are all but gone. The model may have served the nation well in the past but, as the number of students has increased, and is no longer applicable in the way that it once was, in that large amounts of accommodation are off-campus, it has become much too expensive, much too unwieldy, much too environmentally problematic, and, most importantly, no one has been able to decisively show that the residential model has a pedagogical imperative.[2] Given the strides in online learning, it also risks becoming increasingly irrelevant. Gradually the residential model of university education which has been dominant in UK higher education for so long, one in which 'a university without [student] hostels is not a University' (National Union of Students, 1938, cited in Whyte, 2016, p. 195), will likely erode and it may even wither away over time. It has lost much of its rationale in many universities without gaining a new one, while at the same time making higher education much more expensive and less approachable than it needs to be: abolishing it or diminishing its hold could be a way of reducing the expense of higher education in the least harmful way.

> Beyond a general sense that moving to university will grant the 'freedom to be oneself' and a more or less accurate belief that life is more fun away from mum and dad, it is difficult to say what migrating from home is intended to achieve – especially given the relatively short distances most students actually travel. (Whyte, 2019, p. 38)

At a minimum, it might be good to see some private accommodation nationalised, as Dickinson (2019) mischievously suggests. After all, it is difficult to defend so much government funding being poured into the private residential sector in the way that it currently is.

Accordingly, encourage more universities to draw predominantly on their surrounding student catchments, as in Australia. Some might become chiefly student hubs,[3] with a good part of their activity taking place online. Online teaching in universities like these universities could, as Chirikov et al. (2020) suggest for the US, rely on a national online education platform or platforms which will aggregate the best courses from around the country. (All kinds of student payment models will exist as a result, including subscriptions. The notion of a tuition fee will therefore have to become much more flexible, not least because students will take very different times to complete a degree.)

As personalised information grows in quantity and quality as a result of online teaching, so it becomes possible to think about individualised learning pathways. The rise of competency-based education, which I think will become general in many universities over time, can only strengthen this tendency. The divide between higher and further education (which is already diminishing as higher education institutions teach apprentices and as further education institutions teach higher education students) will diminish even further and, because of competency-based learning, many degree courses will pan out according to each individual student's aptitude and interest and will involve transferable credits. These developments will be dominated by institutions that are fleet of foot. Courses will be taught through a variety of institutions which were formerly separate – not just universities, but further education colleges and other institutions too. Many of them will join up as chains or will franchise courses in student hubs, a development that is already beginning to happen.

To increase the quality of teaching in research universities, institute the Princeton system whereby prospective faculty are given separate research and teaching interviews, remembering that many research academics are very good teachers.

For research universities

Recast research universities' governance. It doesn't work properly for large research institutions. Once upon a time, the academic side of the house was run by a senate, a representative body which made all of the academically-related decisions. The council, made up in the past of some academics, a sprinkling of business people, and very often some local worthies, took the business decisions. All this has now changed. The powers of senate have been eroded. The powers of a slimmed-down council, made up chiefly of business people and the general pool of non-executive directors, with a few token academics thrown in, have increased markedly. The council now not only has responsibility for finance and strategy but has also taken on responsibility for oversight of teaching and research, marking the end of any residual pretence as to which of senate and council was the pre-eminent body. But the change to a slimmed-down council has produced substantial difficulties, with decisions taken farther and farther from the coalface – a risk in any organisation but especially in a research university – by council members who often have a less than full appreciation of either what is at stake or how the institution runs. Lay members of council tend to fix on what they know best and that is usually business and finance, followed by students, followed by research. Retreating from the model of an over-dominant council will be hard. One way might be for council to be made up of an equal number of non-executive and academic members. Another would be for research universities and the Committee of University Chairs (CUC) to set up another constitutional commission.

Start to bulk up the institutional capacity of research universities to increase their influence. For example, the Russell Group could become an institution that leads rather than follows. The Russell Group needs a proper strategy that sets out its vision of the future in a way which means that it leads the debate. (So, for example, April 2021 was an absurdly late time to be making an intervention into the debate on freedom of speech by bringing out a 'statement of principles on freedom of speech'.) It also needs to develop a constitution for research universities that will give it genuine commonality and provide a bulwark against unwarranted interference, a constitution that states the basic principles, powers and duties of a research university that both guarantees certain rights to the people in it and the expectations that a public may expect from it, in other words a constitution which emphasises both rights and responsibilities. Some may argue that a combination of charters and charity law already achieve this goal. I disagree. The group also needs a public-facing leader, as I have already argued, one who is not beholden to any individual institution and who is given the space to lead.

Research universities should jointly set up their own independent institution to produce research agendas and research priorities which highlight the radically new and inventive. With the advent of the new Office of Science and Technology and the National Science and Technology Council the pressure will increase to produce large research initiatives that are strongly related to economic imperatives. This kind of strategy is all very well when conducted in moderation but it runs the risk of crowding out the really innovative research that follows unusual and really difficult questions (and thereby produces very different accounts of the world, discoveries that galvanise our understanding, and technologies that are genuinely disruptive) in favour of boosting exactly the same research priorities as other governments and economic actors around the world. Important though these undoubtedly are, they are nearly always instrumental and short term. They will produce results but not revelations. Witness the government's recent Life Sciences (for which, read medicine) Strategy. Its research priorities are all blisteringly obvious and, as academics strive to obtain grants which are fixed by these horizons, may actually constrain new thinking.

Redesigning universities

Let's move on to what forms individual research universities could take after a period of intense growth and when their spirit and purpose is under question. Obviously, there is no one right answer. Rather, the answers come in a number of guises. But one thing is certain. What cannot happen is just going back to the future. Many years ago, Halsey (1971) argued that, even though he longed for such an outcome, a reversion to a university as a small community of scholars, except in the guise of an Oxbridge college, was near to preposterous. The situation has become much more intractable since then in terms of scale, funding, and general outlook. This kind of nostalgic turnabout cannot stand. But what, then, are the alternatives, alternatives which might at least keep some of the flavour of small research communities but set within what is now the equivalent of a metropolis not a village? There are a number of possibilities.

Go small

At the very smallest scale, two models come to mind from history. First, there is the guild. The earliest universities like Bologna, Oxford and Paris originated in guild structures, either guilds of students or guilds of masters, who owned collective legal rights, rights usually guaranteed by charters and issued by princes, prelates, or the towns in which they were located. (Indeed, in the original Latin *universitas* referred to 'a number of persons associated into one body, a society, company, community, corporation, guild, etc'.) Guilds were self-regulating and they could determine the qualifications of their members, setting up barriers to membership and, to an extent, their members' life course through a career trajectory (for example, apprenticeship, journeyman and finally master). They transmitted craft, in other words, but this did not have to mean manual skills, as is often assumed. There were, for example, guilds of judges and notaries.

A more realistic organisational structure is provided by cooperatives. These have been a feature of history for a long time now, at least since Fourier's phalanstery. Perhaps the most obvious and successful example of a contemporary system of cooperatives is provided by Mondragon. Though it is unlikely, there are ways in which cooperatives could become features of academic life again.

Scale back

More pragmatic solutions would work with the grain of scale. There are several that come to mind. One is to step back from student number growth and even cut numbers. There is no reason at all why all research universities need to grow student numbers as if night follows day. Smaller research universities can decide to specialise much more heavily on disciplines, interdisciplinary topics, and global challenges in which they truly excel and these strands can be at the forefront of a push for more research funding. Princeton, Caltech and Brown all show the way. Not just research but teaching opportunities can follow from restraint. A smaller institution would both find it easier to bring research and teaching together and become attractive to those students looking for a more friendly atmosphere and smaller class sizes. Perhaps it might be possible to bring back a core curriculum. It is tragic how this option has faded away under the banner of student choice Again, it might be possible to follow the lead of entities like the NYU Gallatin School of Individualised Study (and other universities like UBC, Penn and ASU) and institute degrees based on genuine individualised (but curated) degrees. In turn, research-led teaching could become a genuine possibility, rather than something that is more of a goal than an actuality. Research and teaching would genuinely feed off each other.

Grow substantially

Another possibility is to use size to beat size – the answer to scale might just be scale – by adding students to the point where there is enough volume of students from what are often very narrow margins to set up and finance what is increasingly a separate research university: a research university within a university, in other words. This is, in effect, the Arizona State University model. ASU is held up as a model for a new wave of large American universities which will provide access for all who deserve it, produce research that is useful, and teaching that is tailored and produces an inquiring mind (Crow and Dabars, 2020). It is aimed at specifically American circumstances in that it is – admirably – trying to correct some of the specific shortcomings of that university system, shortcomings which do not exist in the same way in the UK. But it is still instructive. Strip away some of the rhetoric and there is another way of looking at ASU – as a tiered model of higher education which includes each contemporary moment of higher education within its bounds. It is a research university, a vocational university, an online university. ASU has large numbers of faculty, about 4,700, nearly 20,000 postgraduate students, some 90,000 undergraduate students spread across five campuses and four regional learning centres, and over 38,000 undergraduate online students. It's true that, in part, it is an answer to a problem that the UK doesn't have – a relatively low proportion of young adults going to university – but it could still serve as a model. In particular, the increasingly successful research part of the university is, in effect, sectioned off. So are the best undergraduate students in Barrett, a residential honours college with a lower student–faculty ratio. However, this option is only open to very large universities which can aggregate narrow margins because of volume. Monash, at 78,000 students (spread across a number of campuses) would be another possible example, as would Ohio State (61,000 students or 68,000 including all campuses) or Sydney (61,000 students). No UK research university gets near to these kinds of student numbers at present though UCL and Manchester seem to be aiming in this direction.

Different forms of collaboration

This level of scale and partitioned organisation could be achieved in a different way from simple growth, however, by joining up several universities. That brings me on to another possibility – one that I have foreshadowed already – more collaboration. There needs to be much greater experimentation with models of 'university' which understand universities as cooperative entities. After all, as a matter of routine, university academics cooperate with academics from other universities at home and abroad so collaboration ought not, in principle at least, be a big problem. But it is. There are numerous obstacles, including:

1. *The other university isn't good enough for us syndrome.* This is a perennial. There can be quite a bit of snobbery. Universities carefully monitor their relative performance and they can be wary of cooperating with other universities that they do not see as their equals or betters. In my experience, academics mainly think the university they are in is better than it is. Meanwhile, the really elite university academics can sometimes tend to think they are up there with God.
2. *The cultures of the university are too distant.* University cultures are often very different from one another as I have shown with the example of Warwick. Such differences have often been fostered over many decades or even centuries. It doesn't matter what the superficial attractions of the tie-up may be, if the universities' cultures do not align you will likely get a lot of talk and not much action. Some universities are pushy and expansionist but there is no point in universities like these joining up with institutions that aren't. It will just produce frustration on both sides.
3. *Collaboration takes a lot of management time and resource.* In my experience, universities do not allocate sufficient time or resources to the task.
4. *Lack of appropriate management skills.* Producing collaboration requires an amalgam of skills which not all management teams can lay claim to. Best not to start on a project if these skills are lacking.
5. *Members of the management team in each university have limited buy-in or even oppose the collaboration on the sly.* Academics, in particular, are often apathetic or oppose these ventures, worried about resources being diverted.
6. *The leadership changes.* The new leader sees the collaboration as the previous leader's initiative and wants a newer, whizzier toy. The new leader doesn't get on with their counterpart. The new leader lacks the courage to commit properly. The permutations are endless.
7. *Bad timing.* A crisis blows up in one or other of the universities which means that the intended partner institution's attention goes off the boil.
8. *Finance.* Universities are marginal financial concerns and the risks of cooperation can be substantial, especially in the early years.

Even given these obstacles, in recent times universities have been collaborating to a much greater extent than formerly, stimulated in part by bodies like the research councils which are increasingly insisting on collaboration. A series of forms of collaboration are available, which can be made with differential levels of fuss to build both concerted intellectual capacity and the level of political protection and consequent bargaining power that is more easily attained by being a large actor spread over multiple locations.

Testudo

One form of collaboration is to produce what I call a *testudo* because it combines defence with attack. *A set of research universities would combine their powers to produce a really substantial national research asset with the general aim of reaching the same level of research income and research power (and political clout) as the two clearly and unproblematically national universities of Oxford and Cambridge (research income £653 million on an overall income of £2.4 billion and £589 million on an overall income of 2.1 billion respectively).* A testudo would consist of three or four research universities that are able to closely align and gradually interdigitate so becoming national universities in their own right. There are plenty of opportunities for novel divisions of labour that can arise from this form. For example, in research very few institutions now run the whole gamut of academic disciplines or indeed would think of doing so, and the tendency is to fewer disciplines rather than more and to more interdisciplinary overlap between the disciplines that are left. Equally, in teaching most institutions are cutting courses that do not get requisite student sign-up unless, that is, they are bolstered by endowments. There is no reason why a division of labour between institutions could not be introduced which allowed each participating university to play a somewhat different role but one which, as a joint operation, added up to more than the sum of its parts. Again, there is no reason in principle why common back offices could not be set up for some administrative functions.

This kind of cohesion has happened already, at least to a degree, and may well happen more in the future. Probably the most obvious candidate for this kind of close amalgamation is a set of 'regional' research universities ('regional' is in scare quotes because regions are amorphous and porous things at the best of times) amalgamating to become a national university. Given how different 'regional' research universities are, and the chequered history of amalgamations more generally, this will be challenging. But there are straws in the wind. To begin with, British universities have been continuously amalgamating come what may, especially in London. Then there have also been attempts at regional consortia. (For example, there is the N8 consortium consisting of the eight most research-intensive universities in the north of England. N8 has two main research foci, agriFood and urban and community transformation, and three emergent research communities: industrial technology for the bioeconomy, targets for new medicines, and robotics and autonomous systems. Currently, the consortium is on a relatively small scale but it doesn't have to be.[4]) And, last but not least, government itself has fitfully offered incentives towards greater amalgamation. That has involved universities opting into particular pots of money according to the propensity to amalgamate or become more specialised as well as research councils increasingly demanding the sharing of equipment between research universities. Comings together of these kinds might at least provide a nucleus for growing larger research institutions which can mirror the research power of universities in London and the south-east.

Another possibility. Government could, I suppose, simply gazette the process of cooperation by amalgamating research universities into regional super-universities on the European super-university or the Californian UCal model. That is both the simplest and the most difficult course. There have been instances of successful government-supported mergers of this kind, especially in London. But the example of the merger of Manchester University with UMIST shows that this scale of amalgamation requires very considerable investment and can be the work of decades.

International cooperation

There is a further complication arising out of an imperative towards cooperation. Universities are generally thought to be relatively geographically concentrated – after all, they are still all generally named after single places. But, increasingly, they're not single places. Many universities have become multilocational not just within but between nations which is one reason why, for research universities in particular, with their serried national and international footprints, conforming to the role of a civic university is bound to be problematic. Instead, increasingly it will be necessary to think about what a university is as a more general space of interaction, one which can certainly serve a particular city or region but always tempered by the fact that a part of the university is likely to be elsewhere (Knight, Jones and Gertler, 2020). The point is particularly salient when it comes to research. Where research is concerned, it is possible to argue that there is no longer such a thing as an individual university located in one place. There are probably more interactions by academic staff between institutions than within them. So far as students are concerned, the situation is beginning to catch up, not least because universities are increasingly populated by international students who, having moved once, have a greater propensity to move again. Already, a degree in some universities may well include a period of time in another location as a matter of course. What is the spatial limit of the research university in these circumstances? Does there need to be one, indeed? They are circulations as well as places.

Instituting cross-border cooperation so that UK research universities grow via gradual amalgamation with research universities overseas is another obvious possibility, therefore. In principle at least, there is no reason why universities should not become genuinely multinational and indeed some individual research universities already have quite substantial international operations like overseas campuses as well as partnerships with overseas research universities which include both research and teaching ranging from being members of international conglomerations of research universities like LERU (23 European universities), WUN (23 universities) and Universitas 21 (21 universities) to more substantive forms of joint operation.

Notwithstanding all the difficulties, which have become much more substantial as geopolitical constraints have closed in, effectively closing off certain countries for consideration, making others even more risky, and leaving a nucleus of Western Europe and Scandinavia, North America, Australia and New Zealand, and a few other countries like Singapore as a genuinely safe space (whilst remembering that it is incumbent on universities in the Global North to take actions that don't simply replicate their privileges), belonging to a multinational university built through cross-border cooperation could have all kinds of advantages such as: academic and administrative staff being able to work in numerous jurisdictions; accelerated career opportunities; mass student exchanges; syllabuses taught in multiple locations using those locations as pedagogic opportunities; and, not least, being able to access multiple new sources of research funding. It is entirely possible to gradually deepen existing partnerships so that they bear these kinds of fruit. The Monash–Warwick Partnership, the Plus Alliance, and similar arrangements show the real possibilities that there might be. But this is not a road for the impatient. Different timetables, different educational systems and jurisdictions, even time differences, all provide barriers that have to be overcome. The failure of attempts at Berkeley and Warwick to provide lodging rights for other overseas universities on land that they owned so as to promote more research and teaching cooperation shows the rub.

Conglomerating research centres

Another possibility for collaboration exists. It is also feasible to conglomerate various research centres in different universities that are working on the same topics. After all, there are numerous currently separate China research centres, climate change research centres, nanoscience research centres, and goodness knows what else.[5] And there are many precedents for such a move. Competitions for research centres often produce a multi-site solution with a central node and a number of satellites, for example. A number of laboratories like the Crick and the Turing and the Royce and the Franklin and the Faraday Institutes are, in part, made up of a number of research universities and research organisations working in concert, some of them like Royce with sites in each member university. The much-prized Leverhulme Research Centres (prized because they allow concentrated discovery research in genuinely new research areas over a number of years) do something similar, if on a smaller scale. More such centres could be created.

Such arrangements do not have to be restricted to the sciences and medicine. For example, the 21 mainly humanities-based Institutes of Advanced Study in the UK and Ireland could be forged into one operation. For a while, it was de rigeur for a research university to have an institute of advanced study. Modelled in part on the famous institutes at universities like Harvard, Princeton and Stanford (but without the same funds), the goal was to supercharge research, especially in the arts and humanities and social sciences. Truth to tell, these institutes haven't all worked quite as well as they should have, mainly because of resource issues. However, they might work as a joint research university body, perhaps building on the already extant Consortium of Institutes of Advanced Studies.

Give up the ghost

The final possibility? It may be time to give up the ghost and agree that research universities aren't necessarily going to be the best places to do at least some kinds of research in the current circumstances. After all, the UK is already unusual in having so much research being carried out in universities. Like it or not, the best academics just aren't going to go to research universities that demand heavy teaching and administrative loads. Perhaps what is needed, therefore, is a UK version of Max Planck. In Germany, there are currently 86 Max Planck institutes and facilities conducting discovery and applied research in the natural sciences, life sciences, social sciences, and the humanities. Max Planck institutes focus on research fields that are particularly innovative, or that are especially demanding in terms of funding or time requirements. Their research spectrum is continually evolving: new institutes are established to find answers to seminal, forward-looking scientific questions, while others are closed when, for example, their research field has been widely established. The institutes have three main qualities: people, facilities and the time to do research. There are British analogues, of a sort. As just one example, take the aforementioned Francis Crick biomedical institute, a Medical Research Council (MRC), Cancer Research UK, Wellcome, UCL, Imperial College London and King's College London initiative comes to mind. So does the Alan Turing Institute, the national institute for data science and artificial intelligence. And the Rosalind Franklin Institute, a national institute for transformative changes in life science And the Royce

Institute, a decentralised national institute for advanced materials research. And the Faraday Institution, concentrating on battery research. I suspect there will soon be others as some university research is, in effect, offshored. I would, at one point, have thought this to be a bad thing, subtracting from many research universities' own research efforts and, to a degree at least, parasitising on their staff's talent. Now, as these staff's time is remorselessly chipped away at, I am less sure. It may be that a network of such centres spread across the country through which cognate academics would be able to cycle for, say, five years or even longer, thereby getting concentrated time to do research might, at this difficult time, be a very good way of providing research academics with the boost that they need away from the distractions that now beset them.

A parting shot

By way of a conclusion, I want to address two issues, both of them the result of the backdrop against which we now live. It is no exaggeration to say that the world is in an unholy mess – climate change and a biosphere that is rotting, the fag-end of a 10,000-year war on the environment, pandemics, the end of a period of a comparative period of world peace, as the situation in Ukraine has shown only too well, a world economy that sits on the brink of another downturn, rampant authoritarianism and with it the disappearance of even a semblance of freedom to say what you think in many countries, over-use of precious resources, high levels of inequality, fake news and general gaslighting – the list goes on. It's not an apocalypse, and there is still time to ward off the worst effects but, all that said, some concerted action is needed now, especially by universities.

Universities have traditionally not become directly involved in issues like these – except in wartime – leaving it to their staff individually to do the research that informs each issue, sit on the boards of international and governmental organisations, act as commentators, and sign letters to editors demanding change. But, and this is the first issue, universities can't just be bystanders any longer. The times demand something more. There comes a point where bystanding becomes complicity. The university is

> a good example of the great vulnerability of an institution which has entertained the confidence that its own value was able to stand by itself and be respected as such. We have not even been able to devise common ways of resisting our redefinition in terms of 'the economy.' Most [universities] are now so busy [in a] struggle for survival that they have … no time to … wonder what kind of body we and our different research organs could compose together. … Our case has nothing exceptional about it. … But it may be said that our example is

particularly scandalous since our charge is also to equip students who will have to live in the coming times. (Stengers, 2017, p. 8)

We now face existential issues from which it is not possible to hide away. We are passing into a kind of undeclared war as climate and biosphere change bites and as the need for large-scale planetary restoration becomes apparent, at sufficient scale that it might be described as terraforming. But, so far at least, universities have not risen to the challenge posed by their own academics' research and practical contributions. In fact, there are solutions on the table to threats like climate change, many of which originated in universities, but most of them require political will to put in to place. Yet universities as institutions tend to stay in the background. That's for someone else to do. Universities have never been ivory towers. That was always a convenient myth (Shapin, 2012). But now they need to find the nerve to intervene cooperatively in a much more concerted way.

You can see why universities have left the heavy lifting to their academics. There are real risks in trying to intervene in climate and biosphere change in a concerted way, a course of action which, though it might be regarded as simply a survival agenda, and one based on brute fact to boot, almost inevitably runs the risk of being marked out as political (Chakrabarty, 2009, 2014). There is bound to be caution about making what may look like political pronouncements, given that the mode of enquiry in universities is based on notions of impartiality and a general scepticism towards fixed answers. But I'm not sure it is ethical to do anything other than try. The times demand it. If the world is clearly, as an objective fact, in bad trouble, universities can't just step back from the fray, not least given that it could be argued that knowledge of climate and biosphere change has in good part been produced by universities. Still, it spooks many people when they think that research comes with a will to action, as it now must. You can hear all the counter-arguments. Universities might appear to be 'over-mighty' institutions (Goodhart, 2019) if they go down this route, puffed up with their own importance, too big for their own boots: research is meant to be a base on which others build rather than universities. Universities need to hold back from becoming involved in the humdrum affairs of the world; they need to keep their distance from the fray. Knowledge comes in a neutral shade. Universities shouldn't deal in bright colours. And, last of all, stepping into the contemporary public arena comes up against all kinds of baggage. Learned knowledge is contested at every turn. All kinds of screwball explanations and pseudo-sciences circulate and gain traction in ways that it was far more difficult to achieve before the internet. Spur-of-the-moment opinions thrive. Condemnation has become an artform. Public shaming has become a norm.[6] These three arguments would have been easier to make a few years ago – now, as adverse events mount up, they can seem like evasions, not least because everyone is quite happy to talk about university research having 'impact'. In the process, some knowledge is going to appear to be 'political', come what may.

Of course, this means universities laying themselves open to the charge of being 'political' entities. The risks are obvious. Budgetary reprisals. More governmental fiats. Media firestorms. It's not a comfortable place to be. But universities have very little choice if they want to stay honest. Sometimes they will get it wrong. But the alternative path of a studied neutrality is now a political decision in its own right. Universities are going to have to fight their corner more effectively in the current epistemic fray – without patronising the public – or their corner will disappear.

Again, the only answer I can see now is to collaborate more, both to give more force to actions that need to be taken and as a means of providing at least some protection. In collaboration lies strength.[7] In particular. the situation with regard to the effects of climate and biospheric change is now so serious that it seems extraordinary, even unethical, for universities not to act in a much more concerted way. 'Where were you, in the war, Daddy?' as the saying goes. I'm not suggesting handing out white feathers to vice-chancellors. But the problems of collaboration are well illustrated by Cambridge's recent Cambridge Zero climate change research initiative and Oxford's relatively similar Oxford Net Zero initiative. Obviously, such initiatives should be welcomed with open arms but it is a pity that Cambridge and Oxford set up these initiatives by themselves. They could have been made in concert with each other and with other universities in the UK and around the world which also have climate change capacity, as the welcome advent of the International Universities Climate Alliance now allows to happen. Institutions that fashion themselves as global and as addressing global problems need to act globally and that means together.

The barriers to acting in such a concerted way are many. Universities compete too much and cooperate too little even though cooperation – rock-solid cooperation – is the only defence they've got. Some universities are always in danger of peeling away in search of one goody or another, so cooperation will always be difficult. Then, in the UK, nearly all universities are charities and that limits their ability to participate in politics though it does not preclude them from campaigning if 'the campaign is likely to be an effective way of furthering or supporting the charity's purposes' (Charity Commission, 2021, p. 3). As in the US, antitrust legislation and competition law more generally also limit the room for manoeuvre. Even divesting from fossil fuel company interests, especially when a number of these companies seem intent on going on pretty much as before, proved much more difficult to do than students might have imagined because charities are expected to obtain the maximum return on their investments, because a charity can refuse a donation but the trustees need to be satisfied, and able to show, that it is in the best interests of the charity to do so, and because many universities invested largely in composite index instruments from which it is difficult to separate out the problematic components (though that is now much easier than it once was with various 'green' indexes having come on line).

Then the second, related issue. Universities are long-term institutions. There is a growing body of literature on long timescale institutions which stresses just how important they are, especially in a world where we can predict some of what is to come with a degree of certainty and prepare for it (Boston, 2016, Ialenti, 2020, Kznaric, 2020, Robinson, 2020). And it is not as if universities are the only long-term institutions going against the cultural tide flowing towards the short term and ephemeral. A whole series of other important entities are also designed to keep faith with humanity over hundreds or even thousands of years — some kinds of conservation body, some faith institutions, even sites earmarked for geological disposal of radioactive waste. They have been set up to outlast normal human cycles. Their whole presence can be interpreted as a theory of duration.

Modern life is often characterised as everything in flux and nothing certain — especially by managers and consultants whose jobs often depend on this 'fast' characterisation which underlies and bolsters modern tech and consumerism. Accordingly, for them, the main values tend to be organisational efficiency, speed of response and ability to compete. But because universities are designed for the long term, their main purpose is not just different, it is strikingly at odds with the 'pathological presentism' (Davis, 2022) that infects so many modern societies in which 'we treat the future like a distant colonial outpost devoid of people' (Krznaric, 2020, p. 4, Krznaric, 2019), a future on which we dump our problems and which we feel free to plunder as we please. To imperialism in space must be added imperialism in time. Wealth is there for the taking and accumulating in both dimensions.

The time universities live in is different. It is one which protrudes farther into the future (and farther into the past) than does the time of most institutions, a time which values past and future generations in a way that most modern institutions do not. Universities cannot airbrush future generations. The very act of teaching is an act which is about fashioning a future for them. Then again, research is an activity which relies on trust in the future. It is, generally speaking, wending towards goals which are often indistinct but rely on an understanding that our knowledge of the world can be improved and used to improve things — a future held in trust on trust. To cease cultivating the qualities universities have as long-term institutions in favour of short-term gains would be something approaching a crime.

It may well be those institutions like research universities, designed to last hundreds of years, represent something of an oddity in a world in which there is 'a peculiar propensity for understanding time that passes as if it were abolishing the past behind it' (Latour, 1993, p. 68) and the future as if it can be solved by just adding more stuff. Such views are utterly alien to a university's values which are concerned with a flow not a point, and which therefore rest in the past and the future as much as the present. They 'belong in all tenses' as de Waal brilliantly (2021) puts it. Modern societies desperately need more of these not just longer-term but longer-time institutions (UNEP aside, there is no World Environment Organization, for example), institutions that are trying to go forward in a different way. But, in their absence, we need to preserve the ones we've got.

One of my worries is that recent developments are turning research universities into institutions with shorter and shorter time horizons – just as has happened to so many other modern institutions. But for universities the danger is much greater because one of their main roles is as stewards of a future which is alive to the astonishments of the world. Modern societies often look down on a tradition of stewardship. They are liable to interpret it as a fusty hangover from another age. It isn't. It's a declaration of care for the world arising out of a determination to learn from past blind alleys and cul-de-sacs made through the application of a practice of continuous unlearning born out of being 'a fighter for ends, of which many, but for [their] presence, would not be ends at all' (James, 1890, p. 141). As we head towards an uncertain horizon burdened with multiple problems arising from our greedy grasshopper past and our cavalier disregard for the impacts of our actions on future generations – and indeed the planet – research universities will become one of the most important ways of learning how to set things aright. Let's not throw that away.

Notes

Chapter 1

[1] Even now it is still possible to read accounts which accuse modern universities of being 'ivory towers' (Shapin, 2012). Why? Because the jeremiads which are typical of the sector are usually concerned almost wholly with the arts and humanities which are regarded as constituting the soul of the university (cf. Nussbaum, 2010). But, although the humanistic argument has some undoubted merits, especially in the attention it pays to universities as means of promoting good citizens who understand the difference between rational argument and hyperbole, it is anchored in a particular reality which, like it or not, has little to do with many contemporary big science universities.

[2] I do not intend to define exactly which universities these are. A world of pain would follow! I use the Russell Group universities as a surrogate for convenience while recognising that a good number of other universities can claim to be a research university who are not in the Group. But using just this group as a guide, Russell Group universities won 74.4 per cent of all university research grants and contract income. 91 per cent of the Russell Group universities' research activity was classified as either 'world-leading' or 'internationally excellent' in the 2021 Research Excellence Framework exercise. Authors like Frank, Gowar and Naef (2019) split an elite group of universities off from the Russell Group (Cambridge, Oxford, Imperial, LSE, UCL) for reasons which seem to be more concerned with making an argument that there are some good research universities that are not included in the Russell Group and this move makes them look better. Others like Scott (2021, p. 87) argue that Russell Group membership is arbitrary and that 'many non-Russell Group universities [have] equally impressive research reputations'. Some agreed, but not many surely? I prefer to go with a number around 40 which takes in most notable research universities.

[3] Byrne and Clarke (2019) argue for around 60 such universities.

[4] Everyone talks about 'research-led teaching' as a salve but that is almost impossible to achieve when staff–student ratios are so high.

[5] Of course, this was always a bit of a myth: even in the heyday of the research and teaching academic, there were academics who had pretty well given up on research though they were still doing good teaching. But it was an important myth.

[6] They were thinking of provision of places for '20, 30 or even 40 per cent of the age group' (Halsey and Trow, 1971, p. 464).

[7] Equally, the experience of university around the world has been variegated, to put it but mildly. University systems and the institutions they have sired vary widely. Some are inherently statist. Others have always had a much greater private influence. Some were founded in societies where the pursuit of knowledge was born out of religion as much as Enlightenment. Some were responsible for producing a specific intelligentsia. Some were inherently more egalitarian in tone. In others, elitism ran amok until quite recently. And so on.

[8] In some ways, they may even be too competitive in that many strategies have become a classic follow-my-leader 'if they've got this, we've got to have it too', 'if they're growing we have to grow too', 'if they're announcing this new initiative, we'll announce something similar but not too similar', 'if they've got a big new piece of kit, we will get it too' gambit. The most elite research universities like Princeton don't think like this – they are confident of their ground and their standards are engrained.

[9] The idea that matter is inert has been laid to rest as the enlightenment has been followed by the 'enlivenment' (Weber, 2019).

10 When the five rules were tested against 5,000 oxide structures only 13 per cent satisfied even four of the five.
11 That said, when a number of different methods support a conclusion (so-called consilience) this counts as a powerful indicator.
12 Especially because it can mistake the proliferation of data - which is a hallmark of modern science – for understanding, it can produce an untoward theoretical optimism which can be dangerous when phenomena are complex, and therefore have more – and more varied – associations.
13 This insight is particularly important in the social sciences which are prone to make inflated and sometimes reductionist claims for theory which need to be leavened by using evidence to carefully sort out the influence of each cause. Luckily, new statistical methods and other means of addressing complexity make this easier to achieve.
14 Foucault argued that every society has a 'regime' and a 'general politics' of truth but this way into a history of ideas has then too often been hijacked to legitimate personal knowledge and perspectives as a route to objectivity. That is not something that Foucault would have countenanced.
15 I realise that I am hijacking a phrase from Keats for my own purposes and using it in a different way though Keats' emphasis on 'being in uncertainty' means that I at least dip into his meaning.
16 Though the exchange of knowledge dates from much earlier. In Europe it was already well advanced by the twelfth century where classical works on, for example, mathematical astronomy were copied and recopied, gaining wide circulation among a small group of scholars in places like Oxford, Bologna and Paris (Moller, 2019).
17 This is not as strange a thought as all that. Mansfield boasts of its devotion to state school students, for example.
18 However, when it comes to research degrees the US system is much more hierarchical than the UK: for example, only 282 US universities can award PhDs. Even assuming that this kind of hierarchy might be a good thing (which I doubt) I cannot see it as ever being achieved in the UK, where there is jealous guarding of the accoutrements of research in order to assure status, even by universities that do very little of it.

Chapter 2

1 In Robbins, universities were expected to carry out four main functions: to provide necessary labour market skills, to promote 'the general powers of the mind', to advance learning through research, and to facilitate 'the transmission of a common culture and common standards of citizenship'. This set of criteria was later redefined by the Dearing Report as 'to inspire and enable individuals to develop their capabilities to the highest potential levels throughout life, so that they grow intellectually, are well-equipped for work, can contribute effectively to society and achieve personal fulfilment', 'to increase knowledge and understanding for its own sake and to foster their application to the benefit of economy and society', to serve the needs of an adaptable, sustainable, knowledge-based economy at local, regional and national levels', and 'to play a major role in shaping a democratic, civilised, inclusive society' (National Committee of Inquiry into Higher Education, 1997).
2 However, the fact that quantitative metrics can be problematic is not an argument for never using them. For example, examining citation counts for individuals can be legitimate when they are used as one of a number of indicators. To say that they convey no information, especially when the counts are high, seems to me to go too far. There are at least a couple of league tables based on information on citations of highly-cited individuals which are fairly reliable, of which Ioannidis et al. (2019) is likely the best.

Notes

3   Part of the problem is that we often don't know what people in universities *really do*. There is remarkably little academic work on the nitty-gritty of life in universities in the Howard Becker and Bruno Latour mould. Instead of detailed ethnographies, we tend to deal in folk theories of what people in universities are doing: kindly academics versus evil administrators, 'impure' industry infecting 'pure' academia', the noble pursuit of truth versus hackneyed applied research, and the like (Tuchman, 2009). But, as Becker (2014) points out, it is often much better to reason from cases rather than use overarching theories, theories which are usually, let's face it, simple models involving homogeneous classes of activity linked in some way. These theories often cultivate a false sense of familiarity because we are not aware of alternatives – the theory has blotted them out as it searches for the alike rather than the unalike. But note Les Back's (2016) *Academic Diary*, a set of meditations on academe which shows another way of doing things.

4   In this latter case, it is important to note that each kind of microscope involves a compromise and so produces a demand for even better machines. For example, fluorescence microscopy, in which fluorescent molecules are used to light up target proteins, cells or cellular components, allows live samples to be observed in real time. However, visible light cannot distinguish between objects closer than 200 nanometres to each other, so it is not, by itself, sufficient to reveal the really detailed structures of cells. Electron microscopes can achieve much higher resolutions, but they require a vacuum which means they cannot be used on live samples. (I have even come across specially constructed microscopes that can image all of the things going on in a drop of seawater.)

5   Which is not to take away from the civic service done by many universities, most notably of late in the Covid-19 pandemic where universities like Southampton rolled out a track and trace service to parts of the city, rather as UC Davis did in the US.

6   www.ox.ac.uk/about/departments-a_z.

7   An interesting by-product of this heterogeneity is a question mark over the whole notion of authorship. We may well be moving from a time when individual authorship was the norm to a time when group authorship is the yardstick of progress – from the novel to Pixar in other words.

8   Indeed, the scientific image boosted by information technology is often better than the data it is based on, joining a long line of scientific rhetoric based around making images convincing.

9   Probably the best source I know for understanding academics are all the obituaries to be found in the *Biographical Memoirs of Fellows of the British Academy* and the *Biographical Memoirs of the Fellows of the Royal Society*.

10 Only a fifth of the British population – about 14 million people – are on Twitter. 80 per cent of tweets are written by 10 per cent of users.

11 See Barber (2021). I have to say that in all of my time sitting on far too many appointment committees to count, I have only come across one instance where I thought a candidate's political views were being explicitly held against them by a member of the committee and the rest of the committee soon scotched this tendency. Much more important for committees is the issue of whether a person is going to add to a department's research reputation!

12 One counter sometimes made is that the views of some people are so beyond the pale or counter to human rights that they should not be given exposure on campus. And it is true that some views (outright misogyny or racism, for example) are sufficiently offensive that they do not need to be exposed to the air but, even so, care needs to be taken not to over-reach.

13 Zadie Smith's *On Beauty* also has the merit of being a campus novel which is clear-headed about themes which have only become more relevant. If you're feeling really depressed, there is always John Williams' campus novel *Stoner* to make you feel suicidal.

14 And 66 per cent of part-time academics.
15 Like Gilroy, I am concerned by the apparent rise of ethnic absolutisms built around a category, race. This is not, of course, to deny the presence of racism built out from skin tone but it is to argue that racial categories are neither intrinsic nor immutable and are a product of processes of racialisation. Equally, I worry about blanket terms like structural racism which 'could turn out to be to the 2020s what the invention of the underclass was for the 1980s, a lumpy notion that stops analytic work just where it should begin, confuses and conflates mechanisms of ethnoracial domination, … and thus forms a practical obstacle to the surgical removal of operative sources of racial inequality' (Wacquant, 2022, p. 86, see also Wacquant, 2022b).
16 See www.ethnicity-facts-figures.service.gov.uk/uk-population-by-ethnicity/demographics/age-groups/latest).
17 Chinese universities used to conduct a battle to see how many Nobel prizewinners they could attract to their various ceremonies which didn't help matters.
18 Harvesting Academic Innovation for Learners: see https://thehailstorm.org/.
19 Though there are issues. As many as 20 per cent of US undergraduate students have only partial connection to the internet and associated technology, for example (Gonzales, Calarco and Lynch, 2018).
20 In some Scandinavian countries, the thesis is publicly defended in front of an audience which can include the candidate's family – a far worse state of affairs!
21 A PhD in Germany is also generally free to study, even to overseas students. That isn't the case in the UK (though there are numerous scholarships.)
22 In the US, it has been noted that many university and research funder administrators seem to have become more radical over some of these issues than academics. While I don't think similarly minded administrators are as radical or have quite the same purchase in the UK, the issue remains a live one.

Chapter 3

1 Students are good at saying one thing while doing another. For example, many of them strive to get into institutions which differentiate them from the mass of students, even as they argue for widening access.
2 Though Katz et al. (2021) show that the vocabulary that students have to deal with issues of inequality centres mainly on gender and ethnicity. Class differences mean much less.
3 Some commentators have blamed many of these mental health issues almost exclusively on the internet (and it is true that the large-scale LSE Mappiness project finds that, out of 27 leisure activities, social media ranks precisely last in how much happiness it brings). But it is important not to exaggerate. See, for example, Orben and Pryzbylski (2019).
4 So lectures can be made more entertaining: you can undoubtedly increase your student assessment scores by acting up.
5 The roots of the word may be in *gnosis*, the Ancient Greek for understanding, but the word itself comes from the Middle English, *knoulechen*, to find out about or recognise. The sense of knowledge as 'an organised body of facts or teachings' only dates from circa 1400.
6 It is hard to believe that senior management of universities read through some of this course content.
7 Take the issue of student protests – marches, sit-ins, and the like – on campus. Every vice-chancellor will regale you with some story or the other about what is now a university tradition as fixed in amber as graduation ceremonies, a tradition which in some universities can seem like it is as much about the practice of protest as its aims. But

where do things stop? Should student protests be allowed to threaten the livelihoods of working people on campus who are trying to earn a crust, for example? Equally, I am realistic enough to know that protest may sometimes step outside the law of the land but, if that's what happens, students, as adult citizens, should be prepared to own the consequences. Unfortunately, largely middle-class students often have little or no idea of what these consequences are.

8. Thus, a new law in Florida mandates each state university to conduct an annual survey 'which considers the extent to which competing ideas and perspectives are presented'.
9. Which, by the way, is not to argue that there is no subjective element to racism.
10. Such a move reminds me of Nicholas Christakis's response to Brown University putting in place an online reporting system that allows students to make allegations of sexual assault and harassment anonymously: 'What could possibly go wrong?'.
11. The UUK report (2020, p. 6) rightly acknowledges that 'regular, national data on the nature, scale and prevalence of racial harassment in higher education is not available and, as in wider society, many incidents of harassment go unreported'. It is scandalous that these data do not exist since it makes it very difficult to formulate the right policies. The UUK report relies for data on an Equalities and Human Rights Commission (2019) report which in methodological terms leaves a lot to be desired.
12. Other forms of pressure on students compound the problem. Peer pressure is a real force: a recent study found that a quarter of students are afraid to state their real views for fear of what their peers may think (Grant et al., 2019). Though what this means is open to interpretation, it suggests that universities still have a job of work to do instil independent thinking into some students' outlook, though I think there are few of us who could claim we have never succumbed to peer pressure!
13. Perhaps the strangest manifestation of this tendency was the furore in the US in 2020 over a book by a white author which had the temerity to feature Latino characters. As Zadie Smith (2019, p. 7) puts it: 'what insults my soul is the idea – popular in the culture just now and presented in widely variant degrees of complexity – that we can and should write only about people who are fundamentally "like" us: racially, sexually, genetically, nationally, politically, personally.' Taken to an extreme, this attitude would debar most fiction and most history, anthropology and geography from having anything to say.
14. Universities have a generally honourable record when it comes to these kinds of issues, it's true. But it isn't without blemish. Many of the most egregious instances seem to have come from within the small world confines of colleges. Charles Babbage wasn't allowed to graduate with honours from Peterhouse, probably because his thesis was deemed blasphemous. Trinity dismissed Bertrand Russell for being a conscientious objector during the First World War.
15. They might not want to go so far as Senator Ted Cruz – the man who while at Harvard Law School spurned students from 'minor Ivies' for not having the intellectual chops who then went to as good as accuse the school of harbouring a communist cell called critical law studies.
16. You can't win on this. The Adam Smith Institute (Young and Dube, 2020) proceeded to argue that no student union should have the power to make 'political' decisions on who can speak and who can't because they are effectively illegitimate institutions when they move away from providing basic member services. As a matter of record, some students unions have now proposed a freedom of speech code.
17. This stricture can apply equally to behaviours like sexual harassment or racism or to certain instances of 'hate speech' which are forms of compulsion (though people's understanding of what constitutes these behaviours still varies considerably). On the whole, universities have

striven to delete these kinds of behaviours but this is no easy task when such behaviours occur across society and not just on campus.

18. For example, think of the contribution of Islamic scholars like Abul-Walid Muhammad Ibn Rushd, also known as Averroes, on Western philosophy, letters, science and religion as well as the encyclopaedist, Shihab al-Din al-Nuwayri, and the novelist, Abu Bakr Muhammad ibn Tufayl. This decolonisation doesn't stop at the arts and humanities and social sciences, of course. As the example of Averroes shows it applies equally to the history of science and medicine (Poskett, 2022).

19. I sometimes wonder if a kind of psychological break point has been reached which means that the middle class is increasingly dissatisfied with higher education because it is seen as one more symptom of a set of wider changes which adversely affect them. So far as universities are concerned, it is increasingly likely to judge them less in terms of general welfare and more in terms of means and ends, and it is likely to judge them more harshly as a result.

20. Through the good offices of the founder of WMG, Lord Bhattacharyya, the University of Warwick had a strong and lasting connection with the automobile industry and especially Jaguar Land Rover. It also had a strong connection with Tata Motors which helped to stimulate that company's takeover of JLR. This, in turn, produced all kinds of new possibilities like, for example, the National Automobile Innovation Centre (co-funded with government and JLR.)

Chapter 4

1. It's true that this was nominally a variable fee but most institutions chose to charge the maximum from the outset.
2. Or 2,697,380 students if those registered in further education colleges are included.
3. Slightly different figures using the same source can be found in Bolton (2021a).
4. This state of affairs is not quite as unusual as some commentators like to make out. The degree of private sector involvement in higher education varies around the world but it is increasingly rare to come across a system which has none. Even France educates 10 per cent of its students through private providers.
5. The ERC is very competitive with only a 13 per cent success rate but an independent evaluation in 2020 concluded that around 80 per cent of ERC-funded projects had made scientific breakthroughs or major advances.
6. www.gov.uk/government/publications/uk-research-and-development-roadmap/uk-research-and-development-roadmap.
7. Some commentators have argued that the rest of the overhead was to be found in QR. This is incorrect.
8. Perhaps the most distressing aspect of this recent cut was that it came about in part because of the cut in overseas aid funding.
9. Though not surprising, as Carvalho (2017) makes clear.
10. The same study found that 31 per cent of universities' income came from the public sector in 2014–15.
11. Thus, one significant impact was the volume of personal off-campus expenditure of overseas students, which amounted to £5.4 billion in 2014/15 (see Universities UK, 2017).
12. Including a substantial and growing online component led by students in places like Singapore, Hong Kong, Nigeria, Malaysia and the US.
13. www.obhe.org.
14. Research by Elsevier shows that most highly cited papers are produced by academics with international careers. The problem with this observation is, of course, its causality.

Notes

[15] In the Nature Index the same picture of internationalisation of connection occurs but the order of countries with the largest number of co-authors was the US, Germany and the UK.

[16] What is remarkable is that only the UK and Australia put so little government money into their universities as a proportion of GDP and get so much money back from their export and other earnings in return. Thus, whereas universities in other countries are expanding internally and overseas backed by government funding (or, in the case of the US, by large endowments), UK universities have to compete without much in the way of backing, especially given cuts to the British Council.

[17] Ventures like the Athena Project tried to do something novel by mixing online with multiple international sites in a kind of digital replicant of the Grand Tour.

[18] Not only is alumni loyalty to the top research universities probably much greater in China than in the US or the UK but some of the top research universities have been able to garner extraordinary levels of resource, not just through favourable government funding but also from interesting commercial dealings all the way from property ownership to sponsoring IPOs. And now they are also beginning to reap the rewards of philanthropy. The upshot is obvious. Take Tsinghua (Andreas, 2009). It has used its resources to build more and more research facilities, start-up and tech transfer zones, a liberal arts college and honours colleges, specialist international student accommodation for its many international students, a major art gallery, and it also has a series of important international industrial collaborations, for example with Microsoft.

[19] I reference China here but universities have been involved with other suspect regimes too.

[20] One desperate, almost unbelievable, reaction was to start converting conditional offers to domestic students into unconditional ones. Quite rightly, this ploy was stopped in its tracks and the whole issue of conditional offers of whatever kind has now been now been the subject of formal intervention via the 2022 UUK Code of Practice on Fair Admissions.

[21] A sudden downturn in student demand was probably to be found in most risk registers. But I'm not sure that helped. Indeed, it may have acted to soothe any concerns: we've thought about it, somehow that means we've got it covered.

[22] Degree apprenticeships are on average held by young people of a higher social status than students as a whole.

[23] These universities are experimenting with forms of pedagogy that are relevant to the changing industrial world but which also provide an intensive academic experience. Specifically, they are investing in project-based teaching of a new kind. Beginning with Olin in the US and Quest in Canada (now defunct), a different kind of model is gradually spreading. Olin, founded in 1997, has no departments in order to encourage interdisciplinarity. The faculty act as coaches, mentors and advisers and do a lot of co-teaching. The ethos is 'to start doing stuff straightaway'. All students take an arts, humanities and social sciences course in the first year in order to hone communication skills, as well as an introductory entrepreneurship course. Large amounts of teaching take place through small group projects and there are almost no lectures. Each student can design their own academic path. By the final year, students are ready to address real problems for companies and communities through capstone projects. Elements of this model can be found cropping up in a number of new engineering ventures in the UK: NMITE in Hereford, the Dyson Institute of Engineering and Technology in Malmesbury, and the PLuS Alliance Venture, TEDI-London, in Canada Water, London. I would expect to see more experiments along these lines. For a certain kind of student, they are a revelation. However, they are heavy users of faculty and resource and this will provide a limit on the adoption of their model.

Chapter 5

1. It is interesting to consider private equity which has often become a shadow state, providing many services that would have been deemed public in the past.
2. The same strictures apply more generally to high pay in universities. To read most media accounts, which tend to take the figure of £100,000 or more as holy writ, pay over this amount is all going to 'top managers'. In fact, a good number of these salaries are being paid to academics, the best of whom can easily command such amounts in what is an international market for research talent. That said, I know of one department at Oxford where the professors have all decided to take the same salary.
3. I was from what was probably, at the time, a lower or middle middle-class background. Both of my parents were teachers. Now, for nearly the first time, I came into sustained contact with people who weren't from this background. I still remember the shock of listening to really explicit sexual 'banter'.
4. When I was at school, which started out as a state grammar and then went comprehensive, thus allowing me to claim to be the product of either 1960s upward social mobility or an elitist system, I can't, for the life of me, remember anyone ever even mentioning going to Oxford or Cambridge as a possibility.
5. Against the background of a general decline in social mobility. For example, absolute social mobility into elite occupations has declined. One in five men in professional and managerial occupations who were born between 1955 and 1961 became socially mobile, but the figure for those born between 1975 and 1981 is only one in eight. For women the figure has hardly changed. As the work of Mike Savage and others show, this decline is based on dramatically increased income rewards in a few occupations, mainly in finance, as well as accumulating rewards from wealth. Unsurprisingly, these elites, whose stronghold is London, hold a strong belief in meritocracy.
6. www.ethnicity-facts-figures.service.gov.uk/education-skills-and-training/higher-education/entry-rates-into-higher-education/latest.
7. For example, it runs the risk of tensions arising from poor white students who feel that they are being actively excluded by ethnic minority students, as has happened at some Ivy League universities in the US.
8. This latter suspicion surfaces yet again in the latest government higher education policy which, roughly translated, would have it that many potential students would be better suited to vocational education in colleges. Dressed up as it might be with statistics about the value for money of some courses, it still contains a strand of thought which would have it that some people just aren't suited to higher education.
9. So, for example, 85 per cent of MPs have degrees. But this example shows the rub: having a degree doesn't necessarily lead to better government. Indeed, there is a case to be made that it leads to worse government. In the US, for example, where all House members have bachelors degrees or higher and 95 per cent of Senate members too (Senior, 2020), government decision-making has included 'stagnant wages, financial deregulation, income inequality, the financial crisis of 2008, a bank bailout that did little to help ordinary people, a decaying infrastructure, and the highest incarceration rate in the world' (Sandel, 2020, p. 67). Indeed Carnes and Lupu (2015) found no evidence that formal education made political leaders better at their jobs. Bring back Ernest Bevin!
10. I was privileged to meet Michael Young at Dartington Hall several times later in his life when he and I shared a mutual interest in the study of time. He could have rightly claimed to be the colossus bestriding British higher education.
11. In 2019, London Economics estimates (Conlon, 2019) suggested that 53.9 per cent of the money that was being loaned out to students would end up being written off, that 88.2 per cent of graduates would still be paying off their loan when the 30-year write-off

of loans occurred, and that 33 per cent of graduates would never make any repayments at all.

12. Research in Scotland shows that the number of working-class people going to university has certainly not increased. Indeed, spending on grants has halved in real terms with the result that many poorer students are worse off. In contrast to England, borrowing is higher among students from poorer backgrounds. Even worse, the amount of money going into further education has declined with the number of further education colleges falling. The evidence thus far is that the English system based on income-contingent loans is actually more socially equitable in that it is increasing the number of people from less well-off backgrounds, although at very considerable cost.

13. Some commentators argue that this is one of the major contributors to social unrest in many parts of the world. Certainly, we live in a strange time when more people have been educated in universities than ever before but rational debate still proves a struggle.

14. One signpost to reforming the loan system is provided by the generally overlooked IPPR report of 2013 (Commission on the Future of Higher Education) which produced a set of recommendations which still hold water. Only a few of its recommendations were ever enacted (especially a postgraduate loans scheme and the removal of international students from the net migration numbers). It argued for a gradual increase in student numbers but within the bounds of affordability, a kind of moving cap. Suggestions were made for how to reduce the tuition fee to £6,000, and for the institution of a £5,000 fee for local students, a student premium for those from disadvantaged areas, and mechanisms to privilege vocational education and to promote greater transfers between higher education institutions, all of which still hold good, as well as a set of means for overhauling student finance which still sound sensible.

15. Its counterparts, the Higher Education Funding Council for Wales, the Scottish Funding Council, and the Northern Ireland Department for the Economy do the same.

16. The National Academies – especially the Royal Society and the British Academy – provide considerable funding for fellowships. However, a large part of their funding comes from government.

17. Using another calculation, the cost of the shortfall was £1.4 billion in 2017/18, a figure very close to the total funding from the research block grant to universities (Forth and Jones, 2020).

18. The table of tables of the various national rankings was first introduced in 2008.

19. I won't go here into what constitutes 'government' but it is not just ministers, of course. Civil servants are often immensely influential.

20. Paradoxically, at the same time, many university staff seem to feel more comfortable under the umbrella of the state. It feels safer and more predictable, and therefore less threatening. As importantly, it allows them to argue that another actor needs to 'do something'. There is some cultural bias to this reaction. It reminds me of the old saw that when it snows and the snow needs clearing, an American gets out and clears the sidewalks while a Brit asks what the council is going to do about it.

21. Not too much should be made of this, however. There are examples – and not just a few – of successful research universities which are definitely not autonomous from government. Take the case of China. No one could accuse Chinese research universities of being autonomous from the state (although the various academies of science do have an academic influence on priorities). There, the university bureaucracy includes a parallel party bureaucracy and in the last few years it has become clear that it is the university's party secretary who is in ultimate charge, not the vice-chancellor. Yet these universities are producing some excellent science, anyway you look at it. Or take the case of Singapore. Singaporean research universities have to consult with the Ministry of Education on all

major decisions and their boards include a representative from the Ministry of Education. Yet these universities produce excellent work. Perhaps this is in part because of the way in which academic oversight is exercised through various bodies that include external academic experts.

22 Except when the department prefers to keep a low profile and the responsibility for decisions is loaded back on to universities, as in the case of rental rebates for accommodation during the coronavirus pandemic.

23 Of which the latest example is placing some research funding within a place-based envelope.

24 As Lury (2021) points out, there is an irony in all of this in that the commercial sector, which has often lobbied for open access, keeps a large part of its data firmly locked up behind closed doors.

25 All this said, these contracts cover a wide range of different arrangements, some of which are mutually convenient, such as some part-time language tutors who want to do work as and when, as well as many more who simply cannot get a permanent position.

26 Come in many medical, economics and business school professors, for example. The constant press attention to the salaries of 'senior/fat cat' administrators diverts attention from the fact that some of the 4,423 staff paid more than £100,000 in 2017–18 are actually academics.

Chapter 6

1 If I tell people that when I was applying for lecturer jobs in geography in the late 1970s, there were almost none on offer because of the depressed level of state funding then, they find it hard to comprehend. In fact, it was one of the reasons that I left for a post in Australia (which, by the way, was one of the best things I've ever done).

2 Not that the European Union with its commitment to 'dilute sovereignty without meaningful democracy, compulsory unanimity without participant equality, [and] the cult of free markets without care of free trade' (Anderson, 2021) looks much more attractive.

3 They always have been, of course. But since the days of Peter Swinnerton-Dyer and the UGC they have become larger, much more complex and much more open to public scrutiny.

4 Against a run of dire Brexit and Covid-19 forecasts, the number of EU students has either stayed steady in the case of some countries or declined in others.

5 Though the Australian model assumes that the overhead on government research grants is fully funded.

6 And this number excluded staff who were not paid from general university funds!

7 In particular, these figures were inflated by the rush to make large numbers of offers occasioned by what was predicted to be a likely shortfall in overseas student numbers. Other factors also intervened.

8 For example, tuition fees at MIT are roughly double those at Oxford.

9 It is worth remembering that the government's international education strategy (DfE/DIT, 2019) envisaged an increase in the total number of international students from 460,000 to 600,000 students by 2030, along with an increase in the income generated by international education exports from £20 billion to £35 billion.

10 In 2021, Blackstone and APG joined forces to buy up GCP Student Living and split its property portfolio between them.

11 Of course, things don't always work out as the case of three blocks of Liverpool and Manchester student accommodation being built by the Elliot Group makes clear.

12 Even though it was done once by HEFCE.

13 I don't buy the counter-arguments, for example, that attainment at school has increased so attainment at university will rise in lockstep. The case for the prosecution has been put in an article by Lambert (2019) and though it is overstated it is not as far off the mark

as one might wish. Certainly, at a minimum, the proportion of firsts should be removed from league tables.

Chapter 7

1. In the past, becoming a vice-chancellor was an unusual career track which was often full of mystery. That has changed. As both the number of positions and degree of responsibility has increased, so vice-chancellors tend to follow a well-beaten path. Many academics put themselves on to an administrative career track at some point – as heads of department, as deans, as pro-vice-chancellors, as deputy vice-chancellors, and this is now where most vice-chancellors are drawn from. More so, probably, in the US where an academic administrative career starts earlier. (This can be a problem. Work by Goodall (2009) argues that research universities led by functioning top-rank academics, with high academic standards running in their blood, not people who left their vocation behind early, tend to do better, on the whole. They retain academic values and standards and at least some kind of academically-led vision.) Rightly or wrongly, I detect a drift towards a model of vice-chancellors which is coming closer to the American model.
2. I am well aware of the complexity of the task of describing what a 'typical' vice-chancellor does. Here, I talk only about the vice-chancellor of a research university.
3. It is, of course, possible to become just a little jaded as time goes on, exasperated by the predilections of some colleagues and students (see Times Higher, 2015).
4. In other countries, this transition is sometimes handled with more aplomb. In the US, for example, the erstwhile former president may be given some kind of emeritus position, which at least keeps them quiet.

Chapter 8

1. For Oxford and Cambridge, this is never likely to be a major problem. As I have already pointed out, though they do have substantial undergraduate teaching, their main interest now increasingly leans towards postgraduate students and research, a development signalled by new postgraduate colleges like Reuben. (It is all but inevitable that undergraduate students will become a less prominent feature of these universities, not least given the inadequate amount that they receive in domestic undergraduate fees which, in the case of Oxford, is nowhere near the £18,000 that it has been estimated is the fee that would need to be charged to get anywhere near to a real cost.)
2. Although it is worth recalling Nietzsche's argument that it is the task of higher education 'to turn men into machines', a feat accomplished by means of the concept of duty (Nietzsche, 1990, 9.29).
3. One can go too far, of course. For example, in the UK, for better or more likely for worse, 'impact' is itself becoming a measure of actual academic verisimilitude, as if everyone could and should be a clone of a more instrumental version of John Dewey but one updated for the times.
4. The term eudaimonia originates with Aristotle and this makes it easier to relate to a planetary notion of that term in that Aristotle can also be understood as one of the first to both investigate and mount a defence of the living world: 'there is something awesome in all natural things' (Aristotle in Leroi, 2014, p. 10).
5. Another will be the fact that as the world becomes more 'scientific' in tone and content so the fiction that there is a stentorian venture called Science with a capital S becomes harder to maintain. With science involved in all parts of popular culture, so it becomes a currency which increasingly will be shared in one form or another.
6. Quite rightly, students have pressured universities to fix their own estates so that they are carbon neutral (Facer, 2020). They have also moved in on the culture of international

travel which has become central to modern research. They are right in this too but I suspect that this will be a much harder nut to crack. In the end, though, it's issues like supply chains that are a major culprit.

7. Take just one example out of many. Movebank (www.datarepository.movebank.org/) is an archive which allows the public to access data from academic tracking studies of the movements of animals around the world. It is a treasure trove of information which is continually being added to and it fascinates just about everyone who knows about it.
8. The first journal paper was published in 1665 in *Le Journal des Sçavans*.
9. Though I have my doubts that making academics commit to acting as research council referees if they want research council grants is the right way to go.
10. The number of articles published each year and the number of journals have both grown steadily for over two centuries, by about 3 per cent and 3.5 per cent a year, respectively. However, growth has accelerated to 4 per cent per year for articles and over 5 per cent for journals in recent years. This figure ignores the massively expanding preprint sector, as instanced by the growth of arXxiv and latterly medRxiv during the Covid-19 crisis.
11. I suspect that the figure is higher for the mainly arts and humanities and social sciences journals not covered by Web of Science.
12. https://octopuspublishing.org/. Though, in its current form at least, it seems to me to produce as many problems as opportunities.
13. One of the slightly scary issues that has arisen of late is that funding bodies are increasingly throwing their weight around in this area without much in the way of consultation with universities, even though 30 per cent of every research grant is funded by universities on average.
14. I am not saying that elements like teaching and service aren't important. I am talking here only about research.
15. One can step up a gear, of course. Utrecht University has decided to do without impact factors in making judgements on academics.
16. So a statement in the Wellcome Report (2019, p. 49) such as 'Rewards for those who don't publish – rewarding ideas as well as the final output' sounds good but it is more problematic than it may seem at first glance. Wellcome's move to forbid funding to universities that don't subscribe to DORA (which all do, so far as I know) also strikes me as questionable.
17. Actually this statement is incorrect: they get quite a lot of help.
18. For example, fans of this approach like Forth and Jones (2020, p. 63) suggest that 'at least 25 per cent of the uplift in public R&D funding should, in principle, be devolved to nations, regions and cities'.

Chapter 9

1. www.university-mergers.eu
2. Although Goodhart (2021) argues that it is one of the best features of university education and is a privilege that needs to be extended to those studying in colleges using the space freed up by a decline in university places.
3. Some universities already unashamedly bill themselves as primarily teaching universities.
4. There is also the Greater Manchester Civic University Network but this is not predominantly based on research but rather, as the name implies, on civic priorities.
5. On the whole, colleges in Oxford and Cambridge have only given these universities a relatively limited research boost. Their main historical purpose has been teaching. But that doesn't have to follow for all time. First of all, it's not true of all colleges. All Souls and Nuffield are obvious counter-examples. Second, there is no reason why colleges could not have distinctive research functions. Already, a number of colleges in Oxford have substantial research centres attached to them. For example, there is the China Centre

attached to St Hugh's. Third, colleges ought to be centres of interdisciplinary research in any case, given their mixed discipline fellowships.

6 At least so far as I am concerned, this means that universities naturally fit into efforts to cultivate slow-thinking movements like deliberative democracy. That process could start by producing a round of national citizen juries which tackle particular issues over days or weeks.

7 Collaboration is vital for another reason too. All around the world universities are already being treated as though they were a clear and present danger. Academics in many universities are currently suffering from the attentions of repressive regimes. The list of those living in fear is depressingly long. Yet one hears less than we should from other universities about this situation. Equally, scientists like ecologists can find themselves under threat, sometimes of physical violence. Again, almost nothing. In the US and elsewhere, gag orders on government scientists have limited their ability to openly discuss their work, and politicians ignore or discredit or distort scientific evidence during decision-making processes (Lewis, 2019). The response? Every now and then, a vice-chancellor sends a letter about a postgraduate student detained here or a professor under house arrest there, something that hardly leaves the average strongman or woman quaking in their boots.

References

Adams, R. (2021) 'Tuition fees from undergraduate students fail to cover costs of undergraduate courses at UCL' *The Times*, September 11th.

Adekoya, R. (2021) *Biracial Britain: A Different Way of Looking at Race*. London: Constable.

Ahmed, S. (2021) *Complaint!* Durham: Duke University Press.

Aknes, D.W., Langfeldt, L., Wouters, P. (2019) 'Citations, citation indicators, and research quality: an overview of basic concepts and theories' *Sage Open*, January–March, 1–17.

Aldiss, B. (2013) *Finches of Mars*. London: Harper Collins.

Altman, D.G. (1994) 'The scandal of poor medical research' *British Medical Journal*, 308, doi: https://doi.org/10.1136/bmj.308.6924.283.

Amin, A., Thrift, N.J. (2013) *Arts of the Political*. Durham: Duke University Press.

Amrhein, V., Greenland, S., McShane, B. (2019) 'Scientists rise up against statistical significance' *Nature*, March 20th.

Amrhein, V., Trafimow, V., Greenland, S. (2019) 'Inferential statistics as descriptive statistics: there is no replication crisis if we don't expect replication' *The American Statistician*, 73, 262–270.

Anderson, P. (2020) 'Ukania perpetua?' *New Left Review*, 125, 35–108.

Anderson, P. (2021) 'The breakaway' *London Review of Books*, January 21st.

Andreas, J. (2009) *Rise of the Red Engineers: The Cultural Revolution and the Origins of China's New Class*. Stanford: Stanford University Press.

Appiah, K.A. (2010) *The Honor Code. How Moral Revolutions Happen*. New York: W.W. Norton.

Atewologun, D., Cornish, T., Tresh, F. (2018) 'Unconscious bias training: an assessment of the evidence for effectiveness' Equality and Human Rights Commission, Research Report, 113.

Augar, P., Palmer, J. (2002) *The Rise of the Player Manager. How Professionals Manage While They Work*. London: Penguin.

Bachan, R., Bryson, A. (2021) *The Gender Wage Gap Among Vice-Chancellors in the UK*. Bonn: IZA.

Back, L. (2016) *Academic Diary. Or Why Higher Education Still Matters*. London: Goldsmiths Press.

Baer, U. (2019) *What Snowflakes Get Right. Free Speech, Truth, and Equality on Campus*. Oxford: Oxford University Press.

Barber, M. (2013) *An Avalanche Is Coming. Higher Education and the Revolution Ahead*. London: IPPR.

Barber, M. (2021) *Houses of Wisdom. Universities, Scholarship, and Diversity of Perspective*. King's College Commemoration Address.

Barnett, A., Mewburn, I., Schroter, S. (2019) 'Working 9 to 5, not the way to make an academic living: observational analysis of manuscript and peer review submissions over time' *British Medical Journal*, 367, 1–6.

Barnett, R. (2018) *The Ecological University. A Feasible Utopia.* London: Routledge.

Barnett, R., Peters, M.A. (eds.) (2018) *The Idea of the University: Contemporary Perspectives.* London: Peter Lang.

Barry, A. (2020) 'What is an environmental problem?' *Theory Culture and Society*, 38, 93–117.

Bauerlein, M., Gad-el-Hak, M., Grody, W., McKelvey, B., Trimble, S.W. (2010) 'We must stop the avalanche of low-quality research' *The Chronicle of Higher Education*, June 13th.

Becher, T., Trowler, P. (2001) *Academic Tribes and Territories.* Second Edition. Buckingham: SRHE and Open University Press.

Becker, H.S. (2014) *What About Mozart? What About Murder? Reasoning from Cases.* Chicago: University of Chicago Press.

Bekhradnia, B., Beech, D. (2019) *Demand for Higher Education to 2030.* London: Higher Education Policy Institute.

Bell, T. (2022) 'Why be a poor version of Germany instead of doing what we do best?' *The Guardian*, July 10th.

Ben-Porath, S. (2018) 'Against endorsing the Chicago Principles' *Inside Higher Education*, December 11th.

Bennett, R. (2021) 'Mixed media: what universities need to know about journalists so that they can get a better press' HEPI Debate Paper 26.

Berardi, F. (2009) *The Soul at Work. From Alienation to Autonomy.* Los Angeles: Semiotext(e).

Berman, E.P. (2012) *Creating the Market University. How Academic Science Became an Economic Engine.* Princeton: Princeton University Press.

Bhambra, G., Holmwood, J. (2021) *Colonialism and Modern Social Theory.* Cambridge: Polity Press.

Biagoli, M. (2018) 'Quality to impact, text to metadata: publication and evaluation in the age of metrics' *Know*, 2, 249–275.

Bjornerud, M. (2018) *Timefulness. How Thinking Like a Geologist Can Help Save the World.* Princeton: Princeton University Press.

Blackburn, L.H. (2014) 'The fairest of them all? The support for Scottish students in full-time higher education' ESRC Working Paper.

Blanchard, O., Rodrik, D. (2019) 'Reversing the rise in inequality' Petersen Institute for International Economics. www.piie.com/commentary/speeches-papers/we-have-tools-reverse-rise-inequality.

Blastland, M. (2019) *The Hidden Half. How the World Conceals Its Secrets.* London: Atlantic Books.

Bloom, N., Jones, C.L., Van Reenen, J., Webb, M. (2017) 'Ideas aren't running out but they are getting more expensive to find' *VoxEU/CEPR*, September 20th.

Bloom, N., Jones, C.L., Van Reenen, J., Webb, M. (2020) 'Are ideas getting harder to find?' *American Economic Review*, 110, 1104–1144.

Bloom, N., Van Reenen, J., Williams, H. (2019) 'A toolkit of policies to promote innovation' *Journal of Economic Perspectives*, 33, 163–184.

Boliver, V., Gorard, S., Siddiqui, N. (2019) 'Using contextualized admissions to widen access to higher education: a guide to the evidence base' *Durham Centre Evidence Centre for Education Research Briefing*, 1.

Bolton, P. (2021a) 'Higher education funding in England' House of Commons Briefing Paper 7393.

Bolton, P. (2021b) 'Higher education student numbers' House of Commons Briefing Paper 7857.

Bornmann, L., Mutz, R. (2014). 'Growth rates of modern science: a bibliometric analysis based on the number of publications and cited references' *arxiv.org*. http://arxiv.org/abs/1402.4578.

Boston, J. (2016) *Governing for the Future: Designing Democratic Institutions for a Better Tomorrow*. London: Emerald.

Bourdieu, P. (1984) *Homo Academicus*. Cambridge: Polity Press.

Brabner, R. (2021) 'People want free speech to thrive at universities ... just not for racists, Holocaust deniers or advocates of religious violence' *Hepi News*, May 17th.

Brant, P. (2019) 'It's not (yet?) true that half of young people go to university' *HEPI Blog*, October 9th.

Brazil, R. (2021) What's wrong with research culture?' *Chemistry World*, September 28th.

Brighouse, H., McPherson, M. (eds) (2015) *The Aims of Higher Education. Problems of Morality and Justice*. Chicago: Chicago University Press.

Brink, C. (2018) *The Soul of a University. Why Excellence Is Not Enough*. Bristol: Bristol University Press.

British Academy (2019) *Lessons from the History of UK Science Policy*. London: British Academy.

British Academy (2020) *Qualified for the Future: Quantifying Demand for Arts, Humanities and Social Science Skills*. London: British Academy.

Britton, J., Dearden, L., Waltmann, B. (2021) *The Returns to Undergraduate Degrees by Socio-Economic Group and Ethnicity*. Research Report. London: Department for Education/Institute for Fiscal Studies.

Broecke, S. (2015) 'University rankings: do they matter in the UK?' *Education Economics*, 23, 137–161.

Brooks, D. (2020a) 'The future of nonconformity' *New York Times*, July 23rd.

Brooks, D. (2020b) '2020 taught us how to fix this' *New York Times*, December 31st.

Brown, A. (2022) *What's Next for National Security and Research?* HEPI Report 147. London: Higher Education Policy Institute.

Brown, W. (2015) *Undoing the Demos. Neoliberalism's Stealth Revolution.* New York: Zone Books.

Brynjolfsson, E., McAfee, A. (2014) *The Second Machine Age: Work, Progress and Prosperity in a Time of Brilliant Technologies.* New York: W.W. Norton.

Buckley, W.F. (1951/1986) *God and Man at Yale. The Superstitions of Academic Freedom.* New York: Gateway.

Bukodi, E., Goldthorpe, J.H. (2018) *Social Mobility and Education in Britain.* Cambridge: Cambridge University Press.

Bull, J.W., Taylor, E., Biggs, I., Grub, H.J., Yearley, T., Waters, H., Milner-Gulland, E.J. (2022) 'Analysis: the biodiversity footprint of the University of Oxford' *Nature*, 604, 402–424.

Burnett, K., Thrift, N.J. (2015) *The Future of Higher Vocational Education.* Sheffield: University of Sheffield.

Byrne, E., Clarke, C. (2020) *The University Challenge.* London: Pearson.

Cain, S. (2013) *Quiet. The Power of Introverts in a World That Can't Stop Talking.* London: Penguin.

Callon, M. (2021) *Markets in the Making. Rethinking Competition, Goods, and Innovation.* New York: Zone Books.

Cannadine, D. (2004) 'John Harold Plumb 1911–2001' *Proceedings of the British Academy*, 124, 269–309.

Caplan, B. (2018) *The Case Against Education: Why the Education System Is a Waste of Time and Money.* Princeton: Princeton University Press.

Carey, K. (2016) *The End of College. Creating the Future of Learning and the University of Everywhere.* New York: Riverhead.

Carey, K. (2020a) 'The bleak job landscape of adjunctopia for Ph.D.s' *New York Times*, March 5th.

Carey, K. (2020b) 'Everybody ready for the big migration to online college? Actually, no' *New York Times*, March 13th.

Carnes, N., Lupu, N. (2015) 'What good is a college degree? Education and leader quality reconsidered' *The Journal of Politics*, 78, 35–49.

Cartwright, N., Hardie, J. (2012) *Evidence-Based Policy. A Practical Guide to Doing It Better.* New York: Oxford University Press.

Carvalho, A. (2017) 'Wishful thinking about R&D policy targets: what governments promise and what they actually deliver' *Science and Public Policy*, 45, 373–391.

Cassasus, B. (2020) 'How France overcame the odds to build a research mega-campus' *Nature*, October 27th.

CDBU (2021) *Academic Freedom as a Public Good.* London: Council for the Defence of British Universities.

Chakrabarty, D. (2009) 'The climate of history. Four theses' *Critical Inquiry*, 35, 197–222.

Chakrabarty, D. (2014) 'Climate and capital: on conjoined histories' *Critical Inquiry*, 41, 1–23.
Chandler, J., Housley, C., Rough, E., Hutton, G. (2021) *Research and Development Funding Policy*. London: House of Commons.
Charity Commission (2021) 'Campaigning and political activity guidance for charities' https://assets.publishing.service.gov.uk/government/uploads/system/uploads/attachment_data/file/610137/CC9.pdf.
Chawla, D.S. (2019) 'Hyperauthorship: global projects spark surge in thousand author projects' *Nature*, December 13th.
Chaytor, S., Gottlieb, G., Reid, G. (2021) *Regional Policy and R and D. Evidence, Experiments and Expectations*. HEPI Report 137. London: HEPI.
Chicago Principles (2014) *Report of the Committee on Freedom of Expression*. Chicago: University of Chicago.
Chirikov, I., Semenova, T., Maloshonok, T., Bettinger, E., Kizilcec, R.F. (2020) 'Online education platforms scale college STEM instruction with equivalent learning outcomes at lower cost' *Science Advances*, 6, doi: 10.1126/sciadv.aay5324 (15), eaay5324.6Sci Adv.
Chivers, T. (2020) 'If it doesn't say "registered report", don't trust it' *Unherd*, February 6th.
Christophers, B. (2022) *Rentier Capitalism. Who Owns the Economy and Who Pays For It?* London: Verso.
Cicero, M.T. (1991) *On Duties*. Cambridge: Cambridge University Press.
Clark, T. (2015) *Ecocriticism on the Edge. The Anthropocene as a Threshold Concept*. London: Bloomsbury.
Clark, W. (2009) *Academic Charisma and the Origins of the Research University*. Chicago: University of Chicago Press.
Cole, J.R. (2009) *The Great American University*. New York: Public Affairs.
Collini, S. (2012) *What Are Universities For?* London: Penguin.
Collini, S. (2013) 'Sold out' *London Review of Books*, 35, 3–12.
Collini, S. (2017) *Speaking of Universities*. London: Verso.
Commission on the Future of Higher Education (2013) *A Critical Path. Securing the Future of Higher Education in England*. London: Institute for Public Policy Research.
Committee of Public Accounts (2022) *Financial Sustainability of the Higher Education Sector in England*. London: House of Commons.
Committee on Higher Education (1963) *Higher Education: Report of the Committee Appointed by the Prime Minister under the Chairmanship of Lord Robbins 1961–63*, Cmnd. 2154. London: HMSO.
Conlon, G. (2019) *Fees, Funding and Fairness*. London: London Economics.
Cook, M.C., Newman, N. (2022) 'AI for HE: a student journey map' *HEPI Guest Post*. https://wp.me/p5FB74-521.
Cope, J. (2022) 'We've reached a tipping point on apprenticeships' *HEPI Guest Post*, https://wp.me/p5FB74-4Ym.

Cornell, B. (2020) *PhD Life: The UK Student Experience*. HEPI Report 131. London: HEPI.

Corver, M. (2019) 'Higher education is big business' *WonkHE*, November 11th.

Corver, M. (2021) 'High inflation could devastate universities and leave students overwhelmed by debt' *HEPI Blog*, July 14th.

Cox, G. (2013) *Overcoming Short-Termism in British Business*. London: Labour Party.

Cramer, L. (2021) 'Equity, diversion and inclusion: alternative strategies for closing the award gap between white and minority ethnic students' *eLife*, 10: e58971 DOI: 10.7554/eLife.58971.

Crow, M.M., Dabars, W.B. (2015) *Designing the New American University*. Baltimore: Johns Hopkins University Press.

Crow, M.M., Dabars, W.B. (2020) *The Fifth Wave. The Evolution of American Higher Education*. Baltimore: Johns Hopkins University Press.

Currid-Halkett, E. (2017) *The Sum of Small Things. A Theory of the Aspirational Class*. Princeton: Princeton University Press.

Daniels, R.J. (with Shreve, G., Spector, P.) (2021) *What Universities Owe Democracy*. Baltimore: Johns Hopkins University Press.

Daston, L., Galison, P. (2007) *Objectivity*. New York: Zone Books.

Davies, W. (2022) 'How many words does it take to make a mistake?' *London Review of Books*, February 24th.

Davis, G. (2017) *The Australian Idea of a University*. Melbourne: Melbourne University Press.

Davis, L.J. (2008) *Obsession. A History*. Chicago: Chicago University Press.

Davis, M. (2022) 'Thanatos triumphant' *NLR Sidecar*, March 7th.

Day, R.E. (2014) *Indexing It All*. Cambridge: MIT Press.

Delbanco, A. (2012) *College. What It Was, Is, and Should Be*. Princeton: Princeton University Press.

Department for Education/Department for International Trade (2019) 'International education strategy. global potential, global growth' Policy Paper. London: Department for Education/Department for International Trade.

Deryugina, T., Shurchkov, O., Stearns, J. (2021) 'Covid-19 disruptions disproportionately affect female academics' NBER Working Paper 28360. www.nber.org/papers/w28360.

de Waal, E. (2021) *Letters to Camondo*. London: Chatto & Windus.

Dickinson, J. (2019) 'When did decent student housing become a luxury?' *WonkHE*, 10th December.

Dickinson, J. (2020) 'Will more "free speech" regulation have unintended consequences?' *WonkHE*, March 9th.

Dickinson, J. (2021a) 'Is debate under threat on UK campuses' *WonkHE*, January 20th.

Dickinson, J. (2021b) 'Student finance: it's the interest rate stupid' *WonkHE*, May 31st.

Dickinson, J. (2021c) 'Are universities the right vehicle for schools improvement' *WonkHE*, November 29th.

Dickinson, J. (2021d) 'Students shouldn't pay for things they don't use' *WonkHE*, January 11th.

Dickinson, J. (2022) 'Here's how we get off the campus conflict see-saw' *WonkHE*, February 21st.

Dobbin, F., Kalev, A. (2018) 'Why doesn't diversity training work? The challenge for industry and academia' *Anthropology Now*, 10, 48–55.

Doepke, M., Zilibotti, F. (2018) *Love, Money, and Parenting. How Economics Explains the Way We Raise Our Kids*. Princeton: Princeton University Press.

Donald, A. (2021) *The Research and Technical Workforce in the UK*. London: Royal Society.

Douthat, R. (2021) 'How Michel Foucault lost the left and won the right' *New York Times*, May 25th.

Duncan, E. (2021) 'Britain needs more second-class universities' *The Times*, July 9th.

Duranti, A. (2013) 'On the future of anthropology: fundraising, the job market and the corporate turn' *Anthropological Theory*, 13, 201–221.

Economist (2020a) 'Are left-wing American professors indoctrinating their students?' *The Economist*, January 9th.

Economist (2020b) 'Britain's mixed-race population blurs the lines of identity politics' *The Economist*, October 12th.

Edgerton, D. (2009) 'The 'Haldane Principle' and other invented traditions in science policy' *History and Policy*, Policy Paper 88.

Edgerton, D. (2019) *The Shock of the Old. Technology and Global History Since 1900*. London: Profile.

Edsall, T. (2022) 'America has split and it's now in very dangerous territory' *New York Times*, January 26th.

EHRC (2019) *Tackling Racial Harassment: Universities Challenged*. London: Equality and Human Rights Commission.

Ehrenreich, R. (1994) *A Garden of Paper Flowers. An American at Oxford*. London: Picador.

Elsevier (2020) *The Researcher Journey Through a Gender Lens*. London: Elsevier.

Epstein, D. (2019) *Range. How Generalists Triumph in a Specialized World*. New York: Macmillan.

Errington, T., Mathur, M., Soderbergh, C.K., Denis, A., Perfito, N., Iorns, E., Nosek, B.A. (2021) 'Investigating the replicability of preclinical cancer biology' *eLife*, 10, e71601.

Estermann, T. (2015) 'University autonomy in Europe' *University Education*, 3, 28–32.

Facer, K. (2020) 'Beyond business as usual. Higher education in the age of climate change' HEPI Debate Paper, 24.

Fanshawe, S. (2021) *The Power of Difference: Where the Complexities of Diversity and Inclusion Meet Practical Solutions*. London: Kogan Page.

Finn, M. (2022) 'What's the use of the staff:student ratio?' *WonkHE*, May 24th.

Flaherty, N. (2019) 'Death knell for trigger warnings?' *Inside Higher Ed*, March 16th.

Fleming, N. (2019) 'The microscopic advances that are opening big advances in cell biology' *Nature*, November 27th.

Fleming, P. (2021) *Dark Academia: How Universities Die*. London: Pluto Press.

Forth, T., Jones, R.A.L. (2020) *The Missing £4 Billion. Making R and D Work for the Whole of the UK*. London: NESTA.

Frank, J., Gowar, N., Naef, M. (2019) *English Universities in Crisis. Markets Without Competition*. Bristol: Bristol University Press.

Fraser, F., Blagden, J., Holloway, W. (2021) *Levelling Up Innovation*. London: Onward.

Gabrys, J. (2016) *Program Earth: Environmental Sensing Technology and the Making of a Computational Planet*. Minneapolis: University of Minnesota Press.

Gadd, E. (2020) 'University rankings need a rethink' *Nature*, November 24th.

Gadd, E. (2021a) 'Mis-measuring our universities: why global university rankings don't add up' *Frontiers in Research Metrics and Analytics*. https://doi.org/10.3389/frma.2021.680023.

Gadd, E. (2021b) 'Using REF results responsibly' *WonkHE*, September 27th.

Galison, P., Thompson, E. (eds.) (1999) *The Architecture of Science*. Cambridge: MIT Press.

Ganesh, J. (2019) 'Parenthood should be taken off its pedestal' *Financial Times*, September 21st.

Garcia, T. (2021) *We Ourselves. The Politics of Us*. Cambridge: Polity Press.

Gastfriend, E. (2015) '90% of all the scientists that ever lived are alive today' *futureoflife.org*. https://futureoflife.org/2015/11/05/90-of-all-the-scientists-that-ever-lived-are-alive-today/

Giddens, A. (1991) *Modernity and Self-Identity. Self and Society in the Late Modern World*. Cambridge: Polity Press.

Glennie, P.D., Thrift, N.J. (2009) *Shaping the Day*. Oxford: Oxford University Press.

Godin, B. (2015) *Innovation Contested – The Idea of Innovation Over the Centuries*. London: Routledge.

Godin, B. (2019) *The Invention of Technological Innovation: Languages, Discourses and Ideology in Historical Perspective*. Cheltenham: Edward Elgar.

Goldin, C., Katz, L.F. (2008) *The Race Between Education and Technology*. Cambridge: Harvard University Press.

Goldthorpe, J. (2020) 'The expert in social mobility who says that education cannot make it happen'. Interview with Peter Wilby' *The Guardian*, March 17th.

Gombrich, R.F. (2000) 'British higher education policy in the last twenty years: the murder of a profession', www.damtp.cam.ac.uk/user/mem/papers/LHCE/uk-higher-education.html.

Gonzales, A.L., Calarco, J.M., Lynch, T. (2018) 'Technology problems and student achievement gaps: a validation and extension of the technology maintenance construct' *Communication Research*. https://doi.org/10.1177/0093650218796366.

Goodall, A. (2009) *Socrates in the Boardroom: Why Research Universities Should Be Led by Top Scholars*. Princeton: Princeton University Press.

Goodhart, D. (2019) 'How Boris can cement his new coalition' *Unherd*, December 31st.

Goodhart, D. (2020) *Head, Hand, Heart. The Struggle for Dignity and Status in the 21st Century*. London: Allen Lane.

Goodhart, D. (2021) Tony Blair is still wrong on his 50% university target' *Unherd*, June 2nd.

Gordon, R. (2016) *The Rise and Fall of American Growth*. Princeton: Princeton University Press.

Gore, G. (2018) 'UK Universities turn to private market as debts rack up' *International Finance Review*, October 12th.

GOV.UK (2021) *Entry Rates into Higher Education*. London: Department of Education

Graeber, D. (2015) *The Utopia of Rules. On Technology, Stupidity, and the Secret Joys of Bureaucracy*. New York: Melville House.

Graeber, D. (2018) *Bullshit Jobs. A Theory*. London: Allen Lane.

Grafton, A. (1997) *The Footnote. A Curious History*. Cambridge: Harvard University Press.

Graham, S., Thrift., N.J. (2007) 'Out of order: understanding repair and maintenance' *Theory Culture and Society*, 24, 1–25.

Grant, J. (2021) *The New Power University. The Social Purpose of Higher Education in the Twenty First Century*. London: Pearson.

Grant, J., Hewlett, K., Nir, T., Duffy, B. (2019) *Freedom of Expression in UK Universities*. London: King's College Policy Institute.

Gray, J. (2018) 'The problem of hyper-liberalism' *Times Literary Supplement*, March 30th.

Green, S. (2013) 'Innovation: the history of a buzzword' *The Atlantic*, June 20th.

Green, T.L., Hagiwara, N. (2020) 'The problem with implicit bias training' *Scientific American*, August 28th.

Griffiths, S. (2021) 'Britain's brightest plot a course across the pond' *The Times*, May 30th.

Grove, J. (2020) 'Mark Griffiths: the professor who published a paper every two days' *Times Higher Education*, October 22nd.

Gschwandtner, A., McManus, R. (2018) 'University vice chancellor pay, performance and (asymmetric) benchmarking' University of Kent School of Economics Discussion Paper 1807.

Haldane, A. (2018) *Ideas and Institutions – A Growth Story*. Speech to The Guild Society, Oxford.

Halsey, A.H. (1995) *The Decline of Donnish Dominion. The British Academic Professions in the Twentieth Century*. Oxford: Oxford University Press.

Halsey, A.H., Trow, M. (1971) *The British Academics*. London: Faber.

Haraway, D. (2018) 'Making kin in the cthulucene: reproducing multispecies justice' in Clarke, A.E., Haraway, D. (eds.) *Making Kin Not Population*. Chicago, Prickly Paradigm Press, 67–100.

Hayes, C. (2021) 'On the internet we're always famous' *The New Yorker*, September 24th.

Herb, U. (2019) 'Steering science through Output Indicators & Data Capitalism'. Proceedings of the 23rd Congress of the European Society of Veterinary and Comparative Nutrition, Turin 2019. DOI:10.5281/zenodo.3333395.

HEFCE (2018) *Differences in Student Outcomes: The Effect of Student Characteristics*. London: HEFCE.

HESA (2020) *Higher Education Staff Statistics: UK, 2018/19*. Cheltenham: Higher Education Statistics Agency.

Hewitt, R. (2020) *Demand for Higher Education to 2035*. HEPI Report 134. London: HEPI.

Hicks, D., Wouters, P., Waltman, L., de Rijcke, S., Rafols, I. (2015) 'Bibliometrics: The Leiden Manifesto for research metrics' *Nature*, 520, 429–431.

Hillman, N. (2017) 'Why we must protect university autonomy' Speech to the inaugural G20 meeting at the University of Buckingham, April 3rd.

Hillman, N. (2020) *From T to R Revisited: Cross-Subsidies from Teaching to Research after Augar and the 2.4% R&D Target*. London: Higher Education Policy Institute.

Hillman, N. (2021a) 'A short guide to non-continuation in UK universities' HEPI Policy Note 28.

Hillman, N. (2021b) 'Sex and relationships among students: summary report' HEPI Policy Note 30.

Hillman, N. (2022a) 'Digging in: the changing tenure of UK vice-chancellors' HEPI Policy Note 34.

Hillman, N. (2022b) '"You can't say that". What students really think of free speech on campus' HEPI Policy Note 35.

Hinde, K. et al. (2021) 'Education and outreach: March Mammal Madness and the power of narrative in science outreach' *eLife*. doi: 10.7554/eLife.65066.

HMG (2020) *UK Research and Development Roadmap*. London: Her Majesty's Government.

HMG (2022) *Levelling Up the United Kingdom*. London: Her Majesty's Government.

Hooper, R. (2021) *How to Spend a Trillion Dollars Saving the World and Solving the Biggest Questions in Science*. London: Profile.

Horgan, A. (2020) *Public Higher Education for the Public Good. Addressing the Covid-19 Crisis*. London: Common Wealth.

House, G. (2020) *Postgraduate Education in the UK*. HEPI Analytical Report 1. London: HEPI.

Hudson, L.J., Mansfield, I. (2020) *Universities at the Crossroads. How Higher Education Leadership Must Act to Regain the Trust of Their Staff, Their Communities and the Whole Nation*. London: Policy Exchange.

Hutton, G. (2021) *Research and Development Spending*. London: House of Commons Library.

Ialenti, V. (2020) *Deep Time Reckoning. How Future Thinking Can Help Earth Now*. Cambridge: MIT Press.

Ioannidis, J.P.A., Baas, J., Klavans, R., Boyack, K.W. (2019) 'A standardized citation metrics author database annotated for scientific field' *PLOS Biology*, 17, 1–6.

Irwin, A. (2018) 'No PhDs needed: how citizen science is transforming research' *Nature*, October 23rd.

Jaschik, S. (2017) 'Professors and politics: what the research says' *Inside Higher Education*, February 27th.

James, W. (1918/2010) 'The Ph.D. octopus' in Richardson, R. (ed.) *The Heart of William James*. Cambridge: Harvard University Press.

James, W. (1890) *The Principles of Psychology. Volume 1*. New York: Dover.

Jenkins, S. (2019) 'What are our universities for? Taxpayers have a right to know' *The Guardian*, 31st May.

Jinha, A.F. (2010) 'Article 50 million: an estimate of the number of scholarly articles in existence' *Learned Publishing*, 25, 258–263.

Johnson, J. (2020) 'Universities must do more to attract foreign students' *The Times*, June 15th.

Johnson, J., Adams, J., Grant, J., Murphy, D. (2022) *Stumbling Bear, Soaring Dragon. Russia, China and the Geopolitics of Global Science*. London: King's Policy Institute.

Joice, W., Tetlow, A. (2020) *Ethnicity STEM Data for Students and Academic Staff in Higher Education, 2007/8 to 2018/19*. London: Royal Society.

Jones, L., Hameiri, H. (2021) 'COVID-19 and the failure of the neoliberal regulatory state' *Review of International Political Economy*, 28, 283-294

Jones, S., Blakey, M. (2020) *Student Accommodation. The Facts.* HEPI Analytical Report 2. London: HEPI.

Judge, P.G. (2021) 'The enduring mystery of the solar corona' *Physics World*, September 16th.

Kang, J.C. (2019) 'Where does affirmative action leave Asian-Americans?' *New York Times Magazine*, August 28th.

Kaplan, S. (2019) 'Duke University to pay $112.5 million to settle claims of research misconduct' *New York Times*, March 25th.

Karlsen, S., Nazroo, J.Y., Smith, N.R. (2020) 'Ethnic, religious and gender differences in intragenerational economic mobility in England and Wales' *Sociology*, 54(5), 883–903.

Katz, R., Ogilvie, S., Shaw, J., Woodhead, L. (2021) *Gen Z, Explained. The Art of Living in a Digital Age.* Chicago: University of Chicago Press.

Kennedy, M. (2011) 'Cultural formations of the public university. Globalization, diversity, and the state at the University of Michigan' in Rhoten, D., Calhoun, C. (eds.) *Knowledge Matters. The Public Mission of the Research University.* New York: Columbia University Press, 457–500.

Kernohan, D. (2021a) 'Gravity assist lacks force' *WonkHE*, February 25th.

Kernohan, D. (2021b) 'Where next for higher education funding in Scotland?' *WonkHE*, May 28th.

Kernohan, D. (2022) 'This is fine: regulation, autonomy, and fear' *WonkHE*, May 23rd.

Khan, S.R. (2016) 'The education of elites in the United States' *L'Année Sociologique*, 66, 171–192.

Khurana, R. (2007) *From Higher Aims to Hired Hands. The Social Transformation of Business Schools and the Unfulfilled Promise of Management as a Profession.* Princeton: Princeton University Press.

Kim, E.T. (2020) 'The perils of "people of colour"' *The New Yorker*, July 29th.

Kingman, J. (2021) 'Five years of UKRI'. www.thebritishacademy.ac.uk/events/sir-john-kingman-reflections-on-his-time-as-ukri-chair/.

Kirby, P., Cullinane, C. (2016) 'Class differences: ethnicity and disadvantage' *Sutton Trust Research Brief*, 14.

Knight, E., Jones, A., Gertler, M.S. (2020) 'The public university and the retreat from globalisation: an economic geography perspective on managing local–global tensions in international higher education' *Environment and Planning A*, 53, 210–218.

Kozlowski, D., Larivière, V., Sugimoto, C., Monroe-White, T. (2022) 'Intersectional inequalities in science' *PNAS* 119(2) e2113067119. https://doi.org/10.1073/pnas.2113067119.

Krznaric, R. (2019) 'Why we need to reinvent democracy for the long term' *BBC Future*, March 19th.

Kznaric, R. (2020) 'Four ways to redesign democracy for future generations' *openDemocracy*, July 12th.

Lambert, H. (2019) 'The great university con: how the British degree lost its value' *New Statesman*, August 21st.

Lanchester, J. (2015) 'The robots are coming' *London Review of Books*, 5th March, 3–8.

Landis, S., Amara, S., Asadullah, K. et al. (2012) 'A call for transparent reporting to optimize the predictive value of preclinical research' *Nature*, 490, 187–191. https://doi.org/10.1038/nature11556.

Lapworth, S. (2018) 'Having regard to institutional autonomy' *Office for Students blog*, October 26th.

Lashuel, H. (2020) 'The busy lives of academics have hidden costs – and universities must take better care of their faculty members' *Nature*, March 5th.

Laslett, P. (1967) 'The university in high industrial society' in Crick, B. (ed.) *Essays on Reform*. London: Oxford University Press, 120–143.

Latchman, D. (2021) 'Bringing universities into the 21st century: supporting onsite teaching with virtual learning' *HEPI Guest Post*. https://wp.me/p5FB74-4O4.

Latour, B. (1993) *We Have Never Been Modern*. Cambridge: Harvard University Press.

Latour, B. (2013) *An Inquiry into Modes of Existence. An Anthropology of the Moderns*. Cambridge: Harvard University Press.

Latour, B. (2016) 'Is Geo-logy the new umbrella for all the sciences? Hints for a neo-Humboldtian university' Lecture at Cornell University, 25th October 2016.

Lepore, J. (2020) *If Then: How One Data Company Invented the Future*. London: John Murray.

Leroi, A.M. (2014) *The Lagoon. How Aristotle Invented Science*. London: Bloomsbury.

Leslie, J., Shah, K. (2021) *Wealth Gap Year. The Impact of the Coronavirus on UK Household Wealth*. London: Resolution Foundation.

Lewis, D. (2019) 'Global political climate of fear threatens ecologists' work' *Nature*, 1st April.

Leyshon, A., Thrift, N.J. (2007) 'The capitalization of almost everything' *Theory Culture and Society*, 24, 97–115.

Livingstone, D.N. (2003) *Putting Science in its Place. Geographies of Scientific Knowledge*. Chicago: University of Chicago Press.

Lockee, B. (2021) 'Online education in the post-COVID era' *Nature Electronics*, 4, 5–6.

London Economics (2017) *The Economic Impact of Russell Group Universities*. London: Russell Group.

Lopez, B. (2019) *Horizon*. New York: Vintage.

Lucey, B.M., Urquhart, A., Zhang, H. (2020) 'UK Vice Chancellor compensation: do they get what they deserve?' *SSRN*, January 20th.

Lury, C. (2021) *Problem Spaces. How and Why Methodology Matters*. Cambridge: Polity Press.

MacFarquhar, L. (2011) 'How to be good' *New Yorker*, September 5th.

McCarthy, I.P., Silvestre, B.S., Nordenflych, A., Breznitz, S.M (2018) 'A typology of university research park strategies: What parks do and why it matters' *Journal of Engineering and Technology Management*, 47, 110–122. https://doi.org/10.1016/j.jengtecman.2018.01.004.

McFarlane, B., Burg, D. (2019) 'Women professors and the academic housework trap' *Journal of Higher Education Policy and Management*, 41, 262–274.

McGettigan, A. (2013) *The Great University Gamble. Money, Markets and the Future of Higher Education*. London: Pluto Press.

Mckenzie, C. (2021) 'The re-balancing act of public research and development' *HEPI Blog*. https://wp.me/p5FB74-4JI.

Malchow, H. (2011) *Special Relations? The Americanization of Britain*. Stanford: Stanford University Press.

Mandler, P. (2015) Lecture to the Australian Historical Society.

Mandler, P. (2020) *The Crisis of the Meritocracy. Britain's Transition to Mass Education Since the Second World War*. Oxford: Oxford University Press.

Mandler, P. (2021) '(Yet another) crisis of the humanities' *HEPI Guest Post*, September 28th. https://wp.me/p5FB74-4FW.

Mannix, L. (2022) 'Desperate, despondent, ignored: Australian science at crisis point' *Sydney Morning Herald*, March 20th.

Marcus, J. (2020) 'How technology is changing the future of higher education' *New York Times*, February 24th.

Marginson, S. (2018) *Higher Education as Self-Formation*. London: IOE Press.

Markovits, D. (2019) *The Meritocracy Trap*. London: Penguin.

Marriott, J. (2021a) 'Can't even: how millennials became the burnout generation' *The Times*, January 7th.

Marriott, J. (2021b) 'The new elites are working class wannabe's' *The Times*, January 20th.

Marriott, J. (2021c) 'If you want to get ahead, ditch your creativity' *The Times*, May 12th.

Marriott, J. (2021d) 'Modern life has set us all free in our twenties' *The Times*, October 21st.

Martin, M. (2020) '5 reasons diversity training usually fails' *Fast Company*, August 3rd.

Masschelein, J. (2019) 'Turning a city into a milieu of study: university pedagogy as "frontline"'. *Educational Theory*, 69, 185-203.

Matthews, D. (2020) 'Pandemic lockdown holding back female academics, data show' *Times Higher Education*, June 25th.

Matthews, D. (2021) 'Drowning in the literature? These software tools can help' *Nature*, September 1st.

Mazur, E. (2013) *Peer Instruction. A User's Manual.* London: Pearson.

Mazzucato, M. (2020) 'We socialize bailouts. We should socialize successes too' *New York Times*, July 1st.

Menard, A.D., Trant, J.F. (2020) 'A review and critique of lab safety' *Nature Chemistry*, 12, 12–75.

Millward, C. (2021) *White Students Who Are Left Behind: The Importance of Place.* London: Office for Students.

Mirowski, P. (2011) *Science-Mart. Privatizing American Science.* Cambridge: Harvard University Press.

Mitchell, T. (2015) 'Economentality: how the future entered government' *Critical Inquiry*, 40, 479–507.

Moller, V. (2019) *The Map of Knowledge. How Classical Ideas Were Lost and Found: A History in Seven Cities.* London: Picador.

Morphew, C.C., Eckel, P.D (eds) (2009) *Privatizing the Public University. Perspectives from Across the Academy.* Baltimore: Johns Hopkins University Press.

Morse, A. (2017) 'Preface to National Audit Office' *The Higher Education Market.* London: National Audit Office.

Mulhern, F. (2020) 'In the academic counting house' *New Left Review*, 123, 115–132.

National Audit Office (2022) *Regulating the Financial Sustainability of Higher Education Providers in England.* London: National Audit Office.

National Committee of Inquiry into Higher Education (1997) *Higher Education in the Learning Society.* London: HMSO.

Nature (2020) 'Editorial: Nature will publish peer review reports as a trial' *Nature*, February 5th.

Nature (2021) 'Protect precious scientific collaboration from geopolitics' *Nature*, May 27th.

Nature (2022) 'Research evaluation needs to change with the times' *Nature*, January 11th.

Nelson, N.C. (2021) 'Understand the real reasons reproducibility reform fails' *Nature*, 600, 191.

Nietzsche, F. (1990) *Twilight of the Idols.* Harmondsworth: Penguin.

Norris, P. (2021) 'Cancel culture: myth or reality?' *Political Studies.* doi.org/10.1177/00323217211037023.

Nurse, P. (2021) 'Biology must generate ideas as well as data' *Nature*, 597, 305.

Nussbaum, M. (2010) *Not for Profit. Why Democracy Needs the Humanities.* Princeton: Princeton University Press.

Nuwer, R. (2019) 'This Tarantula became a scientific celebrity. Was it poached from the wild?' *New York Times*, April 1st.

O'Sullivan, S. (2021) *The Sleeping Beauties: And Other Stories of Mystery Illness.* London: Picador.

OfS (2019) 'Unconditional offers: serving the interests of students?' *Insight*, 1. London: Office for Students.

ONS (2022) 'Estimating suicide among higher education students, England and Wales: experimental statistics: 2017 to 2020'. London: Office for National Statistics.

Orben, A., Przybylski, A.K. (2019) 'The association between adolescent well-being and digital technology use' *Nature Human Behaviour*, 3, 173–182.

Oreskes, N. (2019) *Why Trust Science?* Princeton: Princeton University Press.

Osterloh, M., Frey, B.S. (2014) 'Ranking games' *Evaluation Review*, 39, 102-129.

Oswald, A. (2001) 'An Economist's View of University League Tables' *andrewoswald.com*. www.andrewoswald.com/docs/leaguetablespmm.pdf.

Oswald, A. (2017) 'How much should university vice-chancellors be paid?' *andrewoswald.com*. www.andrewoswald.com/docs/VCpayOswaldTimesHigherSeptember2017.pdf.

Packer, G. (2020) 'The enemies of writing' *The Atlantic*, January 23rd.

Page, B. (2020) 'Streaming is stalling: Can music keep up in the attention economy?' *Billboard*, December 16th.

Pelfrey, P.A. (1984) *A Brief History of the University of California*. Berkeley: University of California Press.

Peters, M.A., Barnett, R. (eds.) (2018) *The Idea of the University: A Reader*. London: Peter Lang.

Plumer, B., Davenport, C. (2019) 'Science under attack: how the Trump administration is sidelining researchers and their work' *New York Times*, December 28th.

Poskett, J. (2022) *Horizons. A Global History of Science*. London: Viking.

Price, C.C., Edwards, K. (2020) 'Trends in income from 1975 to 2018' *Rand Working Paper* WR-A516-1.

Rawlinson, S. (2019) 'Growing pains: It is possible that the UK higher education sector is approaching "peak campus"?' *Building*, September 9th.

Reich, J. (2020) *Failure to Disrupt. Why Technology Can't Transform Education*. Cambridge: Harvard University Press.

Reisz, M (2015) 'Humanities crisis? What crisis?' *Times Higher Education*, July 6th, 10.

Ribeiro, L.C., Rapini, M., Silva, L.A., Albuquerque, L. (2018) 'Growth patterns of the network of international collaboration in science' *Scientometrics*, 114, 159–179.

Riskin, J. (2016) *The Restless Clock. A History of the Centuries-Long Argument Over What Makes Living Things Tick*. Chicago: University of Chicago Press.

Ritchie, S. (2020) *Science Fictions. Exposing Fraud, Bias, Negligence and Hype in Science*. London: Bodley Head.

Rivera, L.A. (2015) *Pedigree. How Elite Students Get Elite Jobs*. Princeton: Princeton University Press.

Roberts, A. (2022) *The This*. London: Gollancz.

Roberts, G. (2021) *The Humanities in Modern Britain: Challenges and Opportunities*. HEPI Report 141. London: HEPI.

Roberts, J. (2009) *Wilhelm von Humboldt and German Liberalism*. Oakville: Mosaic Press.

Robinson, K.S. (2020) *The Ministry for the Future*. London: Orbit.

Rose, N. (2019) *Our Psychiatric Future. The Politics of Mental Health*. Cambridge: Polity Press.

Russell Group (2020) *Russell Group Analysis Based on Data from the OfS Shows Declining Funding for Undergraduate Teaching*. London: Russell Group.

Russell Group (2021) *Realising Our Potential. Backing Talent and Strengthening UK Research Culture and Environment*. London: Russell Group.

Şahin, M., Kurban C.F. (2019) *The New University Model: Scaling Flipped Learning in Higher Education*. New York: Global Publishing.

Salovey, P. (2019) 'A culture of curiosity' https://president.yale.edu/president/speeches/culture-curiosity

Sandel, M. (2020) *The Tranny of Merit. What's Become of the Common Good?* London: Penguin.

Savage, M. (2021) *The Return of Inequality. Social Change and the Weight of the Past*. Cambridge: Harvard University Press.

Schmidgen, H. (2015) *Bruno Latour in Pieces. An Intellectual Biography*. New York: Fordham University Press.

Schmidgen, H. (2018) 'History of the beginnings of the laboratory in the modern world' *brewminate.com*. https://brewminate.com/history-of-the-beginnings-of-the-laboratory-in-the-early-modern-world/.

Schweinsberg, M. et al. (2021) 'Same data, different conclusions: radical dispersion in empirical results when independent analysts operationalize and test the same hypothesis' *Organizational Behavior and Human Decision Processes*, 165, 228–249.

Scott, P. (2021) *Retreat or Resolution? Tackling the Crisis of Higher Education*. Bristol: Policy Press.

Seldon, A. (2018) *The Fourth Education Revolution*. Buckingham: University of Buckingham Press.

Seldon, A. (2019) Universities have lost the country. Here's how UUK must reform to win it back' *HEPI Blog*, March 14th.

Senior, J. (2020) '95 per cent of representatives have a degree. Look where that's got us' *New York Times*, December 21st.

Shapin, S. (1994) *A Social History of Truth. Civility and Science in Seventeenth Century England*. Chicago: University of Chicago Press.

Shapin, S. (2012) 'The Ivory Tower: the history of a figure of speech and its cultural uses' *British Journal of the History of Science*, 45, 1–27. doi: https://doi.org/10.1017/S0007087412000118.

References

Shapin, S. (2020) 'The rise and rise of creativity' *Aeon*, October 16th. https://aeon.co/essays/how-did-creativity-become-an-engine-of-economic-growth?utm_source=Aeon+Newsletter.

Shattock, M., Horvath, A. (2019) *The Governance of British Higher Education*. London: Bloomsbury.

Shostya, A. (2015) 'The use of time among college students: a US–China comparison' *International Journal of Education*, 7, 195–208.

Simpson, R. (1983) *How the PhD Came to Britain: A Century of Struggle for Postgraduate Education*. Guildford: Society for Research into Higher Education.

Simpson, R. (2009) *The Development of the PhD Degree in Britain, 1917–1959 and Since. An Evolutionary and Statistical History in Higher Education*. New York: Edward Mellon Press.

Singal, J. (2019) 'Rightside norms, accuracy norms, and internet garbage-fights' *Substack*, January 20th.

Sloterdijk, P. (2011) *Neither Sun nor Death*. New York: Semiotext(e).

Sloterdijk, P. (2020) *Infinite Mobilization. Towards a Critique of Political Kinetics*. Cambridge: Polity Press.

Smith, E. (2020) *No Platform. A History of Anti-Fascism, Universities and the Limits of Free Speech*. London: Routledge.

Smith, Z. (2019) 'Fascinated to presume: In defense of fiction' *New York Review of Books*, October 24th.

Smits, R., Pells, R. (2022) *Plan S for Shock: Science. Shock. Solution. Speed*. London: Ubiquity.

Social Mobility and Child Poverty Commission (2015) *State of the Nation 2015*. London: HMSO.

Social Mobility Commission (2017) *State of the Nation 2017*. London: HMSO.

Social Mobility Commission (2021) *State of the Nation 2021*. London: HMSO.

Somers, J. (2018) 'The scientific paper is obsolete' *The Atlantic*, April 5th.

Speech by the Minister of Science (2020) 'The research landscape' Hepi/Elsevier Webinar, October 20th, https://www.hepi.ac.uk/2020/10/06/hepi-elsevier-webinar-on-the-research-landscape/

Spence, M. (2021) 'Universities must learn how to disagree again' *The Times*, March 8th.

Sperlinger, T., McLellan, J., Pettigrew, R. (2018) *Who Are Universities For? Re-making Higher Education*. Bristol: Bristol University Press.

Steele, T., Taylor, R. (2008) 'R H Tawney and the reform of the universities', *History of Education*, 37, 1–22.

Strathern, M. (ed.) (2002) *Audit Cultures*. London: Routledge.

Stengers, I. (2008) 'History through the middle: between macro and mesopolitics' Interview, November 25th. www.inflexions.org/n3_History-through-the-Middle-Between-Macro-and-Mesopolitics-1.pdf.

Stengers, I. (2012) 'Reclaiming animism' *place-x*, 36. www.e-flux.com/journal/36/61245/reclaiming-animism/.

Stengers, I. (2017) *Another Science Is Possible. A Manifesto for Slow Science.* Cambridge: Polity Press.

Stevens, S. (2021) 'Becoming a science superpower' *HEPI Blog.* https://wp.me/p5FB74-4Ia.

Stevens, S. (2022) 'The government has chosen to back research and development – now it's time to progress some priorities' *WonkHE*, January 10th.

Stoknes, P (2015) *What We Think About When We Try Not to Think About Climate Change. Toward a New Psychology of Climate Action.* London: Chelsea Green Publishing.

Storper, M. (2016) 'The neo-liberal city as idea and reality' *Territory, Politics, Governance*, 4, 241–263

Strevens, W. (2020) *The Knowledge Machine. How Irrationality Created Modern Science.* London: Liveright.

Student Futures Commission (2022) *A Student Futures Manifesto.* London: UPP Foundation.

Synge, M. (2021) 'Regulation of universities as charities: one step forward, two steps back' *Legal Studies*, 41, 214–233.

Taiwo, O.O. (2022) *Elite Capture. How the Powerful Took Over Identity Politics.* London: Pluto Press.

Taylor, M., Pellew, J. (eds.) (2020) *Utopian Universities. A Global History of the New Campuses of the 1960s.* London: Bloomsbury.

Teichgraber, R.F. (2015) 'Introduction' in Veblen, T. (ed.) *The Higher Learning in America. A Memorandum on the Conduct of Universities by Business Men.* Baltimore: Johns Hopkins University Press, 1–29.

Thrift, N.J. (2016) 'Universities 2035' *Perspectives. Policy and Practice in Higher Education*, 20(1), 12–16.

Thrift, N.J. (2016) 'The university of life' *New Literary History*, 47, 389–417.

Thomas, K. (2010) 'Working methods' *London Review of Books*, June 10th.

Thompson, E.P. (ed.) (1970) *Warwick University Ltd*. Harmondsworth: Penguin.

Thompson, L. (2020) *UK Research Landscape – Food for Thought.* Powerpoint presentation to HEPI/Elsevier Webinar, October 20th.

Times (2020) 'The Times view on the reliance of British universities upon China: cooking the goose' *The Times*, June 8th

Times Higher (2015) 'A vice-chancellor's survival guide' *Times Higher Education*, March 5th.

Tough, P. (2019) *The Years That Matter Most. How College Makes or Breaks Us.* London: Hutchinson.

Truscot, B. (1945) *Redbrick University.* London: Pelican.

Tuchman, G. (2009) *Wannabe U. Inside the Corporate University.* Chicago: University of Chicago Press.

Tusting, K., McCulloch, S., Bhatt, I., Hamilton, M., Barton, D. (2019) *Academics Writing. The Dynamics of Knowledge Creation*. Abingdon: Routledge.

UCAS (2022) *Where Next? The Experience of International Students Connecting to UK Higher Education*. Cheltenham: UCAS.

UKRI (2022) *UKRI Strategy 2022–2027. Transforming Tomorrow Together*. Swindon: UKRI.

Unesco (2015) *Unesco Science Report. Towards 2030*. Paris: Unesco.

Universitas 21 (2019) *U21 Ranking of National Higher Education Systems 2019*. Melbourne: University of Melbourne.

Universities UK (2011) *The Impact of Universities on the UK Economy*. London: UUK.

Universities UK (2017) *Patterns and Trends in UK Higher Education 2017*. London: UUK.

Universities UK (2020) *Tackling Racial Harassment in Higher Education*. London: UUK.

Universities UK/Britainthinks (2018) *Public Perceptions of Universities*. London: UUK.

UPP Foundation and HEPI (2021) *The UPP Foundation and Higher Education Policy Institute Public Attitudes to Higher Education Survey*. London: UPP Foundation.

Van Noorden, R. (2017) 'The science that's never been cited' *Nature*, 552, 162–164. https://doi.org/10.1038/d41586-017-08404-0.

Van Noorden, R. (2020) 'Highly cited researcher banned from journal board for citation abuse' *Nature*, February 6th.

Verhaege, P. (2014) *What About Me? The Struggle for Identity in a Market-Based Society*. Brunswick: Scribe.

Viveiros de Castro, E. (2011) *The Inconstancy of the Indian Soul*. Chicago: Prickly Paradigm Press.

Viveiros de Castro, E. (2014) *Cannibal Metaphysics*. Minneapolis: Univocal.

Vogler, C. (2019) 'A spiritual autobiography' *Comment*, November 1st, 23-34.

Wacquant, L. (2022a) 'Resolving the trouble with "race"'. *New Left Review*, Number 133/134, 67–88.

Wacquant, L. (2022b) *The Invention of the 'Underclass'. A Study in the Politics of Knowledge*. Cambridge: Polity Press.

Wagner, W., Fisher, E., Pascual, P. (2018) 'Whose science? A new era in regulatory "science wars"' *Science*, 362 (6415), 636–639.

Walter, B.F. (2021) *How Civil Wars Start: And How to Stop Them*. New York: Viking.

Waltman, L., Wouters, J., van Eck, N.J. (2017) 'Ten principles for the responsible use of university rankings' *CWTS*. www.cwts.nl/blog?article=n-r2q274&title=ten-principles-for-the-responsible-use-of-university-rankings.

Wang, D., Barabasi, A. (2021) *The Science of Science. Big Data, Metrics and Impact.* Cambridge: Cambridge University Press.

Watson, D. (2009) *The Question of Morale. Managing Happiness and Unhappiness in University Life.* Maidenhead: Open University Press.

Weale, S., Baldwin, J. (2021) 'Edinburgh University admits failings after student kills herself' *The Guardian*, March 16th.

Weber, A. (2019) *Enlivenment. Towards a Poetics of the Anthropocene.* Cambridge: MIT Press.

Weiner, G. (2019) 'Our constitutional emergency' *New York Times*, March 26th.

Weisbrod, B., Ballou, J.P., Asch, E.D. (2008) *Mission and Money. Understanding the University.* New York: Cambridge University Press.

Wellcome (2019) *What Researchers Think About the Culture They Work In.* London: Wellcome Trust.

Whitehead, A.N. (1968) *Modes of Thought.* New York: Free Press.

Whyte, W. (2015) *Redbrick. A Social and Architectural History of Britain's Civic Universities.* Oxford: Oxford University Press.

Whyte, W. (2019) *Somewhere to Live. Why British Students Study Away From Home – and Why It Matters.* HEPI Report 121. London: HEPI.

Willetts, D. (2009) *The Pinch. How the Baby Boomers Took Their Children's Future – and Why They Should Give It Back.* London: Atlantic Books.

Willetts, D. (2010) *Hansard, HC*, Vol 520, December 20th.

Willetts, D. (2017) *A University Education.* Oxford: Oxford University Press.

Williams, P., Stevenson, I., Nicholas, D., Watkinson, A., Rowlands, I. (2009) 'The role and future of the monograph in arts and humanities research' *ASLIB Proceedings*, 61, 67–82.

Willsdon, J. (2015) *The Metric Tide.* London: HEFCE.

Witteman, H.O., Haverfield, J., Tannenbaum, C. (2021) 'COVID-19 gender policy changes support female scientists and improve research quality' *PNAS*. https://doi.org/10.1073/pnas.2023476118.

Wolf, A. (2019) *The King's Lectures 2019.* London: King's College.

Wolf, A., Jenkins, A. (2021) *Managers and Academics in a Centralising Sector. The New Staffing Patterns of UK Higher Education* London: Policy Institute, King's College.

Wolf, M. (2013) 'Britain should not go back to the future' *Financial Times*, April 11th, 11.

Wolf, M. (2016) 'UK university reforms are a betrayal of Conservative principles', *Financial Times*, September 2nd.

Young, M., Dube, L. (2020) *State of the Unions.* London: Adam Smith Institute.

Younis, M. (2022) 'To own whiteness' *London Review of Books*, February 10th.

Zakaria, F. (2015) *In Defense of a Liberal Education.* New York: W.W. Norton.

Zaloom, C. (2019) *Indebted. How Families Make College Work at Any Cost.* Princeton: Princeton University Press.

Zerby, C. (2002) *The Devil's Details. A History of Footnotes.* New York: Touchstone.

Zimmer, R. (2019) 'President Zimmer's message on free expression and federal action' *uchicago news*, March 4th.

Index

References in **bold** type refer to tables.
References to endnotes show both the page
number and the note number (231n3).

A

Academic Diary (Back) 261n3
Academic Freedom Index 147
Academic Technology Approval Scheme 117
access to university 127–135
  educational attainment 130–131
  enhancement/progress in 128–129
  ethnic minority groups 129–130, 132
  intergenerational argument 134–135
  working class and 127–128
accommodation 31
  HMOs 184, 185
  private property companies 184–185
  private sector purpose-built 184
  shortages 122
administrative jobs 68–71
Advanced Manufacturing Research Centre (AMRC) 99
Advanced Research and Invention Agency (ARIA) 140
Alan Turing Institute 253
Aldiss, B. 220
Al-Khalili, Jim 160, 227
Altman, D.G. 229
alumni 94–95
ARIA *see* Advanced Research and Invention Agency
Aristotle 269n4
Arizona State University (ASU) 122, 226, 248
arm's length bodies (ALBs) 242
arXiv 231
assessment/evaluation of research 233–235
  cost and funding 233–234
  judgements 234–235
AstraZeneca 53
ASU *see* Arizona State University
ATHENA-SWAN 42
auditing 110–111
Augar review 138, 141
Australia 115, 173–174
  dual labour market 162
  freedom of speech 80
  income-contingent loans 166
  loan repayment 166
autonomy 60, 148–161, 214
  as concept and practice 150
  creativity and 157, 158
  government and state influence 148–151
  innovations and 157–158
  Office for Students (OfS) and 154–156
  public good argument 158–160
  reasons for 156–161

B

Babbage, C. 263n14
Back, L. 261n3
Barber, M. 261n11
Becker, H. 261n3
Beech, D. 180–181
BEIS 155, 176, 242
Bekhradnia, B. 180–181
Bhattacharyya, Lord 204
Big Repair, The 225
BirdNET 224
Blackstone 184
Blair, T. 105, 166
Boise State University 57
Boyle, R. 28
Bragg, M. 227
Brazil 112, 115–116
Brexit 112, 116–117, 140
Briggs, Asa 26
Bristol, University of 178–179
British Heart Foundation 140
Britton, J. 131
Buckley, William F., Jr. 85
bullying 68, 163, 232
Byrne, E. 9

C

Callon, M. 97
Cambridge, University of 18, 122, 124, 129, 133, 171, 177–178, 187, 192, 193, 202
  built ecology 32
  Cambridge Zero initiative 256
  governance 109, 110
  housing developments 63
  income from teaching 2
  postgraduate students 242
  quarrels within 40
  research funding 238
  undergraduate teaching 269n1
Cambridge Zero initiative 256
Cancer Research UK 140
capitalism 168–169
Chapman, B. 166

China 16–17, 115–117
  as global education power 116
  scientific and technological supremacy 117
Chinese military-industrial complex 144
Chinese students 72–73, 117–118
  financial crisis and 191–192
  remote monitoring of 118
Chinese universities 117, 262n17
  being autonomous 267n21
  expansion of 116
Chirikov, I. 244
Church of England 118
Cicero, M.T. 217–218
citation databases 221
cities and research universities
  growth 185–186
citizen science 159–160, 224–226
  crowdsourced 224
  limits 225
  projects, global repository 226
  UKRI funding 225
civic university 204–205
Clarke, C. 9
climate change 9, 214–215, 254, 255–257
  communication about 225
COCHRANE collaboration 145
code of honour *see* honour code
coercive citation 221
collaboration 249–250
  conglomerating research centres 252–253
  international cooperation 251–252
  publication 115
  team-led 232–233
  testudo 250–251
Collini, S. 7, 209
Committee of University Chairs (CUC) 246
Committee on Publication Ethics 144
communication 160, 223–227
  fact-checking service 226
  radio channel 226–227
  television/ internet channel 226
Competition Commission 172
competitiveness 8, 44, 47–48, 73, 74, 89, 91, 115, 140, 167, 172, 208
  government and 171
  market 105
  meaning of 177
  qualifications 133
contract research staff 62–63
Conversation, The 160, 226
cooperatives 35, 247
Cornell University Lab of Ornithology 224
coronavirus pandemic *see* Covid-19
Corver, M. 123, 193
cost(s)
  assessment/evaluation 233–234

inflation and 192–193
online learning 55, 57
research funding 140–141
council 93–94
  see also research council
Council for At-Risk Academics 17
Council for the Defence of British Universities (CDBU) 214
Covid-19 42, 156, 121–122
Cox, B. 160, 227
creativity 28, 157, 158
CRM Students 184
Crow, M.M. 217
Cruz, T. 263n15
culture *see* research culture
Currid-Halkett, E. 90

D

Dabars, W.B. 217
DARPA *see* Defense Advanced Research Projects Agency
DataExplained 144
data management corporations 183
Davis, Glyn 174
Dearden, L. 131
Dearing Report (1990s) 24
debt, higher education sector 121
Declaration on Research Assessment (DORA) 234, 270n16
Defense Advanced Research Projects Agency (DARPA) 140
Deryugina, T. 42
de Waal, E. 258
Dickinson, J. 109, 244
Didion, Joan 209
Discover Uni 135
discovery research 237–238
dissatisfaction 5–6, 161–164
Dobbin, F 82
donors 95
Douthat, R. 78–79
Drucker, P. 213
Duke University 142
Duncan, E. 240
Duranti, A. 24
duties/obligations 216–228
  communication 223–227
  imparting practical skills 221–222
  notion of 217–218
  research 219–221
  service to community 227

E

eBird 224, 226
Elsevier 183
Environmental Protection Agency 142
Environmental Sustainability Strategy 228
EQUATOR network 145
equipment 28, 29–30

Erasmus programme 116
ethnic absolutisms 262n15
ethnic or minority groups
  academics 42–43
  access to university 129–130, 132
  see also racism
eudaimonism 220, 269n4
European Union (EU) 116–117
  academics 116
  Horizon Europe 140, 237–238
  postgraduate students 116–117
  research grants 116
  super-universities in 241
excellence 19, 236
  internationally 113
  loss of 228–240
Export Control Regulations 117

F

fact-checking service 226
Faraday Institution 254
fees *see* tuition fee
Feynman, R. 9
filopietism 217
financial crisis 191–193
  inflation and rising costs 192–193
  operational deficits 193
  publicly-funded teaching 192
financialisation 170–171
Finches of Mars (Aldiss) 220
Foucault, M. 13, 260n14
France 115
  Paris-Saclay federal university 241
Franciscan model 150
freedom of speech 79–88, 246, 263n16
  Chicago Principles 80, 86
  laws and legislations 80–81
  social media and 86
free market 171, 172
free tuition 136
Frey, B.S. 234
Friedrich-Alexander-Universität
  Erlangen-Nürnberg 147
FTSE 250 123
Fulbright Commission 180
funding
  research *see* research funding
  teaching 135–138
Future Fund 237, 243

G

Garden of Paper Flowers, A (Ehrenreich) 203
Gary, Romain 79–80
gender equality 42
gender wage gap 41, 162
Generation Z 59, 74
Georgia Institute of Technology 57
Germany 65, 67, 115, 253, 262n21
Global Public Policy Institute 147

Godin, B. 158
Goldthorpe, J. 134
Gombrich, R.F. 149, 162
Goodall, A. 269n1
Goodhart, D. 137, 270n2
Google Scholar 231
governance 109–10, 245–246
government(s) 6, 16–17, 171
  autonomy and 148–151
  research funding and (*see*
    research funding)
  university leadership and 186–191
Graeber, David 68–69
Grant, J. 214
Gray, John 40
Greater Manchester Civic University
  Network 270n4
growth 173–182
  actors in 182–186
  follow-my-leader behaviour 176
  funding model 176–181
  international/overseas students
    173–175
  quality of students 181–182
guilds 247

H

hacking 144
Haggett, Peter 47
Haldane, A. 151
Haldane, R.B. 149, 151
Haldane principle 151
Halsey, A.H. 3, 104, 127, 149–150, 236,
  243, 246–247
Hand, Learned 80
Haraway, D. 13
He Jiankui 143
Higher Education Act (1986) 80
Higher Education and Research Act of
  2017 151, 152, 154
Higher Education (Freedom of Speech)
  Bill 242
Higher Education Funding Council for
  England (HEFCE) 139, 152, 155,
  172, 188
Higher Education Innovation
  Fund 238
Higher Education Market, The (National
  Audit Office) 171–172
Hillman, N. 141, 152, 157, 171
honour code 217
Hooper, R. 220–221
Horizon Europe 140, 237–238
houses of multiple accommodation
  (HMOs) 184, 185
Hudson, L.J. 180
Hughes, B. 160, 227
Hungary 17
Hutton, G. 139

hyperauthorship 143
hyper-liberalism 40, 82–83
hypothecation 237

I

immersion labs 56
income 2, 111, 113–114, 124, 125, 138–141, 166, 170, 173, 174–176, 179, 181, 184, 185
  from gifts 95
  from grants and contracts 63
  from international/overseas students 121, 141, 174–175, 191–192
  from tuition fee *see* tuition fee
  see also international students
India 17, 115–116
indigenous knowledge 227–228
Industrial Strategy Challenge Fund (ISCF) 98, 140
inequality 89, 131, 168, 222, 254, 262n2
  educational 128, 133
inflation 192–193
  tuition fee valuation and 179–180
infrastructure 26–34
  facilities 33
  laboratories 28–29
  lecture theatre 31–32
  libraries 27–28
  offices 30–31
  science parks 33
  student habitations/accommodations 31
Innovate UK 139, 237
  Industrial Strategy Challenge Fund (ISCF) 98, 140
innovation accelerators 239
innovations 9, 16, 52, 56, 111, 113, 114, 139, 157–158, 218, 233, 239
  disruptive 54
  individual 44
  methods for creating 28
integrity *see* research integrity
interdisciplines/interdisciplinary research 36–37
inter-institutional leadership 189
international cooperation 251–252
international students 9, 17, 72–73, 104–106, 108, 114, 141–142, 183
  Australian universities and 173–174
  Chinese universities and 116
  growth model and 173–175
  reliance on 174–175
  as a source of income 121, 141, 174–175, 191–192
  tuition fee 191–192
International Universities Climate Alliance 256
IPCC Climate Change reports 226
iQ 184–185
Iran 17

J

Jenkins, A. 70, 110
Jinha, A.F. 229
journals 44, 143, 159, 221, 230, 270n88, 270n10
  predatory 230
  private sector and 183
  referee comments 145
  uncited articles 230

K

Kalev, A. 82
Kant, I. 218
Katz, R. 262n2
Kennedy, M. 160
Kernohan, D. 54, 87, 108, 135, 155
Kerr, Clark 241
King's College, London 183
knowledge economy 16, 113
Knowledge Exchange Framework (KEF) 97, 110
Knowledge Transfer Partnerships 238

L

laboratories 28–29
  equipment 28, 29–30
  protocols 29
  technicians or technical expertise for 64
Lambert, H. 268–269n13
Lashuel, H. 61
Laslett, P. 242
Latour, B. 12, 13, 158, 218, 261n3
Laureate 183
leadership 4
  government and 186–191
  individual 188
  inter-institutional 189
  organisational 187–188
league tables 110, 116, 135, 146–148, 189, 201
learning management systems 56
lecture theatre 31–32
Le Grand, Julian 89
Leiden Manifesto 234
levelling-up policy (research funding) 239–240
Leverhulme Trust 140
liberalism 40, 168, 169, 189
Liberty Living 184
libraries 27–28
Lifelong Loan Entitlement 136, 138
Life Sciences Strategy 246
Lifetime Skills Guarantee 136
Liverpool School of Tropical Medicine 64
local communities 95–96
London Interdisciplinary School 18
Lury, C. 268n24

M

Magdalen College Science Park in Oxford 33
Malaysia 115, 116
Mansfield, I. 180
March Mammal Madness 225
Marginson, S. 72
market 171–172, 182, 200, 208
  labour 125, 131, 162, 200, 242, 260n1
marketisation 9, 32, 97, 163
Marriott, J. 79
Marshall, A. 132
Marshall E-Learning 79
Martin, J. 197
Master's courses/degrees 67–68
Matthew Effect 8, 240
Max Planck institutes 253
Medical Research Council 149
mediocrity 79–80, 200
mental health 61, 76–77, 92–93, 126
meritocracy 89, 90, 132, 133, 236–237, 266n5
Met Office 125
'Mickey Mouse' courses 136
middle class 40, 73, 74, 79, 89–92, 125, 132, 134, 136
MIT 56
Monash 248
Movebank 270n7
Mulhern, F. 110

N

National Audit Office 171–172
National Institute of Health Research (NIHR) 239
National Institutes of Health 142
nationalisation 6, 149, 171–173
National Science and Technology Council 246
National Security and Investment Act 117
Nature Methods 30
N8 consortium 250–251
neoliberal criticism 167–169
neoliberalisation of academia 124–125
New York University 159
NHS 118
Nicholls, Tony 46
Nietzsche, F. 269n2
NMITE 18
NYU Gallatin School of Individualised Study 248

O

Octopus 233
Office for Students (OfS) 80–81, 152–156, 172, 188
  autonomy and 154–156
Office of Science and Technology 246
offices 30–31
Olusoga, D. 160, 227
On Beauty (Smith) 261n13
online learning 54–62, 244–245
  analytics 55
  artificial intelligence (AI) 56, 57
  Covid-19 and 111, 122
  effects of 58–59
  limits/concerns 57–58
open access 159
open science 37, 234
Open University 58
ORCID 25
Ordnance Survey 125
Osterloh, M. 234
Oswald, A. 8
Oxford Economics for Universities UK 113
Oxford Net Zero initiative 256
Oxford, University of 18, 32–34, 65, 95, 122, 124, 129, 130, 132, 133, 171, 177–178, 187, 192, 193, 195, 202–203, 242
  AstraZeneca and 53
  Environmental Sustainability Strategy 228
  governance 109, 110
  housing developments 63
  income from teaching 2
  Oxford Net Zero initiative 256
  quarrels in 40
  research funding 238
  research grants and contracts 63
  student–staff ratios 59
  undergraduate teaching 269n1
Oxford University Press 203

P

Parallel Administrative State 70
parents 89–93
  involvement with children's education 91–92
  mental health issues and 92–93
  visiting universities 92
Parfit, Derek 46
Pauling, Linus 11
Pearce Report 173
Pearson 183
Peel Lecture Theatre, University of Bristol 32
peer pressure 263n12
peer review, system of 142, 145, 147, 148, 221, 234
pensions 89, 145–146, 163
Permanent School Fund 243
Permanent University Fund 243
PhD/doctoral students 65–67
  careers 66–67
  growth of 186
Philippines 17

Plumb, J.H. 40
postgraduate students 64–68
  as a labour market differentiator 242
  Master's courses/degrees 67–68
  PhD/doctoral 65–67
predatory journals 230
Price, Derek de Solla 142
Princeton system 245
private sector 107–108, 125, 182–185, 239
project-based funding 139–140
public and private funding 123–127
Public Attitudes to Science Survey 121
public goods 158–160
PURE 183

Q

quality-related block grant (QR) 111, 139, 170, 237, 239
  decline in 237
quality of research 229–231
quantitative judgements 234–235

R

Race Equality Charter 42
racialisation 82, 262n15
racism 82, 84, 93, 126, 232, 262n15
Rainfall Records 224
Rawls, J. 235–236
replicability 144, 221
The Republic (Plato) 39
research council 15, 38, 111, 139–140, 142, 152, 197, 237, 243, 250, 251
research culture 231–237
  assessment/evaluation 233–234
  bullying and harassment 232
  equality and diversity issues 232–233
  judgement 234–235
  REF and 231
Research England 111, 139, 155
Research Excellence Framework (REF) 62, 110, 139, 147–148, 155, 170, 201, 231, 234, 235, 237
Research Fortnight 183
research funding 139–142, 237–240
  assessment/evaluation 233–234
  charities 140
  cost 140–141
  government increasing R&D expenditure 141
  Horizon Europe 140, 237–238
  levelling-up policy 239–240
  project-based funding 139–140
ResearchGate 25, 231
research integrity 142–145
research-led teaching 248, 259n4
Research on Research Institute 236
research universities 1–5, 213–240
  achievement record 123
  complacency in 8

differentiation 2
duties/obligations 216–228
growth *see* growth
importance of research in 2
income *see* income
problems and solutions 213–215
reckoning/public scrutiny 118–121
worldwide competition 8
research universities, actors in 182–186
  cities 185–186
  government 182
  private sector 182–185
  universities themselves 186
research universities, changes in 103–122
  auditing 110–111
  Brexit and 116–117
  growth in staff numbers 107
  intellectual property and defence-related work 117
  internationalisation 114–116
  private sector in ecosystem 107–108
  proliferation 108–109
  research funding 111–113
  student expansion (growth in numbers) 104–106
  technology in teaching 111
research universities, redesigning 241–258
  collaboration *see* collaboration
  governance 245–246
  policy 242–243
  at smaller level or scale 246–258
  teaching 243–245
residential model of university education 243–244
Robbins Committee 243
Robbins Report 23–24, 190
Roberts, Adam 74
Roberts, Alice 160, 227
Rosalind Franklin Institute 253
Royce Institute 253–254
Ruskin College 18
Russell, B. 263n14
Russell Group 65, **106**, 116, 129, 179, 186–8, 192, 246, 259n2
  economic impact of 113
  ethnic minority students 129–130
  international students 175

S

Sagan, Carl 14
Sage 183
Salovey, Peter 14
Sandel, M. 137
Sanders, Bernie 66
Schleicher, A. 169
Scholars at Risk 17, 147
school meals 129–130
schoolification 161, 163, 190, 242
Science Citation Index 143

science parks 33
Sci-Hub 231
SciStarter 226
Scopus 183
Scott, P. 7, 259n2
'Second Farewell to Cambridge' (Xu Zhimo) 203
Seldon, A. 123, 189
self-citation 221
sequencing technologies 30
service to community 227
sexual misconduct/harassment 93, 126
Shanghai Jiao Tong league table 241
short-term contracts 62, 232
Shurchkov, O. 42
Silicon Valleys 239
Singapore 57, 252
  research universities 267–268n21
single-cell multimodal omics 30
Slido 54
Sloman, A. 244
Sloterdijk, P. 12, 45
slow-thinking movements 271n6
Smith, Zadie 41, 261n13, 263n13
social media, undergraduate students and 74–76
social mobility 127, 128, 134, 266n4–5
Society of College, National and University Libraries (SCONUL) 64
Soros, George 214
Springer 183
SSRN 183
Stanford Encyclopaedia of Philosophy 226
Statista 114
Stearns, J. 42
Stengers, Isabelle 13, 220
Stoknes, P. 225
Stoner (Williams) 261n13
Storper, M. 168
Strength in Places Fund 238
structural racism 262n15
Substack 160
suicide rate 92–93
support staff 63–64

T

TALENT Consortium 63
Tawney, R.H. 104, 132
Taylor, L. 227
teaching
  funding 135–138
  online 54–60
  Princeton system 245
  redesigning or improving quality of 243–245
Teaching Excellence Framework (TEF) 53–54, 110, 135, 173, 188
team-led collaboration 232–233
Technician Commitment 63

technicians 63–64
TEDI-London 18
TEF *see* Teaching Excellence Framework
testudo 250–251
Thatcher, M. 165
Theory of Justice, A (Rawls) 236
The This (Roberts) 74
Thomas, Keith 27
Thompson, E.P. 204
Times Higher 181, 183, 205, 207
Times Higher World Rankings 147, 181
Trow, M. 3, 149, 243
Trump government 16
Truscot, B. 150
Tsinghua Unigroup 117
tuition fee 74, 90, 104, 122, 136, 171, 191–192, 244
  Australian scheme 166
  increase in 152, 167
  inflation and 179–180
  as loans 124
  overseas 191–192
  as voucher system 135
Turing Scheme 116
Turkey 17

U

UCL 32, 33, 107, 163–164, 175, 179, 192, 193, 248
UK Committee on Research Integrity 145
Ukraine war 117
UK Research Integrity Office 145
UKRI (UK Research and Innovation) 65, 111–113, 139, 140, 151, 152, 155, 176, 193, 225, 233, 236–239, 243
UK Shared Prosperity Fund 238
Unamuno, Miguel de 189
undergraduate students 72–79
  American culture and 78
  financial insecurity 74
  growth model and 176–181
  identity and 78–79
  international/overseas students 72–73, 141–142
  mental health 76–77
Unite 184
United States 8, 16, 66
  as a cultural exporter 78
  dual labour market 162
  freedom of speech 80
  learning management systems 56
  online education 57
universal free education 136
Universities and Colleges Admissions Service (UCAS) 36, 92, 108, 128, 129, 141, 175, 179
Universities Funding Council (UFC) 152

Universities Superannuation Scheme (USS) 145–146
Universities UK (UUK) 121, 187
 report on racism in universities 82
 Research Integrity Concordat 145
University Grants Committee (UGC) 149, 152
University Innovation Alliance 56
University of California 18, 209
University of Sanctuary 17
University Partnerships Programme (UPP) 184
unlearning 9–14, 218, 218, 222
United Universities (UU) 220
Utrecht University 270n15
UUK *see* Universities UK

V

van Eck, N.J. 147
V-Dem Institute 147
Veblen, T. 168
venture capital investment 99
veterinary schools 32–33
vice-chancellor 6, 166, 194–209
 aims/objectives of 200–202
 chairing committees 196
 criticism 194–195
 graduation ceremonies 197–198
 international labour market 125
 leading a research university 203–208
 physical stamina 199
 publishing 199
 representing university 196–197
 salaries/remuneration 124, 125
 strategies for success 205–208
 tenure of 199–200
 travelling overseas 196–197
Vitae Researcher Development Concordat 63
vocational education 18–19, 137–138
Voice Thread 56
von Humboldt, W. 23, 65, 216, 218

W

Waltman, L. 147
Waltmann, B. 131
Warwick Arts Centre 205
Warwick Manufacturing Group (WMG) 99, 204, 205
Warwick University Ltd (Thompson) 204
Warwick, University of 99, 193, 204–208
 reputation 204
 strategies for success 205–208
Watson, D. 39, 51
wealth gap 127–128
Weber, A. 234
Web of Science 230
 Science Citation Index 143
Wellcome Trust 121, 140
 report on work culture 270n16
Whitehead, A.N. 9, 51, 209
Wiley 183
Willetts, D. 135, 151
Williams, J. 261n13
Willsdon, J. 234
Wolf, A. 70, 110
Wolf, M. 152–153
women academics 41–42, 162–163
WonkHE 183
Wood, M. 160, 227
workloads, academics and 161–162
Worsley, Lucy 227
Wouters, J. 147

X

Xu Zhimo 203

Y

Young, M. 133, 266n10

Z

Zaloom, C. 89–90, 91
zero-citation papers 230
Zooniverse 226

www.ingramcontent.com/pod-product-compliance
Lightning Source LLC
Chambersburg PA
CBHW071150070526
44584CB00019B/2734